Contents

—— ~ ——

The Baltic states
and
Weimar *Ostpolitik*

For Jessica

THE BALTIC STATES
AND
WEIMAR *OSTPOLITIK*

JOHN HIDEN
School of European Studies, University of Bradford

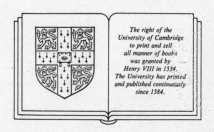

The right of the
University of Cambridge
to print and sell
all manner of books
was granted by
Henry VIII in 1534.
The University has printed
and published continuously
since 1584.

CAMBRIDGE UNIVERSITY PRESS

CAMBRIDGE
LONDON   NEW YORK   NEW ROCHELLE
MELBOURNE   SYDNEY

Published by the Press Syndicate of the University of Cambridge
The Pitt Building, Trumpington Street, Cambridge CB2 1RP
32 East 57th Street, New York, NY 10022, USA
10 Stamford Road, Oakleigh, Melbourne 3166, Australia

First Published 1987

Printed in Great Britain at the University Press Cambridge

British Library Cataloguing in Publication Data
Hiden, John.
The Baltic states and Weimar Ostpolitik.   1. Germany—Foreign relations—
Baltic States   2. Baltic States—Foreign relations—Germany
3. Germany—Foreign relations—1918–1933   4. Germany—
Foreign relations—1933–1945   I. Title.
327.43047′4   DD120.B2/

ISBN 0-521-32037-2

Library of Congress Cataloging-in-Publication Data
Hiden, John.
The Baltic states and Weimar Ostpolitik.
Bibliography
Includes index.
1. Baltic States—Relations—Germany.   2. Germany—Relations—
Baltic States.   3. Germany—Foreign relations—1918–1933.
4. Germany—Territorial expansion.   5. World War, 1914–1918—
Influence.   I. Title.
DK511.B3H53   1987   947′.4   86-14778
ISBN 0-521-32037-2

Introduction

The veritable flood of books and articles on the annexationist policies of Imperial Germany between 1914 and 1918 prompts the thought that historians at least have taken to heart Clemenceaus's advice, that war is too serious a business to be left to soldiers. That monument to German military ambition in the East in 1918, the Treaty of Brest–Litovsk, which Sir John Wheeler-Bennett once described as the 'forgotten peace', is anything but that. That it will continue to be the object of attention has since been assured by those historians of National Socialism who have increasingly located the events of 1918 in the mental world-view of the Third Reich's leaders. Along with the growing number of studies of National Socialist policy in the 1930s, investigations of Wilhelmine Germany's occupation of the Baltic provinces of Russia in the First World War have made a major contribution to the now long-established debate about the 'continuity' of foreign policy aims between Wilhelmine and Hitlerian Germany. Fritz Fischer's pioneering book, *Griff nach der Weltmacht*, dealt extensively with German–Baltic relations in the war and provided a foundation for the more detailed studies of Wilhelmine Baltic policy by Baumgart, Basler, Mann, Volkmann and others.[1]

Apart from Volkmann, few of these historians have followed the thread of German policy through to the 1920s and the startling fact is that today there is still no overall analysis of German–Baltic relations in the inter-war period. There has been, therefore, a serious absence of information to substantiate or refute some of the generalizations made about Weimar *Ostpolitik* in the course of the continuity debate. One judgement, that Germany's socialist leaders simply continued 'the old annexationist policy of the German imperialists', is characteristic of those who have taken the view that in the earlier part of this century German policy concerned the more or less selfish and irresponsible assertion of self-interest.[2] In that respect, at least, there is more common ground than one might suppose between the post-

Fritz Fischer West German scholars of Weimar foreign policy and East German historians, who have long drawn a more or less direct line from Scheidemann to Wirth, Stresemann, Brüning and, finally, Hitler.[3] At the other extreme, it has been argued that the Reich's dreams of annexation vanished with the Armistice concluded between Germany and the Allied Powers on 11 November 1918.[4] Such a view is typical of a long and prominent trend in Western historical writing, one stressing the burdens imposed on the Weimar Republic, the complete military defeat of Germany, its disarmament, the economic restraints of the Versailles settlement and the extent of Allied control measures after 1918. Such studies invariably concluded that there was no German foreign policy as such for the first three or four years of peace and that an 'active' policy was possible only after Germany and Russia resumed direct relations in 1922.[5]

A fundamental concern of the present work is, therefore, to contribute fresh empirical evidence to the overall debate on German foreign policy and on Germany's role in the international system between the wars. What makes the Baltic case-study interesting in this respect is the nature and sheer scale of the readjustment required by Weimar governments, as they were forced to liquidate a wartime administration which had given Wilhelmine Germany political and economic control in a strategically vital area and which had prolonged the historical dominance of the Baltic Germans of Estonia and Latvia. In addition, Baltic problems constitute an essential, if hitherto largely unrecorded, aspect of German–Soviet and German–Polish relations in the 1920s, themes which have long occupied a central position in the study of German policy. Indeed books on Weimar–Soviet relations are legion. Yet in all but a handful of these there is little mention after 1919 of the states destined by geography and history to play a direct part in the relations between the two major powers.[6] It is hoped among other things that some of the conventional wisdom on the so-called 'Rapallo relationship' can be qualified in the present volume.

The study of Weimar *Ostpolitik* has inevitably been concerned with border disputes, particularly those with Poland, and has therefore tended to concentrate on Germany's disruptive role in the region. By contrast, Germany had no direct territorial claims against Latvia and Estonia (which, in this as in other important respects, differ from Lithuania). Although the Baltic states were small and weak powers, covering an area slightly larger than England and Wales, classic examples of faraway countries of which we know nothing, their geographical position makes them ideal vantage-points from which to re-examine the policy re-orientation which Germany had to undergo as a result of its defeat and the threat to its traditionally powerful position in East Europe. An analysis of Weimar–Baltic relations can therefore also broaden our understanding of the effect of the Versailles peace settlement on German foreign policy in general. It will be clear among other things that during such a far-reaching process of readjustment to changed realities, which all the European powers had to undergo after 1918, the so-called smaller states did not in the least behave as pawns in a game conducted by giants. The problems posed for Weimar policy-makers by the Baltic countries provide important clues to the interlocking of the European states system and are a reminder that the new and weak republics did not constitute a *tabula rasa* for the 'great' powers.

Because Germany was politically and militarily weakened in 1918/1919, my study of Weimar policy towards the Baltic countries seeks to assess the relevance of Germany's considerable economic potential to its major goals in the area. The relationship between trade and foreign policy is a theme of growing importance. Again, the Baltic provides a perfect place to study it, not least because it attracted so much European competition after 1918. Beyond the Baltic states lay the hoped for riches of the Russian market, and it is remarkable that until very recently little research was published on great-power commercial rivalry in the region. David Kirby's earlier work on British commerce in the Baltic after the First World War and, much more recently, the studies of the Finnish historian, Merja-Liisa Hinkkanen-Lievonen, have tried to show the British in action in some detail.[7] Their work has been valuable in my own effort to extend my research on Weimar–Baltic relations in the 1920s, because it permits many interesting comparisons between German and British policy to be made in passing. Neither historian has, however, provided a systematic study of the relationship between political and economic goals, between trade and diplomacy in the region. Their concern has been primarily with commerce.

Equally, the very interesting diplomatic studies appearing in recent years on relations between the Baltic countries and on great-power policies towards them – notably that by Rodgers–have on the whole had less to say about economic objectives. Kalervo and Olavi Hovi, Seppo Zetterberg, Tuomo Polvinen and others have considerably extended our knowledge of Finnish, Baltic, Polish and French objectives in the border states. None of these has analysed in any depth the policies of the Weimar Republic.[8] Grundmann's valuable study of the Baltic Germans contains sections on the policies of the Reich government, but his chief concern is to portray in depth the existence of the German minority.[9] My own book, on the other hand, tries to link foreign policy, economic and minority goals in Weimar *Ostpolitik* and to provide an exposition of the development of Weimar–Baltic relations in the light of this trilogy of interests. The developmental aspect of the book is, I think, an important one. The way in which the Baltic republics progressed towards consolidating their independence, the structures of their economic life and their role in the international system was affected by the nature of their relationship with the other European powers; similarly, the policy aspirations of those powers were affected and modified by socio-economic and legislative trends in the Baltic countries as the 1920s unfolded.

To chart this changing interaction chronologically is also a purpose of this book. It seeks to qualify the over-schematic explanatory frameworks which have sometimes been imposed in particular on German economic policy in East Europe.[10] For the determined seeker of 'continuity' it would be easy enough to point to the proclaimed goals of German economic and political influence in the region. But if the language of economic penetration had inevitable echoes of the past, what was the *actuality* behind this in the 1920s? In this respect the present offering is also at least in part a record of the way in which annexationist and revisionist policy goals were transmuted in the face of the changing domestic and international realities confronting Weimar leaders after the First World War. I would hope finally, therefore, to add a small chapter to what has been called the 'new international history'. That is to say, the study seeks to give due recognition to the fact that the Germans did not have a monopoly of nationalism either before or after 1914–18 and that Weimar foreign policy provided opportunities for advancing and defending national interests without automatically threatening the rest of Europe.

It remains for me to express my gratitude to those who have helped towards the appearance of this study. My first debt is to Professor Francis Carsten. Over a number of years he offered invaluable guidance and criticism of the work at a much earlier stage. Other colleagues too numerous to mention individually will recall only too well my encroachment on their time and energy in discussing Weimar foreign policy; this also applies to the many past students of my courses on German history in the inter-war period. I shall always be in the debt of the Institut für Europäische Geschichte in Mainz, which has given both financial assistance for my work in German archives and expert advice on material from its splendid collection of volumes on contemporary European history. As to the Institut's able academics, I should like to acknowledge Claus Scharf, whose expertise I have exploited at various times and who has even put his house at my disposal during my visits to Germany. More recently, my work has benefited from exchanges with fellow Baltic specialists in Sweden and Finland, not least amongst these being Merja-Liisa Hinkkanen-Lievonen and Professor Alexander Loit of the Centre of Baltic Studies in Stockholm. The latter was kind enough to invite me to organize an international study group on the Baltic between the wars during the Conference on Baltic Studies in Stockholm earlier this year. The discussion greatly helped me to finalize some of the ideas in my book. Clearly, none of these is responsible for the shortcomings of my study; these are the exclusive product of my own efforts. Money was provided at one stage of the work by the British Academy; also by the School of European Studies at Bradford University, thanks to the goodwill and encouragement of Professor Kenneth Dyson. Last but not least, my wife and two children have to be congratulated for putting up with me during the writing of the book. It need hardly be said that I could not have completed it without their endless goodwill.

Guiseley, 1985.   John Hiden

PART I: THE POLITICS OF PEACEMAKING 1919–20

I

German–Russian perspectives

In looking backwards to the First World War and the centuries beyond, it is clear that, in the struggle between the European regimes over the Baltic Sea, the position of Germany and Russia overshadowed that of all other powers in the end. With regard to the German Empire after 1871, as to the policy of Prussia before that, the absence of serious Russo-German conflict over the Baltic region owed much to the favoured position formerly secured by the Baltic German aristocracy in what were then the Baltic provinces of Russia. Here, Estonia, Livonia and Courland must be distinguished from Lithuania, with its largely Polish nobility. The local power enjoyed by the great medieval German colonizers of the Baltic remained largely intact after the provinces became part of the Russian Empire in the eighteenth century. The four great Ritterschaften of Estonia, Livonia, Courland and the Islands of Oesel continued to rule loyally for successive Tsars, on behalf of, but increasingly at the expense of, the native Estonians and Latvians. Since the initial failure of the Teutonic Order to subjugate Lithuania closed the provinces to an influx of German farmers, the Baltic barons developed as a dominant caste on the land and in the towns. The long process of readjustment to which this ultimately condemned them was only too apparent by the early nineteenth century, since the land reforms which the German baronial caste felt compelled to introduce then were certain to benefit the Latvian and Estonian peasantry in the long run.[1] Demographic and social trends in general shifted influence and power towards the towns, particularly as the Baltic provinces became important centres of Russian industry in the later nineteenth century.[2] In turn this shift accelerated the growth of a native bourgeoisie

1

and proletariat, providing the basis for a range of parties and ideologies to assume embryonic form and contributing a political dimension to the earlier awakening of Latvian and Estonian cultural and linguistic nationalism.[3]

Any satisfaction of the demands of the native Baltic peoples for a greater share in the administration of the provinces had necessarily to be at the expense of the socially, economically and politically dominant Baltic Germans. In addition, the latter faced the centralizing measures of the Tsarist regime in the last quarter of the nineteenth century. The steady erosion of the privileges once granted by Peter the Great to the German element in Livonia, Courland and Estonia provoked Carl Schirren's 'Livonian Answer' of the 1860s: 'If the spirit of Nystad means anything, it is to rule, not to Russify.' A distinctly beleaguered mentality developed amongst the Germans in the provinces, particularly after the revolution in Russia in 1905, when ferocious attacks were made on the great baronial estates by the Latvians and Estonians. The revolution at least demonstrated that the Baltic Germans and the Tsarist regime retained a mutual interest in keeping Baltic nationalist movements in check, but the experience of 1905 also doomed to failure the efforts of men like Baron Eduoard von Dellinghausen to find a basis for timely reforms involving the native population in the administration of the region. Instead, Baltic Germans closed ranks. From 1905 the relatively new feeling of solidarity between the Baltic German aristocracy and the German urban bourgeoisie intensified. Their combined efforts after the revolution to protect the future of German schools and culture spanned for the first time all three provinces, through the setting up of larger associations (Deutsche Vereine). The defensive mentality also revealed itself in the schemes from 1907 onwards to arrange for the settlement of German farmers (chiefly from Wolhynien) in the Baltic provinces, a project associated above all with the names of Silvio Broederich and Karl Baron Manteuffel. Although the existence of different political currents within the Baltic German camp was an important pointer to post-war developments, prior to 1914 a shared resistance to fundamental change was dominant.[4]

The anomalous and privileged position of the Baltic German Russian subjects was not one which assured them of any great sympathy in the German Empire after 1871. In any case their own traditional values made them equally opposed to the centralized state tradition.[5] After 1905 an active conservative press campaign in the

Reich awakened some public interest in the plight of the Baltic Germans, but the Liberals showed no great concern for their brethren in the provinces, and the hostility of the Social Democrats was overt.[6] Bismarck's policy of avoiding conflict in the Baltic for the sake of the security of the new Germany remained largely intact until 1914. The attempts of prominent emigré Baltic Germans like Theodor Schiemann to involve the German government in his anti-Russian schemes met with scant success. Russia and Germany preserved a mutual tolerance over Baltic issues, although their paramount importance for these was underlined indirectly prior to the First World War by Britain's abandonment of an active naval strategy in the area.[7] It would be premature to conclude that the Baltic Germans had already firmly embarked on the 'road from Tsar to Kaiser' in 1905, but the onset of war in 1914 could hardly leave the Bismarckian policy of non-intervention intact.

War ultimately fostered a growing feeling of solidarity between Reich Germans and Baltic Germans. It finally broke the latter's traditional loyalty to the Tsarist government and provided the opportunity from 1917 for a coalition of powerful interests to be formed in the Reich and in the provinces. In Germany, conservative annexationists, economic interest groups and above all the German High Command (Oberste Heeresleitung = OHL) propounded the view that to secure the Baltic as a power-base would be to hold a standing threat against the feared might of Russia and to secure for Germany the vital sea-route to Finland and Sweden. Land for settlement and food would be provided on Germany's borders; the Reich's major pre-war commercial rival in the Baltic provinces, Great Britain, would be prevented from becoming the dominant influence in the strategically vital area of north-east Europe.[8] Voices were indeed raised early on inside Germany against the attachment of the Baltic provinces in any form to the German Empire. Yet those Baltic Germans, living in the Reich after 1905, who had set up the Baltische Vertrauensrat on 10 May 1915 under Otto von Veh were assured of a hearing when they submitted their memorandum to the German Chancellor, Bethmann-Hollweg: 'We have only one choice; to be annexed by Germany or massacred by Russia.'[9]

The former became more likely as the German armies rolled forward in 1915, overrunning Lithuania and Courland by the autumn of that year. After two years' stalemate along a line stretched between Riga, Dvinsk and Baranovitch, the German armed forces resumed their advance after the revolution in Russia in March 1917 and the collapse of the Tsarist army. Riga was recaptured on 3 September 1917, and in February 1918 the occupation of Livonia and Estonia brought German troops to within one hundred miles of Petrograd. Compelled to make peace with the Germans in order to maintain the revolution in Russia, the Bolsheviks endured the loss of Courland and Lithuania at Brest–Litovsk in March 1918. Although Estonia and Livonia were initially to be 'policed' by German forces, pending the restoration of peace and order, they too were ultimately severed from Russia by agreements concluded between the German government and the Bolsheviks in Berlin on 27 August 1918.

It has, however, become increasingly difficult to maintain that the Treaty of Brest–Litovsk had anything like as broad a domestic consensus behind it in the Reich as Fritz Fischer's work maintained. Of course, the treaty pleased annexationists, the majority of Baltic Germans and the OHL.[10] The great influence wielded by the supreme army leaders after 1916, General Erich Ludendorff and Field Marshal von Hindenburg, was very much in evidence behind the day-to-day running of the military administration covering the Baltic provinces. In the hands of Alfred von Gossler, conservative Reichstag deputy, former Landrat of Prussia and hitherto military governor of occupied Courland, the new military administration in the Baltic (from which Lithuania was separated in the summer of 1918) showed itself determined to convert occupation into permanent German control.[11] Obsessed with strategic issues, the OHL determinedly continued milking the resources of the Baltic provinces. Elaborate settlement projects were planned, both to improve the food supplies of the German Empire and to provide a vital source of reserve manpower.[12] For the German military leaders the Treaty of Brest–Litovsk was but a step towards their goal of permanently weakening Russia by erecting a bulwark of border states. The seizure of power by the Bolsheviks in Russia simply added an ideological dimension to the *Ostpolitik* of the OHL. The menace of Bolshevism also provided a convenient rationale for detaching the Baltic countries permanently from Russia.[13] The proposed barrier of border states, protecting as well as nourishing the Reich, was increasingly regarded by the German military in 1918 as a launching pad for a further decisive action against Lenin and his followers which would achieve the rooting out of communism.

The notion of strengthening German influence in Lithuania and the Baltic provinces, particularly Courland, was appealing to most shades of political opinion in the Reich – that is to say, where it was not overtly welcomed by conservative forces. Outright opposition was unlikely for some time to the 'forward policy' of the OHL which had justified the invasion of the Baltic in the first place. From the moment of occupation, however, Chancellor Bethmann-Hollweg coupled his acceptance of the German takeover in Courland ('the nation's war aim') with an anxiety about hopelessly subverting the Bismarckian tradition of good German–Russian relations over Baltic issues. He was also troubled by the serious constitutional difficulties likely to confront the German Empire in the event of the Baltic provinces' being attached to it. For such reasons the Chancellor favoured the idea of indirect control over a 'buffer' zone, to be realized through advice, aid and influence from Germany, thus avoiding the political problems of annexation.[14] In the Auswärtiges Amt, worry about the military administration causing long-term damage to German–Russian relations was never absent. An appreciation of the strategic advantages of detaching the Baltic provinces from the Tsarist Empire was tempered by a desire to preserve the option of using them as a bargaining counter in any future peace talks with the Russian government. It was therefore logical of the German Foreign Minister, Richard von Kühlmann, to try to insist on a distinction between Courland, the possession of which at least did not cut Russia off from the sea, and Livonia and Estonia. In the event von Kühlmann's resistance to OHL efforts to convert Germany's policing role into full control in Livonia and Estonia helped to force his resignation in the summer of 1918. Yet von Kühlmann's successor, Admiral von Hintze, shared his concern to prevent the OHL from using the Baltic provinces to launch an attack on Lenin's government. Von Hintze was convinced that relations of a sort had to be preserved with Lenin, precisely because the weakness of the Bolshevik regime guaranteed peace in the East, whereas all the other Russian parties based themselves on the Entente and shared a desire to recreate a second front. Bolshevism, by fomenting unrest in Russia, assured German influence the more readily at its outer limits.[15] It is therefore misleading indeed to reduce civil–military conflicts over *Ostpolitik* in 1918 to a debate simply about means, just because of a mutual acceptance of the desirability of maintaining a strong German influence in the Baltic region.

In reality, at the very height of its military power in the East,

Germany's victory created more problems than could be solved. The Treaty of Brest–Litovsk made acute the question of the future status of the Baltic provinces by levering them out of the Bolshevik realm and stipulating that their fate was to be determined 'in agreement with their populations'. Here was the barely concealed response to the political challenge thrown out by the Russian revolution, initially through the provisional government's promise of autonomy to the provinces in March 1917 and later, after the Bolshevik seizure of power, through the Leninist slogans of self-determination. The challenge of self-determination was taken up by the majority parties in the German Reichstag at a time when a national mood of disillusionment and mounting weariness was straining the civil truce achieved in Germany at the outset of the War. After the Reichstag Peace Resolution had called for a peace without annexations in July 1917, there remained a steady insistence on the part of the majority parties that the native Baltic peoples be given their due share in determining their new status, in strict accordance with Brest–Litovsk. How effective such pressures could be is confirmed by the fact that in order to preserve their goal of attaching the Baltic countries to the Reich, even the German military leaders were increasingly compelled to resort to variants of 'self-determination'.[16]

In Lithuania the desire to counter a revival of the old Polish–Lithuanian union persuaded the OHL to deal directly with the native Lithuanians and to recognize the Lithuanian state by 25 March 1918, although it was still under German occupation. In the Baltic provinces, however, the OHL propounded the fiction that the 'interests of the people' could be equated with those of the Baltic German aristocracy. In this fiction the majority of the Baltic Germans wholeheartedly conspired by forming 'representative' provincial councils between September 1917 and March 1918. Dominated by the Baltic Germans, the councils therefore also contained a sprinkling of Latvian and Estonian conservatives. A process beginning in occupied Courland in September 1917 (when its council thanked the Kaiser for liberating their province and duly placed it in his hands) overlapped with events leading to the Brest–Litovsk settlement and climaxed shortly thereafter with the 'election' of a General Provincial Assembly. Composed of 35 Germans, 13 Estonians and 11 Latvians, on 12 April 1918 it duly passed a resolution calling upon the German Emperor to recognize the Baltic provinces as a monarchy and to make them into a German protectorate.[17]

Although the Reich's political leadership remained hesitant, it was compromised by its appreciation of the usefulness of German influence in a ring of border states on its eastern frontiers, as well as by an aversion to Bolshevism, which all parties shared. Yet the Reichstag majority parties, the Auswärtiges Amt and Chancellor Hertling were also to a considerable extent prisoners of the imperial German political structure, which had given the military their power in the first place. The exigencies of war and military occupation had vastly increased that power in the East under the 'silent dictatorship' of Hindenburg and Ludendorff. Quite apart from the fact that the German element in the Baltic provinces monopolized economic power there, the idea of basing policy in the region on the Baltic Germans was wholly consistent with the defence of conservatism in the Reich. The latter goal was central to the concerns of the military establishment behind the war effort. 'Landed nobility and a property owning middle class were the natural supports of a monarchic–conservative form of state.'[18]

The choice of the Baltic Germans on which to base a new political order in the Baltic fatefully determined the structure of the projected giant 'Baltic state' conjured up by the call from the General Provincial Assembly on 12 April. As to Lithuania, the idea of a personal union between that state and Saxony was mooted, whilst the Baltic provinces were marked out for a personal union with the Prussian Crown. In each case, however, the plan was checked at the Bundesrat level; by the rivalry between Württemberg and Saxony over Lithuania and between Prussia and Mecklenburg over the Baltic provinces. More significantly, proposals for extending and reinforcing the archaic voting system in existence in Prussia, through an association with the traditional constitutional order favoured by the Baltic Germans, ran directly counter to the mounting struggle in the Reichstag for socio-political reform. Ultimately it therefore proved impossible to reach any consensus in Germany on the constitutional problems posed by the settlement of Brest–Litovsk. The constitutional dilemma proved indeed to be the 'fatal wound' of German *Ostpolitik*. This was shown beyond all doubt in the summer of 1918, during the frantic activity involved in drawing up drafts of military, transport, customs and currency agreements to try to bind the Baltic provinces to the Reich without too openly violating the doctrine of self-determination. 'There ensued a wasteful confusion of disputed responsibilities and differences of opinion: between Prussia and the other federal states, between the military and the politicians, between the Administration Oberost and the military government in Courland. The personnel in the leading offices changed so often that the preparatory work was continually delayed.'[19]

It would have been surprising on the other hand, if the German government had wholeheartedly endorsed the demands of Latvian and Estonian nationalists before 1918, not least because prior to the Bolshevik seizure of power in October 1917 no clear call had been made by the native Baltic peoples for anything more than autonomy inside Russia.[20] Lenin's coup changed all this. The elected National Council of Estonia, which first met on 14 July 1917 under the presidency of Konstantin Päts, in accordance with the autonomy granted by the provisional government of Russia, had a majority of seats held by the bourgeois/labour group. Only 40% went to the Social Democrats and Social Revolutionaries. The composition of the National Council provides the key to the subsequent failure of the Bolsheviks to gain control of the Constituent Assembly elections after the formal declaration of Estonian independence on 28 November 1917. The ensuing civil war was ended by the arrival of the German armed forces, but in the day left between this event and the departure of the Soviet troops Estonia reaffirmed its independence on 24 February 1918. Latvia's situation was complicated by the much earlier occupation of Courland by German soldiers and by the ensuing departure of literally half of its inhabitants to Russia. It was not until 16 November 1917 that representatives of the different Latvian parties (except for the Bolsheviks) met in the unoccupied territory and proclaimed a Latvian National Council. A second democratic bloc was formed in secret in occupied Riga by Kārlis Ulmanis and others, also without the Bolsheviks or indeed the pro-German elements. The National Council was unable to proceed to the declaration of an independent Latvian republic until 15 January 1918.

The Baltic nationalist movements were therefore checked by the renewed German advance precisely when they were reaching a peak. Yet for the German military administration the maxim formulated by Hindenburg in 1916 still held good: 'The interests of the Army and of the Fatherland are our first priority. In so far as the interests of the native inhabitants do not conflict with these they will also be taken into account where possible.'[21] Such a response was certain to promote a backlash against all things German, notwithstanding the Reich's major contribution to keeping Bolshevism out of the Baltic territories. The determined effort of the Latvians and Estonians to achieve independence by appeals to the outside world were already making an impact, not only in the Reichstag through the majority parties, but also in the cosmetic attempts which the Baltic Germans themselves were compelled to make to involve selected Latvian and Estonian elements in their appeals to the German Empire.

The process of policy reorientation in Germany was therefore first visible in a dawning recognition of the force of Latvian and Estonian nationalism. This recognition above all underlay the growing apprehension of the Reich's political leaders during the closing months of the war: that any policy continuing to frustrate national sentiment in the Baltic would lead to a total loss of German influence. Latvian and Estonian political leaders necessarily looked elsewhere for support for their goal of becoming independent of both Germany and Russia and redoubled their own efforts to involve the Allied Powers in their fate. In the words of the Estonian leader, Kaarel Pusta, the Baltic peoples wanted to bring their cause 'before the arbritration of Europe and America'.[22] As von Hintze commented in the late summer of 1918, 'From liberators, we have become detested conquerors.'[23]

Baltic diplomacy could hardly fail to be directed also against Lenin's White Russian opponents, who still hoped to form the future government of Russia once the temporary inconvenience of Bolshevism had been dealt with. Yet as Allied intervention and civil war in Russia lurched into being the Entente leaders betrayed their uncertainty by simultaneously offering general encouragement to the anti-Bolshevik cause and giving *de facto* recognition on 20 March 1918 to Estonia, a likely constituent of any restored Russia. Clearly, then, the chief motive for encouraging Estonia at that stage was to stiffen resistance to the Reich. Allied anxiety about negotiations between Germany and the Bolsheviks stemmed from an interest in trying to revive a front in the East. At the time of Brest–Litovsk Lloyd George thus reminded his Cabinet: 'Under one name or another, and the name hardly matters, these Russian provinces will henceforth in reality be part of the dominion of Prussia. They will be ruled by the Prussian sword in the interests of the Prussian aristocracy.'[24] E. H. Carr was not quite correct, however, when he minuted that Britain had nothing but sympathy to offer the Baltic states, for the persistent efforts of the Baltic nationalist leaders in the Allied camp throughout 1918 helped at least to ensure that Germany would indeed soon be engaged in a struggle for influence in the region. In January 1918 the

British Chargé dAffaires in Russia had already advised that if the Baltic provinces did not ultimately remain with Russia, they should become independent and form part of a bloc with Scandinavia, Finland and possibly Poland.[25] The outlines of what Lord Bertie of Thane was later to call 'an old fashioned quarantine guaranteeing against infection', were beginning to appear. The irony was not lost in German government circles that the policy of Brest–Litovsk could soon be neatly turned against the German Empire. In the wake of President Wilson's Fourteen Points of January 1918, even moral pressure from the Allied Powers reinforced the arguments within the Reichstag in favour of a timely reappraisal of the whole basis of Germany's border-states policy in the second part of 1918. There is, therefore, considerable force in the argument, advanced in 1927, that the treaty of Brest–Litovsk itself ensured the independence of the Baltic countries; in separating them from Russia it provoked Germany's opponents to do their utmost to prevent her from retaining the territories.[26]

The Allied goal moved suddenly nearer with the dramatic German military collapse following the failure of the Reich's spring offensive in the West. Since military power had kept the provinces in check, the chain of events leading to the German request for an armistice in October 1918 had immediate repercussions in the Baltic. The Reich's first genuinely responsible parliamentary government, under Prince Max of Baden, promptly attempted to end the somewhat dilatory treatment of Baltic issues in the wake of Brest–Litovsk and at last provided the opportunity for the reappraisal of *Ostpolitik* long demanded by the majority parties in the Reichstag. On 5 October 1918, the Baden government's programme proposed to have the military administration in the Baltic replaced by a civilian authority; negotiations would take place for the inclusion of native Baltic peoples in the administration and in the subsequent representative assemblies, in accordance with the will of the majority. Significantly, the reconsideration in October 1918 of Germany's policy in the Baltic provinces involved consultations with a leading member of the Baltic German community, Paul Schiemann. He had been kept out of the area by the German High Command but was to play a key role in Weimar–Baltic relations in the inter-war period (see below, chapter 2). The 'new policy' was signalled by a telegram from the German Foreign Office to its representative with the military administration in the Baltic: 'The government of the Reich is unanimous in respect of the fundamental change in our policy towards the Baltic countries, namely that in the first instance policy is to be made with the Baltic peoples. In this way it might be possible to achieve the formation of governments which survive the Peace Conference.'

Far from expressing a loss of interest in the provinces, then, the prime aim of the new policy-line remained that of securing long-term political and economic influence, as was most evident in the emphasis placed on the survival of the Baltic Germans. The German government insisted that it would be unable to work with any regime in Latvia or Estonia which did not commit itself to the protection of the economic and cultural well-being of the German element.[27] Nevertheless, influence was to be preserved by bonds of friendship between Germany and the Baltic peoples, rather than by chains of subjection. Of course, the new policy received a decisive impulse from Allied pressures and from the need to look ahead to the terms of the peace. Such considerations were expressed in the readiness of the Auswärtiges Amt to abandon its previous insistence on maintaining relations with the Bolsheviks in Russia. In a memorandum dated 5 November 1918, the very day on which the Soviet representative Joffe was expelled from Germany for revolutionary activities, the Russian expert in the Auswärtiges Amt, Rudolf Nadolny, wrote:

Concerning our policy in the East, it should be said that, in the context of the programme of the majority parties and of Wilson's points, and in anticipation of the Entente demands, it seeks as before to decentralise Russia politically with the aid of the nationality principle. And beyond this to create for ourselves possible political sympathy and opportunities for economic activity in the whole Eastern area. In pursuit of the policy it is planned to leave our troops in the occupied border states, with the exception of the Caucasus and eventually Poland, in order to support the setting up in the region of native forces.[28]

Such reactions, it has recently been suggested, were part of a wider search for a Reich foreign policy more able to strike an acceptable balance between German interests and those of the other powers: a product of reformist pressures in the Auswärtiges Amt, in business circles looking ahead anxiously for trade to be renewed, and of course amongst the majority parties.[29] Arguably this is to put too favourable a gloss on Germany's motives as its leaders faced defeat, but it is still more unsatisfactory to view the critical months after the Armistice merely as a sort of annexationist postscript to Germany's Baltic policy. The German socialists who were swept into office as a result of the upheaval had nourished a profound distrust and dislike of the Baltic Germans on whose backs the military administration in the Baltic had been erected. This was true of both the Majority Social Democrats and the Independent Social Democrats. Although the right wing of the former had not expressly rejected annexationist gains in the East before 1918, the stand of the Reichstag faction thereafter was firmly based on the principle of self-determination for the border states. In accordance with its own reformist drive within the Reich, the leadership of the Sozialistische Partei Deutschlands (SPD) had demanded at the first reading of the bill for the Brest–Litovsk treaty that 'from now on in the border states there will be a policy of sincere understanding for democratic sentiments'. The SPD leader, Friedrich Ebert, reaffirmed at the end of August 1918: 'Our position on policy towards the border states is clear. We view the [Berlin] agreement as the continuation of a mistaken policy.'[30] SPD ideas above all had informed the programme of the Baden government. The shift in political power which brought Ebert in as a member of the all-socialist government on 9 November 1918 thus at least guaranteed that the embryonic 'new' policy of October found its due organizational expression. On 14 November 1918, August Winnig was appointed as Plenipotentiary of the German Reich for the Baltic countries. Like Zimmerle, his counterpart in Lithuania, Winnig represented the interim stage between the German military administration and the appearance of governments formed by the Baltic peoples.[31]

Nonetheless, the persistent element of uncertainty and improvisation inside the German policy-making establishment after Brest–Litovsk inevitably continued into the revolution; regrettably, the clarity of vision in taking into account the political realities in the border states was difficult for Ebert to sustain as the German socialists grappled with the tasks of reconstruction at home and preparations for the forthcoming peace talks. Admittedly, another of the preconditions of the policy change was met; namely, the need to help the emergent Baltic states to build up their own defences. Matthias Erzberger, the centre party politician and head of the German delegation to the Armistice talks, succeeded in influencing the wording of Article 12 of the ceasefire. German troops were to remain in the East to help 'in the restoration of peace and good government in the Baltic provinces and Lithuania' and to return to Germany only when the

Allied and Associated Powers thought the moment suitable. This could have been usefully applied to the policy orientation towards the Baltic countries which was slowly taking place in Berlin. In reality, confusion was compounded by the Armistice. It sealed the existing breach in German–Soviet relations by annulling the treaty of Brest–Litovsk and the supplementary agreements of Berlin, and in so doing forged a link between German and Allied policy towards the Baltic. Allied aims, were, however, 'dictated by the requirements of their Russian policy, which called for intervention in the civil war'.[32]

The opening of the Peace Conference in January 1919 made it if anything even more difficult for the Allies to agree on what their policy towards Russia was. The French were anxious in particular to restrict Germany in the East and thus had a strong commitment to pushing back Soviet influence from the border states. On the other hand, President Wilson and Lloyd George both coupled scepticism about a military solution to the Russian problem with a growing interest in the stabilization of trade between East and West. At the same time, Lloyd George had to take account of the pressures on his Conservative–Liberal coalition and of the demands from his back-benchers and from his War Minister, Winston Churchill, who continued to urge the armed overthrow of Bolshevism.[33] The Allies were reluctant to accord the Baltic countries more than *de facto* recognition pending the resolution of the Russian question as a whole. Yet they found it difficult to square even this grudging concession to Baltic self-determination with their support of the White Russian opposition to Lenin, as the abortive conference on the Russian question at Principo in January 1919 showed. In such a setting the containment of Bolshevism was the lowest common denominator of Allied policy, which at best, it was argued long ago, 'never progressed beyond improvisation'.[34]

The situation was not therefore conducive to the consistent development of Germany's October policy-line. The overriding concern of Ebert and the Majority Social Democrats, of the German Military and of the Auswärtiges Amt, particularly once Count Brockdorff-Rantzau became Foreign Minister from January 1919, was to give proof to the Allies of their shared resistance to Bolshevism, chiefly in the interests of securing more favourable peace terms for Germany.[35] Domestic considerations within the new German Republic reinforced this tactic, in that it was used to justify the determined restoration of internal order and the elimination of even the suggestion of Bolshevism at home. Such was the foundation of the working relationship between the SPD on the one hand and, on the other, the Army High Command (OHL), the traditional civil service and the Auswärtiges Amt. The celebrated agreement between Ebert and General Groener on 10 November 1918, duly guaranteed the orderly return to Germany of the troops left outside the frontiers, in return for the army's help in putting down 'extremism' at home.

Objective realities made the likelihood of a Bolshevik-style revolution in Germany remote, as was confirmed by the decision of the Congress of Workers' and Soldiers' Deputies in Berlin on 16 December 1918 to accept Ebert's call for elections to be held for a National Assembly. This vote against revolution was hardly calculated to heal the rifts within German socialism. Once the USPD members had left the provisional government on 27 December 1918, it was a matter of time before force was used against the revolutionary shop stewards and against the Communist movement formed from the Spartacist ranks at the end of that month. Order was conveniently 'restored' in Germany as the Peace Conference convened in Paris early in January 1919, with the deaths of the German Communist leaders, Rosa Luxemburg and Karl Liebknecht at the hands of the newly formed Freikorps.[36] The appearance of these, the basis of the new Reichswehr, confirmed the success of General Groener's strategy, 'through our actions to capture a share of power in the new state for the Army and the Officer Corps'.[37]

BALTIC CAMPAIGN – 1919

The uneasy combination of traditional elites with new political realities at home in Germany was thus necessarily carried forward to the military campaign in the Baltic. In its earliest stages, according to the SPD Defence Minister, Gustav Noske, the venture was, 'summarily handled ... in the face of pressing cares and worries about internal order'.[38] As a result, considerable freedom of movement was created for the military leaders and for August Winnig. The latter found somewhat to his surprise that he could virtually 'make policy' at first, when he was informed by the Republic's first Foreign Minister, Wilhelm Solf, that he would have to deal with problems arising in the Baltic largely on his own initiative; the government was preoccupied with more pressing tasks. A comparable situation existed in London, where it was difficult 'to get the great and the good to attend to problems that to a large extent were of only academic importance to us'.[39] By the time this mistake had been recognized Winnig had also become Oberpräsident of Prussia and had increased his personal power-base. As well as being authorized to act directly in the name of the German government, Winnig was closely involved with the military leaders and civilian authorities in West and East Prussia, particularly over questions of border defence.

When Winnig began to negotiate the required handover of authority to the provisional Baltic governments, military imperatives were paramount, as the Red Army pushed forwards through the gaps left by the exhausted and war-weary German occupying forces. The latter ignored the Armistice provisions and drifted back to the Reich at a pace which presented Winnig with a *fait accompli* in Estonia. On 19 November 1918, he was compelled to approve the existing transfer of power from the German military administration to the government headed by Konstantin Päts in Tallinn. There was more scope to exploit Latvia's desperate need for military aid in order to create better prospects for the Baltic German community. The latter anxiously awaited the setting-up of an administration by the Latvian leader, Kārlis Ulmanis (see below, chapter 2). Sympathy for Bolshevism was stronger in Latvia than it was in Estonia, partly owing to the native reaction against the prolonged German wartime occupation of Courland, which had caused many Latvians to leave for the Russian interior. There was therefore a greater threat of civil war in Latvia, and Winnig had greater leverage over the Ulmanis administration. The Germans formally handed over authority to Ulmanis on 7 December 1918, but Winnig's treaty with the Latvian government on 29 December clearly revealed his long-term hopes for prolonging direct Baltic–German and German political and economic influence in the East.[40]

The treaty offered citizenship of Latvia to any German volunteer fighting for at least two weeks to help clear Latvian soil of Bolshevism. Undoubtedly, the interpretation, both by Winnig and by the Baltic recruitment office set up in Berlin, of this provision to mean the promise of land was essential to attract German fighters to the East. Without such a flow of recruits the terms of the Armistice would have been impossible to meet. Fresh reserves were urgently needed to supplement the volunteer remnants of the retreating German 8th Army, who reconstituted themselves as the 'Iron Division'. Also backing was required for the Landeswehr, formed on 11 November

1918, largely from Baltic Germans but with some White Russian and Latvian troops. The German Workers' and Soldiers' Councils supported Ebert's decision to allow the setting-up of a Berlin recruiting office, primarily to hold the front against the Bolsheviks and to facilitate the return to the Reich of any German regulars who were anxious to leave the Baltic. There was no question of the German councils sanctioning further intervention against the Soviets.[41] Yet the prospect of land was precisely what attracted the military adventurers swelling the ranks of the Freikorps in the Baltic from January 1919. For these men the Weimar Republic had little claim to affection and loyal obedience. The German volunteers were soon joined by White Russian contingents recruited from prisoner-of-war camps in Germany from early 1919 onwards. They were expected to lessen the burden on the Weimar Republic and in due course to replace the German soldiers, who could not expect indefinitely to be allowed to remain outside Germany's frontiers.[42]

The innate problem of maintaining political control over such mixed forces once they moved off towards the East was compounded by the effective shift in decision-making over military matters to the new Army Command (Armee Oberkommando Nord = AOK) set up at Kolberg in January 1919. The move confirmed that Ebert and the Social Democratic leaders accepted the link made by the OHL between the Baltic front and the defence of the Reich's borders. German fears about the new Poland were added to those about the advance of the Bolshevik forces. That a major function of AOK was to improve liaison between the defence of German frontiers and the proposed campaign in the Baltic was confirmed in Winnig's parting instruction on becoming Oberpräsident in East Prussia in January 1919. His deputy in the Baltic, Burchard, was informed: 'As far as military matters are concerned, AOK is to be supported in the organization of the necessary border defence against Russian Bolshevism.'[43] Russia's proclamation between 2 and 22 December of Soviet republics of Estonia, Latvia and Lithuania underlined the military urgency. Although Allied ships arrived at Libau early in December 1918, the German troops provided the only immediate hope of holding the front in the East.

In sum, the combination of a hard-pressed government in Berlin, preoccupied with the coming peace talks, and a collection of political and military figures who were necessarily allowed a considerable degree of initiative in the East provided the perfect recipe for prolonging the unresolved conflict over *Ostpolitik* into peacetime. The debate was all the more protracted in that the absence of any serious prospect of movement in the West, as well as the likely economic constraints there, gave the East the status of a promised land. Winnig, whose standing in the socialist party had commended him for the tricky mission in the Baltic, had also proved acceptable to the military leaders through his ardent patriotism. He remained obsessed with the wartime vision of a vast zone in the East where German economic enterprise would flourish and where the German element would survive and grow stronger. Whilst committed in his official capacity to preparing for Baltic independence, he privately reflected that independent Baltic states made no sense historically.[44] General Quast of AOK and his Chief of Staff, General Hans von Seeckt, had no more understanding of the October policy, viewing independent Baltic countries as a wall separating Germany from Russia.[45]

Such an attitude was even more pronounced in General Rüdiger von der Goltz, who arrived to command the swelling Freikorps in the Baltic on 2 February 1919. Von der Goltz made no secret of his aim of using the Baltic campaign as a last-ditch attempt to preserve a land-bridge to a restored White Russia, which would then support German defiance of the Allied peace settlement. The pursuit of such unreal aims entailed a lofty view of the political force and ambition of Baltic nationalism. Von der Goltz, too, felt perfectly justified in intervening in the domestic affairs of what he had once termed the 'unprepared and wholly non-viable three northern state formations'.[46] Burchard, a survivor of the wartime administration in the Baltic, took a similarly cavalier view of Baltic politics. In his concern to prevent a barrier between Germany and Russia, he was prepared, as was Seeckt later, to contemplate Bolshevism in the border states. The main thing was to ensure Russo-German contact in a world where the Entente was dominant.[47]

Such influential figures were all what the Republic's first Foreign Minister, Wilhelm Solf, has been called: 'wanderers between worlds', who ignored or refused to accept the underlying shift in international power brought about by Germany's resounding military defeat. Clearly they were given unexpected encouragement by the anomalous situation which the Armistice created in the Baltic, and by the widespread acceptance within the German government of the need not to lose sight of a possible White Russia in the future. Above all else was the priority of keeping the Red Army away from the German

frontier. Gustav Noske, the Minister of Defence, Foreign Minister
Brockdorff-Rantzau and the Auswärtiges Amt officials can therefore
all be criticized for the degree of permissiveness with regard to the
distant Baltic campaign which made it so difficult to liquidate the
affair later. Yet it would have been distinctly odd had the German
government not perceived the build-up of its volunteer forces in the
Baltic as a form of insurance, particularly since the process was initially sanctioned by the Allied Powers. Self-interest was not an exclusive monopoly of the German government in 1919. 'Everyone had
schemes, chiefly or at least nominally for their countries' benefit, but
for their own also.'[48] Under the terms of the Armistice, moreover,
Germany had to agree in advance to accept as yet unknown arrangements for Russia. As Wipert von Blücher recalled from his period of
office at the border states desk in the Eastern Department of the
Auswärtiges Amt, such circumstances made 'exceptionally difficult a
future German *Ostpolitik*'.[49] Nevertheless, if such a combination of
circumstances often made for extreme indecision in Berlin, the
German political leadership and the supporters of the Scheidemann
government had a fundamentally truer grasp of the ultimate reality
of Allied power than the men in the Baltic. That much was made
evident after the crisis precipitated by the rapid advance of von der
Goltz in the spring of 1919.

By then Estonia was in the final stages of repulsing the Bolshevik
attack with the aid of Finnish volunteers and the Baltic German
Baltenregiment. Because of the serious situation in Courland, however, von der Goltz developed the case for exceeding his original
instructions to hold the front where it was. In a memorandum which
he forwarded to AOK on 17 February 1919, he argued the case for
moving further east to defend the more easily held line along the
River Aa. In spite of reluctance on the part of both Seeckt and
Groener, the latter being particularly anxious about resistance to the
idea within the Cabinet, von der Goltz eventually received permission to effect his plan. He achieved his stated objective on 23 March
1919, when Mitau was recaptured from the Bolsheviks.[50] Yet the
event also provided the occasion for a coup by the Landeswehr in
Libau, where the provisional Latvian government under Kārlis
Ulmanis was deposed. Von der Goltz insisted that the episode was a
matter of internal politics, but the installation of a pro-German administration in Latvia under Pastor Andreas Needra offered not only
the last chance for the Baltic Germans to secure a firmer grip on the

government, but also the prospect of the Winnig–Ulmanis agreement of 29 December 1918 being interpreted in such a way as to enable the settlement of Germans to take place.[51] Von der Goltz personally had few illusions as to the time's being yet ripe for settlement projects, but he could hardly fail to recognize the advantages of a more secure military base for his planned advance towards Riga.[52] The defence against Bolshevism was being converted into an offensive, and behind the argument for a shorter line of defence lay the familiar OHL vision of 1918.

As we have seen, this had not enjoyed unqualified support even then. The Libau coup prompted the first concerted discussion of events in the Baltic at Cabinet level, as the Scheidemann government had its gaze wrenched from the imminent presentation of the draft peace terms by the Allies. Groener had to counter strong fears about a military reaction when he addressed the Cabinet on 24 April 1919 to keep his colleagues up to date about the situation in the East. 'Premature demobilization', Groener warned, 'is not only dangerous in foreign policy terms, for with it the ambition of the enemy grows, but in domestic terms too. At the moment the East is essentially in our control. All orders from the government can be executed there. The charges of reaction and militarism are unjustified. The OHL insists that there is no question of counterrevolution. It does everything for, nothing against the government.'[53] His assurances did not placate the SPD press and party organization, which expressed its extreme displeasure at the overthrow of the legally constituted government in Latvia. Yet the Cabinet discussion of the points raised by Groener confirmed how far the military leaders could continue to influence policy in the uneasy first months of 1919.

The German government refused formally to recognize the Needra government, but 'without detriment to actual relations'. The important question in Berlin remained the relationship of events in the Baltic to what was perceived to be Allied policy towards Russia. Brockdorff-Rantzau was then adamant in rejecting the suggestion of Erzberger at the Cabinet meeting of 22 April, that Germany should consider the idea of an armistice with the Soviets 'as soon as possible'. The Foreign Minister continued to argue that the struggle against Bolshevism was one of the few agreed points for reconciliation with the Western powers, especially the United States, and that it would seem disloyal were Germany to deal with the Soviets. In the event, a compromise was reached at the meeting of the Cabinet on 24 April.

It was one which took account of the fears voiced by Erzberger and Bell about offending the Soviets and ruled that the front in the East be maintained where it was. No further offensive was to be sanctioned. Consciences could be squared by the belief that to shorten the front would leave Lithuania vulnerable. Noske argued in addition, with some force, that to pull the German troops back from Latvia would provoke civil war, 'directly on our borders'.[54]

The Libau coup and its aftermath thus confirmed the disagreement between the political and the military leadership over events in the East. Further strains were imposed when the draft peace terms were presented on 7 May 1919. Rantzau's objection that these were wholly unacceptable raised the prospect of renewed hostilities with the Entente which would mean, as Zimmerle was told in Kovno, that large troop formations would no longer be allowed outside the Reich.[55] Indeed, Ebert informed an emotional Cabinet meeting on 8 May that German forces in the still occupied areas of Russia would be transferred to the defence of the frontiers against Poland.[56] The Allies were formally notified on 9 May of the German Cabinet's intention to pull back its forces from Latvia and Lithuania in the shortest possible time, a decision originating in Brockdorff-Rantzau's telegraphed instructions from Paris on 3 May. Here he finally dropped his earlier objections to the idea of an armistice between the Soviet and German forces at the front, provided official relations were not restored between Germany and Russia before the peace terms had been finally clarified.[57] The Allied Powers formally rejected Germany's note on 9 May and insisted two day later that German troops fulfil the terms of Article 12 of the Armistice. Yet the German Cabinet decision in principle to liquidate the Baltic campaign had been made. Inevitably, the German military leaders felt apprehensive, sharing as they did Groener's conviction that at the very least the German troops in the East should stay put for as long as possible. Their views were echoed too, in those of the Auswärtiges Amt's Russian expert, Zitelmann, who worried about the effects of any premature ceasefire with the Bolsheviks on the future relations between Germany and a restored White Russian government.[58]

A critical moment had therefore been reached in the reorientation of Weimar *Ostpolitik* when von der Goltz returned to Berlin to give his account of the events leading to the coup in Libau. It is partly for this reason that the General heard conflicting opinions and ultimately chose what most suited his purposes. In his own memoirs he claimed

to have secured the agreement of the German government to the idea
that any further advance of the Landeswehr towards Riga could be
regarded as a matter of internal Latvian politics. Yet Erzberger and
Noske categorically rejected von der Goltz's suggestion that some ten
thousand of the twenty or thirty thousand German troops in the
Baltic should be allowed to join such a 'Latvian' army. They did so
specifically on the grounds that the suggestion was 'no longer feasible
since the [German] government has decided on the evacuation and
nothing can change this'.[59] It is true that Berlin elected to accept von
der Goltz's assurances that he was not personally involved in the
coup against Ulmanis and refused to carry out the Allied demand for
the General's recall. The Allies themselves could, however, be held
partly to blame by continuing to insist that the German troops should
stay where they were, for German government circles worried about
the likely ramifications of von der Goltz's recall in view of his considerable personal popularity amongst the Baltic Freikorps.[60]
Although von der Goltz testified later that a 'high official' in the
Auswärtiges Amt was interested in his notion of building a land-
bridge to Russia through the actions of the German troops in the
Baltic, Erzberger and Noske were not impressed and the official concerned was later dismissed.[61]

Wipert von Blücher later suggested that 'one could not tell if anything politically useful would develop from this [Baltic] undertaking;
it contained a good measure of idealism as well as the elements of
chance and adventure'.[62] No doubt this pessimistic mood imparted
itself to von der Goltz. As he returned to the Baltic front the one thing
he could be sure of was that hesitancy reigned in Berlin. The atmosphere was conducive to a feeling that the Baltic campaigners could
act with impunity in their distant field of battle, and von der Goltz
promptly sanctioned the advance of the troops, who duly recaptured
Riga on 22 May. In retrospect, this was an unsurprising outcome to
the whole train of events set in motion by the April coup. Faced with
yet another *fait accompli*, the Reich Cabinet still failed to discipline
von der Goltz, but it repeated forcefully that the front must be held
where it was and expressly banned Reich German contingents in the
Baltic formations from further advances. There can be no serious
suggestion that the Reich government as a whole actively colluded
with von der Goltz's more fantastic notion of building a land-bridge
to a restored White Russia. Such an active participation in the demise of independent Baltic states would have violated the new policy

proclaimed by the German government in October 1918, would have negated the Cabinet decision in early May to liquidate the campaign (at least as far as Reich German troops were concerned) and would in addition have run counter to the growing pressure within the Cabinet and the Reichstag to re-examine the whole question of an armistice with the Soviet forces. The delay in more effective restraints being imposed on von der Goltz and others continued to derive largely from the government's anxiety about the difficult military situation at the front and from fears, shared by the Allies, that it would be difficult physically to thwart the threatened march towards Petrograd by the Baltic campaigners.

Above all the irresolution of the German government owed much to the still unfathomable Allied policy towards Russia and the Baltic.[63] Blücher's judgement might well have been passed on any of the Allied governments. After all, the Baltic states had been saved from Bolshevism by the defeat inflicted on the Soviet forces at Riga on 22 May. This achievement itself vindicated the provisions of the Armistice. The 'miracle on the Daugava' preceded the rather better-known 'miracle on the Vistula' by a year.[64] Only four days after Riga had been retaken, the Allied Powers reaffirmed their opposition to the Soviets with their decision to support the White Russian Admiral Kolchak and his forces. These were to be provided with 'munitions, supplies and food, to establish themselves as the government in Russia'. In such a setting it is not difficult to see why von der Goltz encouraged the Landeswehr, reinforced by German troops and ostensibly in the service of Needra's 'government', to continue the advance beyond Riga.[65] The situation only changed dramatically when those troops engaged with a joint Estonian–Latvian force supporting the deposed Ulmanis government. The event greatly intensified Allied fears that Russia would be restored under German rather than Allied auspices. The clash finally provoked a decisive display of Allied resistance to the entire Baltic undertaking by German troops; an armistice was imposed on the Freikorps/Landeswehr force on 10 June and again, after a brief resurgence of fighting, on 3 July (at Strasdenhof). The latter document insisted on the Germans evacuating Riga, which duly occurred on 5 July, and repeated the Supreme Council decision of 13 June, that all Reich German soldiers were to leave the region in the shortest possible time.[66]

The armistice of 3 July 1919 marked a climax to the challenge for influence in the Baltic countries mounted by the Allies after the April coup. A direct result of that event had been the arrival in the Baltic states of a veritable flood of Allied agents and missions, not least initially to determine what was actually going on there. The formation in April of an Interallied Commission on Baltic Affairs, to examine the political aspects of the Baltic problem, was followed by the appointment of the British Major Gough as chief of the British, later Allied, Military Mission. A flow of aid in the form of equipment, money and training resulted for the Latvian and Estonian governments. Significantly, and this is of relevance to the subsequent German delays in evacuating the Baltic, the Peace Conference retained its formal commitment to the notion of a restored Russia. Before he left for Latvia Major Gough was specifically warned by Curzon that it was not the policy of HM Government to support full-scale intervention against Russia — contrary to the wishes of Winston Churchill, Gough's superior at the War Office. Instead, Gough was reminded of how important it was not to endanger Britain's relations with Russia's future government. He was instructed to concentrate on trying 'to establish our influence in the countries between Germany and Russia'.[67]

The flurry of heightened activity on the part of the Allied Powers incidentally provided Latvian and Estonian political leaders with an ideal opportunity skilfully to exploit the attention being devoted to their states by the Peace Conference. It was thus possible to begin effectively countering the belief that the existence of independent Baltic countries was less important than the continuation of the West's struggle against Bolshevism. The Estonian socialist, Martna, ruefully commented: 'People held the defensive struggle of our country for some sort of intervention, although the Russians attacked us and we did not want to be subjected.'[68] Under such circumstances the Allied determination to replace the German anti-Bolshevik fighting forces by native formations backed by the Allies provided an unintended but powerful boost to Baltic nationalism. Not without reason, the April coup has therefore been seen as a turning-point in the 'tortuous struggle' for independence. This remained the prime foreign policy goal of the Baltic peoples in 1918/1919.[69]

Meanwhile, the Versailles treaty confronted the German government with conclusive proof that the strategy of collaborating with the Allies over Russia had failed to achieve better peace terms. The conditions of peace made all the more unwelcome to the German government the setback in its attempt to maintain political and

economic influence in the Baltic countries in June and July. Any
lingering hopes of securing the extensive settlement of Germans in
Latvia were also crushed by the armistice of 3 July. It precipitated
the collapse of Needra's administration and opened the way for the
return to power of Ulmanis, an event which at last compelled the
Baltic Germans to adjust painfully to a new era (see below, chapter
2). The final and inevitable decline of Baltic German dominance was
confirmed by the fact that the Landeswehr was placed under a British
officer after it had been purged of its Reich German volunteers.
General von Seeckt's intelligence report for July 1919 graphically
described the German military's response: 'In the Baltic itself an
increase in English influence is undeniable.' The report then
described how the pro-Needra Landeswehr 'began negotiations with
the Ulmanis Latvians. Through the efforts of the Chief of the Allied
Military Mission the talks resulted in the pro-German Landeswehr
being sent to fight Bolshevism under the command of the English
Colonel Alexander – and this after the expulsion of all Reich
Germans and the loss of those rights accorded to them in the Baltic.'
The conclusion of the German military leaders was that 'England
wants in this way to make the Baltic provinces into an English colony
and to destroy at any price the bridge between Germany and
Russia.'[70]

Groener himself now had few illusions about the prospect of successful intervention against the Bolsheviks in Russia, but he retained
his belief in the need to keep a German military presence in the Baltic
area for as long as possible. 'Stay put and wait', Groener's maxim,
remained much as it had been at the outset of the Baltic campaign,
when the presence of German forces had been sanctioned by the
Armistice.[71] His views counted since he remained temporarily at his
post when the army high command was made formally illegal under
the terms of the Versailles treaty and thus transformed itself to the
Kolberg Command Post. By contrast, von der Goltz favoured a more
active initiative precisely because of the setback of the Versailles
terms, arguing that those Germans who did not want to return home
should be encouraged to join the growing army of White Russians
from the German prisoner-of-war camps. These were increasingly
under the influence of the pro-German Colonel Bermondt-Awalof
and effectively constituted part of the overall White Russian intervention.[72] Since this retained the nominal support of the Allies, the
idea of getting the Reich German Freikorps into Bermondt-Awalof's

command appeared to offer the chance to sidestep Allied controls. As early as May 1919, Groener had also shrewdly attempted in the Cabinet to link the continuing German military presence in Latvia with the SPD government's stated goal of supporting independent Baltic countries, by arguing that White Russian troops were the obvious substitute for the retreating German Freikorps, 'if our government has any interest in the survival of the Latvian state'. Von der Goltz was content to raise the spectre of rebellion in the Baltic by suggesting that the White Russian troops could be in conflict with their German counterparts unless they were given equal treatment. That a dangerous and frustrated mood existed in the German Freikorps ranks was recognized by Allied observers. It was confirmed beyond doubt by the mutiny on 23 August of the Iron Division, which refused to obey the German government's recall. A divided Cabinet, in which Noske gave the casting vote, reluctantly agreed to continue payment to the Bermondt troops for September.[73]

Given the choice by von der Goltz of joining the White Russian command or returning to Germany, the majority of the Iron Division chose the former, and indeed von der Goltz handed over the formal command of the volunteer forces to Bermondt five days before he formally sought approval of his actions from the German Defence Minister. The event suggests not so much that the Cabinet positively encouraged the Baltic troops in the last stages of the campaign, as that it dismally failed sufficiently to discourage the 'political General', as von der Goltz referred to himself in his memoirs. Noske has been singled out as one who tacitly supported von der Goltz. It is likely, in fact, that, as in the case of many of the officials in the Auswärtiges Amt, the Defence Minister found it difficult to abandon the idea that in some way or another a basis for collaboration with a restored, non-Bolshevik Russia should be preserved. Partly as a result of such wait-and-see attitudes – originally encouraged, it must be repeated, by the uncertain response of the Allies towards Russia – the impression gained ground in the Freikorps ranks that Berlin was giving orders to evacuate the Baltic simply to satisfy Allied require-ments. Such was the view of Major Stülpnagel after his visit to Latvia to investigate the mutiny of the Iron Division. In his subsequent Berlin lecture, 'The troops in the Baltic', he confirmed that most men would 'delay answering the recall and would wait to see if anything would really be done'.[74] The physical separation of the Baltic troops from Germany and the uneasiness existing between Freikorps and government nourished a mutual ignorance which enabled von der Goltz to act as a two-way filter, carefully presenting one case on the spot in Latvia and another one in Berlin.[75] This was manifestly what happened when he assured the Iron Division, after reproving them for their indiscipline, that he would speak on their behalf to the government at home, but that meanwhile the evacuation was 'interrupted'.[76] Even British sources felt that too much was going on behind the backs of Noske and the German government and cited examples of the old imperial policy machinery surviving, including officials who stamped and signed directives on their own initiative. According to such reports, admittedly, von der Goltz was also 'completely out of hand'.[77]

Indeed, von der Goltz was quite capable of justifying a refusal to obey one of General Gough's orders on the grounds that it showed the British that 'he [von der Goltz] was no Hermann Müller'. Yet the Bauer government, and particularly the SPD Foreign Minister to whom the General here refers had no illusions left about the need to evacuate the German troops after June 1919. Fundamental differences between the political and military leaders were re-exposed once the Allies displayed their determination to force the Freikorps out. In view of the perception of Allied power which had already prompted the Bauer government to shoulder the burden of signing the detested peace treaty it is highly improbable that von der Goltz was as actively supported as some accounts have suggested. Müller had quite specifically discouraged the step which von der Goltz eventually took in handing over his charges to the Russian general. What is more, the Foreign Minister forcefully articulated the growing doubt about the whole process of basing Baltic policy on the outcome of the situation in Russia. He at last again made a central priority of the policy goal of October 1918, by warning that in the long run everything had to be done to avoid incurring the hatred of the Estonians and the Latvians.[78]

FROM INTERVENTION TO COLLABORATION

The Allied Powers did not allow their continuing doubts about the future of Russia to divert them from opposing the German Baltic troops, even if these were reconstituted as part of a White Russian force. Their determination was shown by the renewal of the Allied blockade of Germany in early October. The event was taken with the seriousness it deserved by the Bauer government. German Cabinet records show an urgency about convincing the Allies of the effort being made to enforce the evacuation of the Baltic countries. Ultimately the German government agreed to an Allied commission under the French General Niessel to supervise the measures of evacuation. The Allies could determine for themselves the practical difficulties involved. On 18 October 1919, whilst commending von der Goltz for his services in the East, the Cabinet explicitly acknowledged that the evacuation of the Baltic area had become a 'prestige question' for the Allies. Von der Goltz had to be replaced because 'his name is inseparably linked with the events' in the region.[79] Just as deference to Allied power had sanctioned the campaign in the first instance, so now it demanded its abandonment and provided the Bauer administration with effective leverage to get the Freikorps back to Germany. Von der Goltz revealed his anger at the sabotage of his efforts by the detested SPD leaders by defiantly publishing a final call of encouragement to the VI. Reserve Corps: 'God be with you and your just cause. To the devil with the rule of criminals, Bolsheviks and their friends.'[80]

Although von der Goltz directed his venom at Bauer and Müller, in truth the ability of Bermondt to achieve anything worthwhile had long been open to doubt, even at Kolberg Command, where a report of 17 July 1919 observed that the Russian general was 'scarcely in touch with reality with his plans'.[81] Still more scathing was an appreciation written by the German Chargé d'Affaires in Estonia, Henkel. He felt that during the build-up, existence and liquidation of the forces under Bermondt 'such demoralisation and lack of preparation was revealed on the side of the Russian intelligence and Russian officer corps, that one must doubt whether these circles will ever be capable of conducting any sort of fruitful reconstruction [in Russia]'.[82] Such a judgement is an apt reminder that Bermondt's ultimate defeat at the hands of the Latvians by mid-November 1919 was very much a part of the general decline in the second half of that year of the White Russian intervention as a whole.

It is not therefore without significance that Müller's attempt to check Bermondt's venture in August and September 1919 was paralleled by decisions taken in the British War Cabinet in late September. In the face of strong Foreign Office reservations, the War Cabinet showed that it shared Lloyd George's disillusionment with intervention by refraining from expressing any opinion as to how far the

Baltic governments should respond to the Soviet peace overtures of late August 1919.[83] Effectively this gave tacit approval to the effort being made by Baltic leaders to disengage their countries from the fight against Soviet Russia. The Allies, particularly France, continued to be worried about this process and about the rundown in general of the forces of Denikin, Yudenich and others, but White Russian hopes for a reconstituted Russia inexorably moved a stage further away from reality. Peace treaties with the Soviet forces constituted for Latvia, Estonia and Lithuania the first positive step towards independence in a world of half-promises and prevarications. The readiness of Baltic leaders to seize the opportunity demonstrated their ability to exploit the limited room for manoeuvre between the major powers. In accepting the idea in principle of peace talks with the Bolsheviks on 4 October, Baltic governments themselves shifted the international debate perceptibly towards the recognition of their full independence.[84]

Undoubtedly, such growing self-confidence in the Baltic states derived from their resourceful struggle to clear their territories of hostile forces in 1919. Yet the prospect of peace talks with the Soviets posed in more acute form the question of how best to maintain Baltic independence as the Allies began slowly to pull back from direct involvement in the borderlands between Russia and the West. The long-discussed possibility of some form of regional alliance system at last became an actuality. That this immediately posed urgent questions for Weimar *Ostpolitik* might be inferred from the earliest hopes attached by Baltic politicians to the policy of 'binding themselves to others who most resemble them in the suffering from the past and their ideas about the future'.[85] The three Baltic countries will, an analysis written in 1917 argues, 'strongly resist German expansion … they will build a corridor through which the influence of the Allied countries will penetrate Russia and will soften the eventual friction between Russia and Poland.'[86] Two years later, early in 1919, Čakste, the President of the Latvian State Council, assured the French Premier, Clemenceau: 'Latvia opposes and will continue to oppose, Russian or German domination of the Lettish lands, and sees in the creation of a barrier stretching from the Baltic to the Black Sea the prime condition of political equilibrium in Eastern Europe and the first guarantee against a Russo-German alliance, Bolshevik or otherwise.'[87]

The Allied conference in London, on 11–13 December 1919, which marked the abandonment of effective aid for the White

Russian cause, gave the regional alliance projects a deeper significance for Germany by formally endorsing the idea of a 'cordon
sanitaire' of border states; as Lord Balfour put it, of confining
Bolshevism and keeping Germany and Russia apart.[88] Inevitably,
the idea of a regional bloc involved Poland, a Baltic power of the first
importance in view of its acquisition of the Polish corridor and of
access to the free city of Danzig under the terms of the Versailles
treaty. The Polish leader, General Pilsudski, aimed to reduce the
vulnerability of the new Poland by absorbing the nascent alliance
schemes into his own federal plans, thus ensuring that the 'barrier'
was indeed strong. This was quite evident in the course of Pilsudski's
negotiations with the Latvian Foreign Minister, Zigfrids Meierovics,
late in October 1919, for a joint action against the Red Army. The
signing of a joint Polish–Latvian defence pact to clear the remaining
Bolshevik forces from their respective territories, Poland's perception
of the economic value of exit rights through Latvian harbours, and
additional demands from Warsaw in the first weeks of 1920 concerning how best to deal with future attacks from Russia, amply
supported the view of the Latvian ambassador to Poland: 'The Polish
ideal is a new, powerful Entente Cordiale with an independent
political centre in Warsaw.'[89]

For the German government, for German political parties of all
shades of opinion and for German military leaders, all alike committed to the revision of the German–Polish frontiers after 1919,
Pilsudski's policies were unwelcome to say the least. The French
government's growing interest in Poland followed the collapse of
France's old ally Russia and was likely to impart a stronger anti-
German slant to the Baltic alliance projects. This was reinforced by
the effort which General Niessel expended on laying the groundwork
for a regional system, whilst ostensibly engaged in impartially super-
vising the evacuation of the German troops from Latvia in late 1919.
'It was necessary', Niessel recalled, 'to coordinate action between the
Baltic states, Finland and Poland. If left to themselves they would
never come to an understanding.'[90] Some of Niessel's fears were soon
confirmed. After a successful Polish–Latvian action against the
Bolsheviks in Latgale, the conference of Baltic states met in January
1920 in Helsinki, where the emerging Polish–Lithuanian conflict
over the disputed Vilna area and the Estonian–Latvian frontier dispute concerning Valga frustrated the earliest attempt made to
achieve a common policy with respect to the Soviet peace offensive.[91]

Despite the initial setbacks to the regional alliance discussions, the political ideals which the talks expressed remained very much alive, as we shall see in more detail later. The generally pro-Allied sentiments which prevailed in the Baltic countries at the end of 1919 contrasted profoundly with the anti-German mood there, particularly in Latvia. As a result of Bermondt's offensive, the Riga government had even declared a technical state of war to exist between Latvia and the Weimar Republic from November 1919.[92] To the German military leaders the situation could hardly have looked gloomier, as they contemplated a hostile Western world and the threat that through France's efforts the Versailles system would be extended to the Baltic region, thus further weakening the strategic position of the new Germany. For von der Goltz, the collaboration between the Baltic countries under the auspices of the French and British governments was a direct outcome of Berlin's failure to capitalize on the readiness of the German Freikorps to hold out in the Baltic region. He continued bitterly to regret the 'sabotage' of his attempt to frustrate the execution of the Versailles terms through making physical contact with a restored Russia. Although General Hans von Seeckt, too, remained seemingly indifferent to the force of Baltic nationalism, insisting that a future political and economic agreement with Greater Russia was 'the indispensable aim of our policy', he at least took account of the changing fortunes of the Bolsheviks.[93] In early 1920, as the Baltic republics made peace with the Soviets, beginning with Estonia on 2 February and continuing with Lithuania and Latvia on 12 July and 11 August respectively, the odds shortened on the Soviet forces being concentrated largely against Poland. Seeckt contemplated with apparent relish the prospect of a Russian victory over that state, and with it the restoration of the German–Russian borders of 1914 and therefore the eclipse of the Baltic countries too. He could not resist the temptation of a militarily crippled Germany, tied up by the peace treaty, receiving salvation through the actions of Russia. For Seeckt therefore, neutrality towards the looming Russo-Polish conflict itself constituted an 'active' step.[94]

There were inevitably some parallels with Seeckt's reaction inside the government, for Germany's growing disillusionment with the White Russian forces necessarily overlapped with the slow resumption of contact with the Soviets. A working relationship was established between the German and Soviet leaders through the Soviet agent, Viktor Kopp, from late 1919, together with the repatriation of the remaining Russian prisoners of war. This at least provided a basis for a minimum dialogue about future relations and led in January 1920 to Germany's acceptance in principle of Soviet overtures for economic talks. It is also evident that the overwhelmingly anti-Polish mood of the Reichstag and of public opinion in Germany at large made a policy of neutrality most likely in the event of any Russo-Polish clash in 1920. It should be remembered, however, that the Allied insistence on German troops evacuating the Baltic itself virtually ensured that Germany would not actively intervene in the conflict. During the Cabinet meeting of 3 May, only a week or so after the Poles had launched their counter-offensive against the Russians, the German leaders stressed once more the importance of complying with Allied demands that they should discipline the German officers and men who had been charged with insulting behaviour towards General Niessel's mission.[95] The following day von Maltzan remarked to the Finnish General Mannerheim that 'Germany has undergone expensive enough and painful enough experiences with the campaign of von der Goltz and Bermondt, not to let itself in again for such adventures.'[96] When in addition the Allied conference at Spa had dashed any lingering German hopes of relief over reparations, and any prospect of accommodation in the matter of German disarmament, the formal declaration of neutrality was given by Berlin on 20 July 1920.

It must at least be assumed that in the event of a Russian victory even more moderate German political leaders would have learned to live again with the absence of independent border states, Poland above all.[97] Yet, however one speculates about the likely outcome of a Russian success in 1920, the German government's policy of neutrality did not signify full agreement with Seeckt's line. To the Cabinet's fears about the disgruntled Freikorps in East Prussia exploiting the Russian advance to engineer a coup (a real fear in the wake of the Kapp putsch), was added anxiety about the influence of Bolshevism inside the Republic should the Red Army get too close. Such anxiety found expression in the request of Foreign Minister Simons to the Russians, for a German military observer to be attached to the advancing wing of the Bolsheviks.[98] Clearly, expectations of political advantage were mingled with apprehension about the possible disappearance of the border states. This was no 'resolute knocking on the Russian door', but rather an example of the uncer-

tainty afflicting most of the Western European powers as they came
to admit the possibility of the long-term existence of a Communist
system in Russia, and as intervention gave way to containment.

Germany's policy could be justified in terms both of its military
weakness and of its growing need not to alienate the Soviets. It had
the additional advantage of preserving at least the spirit of the
Versailles provision that the Weimar Republic should recognize the
future relationship between the Allies and Russia, whatever this
proved to be. That the political leadership in Germany did not share
the military's apparent indifference to the border states as a whole
was suggested, however, even by Allied reports, which showed Berlin
attempting to sow discord between Poland and the Baltic countries
during 1919/1920.[99] Notwithstanding the atmosphere of crisis in the
border states and the possibility that Soviet troops would move into
the area, the Auswärtiges Amt demonstrated the importance it
attached to immediately mending its fences with its Baltic neighbours
by holding a meeting on 9 January 1920 to consider the question
of making peace with Latvia. The major Reich ministries, the army
and navy, the Prussian Ministries of Justice, Public Works, Finance,
Trade and Industry and Agriculture, the Directorate of the Reichsbank, various head organizations of industry and business, the
Chambers of Stettin, Königsberg and Tilsit, all sent representatives
to meet von Dirksen and von Maltzan as well as Müller himself.
Nothing could have demonstrated more clearly how much matters
had changed only one year after Winnig had 'made policy'.

Although the immediate objective was to try to clarify the extent of
mutual claims for damages and compensation between Germany and
Latvia, the wider aim was indicated by the Auswärtiges Amt in its
invitation. It expressed the need 'to be equipped for the eventuality of
peace with Latvia. It seems urgently necessary to discuss all questions
of an economic nature which could arise in this connection.' The task
of the German personnel being assembled for the Riga post when
normal relations were resumed was to 'bring German–Latvian relations to the degree of warmth necessary for fruitful collaboration'.[100]
It is clearly not without significance that this process was continuing
even as the Soviet–Polish conflict reached its crisis. It offered a
marked contrast to the line advocated by von Seeckt. Similarly, in
the case of Estonia, with whom Germany at least had *de facto* relations, the Auswärtiges Amt dismissed the fears of the Reich Ministry
of Economics that increased supplies of military clothing to Estonia

would be diverted for the Polish war effort. The German Foreign Office must 'precisely on political grounds, attach the utmost importance to showing the republic of Estonia every accommodation in this matter. The achievement of a good relationship with Estonia is of essential concern for our economic relations with Russia.'[101]

A growing attention to the economic aspects of the post-war German–Baltic relationship will be followed later. They provide an important and neglected counterpart to the more familiar discussion of neutrality and strategy during the 1920 crisis. The influential Baron Ago von Maltzan, from the summer of 1919 the head of the Russian section of the Auswärtiges Amt's Eastern Department, had – like von Seeckt – also remarked on the danger of a bloc of states in the Baltic. In a memorandum of 30 January 1920, he expressed the view that Estonia, Latvia and Lithuania were being used by the Allies as a bulwark against Communism. 'As a secondary aim, the Entente seeks to threaten Germany via the border states in case Germany makes any sort of difficulty.' Unlike von Seeckt, von Maltzan went on to assert that 'in relation to Germany an improvement is shown in all three states since the ending of external interference, whether through occupation or through the Bermondt adventure, as the distrust of the German threat recedes and the force of economic realities makes itself felt'.[102] The political implications of this diagnosis became all the more interesting in view not only of the restrictions imposed on German trade by the Versailles terms (see below, chapter 3), but also of Germany's obligation under the peace terms to accept future Allied arrangements for Russia, including the Baltic countries. Thus both the talks with Kopp and those with the Latvians took place ostensibly with the object of making arrangements for the repatriation of prisoners of war. The Latvian Red Cross committee which left Riga at the end of March 1920 under Albats, the Under-state Secretary in Latvia's Foreign Office, publicly came to discuss the prisoner of war issue but had 'beneath this guise more extensive tasks of a political nature'.[103]

The idea implicit in Maltzan's memorandum, that economic means could help Germany escape from the 'inactivity' in foreign affairs to which the Versailles treaty was felt to have condemned it, was shared by many in the Weimar Republic. It hardly amounted to a policy as yet, but it was reinforced by the influential document circulating in the Auswärtiges Amt under the joint authorship of the industrialists Felix Deutsch and Walther Rathenau, who was later

Foreign Minister in Wirth's second administration. Their memorandum provides one of the earliest and clearest justifications for an 'active' Weimar *Ostpolitik*. 'The undersigned', the memorandum opened, 'venture to bring to the attention of the Reich government considerations concerning foreign policy questions which demand an answer and the solution to which will determine the economic and political future of Germany. It concerns the relationship between Germany and the political units which have arisen on the territory of the former Russian Empire.' Taking for granted that political and economic collaboration with Germany's Eastern neighbours was the aim of German foreign policy and that this was not so much in dispute as how to achieve it as soon as possible, Deutsch and Rathenau criticized the government's policy of passively awaiting the outcome of the Russian question. Whilst appreciating the restraints imposed by the Versailles peace, notably under Article 117, which obliged Germany to recognize future provisions for Russian territory made by the Allied Powers, the authors deplored the obvious aim of the victors of maintaining 'separating barriers' between Germany and Russia. The writers admit the 'theoretical possibility that the Entente will conclude treaties forbidding or at least limiting the traffic between Germany and Russia'. Precisely this danger

ought to motivate Germany to consider the earliest possible relationship with the Eastern states, so damping the tendency of the latter to accommodate themselves to the wishes of the Entente in restricting contacts between Germany and Russia. The peace treaty has not taken away Germany's right as a sovereign state to arrange its foreign relations with the East according to its own needs. If, therefore, no greater significance is attached to the suspected intentions of the Entente over and above what is legally required, no reference can be found in the peace treaty which is opposed to contact with the Eastern states.[104]

Contact was exactly what the Müller government wished to establish once the running-down of the Baltic campaign had removed the dead hand of the German military presence. Apart from preparation for peace talks with Latvia, the selection of personnel was being made for the Baltic posts with a commitment to the cause of good Weimar–Baltic relations.[105] It would have served no purpose gratuitously to increase the number of Germany's enemies in the East. What had been regarded as timely by the German political leaders in October 1918 had become a matter of dire necessity by January

1920, when the Versailles terms came into force. Such perspectives were lost on German nationalists and on the advocates of resistance to the Allies. For all that, they were the only realistic ones when the Poles had turned back the Red Army at the battle of Warsaw in August 1920, an event which brought considerably nearer the international recognition of the full independence of the Baltic countries. At the conclusion of the major conference at Balduri, near Riga, on 20 August 1920, between Poland, Estonia, Latvia, Lithuania and Finland, proposals were made for more detailed agreements, throwing up the outline of a large regional political and economic bloc. By no means without its serious difficulties, the underlying and shared experience of the border states, which lay at the bottom of the alliance projects, *itself* constituted a challenge for Weimar policy. Stategically, the regional alliance projects marked a setback to the Reichswehr's expectation encouraged by the Soviet–Polish conflict, of a handshake with the Russians. There remained in this gloomy situation the recognition in Berlin of the harsh economic realities facing the border states at the opening of 1920, and of the part which Germany had traditionally played there in East–West trade. As the Western powers in general intensified their competition for access to Russian markets via the Baltic states after 1918, the Weimar Republic had a direct stake in the domestic policies and politics of the Baltic republics – particularly in Estonia and Latvia – in the form of the historic Baltic German minority. For this to be an advantage rather than a severe handicap, however, attitudes had to change. A critically important aspect of the reorientation of Weimar Baltic policy during the transition from peace to war concerned the Baltic Germans. They became a vital key to the success of the Weimar Republic's proclaimed goal of friendly Weimar–Baltic relations, given the intensely anti-German mood in the border states in 1920, when, as Keyserling said with regard to Estonia, 'Germany can only slide in today … as it were, through the keyhole.'

2

The Baltic Germans as *Auslandsdeutsche*

───── ⌇ ─────

The physical removal of the last German troops from the Baltic countries in December 1919 marked the opening of the New Year as the beginning of another chapter in German–Baltic relations, an obvious point of departure for implementing the policy of active friendship proclaimed by the Auswärtiges Amt in January 1920 during its peace negotiations with Latvia. History recognizes no clean breaks, however, and the retreating German troops could not take away in their kitbags the legacy of bitter resentment at German occupation. It was never far below the surface in the post-war years; predictably so, for to take issue with their recent conquerors was also for the Latvians and Estonians to define and legitimize their own still vulnerable state forms. In March 1923, when the Latvian Prime Minister, Kārlis Ulmanis, was still probing sore spots in a markedly anti-German lecture on Latvia's recent past, the then German ambassador to Riga, Adolf Köster, was forcefully reminded that it would take years for the Latvians to forget what had happened to them in 1919.[1] Against whom above all was this resentment most obviously, logically and conveniently directed if not against the once dominant Baltic Germans? A glance at the overall scale of the changes imposed on the German element in the Baltic States can make this point most effectively.

Nothing had more obviously symbolized the social and economic dominion of the Baltic German ruling caste than its landholdings, the basis too of its political power in the provincial administration. In 1918 in Estonia, some 90% of the large landed estates had been owned by Baltic Germans and about 58% of all agricultural land had been in the hands of the big landowners.[2] In Latvia, approximately 57% of agricultural land was under Baltic German ownership.[3] Redistribution of the land on a more equitable basis was a manifest necessity for the new Baltic governments on social grounds alone. A belief in more effectively combating the threat of Communism through the creation of small holdings also played an important part. In the harsh post-war years compelling reasons existed for the new political leaders to control and plan available economic resources, including land. To the Latvians and Estonians, however, it was hardly unwelcome that the Baltic Germans bore the brunt of the hardship of agrarian reform. The severity of the agrarian legislation introduced in Estonia on 10 October 1919 and in Latvia on 16 September 1920 reflected above all a determination to break the disproportionate political and economic power of the German element.[4] As far as landholdings were concerned, that particular goal was achieved by these radical laws. In Estonia no less than 96.6% of all the estates, largely belonging as they did to the Baltic Germans, was taken over, together with farms and villas. The question of fair compensation was left open for the time being. In Latvia, in contrast to the implied promise in Estonia, nominal remainders, (*Restgüter*), usually made up of about 50 hectares and in a few cases of 100 hectares, were left to the dispossessed estate owners, as well as an appropriate amount of stock and equipment. The latter concession was seen by most Baltic Germans as offering little more than the life-style of a peasant farmer.[5] Again, compensation was to be the subject of later legislation. As a result of the reforms the Latvian and Estonian governments acquired huge land funds for redistribution in the 1920s, and the Baltic Germans lost at a stroke most of their inherited wealth.

Agrarian reform also affected rural industry, where German losses were put in a later edition of the Baltic German Yearbook at some 80%.[6] Clearly, apart from the landed estate owners, the rural Mittelstand dependent on the old estates was severely afflicted. The expropriation of agrarian banks by the state worsened the prospects for recovery.[7] In turn the reforms accelerated the drift from rural to urban living and work. In Latvia, for example, 50.8% of the Baltic Germans lived and worked in Riga in 1920, a figure rising to 61.7% by 1925, and some 20.2% of the remainder were in other towns.[8] Although the urban commercial and industrial sectors of the German communities had at least relatively good prospects for adapting, as will be clear, the impact of rural employees looking for work in the towns imposed severe strains on the German welfare organizations.[9] Paul Schiemann's later polemic against the Bank of Latvia came to the conclusion that 90% of Baltic German wealth had gone into the coffers of the Latvian state.[10]

Facing towards the 1920s the Baltic Germans had good enough reason to regard themselves as a 'barely tolerated minority', numbering some 58 000 in Latvia in 1920 (or 3.7% of the total population) and 26 000 in Estonia (1.5%) – a situation characterized with some understatement as 'bleak'.[11] The scale of hardship and the prospect of continuing hostility from the Latvians and Estonians in the first period after the war narrowed the perspective down to one of survival for German culture and schooling and of the preservation of an economic base sufficient to sustain and nourish this endeavour. Baltic German historiography has rightly painted a gloomy picture of the 'turn of fate' experienced by the German element as a result of Latvian and Estonian independence. The hardship experienced by the German minority also needs to be seen, however, in relation to the extreme post-war suffering and dislocation facing even the dominant Baltic nationalities in 1920, though this is not to deny the racial dimension to the socio-political conflicts in Latvia and Estonia in the early independence period. For the first time the Baltic Germans experienced the full drawbacks of their numerical weakness, which before 1914 had always been concealed by the inverse relationship between their smallness and their political power. As the Estonian socialist, Martna, exclaimed with understandable scorn, 'We are supposed to assure the German element half the mandates in the Estonian parliament! Estonian population circa 1 680 000, Germans circa 26 000!'[12] Nothing could prevent the Estonian and Latvian parties from pressing home the attack on Baltic German wealth, which for so long had helped them to thrive and rule in spite of their waning numbers. More rational reflection convinced many Baltic Germans of the need for changes but the political hostility behind these and the spirit of revenge detected there were described as intolerable in the initial responses of the German minority to the agrarian reforms.[13] Protest was in vain. Baltic leaders were rightly convinced of the need for drastic reform and they felt able to manage 'without the approval of old Balt opinion'.[14]

The American Commissioner to the Baltic in 1919 may have exaggerated when he said of the Estonians: 'German Balts are their pet aversion, more so really than the Bolsheviks.'[15] On the other hand his remark well conveys the extreme sensitivity of the Baltic peoples on the subject of the 'Baltic barons'. Governments of the Weimar Republic could no longer be indifferent to the fate of the Baltic Germans, in view of wartime experience and the political link thereby forged between the Reich and the German minority in Estonia and Latvia; indeed Winnig made this clear when handing over the administration at the end of 1918. The first priority for German governments after 1919 remained, however, collaboration with the Baltic countries. It was unhelpful in this context that in the heated post-war mood Latvian and Estonian public opinion often made little distinction between the Reich Germans and Latvian and Estonian citizens of German origin – or, more precisely, to use the German terminology, German Balts. In the Baltic states, as an Auswärtiges Amt memorandum testified, 'the centuries old enmity of the nationalities now in power, against the old elite of German origin, has today been transferred to us'.[16]

This was a formidable obstacle for German policy to overcome. That it had to be overcome was certain in view of the anxiety in the Weimar Republic to resume economic penetration in the East, which was dependent on better relations with the border states. With compelling if unendearing logic, the economic and entrepreneurial interests in Germany who were pressing anxiously for access to Russian markets urged the government in 1920 'finally to throw overboard the policy of the German Balt barons and to conduct a purely German policy in Latvia and Estonia, on an honourable basis'.[17] This was knocking on an open door as far as the Auswärtiges Amt was concerned. When in 1923 Ago von Maltzan still felt it necessary to urge Wedding, the new German representative in Reval, not to be seduced by the social charms of the Baltic German community in Tallinn, lest he offend the 'endlessly sensitive Estonians in this matter', he recalled: 'We must base our policy in Estonia on the Estonians and not on the German Balts. I initiated and carried out this policy three years ago with great difficulty.'[18]

The corollary of such a policy was to convince the new leaders of the Baltic states that Germany was no longer following the policy of the German Balts in insisting rigorously on the legal distinction between 'Reich Germans' who happened to live and work in the Baltic countries and those of 'German origin' who, after centuries of settlement in the region, opted to stay in their 'homeland' as citizens of the new states of Latvia and Estonia. As never before, it became important to establish in Latvian and Estonian eyes the difference between the Reich German and the German Balt, a distinction which in practice had been blurred by the use of general terms like 'Baltic German' or 'German element'. The Auswärtiges Amt identified as a major contribution to 'removing the poison' of the anti-German mood in the Baltic countries 'a judicious emphasis on the distinction between Reich German and German origin'. This approach was also intended to minimize resistance to the direct efforts which the German government was entitled to make on behalf of its own citizens working in Latvia and Estonia, in representing, for example Reich Germans dispossessed by the Baltic agrarian reforms. 'In cases where, as a result of the prolific legislation of the young [Baltic] states, Reich Germans and those of German origin were similarly disadvantaged by laws which make a mockery of West European legal practice, we could not safeguard the interests of those of German origin.'[19]

This was not acceptable to rightist opinion in the Weimar Republic or to the vociferous Baltic Germans emigrés in Germany who maintained links with the nationalist parties in the Reichstag. The difficulties which the German government experienced in restricting its public action to the defence of Reich German interests in Latvia and Estonia, thereby deliberately maintaining an ostentatious display of non-intervention, were considerable. It was significant that, as distinct from the shift in political power which took place amongst the German Balts electing to remain in the Baltic states, the old baronial aristocracy retained the political upper hand in the emigré centres in the Republic, particularly in Berlin. The counterpoint to their bitter conflict with the Germans who were 'staying on' in their old Baltic homeland was their sharp criticism of what they felt was the German government's failure to do more directly to represent German Balt interests in the face of the draconian socio-economic legislation pushed through by the Estonian and Latvian governments in 1919/1920. A magnificent display of how not to learn the lessons of history was provided, by the prominent emigré, Baron Wrangell, who from March 1919 had increasingly assumed the role of spokesman for the German Balts at the Auswärtiges Amt. In December 1920 he attacked von Maltzan with the charge that 'present practice' conflicted with the best protection of the interests of the 'Germans in Russia'. Conjuring up the prospect of a future Russia of extreme nationalism, Wrangell harked back to the Treaty of Nystad and to the guaranteed position of the German minority in the Baltic. Wrangell saw the distinction between 'Reich German' and 'German Balt' in rather different terms: 'The only element in the Russia of the future who can direct the waves of the Slavic sea into more peaceful, less dangerous channels for Germany, is the German Balt element, not the Reich Germans ... These have no hold ... and sink in the Slavic ocean, unlike the Balts, because the latter are rooted to the soil.'[20]

The angry refutation of Wrangell's closing charge, that the German government welcomed the Estonian and Latvian attack on the German Balts, provides a glimpse of the long-term strategy which underlay the pointed tactical differentiation between Reich German and German Balt in 1919/1920. After he had been told once more that direct diplomatic pressure could not be exerted on behalf of the German Balts in Latvia, Wrangell was reminded that, nonetheless, 'everything is being done on our side in a confidential way to relieve the heavy fate of the German Balts'. There followed what was under the circumstances an impressive list of recent actions, beginning with the fact that the German–Latvian provisional agreement of 15 July 1920 contained a clause, inserted by the efforts of the German negotiators, 'which made possible an advantageous compensation of the German Balt element' (see below). In addition, the Auswärtiges Amt had taken the initiative to ensure that German Balt claims for losses due to German troop requisition in the war should get the same treatment as claims from Reich Germans; out of its own budget, the Auswärtiges Amt had already set aside the sum of 50 000 marks to help towards the recovery of the shattered German schools system in Latvia. Finally, it was also trying, 'secretly and with some success', to persuade the Latvian passport authorities to accept visa applications from those German Balts anxious to return to Latvia.[21]

In short, the German government continued to be manifestly interested in an existence for the German element *as a whole*. The first duty of the German representatives in the Baltic, to look after the Reich Germans there (of whom there were, for example, 2 000 in Riga in 1920), could only make sense in terms of the survival and readjustment to new conditions of the far more influential and numerous German Balts.[22] As one of Germany's representatives was to report later, when reviewing his progress in getting the Latvian government's trust that he was conducting a German policy and not that of the Baltic barons, the effort was ultimately aimed at exploiting the better mood to make it easier for German Balt emigrés to come back – a pre-condition, in Wever's view, for the long-term survival of Germandom as a whole in Latvia.[23] The implication here was, first, that the strictly legal distinction between German Balt and Reich German, which the Weimar Republic was compelled to observe after 1919 on political grounds in order to maximize the chances of collaboration with Estonia and Latvia, would be blurred once more in the long run, as inflamed passions abated and the German element as a whole came to make the most of its 'turn of fate'. To appreciate this strategy it is essential briefly to set the Weimar Republic's changed relationship to the German element in Latvia and Estonia against the general role which Germans abroad were expected to play after the First World War.

It has been said that war was 'the hour of birth' of the *Auslandsdeutsche*, or German abroad.[24] So it was, in the sense that the struggle within German minorities in Europe, between their cultural and racial affinity to the new 'Fatherland' after 1871 and their existence in their current 'homelands', was made more acute by the enormous surge of anti-German feeling in Europe when the fighting came to an end in 1918. Large new groups swelled the ranks of the *Auslandsdeutsche* as a result of the territorial changes made by the peace settlement.[25] In the case of the Baltic Germans, to use the general term again, the relationship to the German Reich had been dramatically changed by the outbreak of war and particularly from 1917, as the old ties with Russia fell away with the disappearance of the Tsar and his system of government. 'The consciousness of belonging to the German people', Jürgen von Hehn recently wrote, 'was no longer merely a question of their cultural affinity, but increasingly acquired political overtones.'[26] The Baltic Germans paid the price for this, like other German minorities, with the loss of prestige and influence and the personal hardships which were inevitable in view of the charges of 'war guilt' levelled against the German nation as a whole. The more strongly was a shared community of interest perceived between Germany and its minorities by opinion within the new Weimar Republic. 'War, this great teacher of history, awakened us to the importance of Germandom abroad and our relations to it.'[27] The clear proof of this was the enormous interest in all sections of German public and political life which sustained the remarkable number and mushrooming growth of organizations inside Germany concerned with the future welfare and survival of the *Auslandsdeutsche* after 1918.

That such energetic but initially uncoordinated activity assumed a central importance for German foreign policy in general, was apparent in the German government's attempts to exercise a measure of centralized control over the various organizations. The Auswärtiges Amt reported early in 1922 that it had already been engaged 'for a considerable time on the plans for a rationalization of the overall care of the *Grenz-und Auslandsdeutschtum.* This is to be achieved on the one hand in financial terms, through an agreed distribution of all public and private funds for this purpose, and on the other hand through practical work, especially the concentration of the divided associations.'[28] The so-called 'Administrative Union of Free Germandom Associations', which was set up under the Auswärtiges Amt influence in March 1922, covered all but 10% of the various private organizations involved with the *Auslandsdeutsche*, according to its own reckoning. This at least gave a measure of direction to the German Foreign Office – although in post-Versailles Europe much of the work of the organizations had to remain on a private basis and to aim to support its own efforts largely.[29]

In the field of private organizations, therefore, the Auswärtiges Amt was unable to achieve the degree of above-party, centralized control which seems to have been its ideal, judging from an internal plan referred to on 14 February 1922. This projected a sort of 'Parliament for Germandom', representing private organizations for the care of the *Auslandsdeutsche*, regional authorities, trade unions, industrialists and so forth, from which a working committee would be drawn to supervise the distribution of available funds and to determine priorities.[30] Nevertheless, the more modest goals which had to be set in relation to the private organizations need to be seen against the far more effective Auswärtiges Amt control of the influential Deutsche Stiftung. This successor to the so-called 'Ostschuss', originally founded in 1919 to prevent the threatened areas in the East from falling under Polish control, eventually supervised the distribution of aid to German minorities in Europe. Ostensibly a 'private' organization too, the Deutsche Stiftung functioned as a concealed official body, with regular consultations taking place between its business management, the Auswärtiges Amt and the Ministries of the Interior and Finance. Unlike the other private organizations, the Deutsche Stiftung was subject to parliamentary control through its advisory body, on which sat representatives from all the parties, with the exception of the Independent Social Democrats (USPD), the Communists (KPD) and the National Socialists (NSDAP). In practice, the advisory body was a device to forgo further parliamentary

scrutiny of the Deutsche Stiftung's activities and government funding, and to keep the work of the *Auslandsdeutsche* above party quarrels.
The private organizations could not of course match the scale on
which the Deutsche Stiftung operated.[31]

The elaboration of the organizational network inside the Weimar
Republic which catered for the *Auslandsdeutsche* need detain us no
further here.[32] It is merely necessary at this stage to beware of the
glib assumption, made in the light of Hitler's eventual exploitation
and abuse of the *Auslandsdeutsche* organizations, that the care of the
Auslandsdeutsche from the earliest days was geared more or less exclusively to the cause of militant revisionism; that Germans abroad were
fifth columns.[33] True, German minorities abroad were certainly
expected ultimately to contribute to Germany's own recovery and to
restoration of its international influence. Indeed, Carl Becker,
Prussian State Secretary and later Minister for Culture, argued in
his, *The Cultural policy tasks of the Reich*, published in 1919, that for the
foreseeable future German foreign policy would have to be, in good
measure, 'policy towards Germandom abroad'.[34] To have allowed
this to become the policy of open irredentism, whatever nationalists
might want, would have been politically self-defeating in the highly
charged post-war atmosphere. It is worth stressing that a good deal of
the secrecy and the reliance on verbal exchanges which characterized
much of the work for the *Auslandsdeutsche* – including the Baltic
Germans – reflected the sensitivity of the issues rather than inherently
sinister motives at work.[35]

Collaboration necessarily remained the watchword of official
policy towards the *Auslandsdeutsche*. German minorities had to play an
active part in improving relations between their 'host' country and
the Weimar Republic. Economic imperatives ruled here. In the
words of the Bund der Auslandsdeutschen, which had been called
into being under the auspices of the Auswärtiges Amt in 1919, and
which played a role in the machinery of compensation for Germans
abroad damaged by the war, 'Germans abroad had once been a more
significant factor in the world's economic life.' These, 'if properly
used would help Germany recover its former standing.'[36] The idea
was a dominant one in the pamphlets, speeches and exchanges
between the *Auslandsdeutsche* organizations and official bodies, from
the moment they came into being. As another speaker argued at the
First Congress of Germandom Abroad, held in Hamburg in
December 1919, few were aware 'to what a high degree the *Auslands-*

deutsche prepared the way for our industrial exports abroad'.[37] Faced by the post-war economic problems, the Weimar Republic had to become once more a 'gigantic industrial undertaking', with the *Auslandsdeutsche* 'as its agent and propagandist'.[38] Carl Becker might regret the harsh economic emphasis in the *Auslandsdeutsche* movement, but if the German minorities were reduced after 1919 to concentrating on their cultural and economic survival, the latter was manifestly a pre-condition of the former. In any case, the overwhelming need of the Weimar Republic was to recover its foreign trade. The Managing Committee of Reich Germans from Russia, which worked with the Bund der Auslandsdeutschen in the immediate post-war years, and on which sat prominent German industrialists from Riga and Tallin, notably Hermann Peterson, Eugen Busch and Gerhard Krull, argued strongly in December 1919 that, 'owing to the force of circumstances our foreign policy in the foreseeable future can only be an economic policy'. In relation to the West it would regrettably have to be passive by and large, confined to tactical manoeuvring, 'whereas in the East there should be an opportunity for a purposeful economic policy'[39] (see below, chapter 3).

The intention of the writers of this letter was to put their expertise at the disposal of the German government. That the latter took their advice at the highest level was confirmed by the presence of Baltic German industrialists in the early talks concerning the peace treaty with Latvia. The Baltic Germans as a whole exemplified *par excellence* the model of a German minority which had enjoyed a long-standing and prominent economic role abroad and which might be expected to pick up the threads again after 1919. Riga industry in the pre-war era had been to all intents and purposes a branch of German industry, offshoots appearing in the Baltic capital to circumvent the high tariff barrier erected by Tsarist Russia in its later years. The central role in East–West trade of German commercial enterprise in Riga was what Dr Bach emphasized when trying to secure German government help in re-starting the damaged Baltic industries early in 1920 (see below, chapter 3). Arguments in a similar vein were advanced by Graf von Medem, a former judge in the Provincial Administration of Courland. He increasingly played a leading role as a spokesman of Balts in the Reich and in 1919 became a section leader on the German Winding-Up Authorities for the Baltic Countries. Assuming 'a German economic policy gravitating eastwards, particularly towards Russia', he stressed the importance of the

German element as a vital 'sphere of influence' by reference to the pre-war economic role of such German-controlled firms as Waldhof and Mannheim, which were among those concerns involved in the supply from Russia and the Baltic of 90% of the wood used in the Prussian wood industries. Like Bach, von Medem wanted the German government to take account of the German element as a whole in its dealings with Latvia, urging that the Berlin administration should make special arrangements with Latvia for compensating German Balts for war damages. Significantly, von Medem's defence of Germany's need for footholds in the Baltic argued: 'With the rebuilding of Latvia German craftsmen and such like will find their way to the Baltic states, so that the policy of settlement will, unnoticed, find a rich field for action alongside the economic policy.'[40]

That the German government supported the general drive of the *Auslandsdeutsche* organizations and of political parties and interest groups to facilitate the return of Reich Germans and German Balts to Latvia and Estonia was assured by its wider interest in maintaining Germandom abroad and by its awareness of the likely international competition for renewed trade with Russia and the East (see below, chapter 3). In any case it made sound financial sense to reduce the number of German Balt exiles in Germany. Earlier efforts had been made to discourage the influx of refugees expected from the Baltic after the war because of the hopeless employment situation inside Germany. Something like a quarter of the overall total of German Balts from the border states had to be dealt with initially through refugee organizations and by means of setting up funds in accommodating capitals like Stockholm. Here, early in 1919, a fund had been authorized by the Reichsbank from the occupation currency of the wartime German Military Administration in the Baltic, which was distributed via the Stockholm Trade Bank.[41] The German Balt refugees inside the Weimar Republic formed a bridge, as it were, to the German element in the Baltic countries, but the return of as many emigrés as possible was the aim of the German governments from 1919 onwards. Here the tactical distinction between 'Reich German' and 'German Balt' can be briefly re-examined with this particular issue in mind, to better illustrate the long-term strategy behind it.

All 'Germans', German–Balt and Reich German, could draw on limited sums from the Rückwanderhilfe, whose collections began in 1919, although these benefited chiefly those whose material need was not great.[42] An important source of larger funds – on which, strictly speaking, only Reich Germans could draw – was made available under a scheme publicized on 15 November 1919, by the 'Announcement regarding the use of government funds for Germans suffering damages abroad'.[43] Although the German authorities argued that no legal grounds existed for compensating Germans outside the Reich who suffered damages as a result of the war, it was recognized that the Versailles Treaty, by referring to general damages to private property in enemy lands (article 297b, 439), made Germany responsible for the losses of its citizens abroad. Since the Versailles Treaty was made between nations, however, the basis of individual claims had still to be created by law, as it was on 31 August 1919. The scheme was eventually publicized in the 'Announcement' of 15 November.[44] Essentially, the aim was to sift claims and to make advance payments pending a future resolution of the whole problem of German property in enemy lands.[45]

The task of processing claims was allocated to the Bund der Auslandsdeutschen. The rationale for making the advances was that it enabled Germans to return abroad as quickly as possible and to begin standing on their own feet. Predictably, the scheme aroused great enthusiasm and interest in, and generated constant pressure from, nationalist circles in the Reich. Stresemann's personal query about the procedure in February 1920 was met with the assurance that the whole matter was being handled as quickly as possible so that Reich Germans returning abroad could resume their former activity in the interest of German trade. [46] Indeed, the limited nature of the funds available dictated that priority be given to those Germans who had already worked outside the German borders earlier. 'The return abroad of these people is in the urgent economic interest of Germany, since the recovery of German economic life is dependent to a high degree on the growth of German foreign trade.'[47] As the Bund der Auslandsdeutschen was later to testify, economic priorities were uppermost in the early years, and preference was given to economic rather than to cultural survival.[48]

The inclusion in the scheme of German Balts wanting to return to Latvia and Estonia, as well as Reich Germans, was seriously considered by the German government. In the end the financial burdens likely to be imposed on the Republic if all those of 'German origin' claimed as a result of a precedent's having been set with the German Balts proved decisive in excluding the latter.[49] Another aspect of the compensation mechanism appeared to offer more scope, namely that concerned with the work of the Reich Compensation Commission, which came into existence on 25 April 1915. It handled claims of owners of property abroad which had been seized in the name of the Reich as part of its war effort. In respect of the border states such claims were not, therefore, confined to German Balts, but were open to Latvian and Estonian citizens in general. They were dependent for their settlement on an overall agreement on war damages as a whole between the German government and the governments of Latvia and Estonia. A further legal complication was that until the recognition of the Baltic countries by the Allied Powers in 1921, and indeed afterwards for a while, the question remained open as to what Latvia and Estonia, as former constituents of Russia, could claim on the basis of article 116 of the Versailles Treaty. The article in question reserved reparations rights to Russia (see below, chapter 3).[50] The chief worry, Henkel warned in June 1920, was that the detested German Balts might not, as citizens of Estonia and Latvia, get their share of any war damages paid directly to the Baltic governments.[51] The problem first became pressing with Latvia, however, because of the need to restore normal relations and to end the state of war existing between that state and the Reich until July 1920. It was to this problem that von Medem had referred in his memorandum of 20 January (see above, note 20).

Further detailed discussion of the points raised by von Medem took place on 16 January 1920. It was apparent that giving cash advances to the German Balts by way of the Reich Compensation Commission raised problems for the German government, in that it planned to offset the value of war and of materials left behind when the Reich German Freikorps evacuated the Baltic area against the claims put forward by the Baltic countries. This ruling provoked the displeasure of Erich Koch-Weser, Minister of the Interior. Along with the Auswärtiges Amt, the Ministry of the Interior had a major interest in the welfare of the *Auslandsdeutsche*. Friction between the two departments of state had already made itself felt over the organization of the *Auslandsdeutsche* network as a whole. Koch regretted that he had not been invited to the talks on 16 January in view of the central concern of his office in the problem, and argued: 'I regard it as absolutely imperative that the German Balts, in so far as they have preserved and confirmed their German character, are compensated for requisitions against them according to the same principles applied to Reich Germans and indeed without regard to whether or not they are dwelling in Germany.' Not only did Koch-Weser insist on the government's duty on this issue; he also asserted that in any event the action would help materially 'to strengthen the much diminished German influence and standing in the Baltic and to foster trade with the East, which is profoundly important for the German economy' – a sentiment with which the President of the Compensation Commission, Hiekmann, agreed wholeheartedly.[52]

The Finance Minister made it perfectly clear, however, that financial grounds precluded preferential treatment of the German Balts, and the resultant compromise emerged in the discussion of war damages between the German and Latvian negotiators in the spring of 1920.[53] According to a report on 4 May 1920 by the head of the Eastern Department of the Auswärtiges Amt, Behrendt, the Latvians had been persuaded to agree that in mutual reparation claims room should be left for a direct agreement between the German government and those German Balts claiming damages.[54] On this basis – under paragraph 3 of article 5 of the German–Latvian Provisional Agreement of July 1920 (see below, chapter 3) – cases were excluded from the working of the mixed German–Latvian commission set up to deal with damages, where compensation had already been paid directly or where separate agreements to this effect had been made with the parties concerned. The German government was thereby enabled to make arrangements for direct payment to those German Balts accepting the procedure. Koch's overall wish had been met in a more acceptable form.[55] The Auswärtiges Amt affirmed later that the article in question was introduced expressly 'to ensure compensation directly to the German Balts, which was desirable on political grounds'. Even so, damages caused by German troops before the Latvian state formally came into existence were excluded from this procedure, as were claims for losses caused by the transfer of German church and school property to the Latvian Republic. 'It could have the most fateful consequences if, whilst protesting its exceptionally limited capacity to pay to the enemy coalition, Germany nonetheless made payments for purposes where there was not even a direct obligation.'[56] These arguments did not prevent the Auswärtiges Amt from regretting that the German Balts could not claim for the period before the 'birth' of Latvia, 18 November 1918.[57]

What emerges only too clearly from this first confrontation with the reparations issue in the East is the inverse relationship between the importance attached to the survival of the Baltic German community as a whole and the inability of German governments to add indefinitely to the resources provided by the private organizations for the care of the *Auslandsdeutsche*. It is for this very reason that so much emphasis was placed on the *Auslandsdeutsche*'s ability to become self-supporting. An extract from the journal of the Deutsche Schutzbund for 1920 is worth quoting at length, for it exemplifies the way in which the *Auslandsdeutsche* issue played its part in helping the German state to readjust to its post-war demotion:

The minorities ought not, in their economic struggle, to bank on material aid from Germany ... Minorities must be able to lead an independent economic existence. Conditions will vary, inevitably, in each state, according to whether the [German] minority is made up of farmers, landlords, industrial labour or the middle classes ... In each case the effort must be made to bind the German minority to the land. The attempt must be made to ensure that when making new trade treaties the large German minorities are called on by Germany to give advice, so that the self-help of the *Grenz-und Auslandsdeutsche* will be given strong backing through such treaties.[58]

How closely German policy towards the Baltic Germans echoed this sentiment can be seen from the words of Wipert von Blücher's explanation to the Reichstag's Foreign Affairs Committee on 20 May 1920. Once the German–Latvian provisional agreement had been made, Germans 'will return to Latvia and German trade will follow'.[59]

Where grounds of extreme political sensitivity reinforced the case for financial limits on the support of the Baltic Germans as a whole, the reaction of the more numerous German Balts was of great importance to the success of the strategy imposed on Weimar governments by the constraints of the post-war order. Adolf Köster, in turn German Foreign Minister, Minister of the Interior and ambassador to Latvia, rightly argued that the support of the German Balts had to take other forms but that it was more important for German interests in the East than that of the relatively small number of Reich Germans in Latvia and Estonia.[60] It is impossible to imagine how the German policy-makers could have pursued the strategy of active cooperation with the Baltic countries, had not those German Balts who elected to stay on themselves faced up to the burdensome task of building a new existence, so that they were enabled to make the most of those 'other means' to which Köster referred. In spite of difficulties created by the anti-German mood in the Baltic and the old fears about the German Balts as the agents of German imperialism, there was one field of activity which remained at least relatively free of serious friction, namely that of cultural support for the German community as a whole in Latvia and Estonia.

As Baltic governments defined the parameters of German activity in their states between 1918 and 1920, it was all the more important that in Latvia and Estonia there was a wide measure of agreement across the political spectrum that cultural autonomy was a desirable goal. This was partly related to the pursuit by both states of entry into the League of Nations, but in general it could be argued that the question was one of survival. In Latvia in 1920, almost a quarter of the population was composed of different minority groups, the figure for Estonia being about 14%.[61] The struggling new states could hardly dispense with the support of these groups and in particular needed the expertise of the German element, given the relative inexperience of many of the native administrators in 1919. As a contemporary observer suggested, the new states could either face 'tribalism and ruin, or alternatively, racial tolerance and prosperity'.[62] In Latvia the passage of the School Law, on 8 December 1919, counted as the first success of the Baltic German community in the new state. In Estonia, too, Baltic German drafts and preparatory work helped to ensure that cultural autonomy was enshrined as a principle in the constitution of 1920.[63] In comparison with the minority treaties which the Latvian and Estonian governments signed when they joined the League of Nations in 1921, their own legislation was an advance, since the League arrangements were concluded between states and this generally made it hard for minorities to find an outlet for their individual cases on the international level.[64]

Turning the promises and projects of the Baltic governments into practical policies was a central goal of Baltic German activity after 1919. The German community in Latvia was at once put into a position of at least starting to try systematically to rebuild the private German school network, as a result of the School Law, which sanctioned the setting-up of education authorities by the German and other minorities. Although the chief of the German authority was elected by the German element, he had access to the cabinet in Riga through his attachment to the Latvian Education Ministry. Such cultural 'defence' was crucial to the very survival of the German minority in the Baltic countries, for it had implications for long-term developments and economic security. This was a lesson well learned from the Baltic German experience of Russification before the First World War. The echo was strong of Carl Schirren's dictum, that cultural autonomy was 'the innermost nerve' of Baltic German life.[65] It has been argued that cultural autonomy was the goal of Baltic German politics, that the maintenance of German schools constituted the essence of the German minority's work in Latvia and Estonia; that it was the 'legacy' of the Baltic Germans, the reward, as it were, of their own historical tradition of not attempting to Germanize the Latvians and Estonians.[66]

Of course, the acceptance in the Baltic states of the principle of cultural defence provided the German government with legitimate grounds on which to help financially the cultural and social welfare activities of the German communities there. By the end of 1920, Wolfgang Wachtsmuth, a member of the German education authority in Latvia, began his yearly journeys to Germany in order to raise funds for the support and development of German schools in Latvia, of which there were only 45 in 1919/1920. He also negotiated with German publishers for textbooks and elsewhere made efforts to get recognition from the Weimar Republic of the diplomas offered by the German Higher Schools in Riga. Not only did the Reich cultural authorities give their approval to German Balt activity in this field, but the Auswärtiges Amt promised the sums of money requested, 'whereby a beginning was made with the yearly subsidies'.[67] In the case of Estonia, the Auswärtiges Amt had already started making advances for the school year 1919/1920.[68]

These were necessarily modest sums in terms of the Weimar Republic's overall budget. In the first post-war years the sums gained through the contacts and overtures of the Baltic Germans to the Weimar Republic and the organizations caring for the *Auslandsdeutsche* were sporadic. Detailed figures are hard to come by before the mid-1920s, when the Baltic Germans' own organizational network for care and welfare was put on a more solid footing (see below, chapter 7). The basic principle of the aid channelled through the Cultural Department of the Auswärtiges Amt was that subsidies were intended initially to help the German community over a lean time until their own organization was completed. One interesting example of such *ad hoc* funding is provided by the agreement of Koch-Weser in October 1920 to a request from the Verein für das Deutschtum im Ausland (VDA), that 600 000 marks be allocated from the surplus funds of the German Winding-Up Authorities of the formerly occupied areas. The claim was advanced with regard 'to the great importance of maintaining the German school system in the Baltic countries'. After a high-level meeting involving Wirth, Koch and Foreign Minister Simons, the sum was eventually increased to 12 million marks.[69] It was arranged that the money would be distributed through the Deutsche Stiftung and administered by a committee which would include representatives from the Baltische Vertrauensrat and the VDA. How important this was emerges from the personal interest which Simons took in the matter. He promised also that he would use his influence to ensure that the Reich Compensation Commission met promptly the claims of the German School Association in Courland for losses to the Latvian authorities after the German troops had evacuated the region; and that the money would be sent directly to the Baltische Vertrauensrat, so that 'in so far as the school system is concerned, the return of the Balt refugees from the Reich to their homeland can be set in train'.[70]

Although the financial contributions coming from the Reich were limited in the immediate post-war years, it was important that a network of ties emerged early on between the German communities in the Baltic and the major organizations in the Weimar Republic for the care of Germandom abroad. The VDA, funded largely by the Ministry of the Interior, was much involved. The regional branch of the VDA in Lower Saxony was directly responsible for liaising with the Baltic Germans in Latvia, whilst Max von Radecki, of the German education authority in Latvia, was the official link-man with the Lower Saxony organization. He did not confine his meetings to financial matters, but 'brought out the essential cultural unity of the German element in Latvia with the *Auslandsdeutsche*', in tune with Auswärtiges Amt thinking.[71] The entire logic of cultural support – schooling, subsidies to the German Theatre in Riga (later to the Herder Institute), the school visits, visiting professors and student exchanges – was very obviously to cement together the disparate elements in the Baltic German communities as a whole.[72] The process was furthered too through the work of the German representatives in Riga and Tallinn. Although nominally looking after Reich German interests and the colonies of Reich Germans residing in Tallinn and Riga, the German ambassadors ultimately came to play a key role in the local distribution of funds coming from the Reich.[73] 'A wealth of small means' was indeed required to ensure that; 'something will slowly be accomplished here, and with time.'[74] The

German-language press in the Baltic countries had an important function in the attempt to bring Reich German and German Balt together and more generally to help eliminate ill-feeling between German and Baltic governments. This was reflected in the Reich's financial stake in the largest German-language daily in the East, the *Rigasche Rundschau*, which was ultimately controlled by Reich funds via the cover organization, the Concordia, Literarische Anstalt. Early subsidies were also given by the German government to the *Revaler Bote* and the *Dorpater Zeitung*.[75]

In sum, in 1919/1920, Weimar *Ostpolitik* effected a readjustment of policy towards the Baltic Germans in Latvia and Estonia which paralleled its attempt to work closely with the new Baltic republics. Accepting the drastic reversal of the position of the Baltic Germans as unavoidable, German policy-makers responded cautiously and were influenced by long-term aims, which were clarified within the general context of the *Auslandsdeutsche* as a whole. The twin pillars of cultural and economic support for the German element in Latvia and Estonia were founded literally in the moment of peace. Since Weimar–Baltic German relations were also part of the larger network of Weimar relations with the *Auslandsdeutsche* at large, pressures could never be absent, either within the Reichstag or within the predominantly conservative/nationalist *Auslandsdeutsche* organizations, to treat the support of compact German communities largely as an extension of the long arm of German revisionism after 1919. Here, as elsewhere, it remains difficult to achieve the task of looking outwards from 1919, rather than backwards through the prism of National Socialism, whose doctrines systematically subverted much of the meaning of the *Auslandsdeutsche* movement.

The advantage of examining how German governments first modified relationships with the German minorities in Latvia and Estonia is that it enables the focus to be kept on readjustment rather than revisionism, for the Weimar Republic had no territorial claims against either Latvia or Estonia. It is of course undeniable that Weimar–Baltic relations came to have an important function to play in the revision of the German–Polish frontiers, as will be seen. Yet the significant feature of Weimar support for the Baltic Germans as *Auslandsdeutsche* is that the success of the strategy depended on instilling in the German community the need for constructive collaboration. Although essentially rooted in German weakness after 1918, such a tactic could develop its own positive momentum. At the very least, the above discussion depicts an instructive example of how large powers like Germany adapted to the new 'small states' in the East. Arrogance in German government circles towards what Brockdorff-Rantzau called the *Rand- und Schandstaaten* was perhaps inevitable at times, but the logic of Weimar policy was to throw weight behind the attempt to encourage the Baltic Germans to be loyal to their new masters. The acceptance by Baltic Germans of Latvia and Estonia as independent states was virtually a pre-condition of a successful German *Ostpolitik*; political outsiders were no use to the Weimar Republic's drive to restore trade through the good offices and work of its minorities in the border states. In this respect, it was vitally important that the Baltic Germans of Latvia and Estonia came to follow a road which ran roughly in the direction taken by German governments after 1919.

Of the twenty thousand or so Baltic Germans who fled to Germany at the end of the war, through Stettin, Danzig and Königsberg, almost half had returned to Latvia and Estonia during the course of 1920/1921. Those who stayed away from the Baltic failed, in Paul Schiemann's words, 'to share in part of their homeland's history'.[76] They shared little understanding of the idea that minority protection was not simply a question of right but was, rather, 'the policy of the possible ... also of the attainable'. [77] Formidable criticism and pressure were applied by the emigré Baltic Germans when, after the dissolution of the ancient Baltic German Ritterschaften by the Estonian and Latvian governments in 1920, men such as Eduard von Dellinghausen, von Stackelberg, Oettingen and Manteuffel elected to remain in the Weimar Republic, thus ensuring that the 'old Balt' mentality dominated the political leadership of the Baltic German groups in Berlin and elsewhere in Germany. There was much truth in the polemic which the Latvian M. Walters wrote, characterizing such old Balt attitudes ('Doubting, intolerant; declarations of protest, bitter opposition, demands'), and there was an expectation that the Eastern question would be re-opened.[78] The emigrés 'saw in those staying on (Heimatbalts) compromisers, who through their "adjustment" to new conditions had relinquished something of their national honour by abandoning Balt tradition'. This resentment was matched, however, by that of the Heimatbalts, who tended to regard those who had not returned to Latvia and Estonia as 'deserters, who in the hour of need had left the land where they were born and who shunned taking up the struggle for existence'.[79] It is easy to see why the Auswärtiges Amt had such difficulty in convincing governments in Riga and Tallinn that Germany was no longer following the policy of the German Balts.

In truth, it *was* pursuing such a policy, but it was not that of the 'old Balts'; rather, so to speak, of the 'new' Balts. Readjustment in the Baltic German communities of Latvia and Estonia to the radical changes brought about by Germany's defeat was facilitated by the fact that so much of the old Balt political influence was left outside the Baltic states after 1918. This is not to say that the long-standing class distinctions between the old Balt nobility, the urban patriciate and the professional sectors vanished after the dissolution of the traditional *ständisch* political organizations in the Baltic.[80] On the other hand, the necessary acceptance of parliamentary democracy by the German element in Latvia and Estonia opened up new paths to a career in politics, whereas formerly the route had been through the old corporations on the land and in the towns. The change moved the political centre of gravity towards the urban bourgeoisie, in Latvia especially. It thus followed the shift in economic influence to the urban commercial and industrial sectors of the Baltic German communities which was the result of agrarian reform.[81] It was important for the long term that the Baltic Germans of Latvia and Estonia by and large quickly grasped the need to avoid overtly sectional and selfish interest representation within the German community as a whole. And here the earlier experience of the pre-war associations (Vereine) paid handsome dividends. [82]

In general the political adjustments demanded of the Germans in Estonia proved less problematical, partly because the country as a whole had endured a far less protracted and thorough German occupation in the war than had Latvia. Although perhaps more conservative in outlook than many of the German political leaders in Latvia in the inter-war years, the Germans staying on in Estonia after the 'deserters' had left favoured immediately closing ranks with the Estonians to defeat the joint enemy in the shape of the Bolshevik forces. Nothing demonstrated this more graphically than the way in which the Baltic German fighting force set up at the end of 1918, the Baltenregiment, threw its weight behind the new state. The contrast with the policy pursued by the Baltische Landeswehr in Latvia at that time is marked, as we have seen (see above, chaper 1). Men of essentially conservative outlook, like Werner von Haselblatt, the former lawyer from Dorpat and prominent minority spokesman in

Estonia and Europe in the 1920s, Axel de Vries, then lead writer of the *Revaler Bote*, and Baron Carl Schilling, were able to take the newly formed Deutsch–Baltische Partei (December 1918) relatively smoothly into the Estonian Constituent Assembly. This met on 23 April 1919 under the influential chairmanship of the poet and journalist Christoph Mickwitz.[83] The immediate pressure on the German community was lessened by the acceptance of the principle of cultural autonomy, and this in turn facilitated an early concentration on political activity in the Estonian parliament, the Riigikogu.

The contrast with the Baltic German community in Latvia could not have been greater; there the legacy of the protracted German military occupation and the extension of German action as a result of the armistice provision made it difficult to seize the early chance to return to normalcy, as the Baltic Germans had done in Estonia. The continuing illusory hope of salvation from Germany made it virtually impossible at first for the Baltic Germans to set up a single party to represent the varied interests and political viewpoints in the Baltic German camp in Latvia. It was necessary to establish an umbrella organization, which was announced in the *Rigasche Zeitung* on 9 November 1918. The new National Committee's task was to coordinate the work of the main political groupings of the Germans in Latvia.[84] These included the Demokratische Partei under Paul Schiemann, the Volkspartei under the conservative Baron Wilhelm Firks, a middle party in the shape of the Reformpartei, a small Fortschrittliche Partei under Rosenberg, and the Einigungspartei.[85] Of these, only the liberal Democratic Party had been founded before November 1918. It appeared in April 1917 and was linked with one of the few German Balt leaders who was not burdened by association with the Wilhelmine German occupation of the Baltic countries, Paul Schiemann.[86] His earlier advocacy of the idea of independent Baltic states had ensured that the German military kept him out of Latvian territory during the war, but he had continued to spread his ideas in Berlin. Here he made contacts not only with members of the Reichstag majority and with liberals like Max and Alfred Weber, Hans Delbrück, Theodor Heuss and Paul Rohrbach, but with the Auswärtiges Amt officials, notably von Maltzan. Schiemann's memorandum of 7 October 1918, written in conjunction with the German landowner from Lithuania, Friedrich von Ropp, played no small part in the deliberations leading to Max of Baden's declaration of the 'new policy' in the final weeks of the war.[87]

That Schiemann was correct in refusing selfishly to capitalize on his party's relatively favoured position, and in choosing instead to continue to work with the other political leaders on the National Committee, was confirmed by the fate of the Progressive Party under Rosenberg. The latter headed a political group not unlike Schiemann's in terms of its values and beliefs, but he elected to dissociate his party from the conservatives in the German Balt political camp. In hurriedly accepting five of the eight seats reserved by the Ulmanis government for the German minority in the Latvian Volksrat in November 1918, Rosenberg broke ranks with the National Committee and dealt a further blow to Winnig's vain effort to negotiate a disproportionately large share of the seats for the Baltic Germans. It is tempting to sympathize with Rosenberg against the overwhelming weight of the Baltic German historiographical tradition, and with his view that Winnig was a 'very, very small man, with a very, very limited outlook'. Rosenberg openly scorned the collapse of the German Balt 'laboriously erected house of cards' before the wind of Latvian nationalism.[88] Yet in the last resort, with the mortal blow to the old Balt position in June 1919 (see above, chapter 1) the more difficult path urged by Schiemann was vindicated. After his return to Latvia in July 1919, Schiemann's patience facilitated the collaboration between his own movement and that of the conservative leader, Baron Firks. The partnership provided the foundation of German–Balt political activity within the new Latvian state. Negotiations between a three-member commission of the National Committee and the second Ulmanis government took place on 25 June 1919 in the name of the German community as a whole. In the interests of *Realpolitik* the Latvians dropped Rosenberg. With the acceptance of two ministerial posts in the Ulmanis administration, Dr Erhard as Finance Minister, E. Magnus as Justice Minister, 'the integration of the Baltic Germans into the state was accomplished'.[89]

It is worth stressing, the better to understand the collaboration between Schiemann and Firks, that the former came from an old-established lawyer's family from Courland and had a secure place in Baltic German society before the war, being also the nephew of the celebrated historian Theodor Schiemann. In a real sense, therefore, Schiemann's skill related to his ability to conserve and adapt 'old Balt' values within the new democratic forms. Important as Firks was to Schiemann's standing within the Baltic German community as a whole, the democrat leader's conceptions remained paramount in guiding the day-to-day political work of the Baltic Germans after 1919. Schiemann's commanding position was given more tangible expression in the Committee of German Balt Parties which succeeded the National Committee early in 1920. The Committee was created on the initiative of Schiemann and Firks expressly to secure a broad measure of agreement within the Baltic German camp on cultural matters and in dealings with the Latvian state. The original idea of switching the chairmanship of this coordinating committee resulted in practice in Schiemann's duly allotted six-month term of office being extended by popular consent to ten years.

Whilst the separate [Baltic German] parties continued formally but in practice assumed the character of organs giving political and technical advice, the
Committee of German Balt Parties ensured, under Schiemann's leadership, a
uniform political formation, a compact German fraction in the parliament
and knit so closely together that it [the committee] itself assumed the character of a 'party' without ever formally becoming one. As such – as the German
Party – the Latvians also termed it and accepted it. The German deputies
were responsible to the Committee rather than to the individual parties. So
arose the paradox that Schiemann was leader of a 'party' which consisted
chiefly of members of other parties.[90]

Admittedly the number of German Balts who had seats in the assemblies of Estonia and Latvia, respectively the Riigikogu and the Saeima, was small in itself, being three in Estonia in 1920 and five in Latvia. This has to be seen against the background provided by the large number of political parties in both states. Furthermore, the constitutions in the Baltic countries were notable for their ideally democratic form, particularly in Estonia where it has been argued that the bias towards parliament was so great 'that in effect the government was little more than a parliamentary commission'.[91] In view of the number of small parties, including those representing the minorities in both states, the more tightly organized Baltic Germans could anticipate tactical voting to some extent. In Latvia and Estonia a conservative agrarian party was opposed by a Social Democratic Party, with the middle ground occupied by one or more liberal parties. In Latvia the centre was vital in all cases, since the forces of right and left were too evenly balanced to form wholly independent administrations.[92] Baltic German parliamentary activity was an essential dimension to the work of building up the network of organizations for the care and welfare of the minority in the first months of

peace. Although much of the work in this field – through, for example the League of German Associations founded in Estonia in 1920, the Welfare Central which emerged in Latvia in 1921 and, later the Zentrale deutsch-baltischer Arbeit, – had to be a-political, nonetheless political activity and influence provided an essential focal point for the overall involvement of the Baltic Germans in the rebuilding of the states.

It must be emphasized at this stage that in Latvia especially wider opinion did not automatically see Baltic German parliamentary activity in the way Schiemann portrayed it. For Schiemann it was in the parliamentary field above all that the Baltic Germans could openly contribute towards that solution of the conflict 'between belonging to a state and belonging to a people' which he saw as 'the task and goal of the nationalities movement' and as 'the essential nature of the minority problem'. By contrast a Latvian analysis of the political parties urged that Schiemann was in effect adapting old Balt ideology to newer times, in his demand for autonomy for the minorities in the cultural field and for the revision of agrarian legislation, and in his conscious attempt to prevent social splits in the ranks of the Baltic Germans. 'Thus the tendencies of the [German] Party in the first instance are towards fostering the economically strong sectors of Germandom, big business and large scale industry ... directed among other things at bringing all Germans under one direction and command, in keeping with the old traditions.'[93]

Yet Schiemann remained one of the most articulate defenders of the 'new Balt' policy, and it was crucial to the success of Weimar Baltic policy that he should have used his influence so decisively to persuade the majority of German Balts staying in Latvia to see their own struggle for survival as linked with that of the Latvian state. The same can be said of the German Balt leaders in Estonia. 'If in this hour of crisis ... we ... leave the posts we have been given, we are lost. By demonstrating the strength of our culture in working for the state we will best protect [that culture].'[94] These beliefs were set out in Schiemann's 'Guidelines', published in the *Rigasche Rundschau*, of which he was then editor, on 12 January 1920. These professed the struggle against class privilege and demanded an organization of various professional interests to help rebuild the economy. Among other things it called for social solidarity and a recognition by the party of the national interest and urged the need for regulation of the economy. Whilst preserving German interests, the party was to avoid collision with the state. 'The party is striving to realize its political and national aims within the bounds of an independent Latvian state.' Schiemann remained anxious to involve 'all the forces of the German Balt population in Latvia' in the overall 'reconstruction and consolidation on a democratic basis' of that state.[95] His aims were publicized in his considerable body of writing on minorities in inter-war Europe. Ultimately he wanted such groups to be given full autonomy as far as culture was concerned, and he projected a vision of care for minorities which was doomed to disappointment by the end of the 1920s. It needs to be emphasized, however, for it underlined the commitment of many of the Baltic Germans to making the most of their 'turn of fate'.

How far they were able to achieve their main goals of cultural and economic survival can be re-examined later in this book. That the process of readjustment would not be acceptable to all those staying on, let alone those who had left their homeland, was certain. The significant fact is that the Baltic German leadership in Latvia and Estonia had set the points in the direction best suited to the Weimar Republic's own goals in the region. It is impossible to imagine a German policy based on collaboration with the Baltic countries with-out the parallel effort of so many Baltic Germans to work in and with the new states. For Germany, more was at stake than the survival of the Baltic German community. The link had already been made between that minority and Germany's own economic prospects. The Baltic German community as a whole, its power gone on the land, had not been displaced from the commercial life of the towns, and there seemed sufficient reason to hope that it would help German trade recover in the region and in so doing help itself too. Behind all this was the prospect of the German element giving Germany an advantage in making Estonia and Latvia into 'springboards' to the Russian markets beyond. Here the Germans needed all the help they could muster, for they were in direct competition with the other powers, notably Great Britain. That Germany was only one of the ardent suitors pursuing Estonia and Latvia from 1920 gave the Baltic governments a degree of freedom in playing off the bigger powers, thereby suggesting that small countries are not always best under-stood by treating them as pawns in a game of diplomacy.

PART II: TRADE AND FOREIGN
POLICY 1921–3

3
The springboard concept

'The Germans are divided financially into two camps: the businessmen on the Rhine whose factories are working (thanks to the occupation) are largely looking westwards. The rest of Germany is looking
East.'[1] This appreciation by the British Foreign Office neglected to
point out that the view in question was being watched with equal
interest by the rest of Europe. In the present climate of East–West
uneasiness it comes as something of a shock to record the veritable
clamour for business with Russia which developed in Europe after
1918 and to chart the inflated expectations attached to this commerce. The prospect of competition in this area was a deadly serious
one for post-Versailles Germany. As with the *Auslandsdeutsche*, so
with its foreign trade the Weimar Republic sought to exploit what
resources it had to offset its international weakness after 1919.
General Groener might well lament in May 1919 that a foreign
policy needed 'power, an army, a fleet and money, all of which we no
longer have'.[2] Others were more aware of the leverage to be gained
by an active trade policy, above all in East Europe. Stresemann put
the matter succinctly later by writing: 'Now that we no longer have
our army there are only two sources of German power. One is our
united national will and feeling. The second is the German economy
… Our economy is the most powerful source of potential today … in
the last resort every German government must cooperate with the
German economy.'[3] Doubtless, Foreign Minister Friedrich Rosen
had such considerations in mind when he said of Germany after 1919
that 'economics alone were decisive and foreign policy as such
pointless'.[4] In reality, an active foreign trade policy was effectively
also 'foreign policy'.

This had long been recognized inside Germany even before defeat heightened the importance of its foreign trade. Since 1917 especially, reformist pressures had developed in the German business community and in the Reichstag and even within the ranks of the Auswärtiges Amt bureaucracy, in favour of broadening the expertise and training of the German foreign service to make it more aware of the needs of German commerce abroad.[5] The reforms of the Auswärtiges Amt which were completed by 1920 and which took their name from the then director of the office's personnel department, Edmund Schüler, duly gave expression to, among other things, such demands for fundamental change. The fusion of political and economic matters within the new regionally organized departments of the Auswärtiges Amt furthered a closer relationship between foreign and economic policy and allowed the Foreign Minister to have a decisive voice in economic issues affecting Germany's foreign trade. Schüler's ambitious scheme for a separate department to function as a continuing forum for civil servants, academics and businessmen to analyse and advise on foreign economic relations found brief life between 1920 and 1921 in the shape of Department X (Aussenhandelstelle) before it foundered on largely internal conflicts in 1921. Nevertheless, it played a crucial role in the very early resumption of trade contacts in the immediate post-war years, and its values lived on.[6]

Such restructuring recognized, therefore, the truth that the economy was Germany's 'last trump and the basis of existence of the otherwise powerless Reich'.[7] The Weimar Republic's trade policy was moreover inextricably tied up with the whole question of how the terms of the Versailles treaty would be carried out. At the most basic level, the rate of recovery of Germany's foreign trade was linked to its ability to finance the reparations payments demanded by the Allied Powers. Additional burdens were imposed by the Versailles treaty's requirement that for a five-year period the Germans should grant one-sided, most-favoured-nation treatment to the Allies – a restraint on Germany's foreign trade which was felt to be the more intolerable in view of the other economic penalties of the peace settlement. At a stroke, the Versailles provisions dampened the initial hope in the Republic that at least it would be allowed fully to restore its pre-war trade network and thereby regulate its own economic destiny. Effectively, the only path towards the goal of recovering sovereignty over its trade policy was for the Weimar Republic to negotiate a whole series of individual treaties with its foreign trading partners, thereby extending most-favoured-nation treatment for the Reich and gradually recovering its equality of status on the international level.[8]

Such gradual 'revisionism' was a logical enough response to economic provisions in the peace treaty, which undoubtedly pursued the political goal of postponing Germany's economic recovery.[9] That political implications of the first order of importance would follow in East Europe, the chief target for Germany's trade offensive and the region where its major revisionist hopes centred, was inevitable. It should be stressed, however, that for the Reich in the immediate postwar months the emphasis was heavily on recovery and the development of markets in the East, a point which enables comparisons to be made with the other European powers and helps to provide a fuller context in which to assess the nature of Weimar revisionism. Germany was not alone in its *Drang nach Osten*, and the Baltic countries here assume an importance far beyond their size. It is astonishing that the overwhelming majority of studies of early Weimar–Soviet relations not only give far less attention to this comparative context but signally fail in most cases even to mention Latvia and Estonia after 1919, though these were areas destined by geography and history to be at the very point of contact between the capitalist West and Communist Russia. Formally unrecognized by the Western Powers until 1921, the Baltic states were necessarily central to the earliest stages of Western policy towards Russia, and a fuller appreciation of their role in general can therefore hardly fail to qualify a good deal of the conventional wisdom about the much discussed 'Rapallo relationship' between the Weimar Republic and the Soviets in the 1920s.

West European economic expectations of the Baltic countries after the war derived in the first instance from their vital pre-war function in East– West trade. The major Baltic ports of Riga, Libau (Liepaja), Mitau (Jelgava) and Windau (Ventspils) in Latvia, and Reval (Tallinn) and Narva in Estonia, were favoured by location and climate as major access and exit points to and from the Tsarist Russian interior. By 1912, Riga, Libau and Windau together handled more shipping than St Petersburg.[10] Between 1908 and 1911 those same ports, on which converged three of Russia's great railroads, dealt with no less than a third of all exports and imports of European Russia.[11] A rich and profitable trade thus flourished prior to the outbreak of war in 1914, involving exports from Russia and the Baltic of millions of tons of flax, timber, hides, rye, butter and eggs and the unloading of foreign ships carrying raw materials such as rubber, steel and coal. These were for conversion by Baltic industries and largely for sale as finished products in the Russian Empire. Riga, that particularly favoured port, offered great attractions to foreign shippers, whose vessels not only could be used to bring in raw materials but could leave full again, this time with timber. On such a basis Riga became the biggest wood-export harbour in Europe and was duly rewarded by a doubling of its shipping trade between 1900 and 1913.[12]

Western interest and participation in Baltic transit trade was supported by the presence before the war of French, Dutch, Belgian, British and, above all, German capital. Such funds helped to make possible the concentration of industry and commerce in the major towns of what were then the Baltic provinces. This, together with the practice of setting up branches of German and West European industry in the Baltic to circumvent Russia's high tariffs, ensured a lively industrial development. Estonia could boast in Tallinn, for example, the Dvigately Railroad Car Factory and one of Russia's most important shipbuilding centres, the Baltic Shipyards. Narva housed the world's biggest cotton works, the famous Krainholm Mills.[13] Latvia, the 'Belgium of the East', supported, like Estonia, a range of metal, chemical and wood industries.[14] In Riga alone were the world's largest file manufacturer, the Salamandra plant, the huge Provodnik Rubber Factory, the Felser Shipboiler Works and the Phoenix Railroad Car Factory. These, along with other concerns and with the necessary commercial and business network, helped to ensure that two-thirds of the inhabitants of Riga were dependent on industry for their livelihood.[15]

Dramatic changes were wrought by war and revolution and by the setting-up of three separate economic units as a result of Baltic independence movements.[16] The lucrative transit trade dwindled to nothing as a result of the war. With Bolshevik seizure of power, ensuing civil war and early socialist 'planning', the great Russian markets, which had given meaning to Baltic industry, disappeared to all intents and purposes. The once flourishing big industrial concerns stood largely empty and lifeless, victims of Russia's determination to evacuate machinery, equipment and industrial labour as its troops pulled back before the German wartime advance. A large question-mark therefore hung over the future of Baltic industry in 1919. Similarly, the banking and financial network which had served Baltic trade and industry, but which had been greatly dependent on parent companies in Russia, virtually collapsed (see below, chapter 4).[17] To all this must be added the strains of Baltic involvement in the Allied intervention in Russia, the further disruption of trade caused by the blockade of the Allies and the absence of any worthwhile Baltic currency. Indeed, independence was proclaimed by the Baltic countries with ruined industries, empty coffers and largely agrarian economies.[18]

Such harsh economic realities did not dispel the conviction in West Europe that the older and deeper rhythms of East–West trade would slowly reassert themselves in the post-war period. In this context it is relevant that the three big industrial powers in Europe, Britain, France and Germany, remained vitally interested in intra-European trade after the war. All of them were net exporters of manufactured products; equally, the largely agrarian states of East Europe were committed to the provision of primary products in exchange for Western manufactures. In spite of the disruption caused by war there remained a congruence of interests between the Western industrial powers and the underdeveloped East.[19] Rivalry could be expected between the European powers. Although much emphasis has been placed in studies of the international system after 1919 on Britain's relative leniency over the peace terms imposed on Germany, the British were the chief economic adversaries confronting the business-men of the Weimar Republic in the post-war race for East European markets. Germany and Britain between them accounted for some 50% of total trade between the European powers in the inter-war period, and long before 1914 the two states had been involved in active competition for Russian and Baltic trade. Germany had cap-tured 38.2% of Russia's foreign trade by 1913, and by this date she was also challenging Britain's position in the imports and exports going through Baltic ports. Germany sent 133 million marks' worth of goods to Riga in 1913, receiving in turn some 91.8 million marks' worth of materials. The corresponding figures for Britain were 171.4 million marks and 187.2 million marks.[20] After 1918, therefore, Britain and Germany were resuming a long-standing battle for Baltic markets. Mutual hostility was a factor in the policies of both powers, as can be seen from the respective German and British analyses of economic prospects in the Baltic region during the second half of 1919.

The Allied political ascendancy in Latvia and Estonia from the summer of 1919, the Allies' blockade of Russia, the role of such men as Sir Stephen Tallents as temporary governor of Riga in early July 1919 and the strong British naval presence in the region in 1919/1920 all appeared to give substance to the view that by the turn of the New Year Britain virtually 'ran the Baltic'.[21] The attempt to convert political influence into tangible economic benefits was made early on, when both British and French representatives tried to link Allied advances of money and military equipment with future deals to secure Baltic raw materials – notably flax and wood.[22] General Niessel's mission also drew attention to the economic stakes. At the end of August 1919, he secured the support of the French War Ministry and the Quai d'Orsay for a plan to supply eleven million francs' worth of military equipment to Latvia against later payments in wood.[23] British and French rivalry there certainly was, but both had Germany as the main target of their competition. Niessel's aide, Du Parquet, frankly admitted the link between Allied help and the desire to oust the Germans in order to secure a pro-Entente Latvia.[24] Nor did the English have any hesitation in insisting in July 1919 that the German flag be excluded from shipping in the Baltic for the time being.[25] Evidence continued to mount of the British government's encouragement of preparations for the resumption of contacts between private traders; persistent reports reached Germany of British meetings with Riga industrialists and of discussions in British business and banking circles on the possible restarting of Riga industry.[26] They had intimated that they would 'rather advance half a milliard than leave it to German capitalisation'.[27] That one or two at least of the larger concerns in Tallinn were soon operating with British capital is confirmed by a list forwarded by Henkel to the Auswärtiges Amt a year later.[28]

Late in 1919, in fact, *The Times* could still charge the British government with being insufficiently energetic in countering the German presence in the Baltic.[29] Yet German sources unequivocally reflect the gravity of Britain's attempt to secure an economic foothold in the Baltic countries. Like the British, the German experts and advisers – men such as Lorenz-Meyer, the German commercial attaché in the Baltic, and Schneemann, a member of the German Treasury commission in the Baltic in 1919 under the Riga industrialist Dr Bach, all stressed the great potential for economic penetration of the Baltic states, because of their shortage of currency and their demand for all goods.[30] In June, to Lorenz-Meyer's regret, Germans were also showing a lack of initiative in the face of the foreign business activity which was building up in Latvia and Estonia, particularly since the Allied blockade meant that the East 'offers at the moment the one large scale area of operations for our foreign trade'.[31] By the end of July he was reporting on Britain's use of its political weight to wrest flax concessions from the Latvians. 'If the Reich permits the most extensive exports to Latvia, the competitive gains of the Allies will be cancelled out in the shortest possible time.' The repeated line in such reports was the insistence that existing obstacles to the restoration of a regular flow of trade should not be allowed to hold up active preparations; that irrespective of the political future of Latvia and Estonia their economic need would remain. German trade and banking circles had to be made aware how important was 'the undermining of Allied influence and the quiet domination of the Latvian market as a preparatory measure for securing our economic outlet to Russia'.[32]

Two days later Lorenz-Meyer urged that in pursuit of such goals, 'a trade espionage network' had to be set up over the region. It was to be composed of private German businessmen and travellers using assumed names because of the anti-German mood in the Baltic countries. In addition Lorenz-Meyer called for the setting up in Königsberg of a branch of the Reich Commission for Imports and Exports. This could maintain closer contacts with the German commercial travellers than could the trade section of the German embassy and would thereby avoid inflaming highly sensitive public opinion in Latvia and Estonia.[33] His advice was underlined by his discovery, at the end of August 1919, that a British economic mission under McDuff and Fortington intended to set up an information network on Baltic economic prospects. In effect, Lorenz-Meyer was adding arguments to the political pressures building up against the German Freikorps in the Baltic in 1919, by stressing that the troops were undoing any good achieved by German business and that they were 'providing the Latvians with propaganda material for their dearest wish, namely to see the Versailles peace terms extended to the East'.[34] Schneemann also insisted shortly afterwards that 'the question of evacuating Courland and the financial plans for Latvia ... are interlinked'.[35] His talks earlier in August with Paul Schwartz, of Riga's Great Guild, confirmed that the British mission was equipped with detailed lists and charts on Latvian firms needing capital and that particular interest was being shown in concerns

which had once had connections with markets in Russia. Schneemann warned that, unless Germany prepared more actively, 'the
door to Russia will be closed and in addition to our military and
political failures we shall also finish up with a catastrophic trade
policy setback in the Baltic'.[36]

British and German preparations were at first frustrated by the *ad
hoc* emergency legislation which the Latvian and Estonian governments pushed through in the period between the end of the war and
the recognition by the Allied Powers of fully independent Baltic
countries in 1921. In both countries in the immediate post-war
months, the combination of fervent nationalism and constituent
assemblies, with socialist parties initially holding the largest number
of seats, produced radical approaches to what were horrendous problems of reconstruction – as the discussion of agrarian reforms has
illustrated already. As well as imposing a number of import and
export regulations and *ad valorem* duties which were intended to keep
a tight grip on available resources, the Estonian licensing system
permitted only absolutely vital goods to enter the country. The state
monopolized the valuable raw materials.[37] Similar restrictions on
foreign trade were imposed in Latvia on 12 December 1918, and a
period ensued where private initiatives were reduced to a minimum.
Priority was given to the survival of the new state and to securing
food supplies. Non-essential goods were effectively banned too, since
licences were given only for necessary supplies and machinery,
particularly agricultural machinery. The Latvians also planned to
monopolize wood, flax and spirits for the state; in this context the
agrarian reforms played a part by taking over woodland. Much of
the emergency legislation was retained until the middle of 1921.[38]

Trade between the Weimar Republic and the Baltic countries was
therefore certain to be fitful initially. For this reason Berlin attached
importance to negotiating arrangements for trade which would at
least achieve a relatively secure legal basis for the activity of German
entrepreneurs and interests in Latvia and Estonia. Even a detested,
defeated and weakened Germany retained sources of potential
strength in relation to Latvia and Estonia. These advantages had
become only too apparent to the British by the end of 1921, as we
shall see later (see below, chapter 4); but, briefly, they derived from
Germany's geographical proximity and the long experience of
German businessmen and travellers with Baltic market conditions
and above all from the degree of encouragement given by German

governments.[39] In view of the great uncertainty in East Europe after 1918 much depended on the extent of private enterprise commitment to the opening or re-opening of business ventures in the Baltic. Even during the Baltic campaign in 1919, German governments were being subjected to continuing pressure. 'Nordexport Robert Schnabel' spoke for countless similar concerns when it reminded the Auswärtiges Amt of its long-standing business interests in the Baltic and voiced the expectations in German export circles that the government would do its utmost to revitalize such trade.[40]

The sentiment was heartily shared by the 'Feldmühle Paper and Cellulose Works' and the Hamburg-based company of 'Meissner & Company', who planned in September 1919 shortly to renew trade to the Baltic countries, and who added to the growing clamour for detailed and updated information on the conditions in Estonia and Latvia in the second half of 1919.[41] How scarce well-organized and up to date information was on the new circumstances prevailing in post-war Baltic trade was confirmed by a reference in one of Lorenz-Meyer's reports to the efforts of a certain Reich German to set up a journal, to be called *The Pioneer*. The proposed journal intended to collate information on current conditions, which were liable to change with lightning speed. The important point is that the German commercial attaché wanted the journal funded because it was then, in July 1919, the only one of its kind.[42] Parallels can be found with British firms pressing for information, which was one reason at least why the British Department of Overseas Trade began to offer practical advice on trading with the Baltic.[43]

The representatives of German economic life, especially in trade, shipping and banking had already assumed an active role in the shape of the Geschäftsstelle für die Friedensverhandlungen, which sought to influence the formulation of German economic demands at the peace negotiations. Yet, as to satisfying private business requests actively to stimulate commerce, the Auswärtiges Amt felt obliged to warn of the difficulties caused by the intervention of the Allies against Russia and the resulting restrictions on trade. One instructive example of the German authorities trying, however, to respond to the urgent calls from private traders under the worst possible conditions concerned the basic problem of financing a flow of goods. German firms were quick to point to the urgent need for a German banking institution to facilitate basic transactions of credit with the Baltic countries.[44] The problem also exercised British businessmen, but the

Weimar Republic had an interim advantage in the form of large amounts of German wartime currency which had first been used in Courland and which had formally replaced the Russian rouble in German-occupied Livonia and Estonia on 28 July 1918.[45] The so-called *Oberostgeld*, or *Ostmarks* continued to circulate in the post-war months, even after the new Estonian state bank, the Eesti Pank, had issued its own mark in 1919, basing it roughly on the value of the German mark. The *Ostgeld* remained in use in Latvia too, although the ill-fated Latvian rouble formally replaced the occupation currency after the Armistice, pending the setting-up of a state bank later in 1922.

The fact was that in the early post-war months both the Latvian and Estonian currencies suffered a loss of confidence and severe depreciation. The Latvian rouble had sunk to 500 to the dollar by mid-1921.[46] To the chagrin of the British, the German *Ostmark* continued to be prized under these circumstances and to be used by Baltic traders to secure credit and goods from Germany. Indeed the British Tilden-Smith group sought at one stage to buy some 20 million *Ostmarks* to purchase flax in Lithuania, which actually retained the German unit as its currency until 1922.[47] Thus the emergency branch office of the Berlin issuing authority for the *Ostgeld*, the Darlehnskasse Ost, originally set up in Tallin early in 1919 to wind down business, rapidly found itself accepting large sums of *Ostmarks* from the Estonian government. These were transferred to Germany, where the equivalent value in Reich marks was then paid to German firms supplying goods to Estonia. Not surprisingly, the German embassy in Riga urged in a report of 25 July 1919, entitled 'Securing a German banking influence in Estonia', that the Darlehnskasse Ost's branch in Tallin should not be closed until German interests were transferred to another suitable institution. Otherwise the absence of banking ties between Estonia and Germany would 'drive the customers into the trade net of the Allies and neutral powers'. The alternative was that German banking capital should take part in the Tallinn-based 'Trade and Industry Bank', recently formed by pro-German traders.[48]

In fact a meeting had already been held in the office of the Reich Commissioner for Exports and Imports on 10 July 1919, when agreement was reached that *Ostgeld* could be exchanged, providing its owners could prove that they had placed 'bigger orders for German goods'.[49] The balance tipped in favour of maintaining the Tallinn branch of the Darlehnskasse for the time being, as opposed to replacing it with Reich funding for the 'Trade and Industry Bank', when the Reichsbank voiced doubts about German capital being tied up in Estonia whilst it was still felt to be directly under Allied influence.[50] The advantages of providing buyers in Estonia with a ready means of purchasing German goods were stressed by the Reich Ministry of Finance and the Reich Ministry of Economics, and this ensured that the branch office of the Darlehnskasse remained open.[51] Once the procedure had been agreed by the Estonian government, discussions continued between the Darlehnskasse Ost, the Auswärtiges Amt and the Finance Ministry on 'the timing and form in which the branch could be transformed into a German banking institute'.[52] The Tallinn office was still functioning in 1921, a fact which prompted the Darlehnskasse director, van Roy, to visit Riga in April. He sought 'to secure permission to set up a branch in Latvia, attached to and under the protection of the German diplomatic representation, as in the neighbouring states of Estonia and Lithuania. Ostensibly this would deal with outstanding claims and withdraw invalid Ost-bills; in reality, it would gradually make the German *Ostgeld* dominant.'[53] In the last resort the plan was abortive because by 1921 the Latvians were wholly determined to eliminate any 'second currency' and to return to normal banking as soon as possible. Thereafter Germany could exploit other avenues of approach (see below, chapter 4).

The preparatory skirmishing between the European powers evolved into a more systematic struggle for a foothold in the Baltic in the early part of 1920, when the Soviet–Estonian peace talks heightened expectations about a surge in transit traffic to Russia. An insight into the hectic process of setting up concerns to exploit the expected opportunities in the East is provided by an assessment written in the Auswärtiges Amt on 9 January 1920. It referred to such recent ventures as the Russian Finance Office, the Russo-German Bank for Trade and Industry, the Trading Society East, the Northern Trading Society and, most recently, the East European Banking and Trading Society. The latter was a stock company formed by the bankers Hardy & Co. of Berlin and S. H. Stern of Frankfurt, together with the Barmen Banking Association and the firm of G. J. H. Siemens from Hamburg. The organization owed its existence to the belief that regular trade with the East was essential, irrespective of political developments there and that in the first instance commercial relations had to be re-established with the Baltic states. The East European Banking and Trading Society was 'an organization which could carry this out systematically'. The group's plan was to secure commissions from the Baltic countries and from the Russian cooperative and economic associations situated in the border states. Armed with these orders, it hoped to secure a monopoly of sales in large machine manufactures in East Europe. The board of the group included experts on East European market conditions, including the Russian Maurice Laserson and Hans Ploeger, a former representative of foreign banks in St Petersburg.[54] Such organization contrasted markedly with the rather *ad hoc* contacts made by private British traders with the Russian cooperatives in the Baltic countries. These were merely encouraged by the British Department of Overseas Trade, on the grounds that such temporary arrangements would be important in due course for trade with Russia.[55]

The ending of Allied intervention in Russia therefore helped to create the conditions for the border states to function as 'springboards' to the still more uncertain markets of Russia. The latter beckoned like a fabled land to the veritable army of German and Allied concerns and individual speculators who were making their way towards the Baltic states in 1920.[56] The Supreme Council's decision on 24 February 1920 to encourage trade with the Soviets, without yet formally recognizing the Bolshevik regime, facilitated the efforts of the British Prime Minister, Lloyd George, to use the border states as clearing-houses pending more organized economic and financial relations with Russia.[57] Lloyd George's vision of a peaceful economic penetration of Russia through the Baltic area was further encouraged by the terms of the Estonian–Russian peace treaty of 2 February 1920.[58] In return for Russia's promised payment of 15 million roubles in gold to cover Estonian claims and for timber concessions, the Estonian government agreed to reserve for Russia in the free docks of Tallinn and elsewhere sites for the transhipment and warehousing of goods in transit. Those goods were to be exempted from import duties and taxes. Similar provisions were later included in the Soviet–Latvian and Soviet–Lithuanian peace treaties. Britain's early trade lead in Estonia was confirmed when the Tallinn government made its first trade agreement with London, in the form of an exchange of notes in July 1920.[59]

Allied policies were inevitably helping to create a framework in which German interests would also operate more effectively. Von

Maltzan observed at the end of January 1920 that an 'economic transfusion' was expected for Estonia as a result of the Soviet–Estonian peace-talks because these effectively broke the blockade round Russia.[60] His expectation was echoed both in Lenin's view of the treaty and in the words of the Soviet Commissar for Foreign Affairs, Chicherin. The latter foresaw the agreement developing into 'a dress rehearsal, so to speak, with the Entente, into the first attempt to break through the blockade and into the first experiment in peaceful co-existence with the bourgeois states'.[61] Henkel reported more cynically that the Soviets expected the treaty to provide a doorway in Estonia to spread trade and propaganda to Western Europe.[62] Under these conditions, the early German moves to secure provisional agreements with the Baltic countries (in the spirit of the Deutsch–Rathenau memorandum) constituted an indirect step towards normalizing relations with the Bolshevik regime, at a time when the direct resumption of relations would have been impossible for the Weimar Republic to contemplate. Henkel was soon in contact with Gukovsky, the head of the Russian trade mission which arrived in Tallinn after the Soviet–Estonian peace treaty. Gukovsky assured Henkel of Russia's great interest in trade with the Weimar Republic because of its cheap currency.[63] By contrast, there were several isolated instances when Estonia expressed disappointment with British traders. Keyserling argued in July 1920 that trade between Estonia and Great Britain was beginning to show some ill effects because the English tended to be too preoccupied with business with Russia.[64]

LATVIA'S ROLE

Notwithstanding such reports, Estonia remained firmly enough in the Allied orbit. Since Lithuania's small land frontier with the Soviets was threatened because of Kovno's conflict with Warsaw over the district of Vilna, and because Lithuania possessed no major port of its own in 1920, the struggle between Germany and Britain for a Baltic foothold was most evident in Latvia, where problems were all the more acute as a result of prolonged German wartime occupation and the Baltic campaign of 1919. The classic argument about Latvia's function as a 'springboard' to Russia is to be found in the series of writings and lectures by Hermann-Felix Crohn-Wolfgang, the German Economics Ministry expert who was responsible for the overall coordination of economic and trade matters in the negotiations with the Baltic countries from 1920. His publications, together with his frequent meetings with German business and banking groups interested in Baltic trade, amounted to a systematic public presentation of Germany's case for staking a claim in the border states.[65] Drawing on the lessons of colonization, Crohn-Wolfgang argued that history had shown that, to open up new areas economically, a beginning had to be made in the frontier regions, which for Russia after 1919 meant the Baltic countries. These 'will be the bridge across which we can reach Russia, whereas the leap from Berlin to Moscow is bound to be a blunder'.[66] Of Riga, Crohn-Wolfgang said what most expert opinion believed, when he urged that the advantages of this most celebrated centre of earlier Russian trade

> were a product of nature which could not be changed by political events and will never be changed by these ... However the political relations in the East develop, one thing is certain, namely that the geographical area constituting European Russia will continue ... to use Riga as its main economic outlet; and here all human reason suggests that Riga's future as a harbour is determined, as is that of Latvia as a transit region. Specifically, the country will continue to be the coastal transit zone for Russia and the bridge between Western Europe and Russia.[67]

How to translate this into practice was a central question underlying the German–Latvian negotiations which opened in Berlin with the arrival of a delegation from Riga at the beginning of April 1920. After the fairly rapid settlement of the problem of exchanging prisoners of war (see above, chapter 1), broad lines of general agreement were hammered out with difficulty on the wider political and economic issues. Slowly, the text emerged of the convention reestablishing diplomatic relations between the two countries on 15 July 1920.[68] An account which Wipert von Blücher prepared on 17 May 1920 for the Reichsrat Committee on Foreign Affairs stressed that the aim behind the talks was to facilitate the return to Latvia of those Germans still waiting in Germany. 'German trade will follow and, hopefully, will be in a position to counter possible English efforts to secure a monopoly.'[69] The wording of the convention paid lip-service to the 'provisional' nature of such agreements with the Baltic countries, which had not yet been legally recognized by the Allies. *De jure* recognition of Latvia by Germany was therefore made dependent on prior recognition by the Entente. As Rathenau and Deutsch had pointed out, however, the content and nature of any 'provisional' agreement in the East could exercise a formative influence on any future settlement.

The German–Latvian convention to resume relations omitted the term 'war' from the preamble to prevent Latvia from claiming damages against Germany as an Allied and Associated Power, but under article 5 Germany accepted liability for damages caused by German troops on Latvian territory. Linked, as we have seen, to the well-being of the Baltic German element, such a commitment was imprecise enough to cause problems. One of these was agreement on when 'Latvia' could be said to have come into existence. There was also the question of how far Berlin would modify its refusal to accept responsibility for damages caused by the Bermondt venture, a matter specifically excluded from the convention of 1920. Early on the German government indicated its readiness to accept the suggestion that material abandoned by the Russian general could be kept by Latvia to offset its losses (article 6). Ultimately, a mixed German–Latvian commission (one of several set up by the agreement) was to give detailed consideration to the extent of damages and to reparations. In order to prepare its own counter-claims, the Reich government had already empowered a consortium, the 'Reich Trustee Company', to begin documenting Germany's case from the records of the German Winding-Up Authorities for the Baltic.[70] The somewhat ill-defined commitment assumed by the Reich government over damages demonstrated the importance attached in Berlin to securing the convention quickly. This could also be said of article 7, whereby the German government undertook to help arrange credit for Latvia to buy German goods. Again, the detailed conditions were to be determined by a further mixed commission. The German Foreign Minister, Simons, justified the article on the proposed credit by reference to the need to save what could be saved of the substantial German investment and wealth in the Reich German communities in Latvia, particularly Riga. This would further Germany's general trade interests as well as its plans to secure raw materials from Latvia for Prussian and German industry. The mutual most-favoured-nation treatment promised in article 4 did not guarantee complete equality of treatment between Latvian and Reich German citizens in Latvia, since the latter were not allowed to acquire land, but at least a more secure legal basis was provided for each state's nationals.[71] Even a normally hostile source saw the agreement as being important for the Weimar Republic as 'a first step towards settling old differences'.[72] By providing a starting-point for a series of negotiations intended to lead towards an economic agreement, the German–Latvian convention of 15 July 1920 represented an early and active challenge to British and Allied policies towards the Baltic countries. That was important in terms of the overall strategy of building up a network of agreements to offset the restrictions of the Versailles treaty on German commerce. The German–Latvian convention of 1920 might therefore usefully be compared with an equivalent British attempt to secure a preferential position in Latvia's economic life.

The scheme in question was outlined at the end of 1919 by the Chairman of the National Chemical Bank, Richard Tilden-Smith and was initially supported by the British Board of Trade and the Foreign Office. It involved an agreement combining capital help in founding a bank of issue in all three Baltic countries with securing a monopoly in timber and flax concessions. Crohn-Wolfgang rated the British attempt to monopolize export contingents from the Baltic states as a measure of their determination to oust Germany. Indeed, the attraction of the Tilden-Smith project to the Foreign Office was precisely that it promised to frustrate German efforts and establish British influence as paramount. The Foreign Office firmly rejected Tilden-Smith's later idea of allowing participation by the German capitalist Stinnes, 'since the introduction of a German element would seem to be the very thing we set out to obviate'.[73] Yet, after some progress in Lithuania by April 1920, the Tilden-Smith scheme had made no significant headway in Estonia or Latvia. Government and public opinion, particularly in the latter country, reacted violently against the overtly monopolistic nature of the British project. Foreign Office doubts about the plan also grew on account of the resolution of Baltic governments not to allow such far-reaching foreign control of vital raw materials. The episode did result in Britain getting a majority of Latvian flax exports from November 1919 until April 1920, but this fell far short of what had been intended. A recent investigation of Britain's commercial policy towards the Baltic states called the Tilden-Smith venture a 'significant chapter' in the development of British–Baltic relations, but its main significance seems to be in underlining the relative heavy-handedness of British policy.[74]

The very fact that Germany, unlike Britain, could not expect goodwill from Latvia instilled in the Berlin government extreme caution. That helped to produce a more flexible response towards Riga than the British negotiators seemed capable of, and this no doubt also reflected the German government's care to include on the commissions for the economic talks with Latvia men who were knowledgeable about Baltic market conditions. At the inter-ministerial conference in the Auswärtiges Amt on 27 August 1920, to consider the execution of the clauses of the July convention between Latvia and Germany, nominations were accepted from the Deutsche Industrie und Handelstag for the proposed commissions. These included Hermann Eschenburg, president of the Lübeck chamber of commerce and Hans Litten, vice-president of the Königsberg chamber of commerce. They joined the representatives from the Reich Ministries of Economics, Finance and Food and from the Prussian Ministry of Trade and Commerce. On the important commission for war-damage claims, under the leadership of the Auswärtiges Amt, were members from the Reichswehr and the Ministries of Finance and of Reconstruction and from the Reich Compensations Office.[75] By the time the full list of members had been drawn up for the meeting of 13 November 1920, procedures had been further adjusted to take account of likely delays in the convening of the two commissions on compensation and credit, but it was felt that the group concerned with general economic relations could begin its work at once. Its leader, Crohn-Wolfgang, confirmed that soundings of German business interests had already been taken in July. In contrast to the presumptions of Tilden-Smith's scheme, Crohn-Wolfgang warned at once that 'the extent of our demands is closely related to Latvian financial and economic legislation'.[76]

In 1920 Latvia appeared to be encouraging both British and German commercial overtures in the hope that the two powers would outbid each other for Riga's favours. Much the same could be said of Estonia's hints to German sources of its dissatisfaction with the extent of British trade and credit and of the request from Tallinn on 4 October 1920 for negotiations for a trade agreement to be arranged with Germany.[77] Inevitably, Britain in fact continued to enjoy the benefits of a prompt start and in 1920 secured a clear lead over the Weimar Republic in the foreign trade of both Estonia and Latvia. The extent to which Britain had its hands on Latvian raw materials can be seen from the fact that it received 67.5% of Latvia's exports in 1920, compared with Germany's pitiful share of 1.24%. On the imports side the situation was less bleak, at least in relative terms.

Crohn-Wolfgang's figures showed that about 50 million marks' worth of German goods had been sent to Latvia in the last few months of 1920.[78] In the long run Germany's natural advantages might narrow the gap, particularly as the Weimar Republic built up the exports offensive which was made possible by the compromise in Germany in 1919 between industry and labour and by Germany's cheaper currency (cf below, chapter 4). As to the emergency legislation of Latvia and Estonia, both Britain and Germany, like other would-be foreign investors, had to cope with the determination of Baltic leaders to strike a balance between their need for foreign aid and their understandable refusal to be dominated by outside economic interests. Latvia's currency laws in 1920, for example, which enforced a highly unfavourable rate of exchange between the Latvian unit and foreign currencies, could be represented, like the Baltic agrarian reforms, as applying to all foreigners. In practice they affected German interests most profoundly, not least because of the effects the legislation had on the settlement of debts. Yet the welfare of the German minority was precisely what provided the German government with the sort of incentive and patience to tackle the trials of Baltic legislation which the British could hardly hope to match.

Here, as in the case of East–West trade, the tendency existed to cling to pre-war patterns. It was felt in German government circles that the revitalization of Estonian and Latvian economic life would also help to preserve something at least of the position which the Baltic Germans had maintained in the business and commerce of the Baltic provinces before 1914, particularly since economic power within the German communities of Estonia and Latvia shifted still more decisively towards the larger towns after 1918 (see above, chapter 2). In Estonia, where Germans were more heavily concentrated in commerce, industry and the professions than their share of the population figures warranted, it was important, too, in the mood of chauvinism after 1918, that links persisted between the German element and the native Estonian establishment. A notable case was that of the Baltic German Scheel Bank, which became the leading private bank in the Baltic states and through its holdings in other financial institutions ultimately played a salient role in the economic life of Estonia.[79] In 1920, it was to the Scheel Bank that the Russian delegation in Tallinn turned after the Soviet–Estonian treaty. The resulting extra business significantly boosted the wealth of the bank, causing the Auswärtiges Amt to refer to Scheel as the 'banker of the

Soviet regime'.[80] In Latvia the attempt to preserve the position of the German community in Riga's economic life, which had been central to pre-war East–West trade, involved even higher stakes. There was no shortage of support in the German government for the arguments advanced by the then director of the Riga Stock Exchange, Wilhelm von Bulmerinq, in a memorandum to the Reichsbank, 'The influence of Riga's industry on the formation of Riga's trade'. Unless aid were given to restore the shattered industries of Riga, Bulmerinq affirmed, German capital and work would be lost and Riga would be robbed of its most important source of existence as a trade centre. Dire results would ensue for Germans living in Riga.[81]

The Auswärtiges Amt did help to arrange for German industrialists from Riga to make a return visit to Latvia in 1920 to examine their concerns and to assess their needs. One of those industrialists, Dr Bach, was also brought into the preparatory discussions in Berlin on implementing the terms of the provisional agreement with Latvia. Like the Reich Ministry of Economics and the German industrial representatives involved in the talks in the second half of 1920, Bach argued the need for the momentum to be stepped up by opening economic talks with Riga even before satisfaction had been given by the Latvians on the matter of compensation for Germans affected by the agrarian reforms and the currency laws. By contrast, the Auswärtiges Amt's Eastern Department, then under Behrendt, wanted to link the contentious issues to the talks for a trade agreement, preferring tangible concessions for the Reich German element in Latvia before Germany gave large credits. What was in reality a clash over timing and tactics rather than long-term aims was resolved for the time being by a compromise suggested by Fritz Beusten, the director of the Atlantic Speditions und Lagerei AG, and a member of the commission on transit problems: namely, that four businessmen and three government spokesmen should go to Riga for 'unofficial' soundings on economic relations.[82] German business circles were also excessively worried that delays in providing credit would prejudice any export offensive. This at least was recognized in December by the merger of the German commission on the proposed credit with that responsible for general economic and trade relations with Latvia.[83]

At the opening of 1921, therefore, the Auswärtiges Amt's initial reluctance to send a delegation to Riga before clarification of the damages done to Reich German landowners and creditors in Latvia had been overcome, although for the time being it was felt that any credit to that country would have to be in the form of an exchange of goods from merchant to merchant. The way was open at last for Crohn-Wolfgang to arrange a major meeting with the assembled representatives of German industry and finance on 26 January 1921. The aim was to provide information and direction on the economic policy objectives in Latvia in the immediate future. Nothing could have provided a greater contrast to the ill-coordinated, *ad hoc* approaches of British private traders to the Baltic and the relative absence of overall governmental guidance in London. When Crohn-Wolfgang turned to the problem of maintaining wood supplies for the Prussian timber industry, he emphasized that the Riga government would probably continue to exercise its monopoly over Latvia's timber. Germany would therefore try at least to secure quotas in its negotiations with Latvia. Additionally, if it proved impossible to persuade Latvia to remove tariffs from its wood exports, the German government was prepared to argue for a maximum tariff on finished wood products and for a range of lower duties on raw timber, paper and pit-props. Other German demands would concern the unimpeded passage of timber shipments and the recognition by Latvia of agreements concerning the securing of wood by Germany or for German interest groups. Similar efforts were to be made to obtain flax supplies. Turning from the issue of raw materials to that of increasing German exports to Latvia, the speaker urged that the most-favoured-nation agreement which Germany wanted would help, whilst Germany also planned to insist on the right to set up transit depots in Latvia for the free import and re-export of German goods.

On the subject of rebuilding Latvian industry, 'which before the war was largely in German hands, at least 85% under German management', Crohn-Wolfgang delivered an emphatic message. The problem was important

not only for those Germans who had been active earlier as industrialists in Riga and who were robbed of their livelihood by the war, but from a general economic viewpoint. There must be encouragement in all ways for the German element in Latvia to be firmly based, for Latvia is one of the main trade routes to Russia. Here, for the foreseeable future, a good deal of our business will be carried out. It is therefore of the utmost importance for our entire economy that an economically strong and influential German element is on hand.

Much of what Crohn-Wolfgang had to say on the subject derived from an earlier memorandum written by Dr Bach, who in the new conditions of independence envisaged industry being re-established on the basis of cooperatives jointly run by Germans and Latvians. The Riga government would be expected among other things to tolerate Reich German management of the joint ventures, as well as access of German insurance companies to Latvia and the return of Reich German property taken by Russia from the Baltic provinces. The Latvians would also be requested to guarantee some stability in taxes imposed on trading companies. In this context Crohn-Wolfgang made it clear that the German government's promise to arrange credit through the Reich's industrial and banking circles was undertaken not simply to boost German exports, but also as an inducement to the Latvians to take account of German wishes when legislating. The German banks, Crohn-Wolfgang urged, were expected to help in arranging credit, and he stressed that a banking institution which Germany could trust would have to be set up in Latvia.[84]

Crohn-Wolfgang's speech must be seen against the background of the intensified pressure coming from German industry in 1921, particularly from the electro-technical industries like Siemens and the AEG, for economic penetration of Russia. This drive continued to gain momentum for a number of reasons. First, the Allied London Ultimatum in March 1921 increased the pressures for an overall trade expansion to finance reparations payments.[85] The Allied occupation of the Ruhr ports began a process eventually leading to the collapse of the Fehrenbach administration and the emergence of a new coalition under the Centre Party Chancellor, Josef Wirth, whilst the British government's imposition of a 50% charge on its imports from Germany stimulated even greater interest in the Weimar Republic in trade with the East. In the words of the then Reich Minister of Economics, Scholz, 'The enemy fails to appreciate that Germany can purchase less from its opponents, especially England, if its foreign trade is throttled by the required 50% export tax. Foreign trade will have to adjust to the changed conditions and find other ways. It is to be hoped that East Europe will be receptive to German goods.'[86] Britain's competition for East European and Russian trade caused the British–Soviet trade agreement of 16 March 1921 to act as a sharp stimulus to Germany's economic negotiations, and the Weimar–Soviet trade agreement followed shortly afterwards on 6 May 1921.

A receptive mood was thus created in German industrial and trading circles for Crohn-Wolfgang's pleas to regard the Baltic countries as vital staging-posts to Russian markets. His closing request at the lecture of 26 January 1921 was for urgent preparations to be made in view of the speed with which events could change in the East. The argument was given added force by the fact that on the very day of his talk with German businessmen the Allied Powers at last formally recognized the independence of Latvia and Estonia. To German export circles this added substance to the charges of Foreign Minister Simons in the Reichstag a few days before, that the Allied attempt to erect 'barriers between Mitteleuropa and the large territories in the East' threatened to frustrate Germany's historic role as the natural mediator in East–West trade. Simons was not implying hostility towards the Baltic states as such, politically tactless as his speech was, and he had to go to considerable lengths to calm a highly sensitive public opinion in the Baltic capitals.[87] In reality, the international acceptance of independent Baltic countries in January 1921 vindicated the policy of using them as stepping-stones to Russia, precisely because of the still greater uncertainty of market conditions inside the Soviet state. Although the introduction of the New Economic Policy in Russia manifestly recognized the need for at least temporary accommodation with Western business and capital, the Soviet regime retained control of the economy's 'commanding heights'. Whilst NEP stimulated a substantial rise in Soviet foreign trade, this did not lessen the importance of the Baltic countries as intermediate zones for Western entrepreneurial activity and investment. On the contrary, for all the Western dislike of state interventionist policies in Latvia and Estonia, the two countries remained, in spite of the radical nature of their early financial and economic legislation, parliamentary democracies and private enterprise economies. As such they were sooner or later bound to be susceptible to pressure from the Western industrial powers. It is erroneous to assume that the direct talks in the spring of 1921 between Britain and Russia on the one hand, Germany and Russia on the other, diminished the value of the Baltic countries as 'springboards'.[88] Compared with Russia in 1921, the Baltic countries did stand out 'like rocks in a stormy sea'.[89]

At least from early 1921, the Baltic countries were sovereign powers, and during the course of the year they began the painful move towards longer-term planning of economic resources. In Estonia, the banking entrepreneur and Farmers' Party leader, Konstantin Päts, formed a government which professed a more lenient line over export licences and identified foreign trade as a priority in its plans for economic reconstruction.[90] Latvia also had an urgent need to revitalize its foreign trade, in order, like Estonia, to increase its financial resources so that it could develop its industrial sector. If anything, the scale of the problem was greater in Latvia, which suffered a protracted inflationary crisis in 1921. Party-political squabbles spilled over into the economic management of the state, a process which the new 'strong man', Finance Minister Ringold Kalņiņš, was determined to arrest on his appointment in April 1921. It was expected that his impact on the Latvian economy would be as striking as that of his physical appearance on those who met him. To the German representative in Riga, Wever, Kalņiņš was simply 'the most repellent person he had ever had official contacts with'. With his unkempt hair, unwashed eyes, the sort of clothes that 'only workers wear', Kalņiņš's one obvious indulgence were the enormous gold fillings in his upper teeth, 'a grotesque sight'. Wever felt that Kalņiņš looked every inch the classic miser, 'for a Latvian finance minister, no bad thing'.[91] The programme which Kalņiņš intended to pursue was outlined in the journal of his ministry, the *Ekonomist*: 'The monopoly of economic life by the state is to be ended. In this way, together with other drastic measures, the budget will be balanced as far as possible. At the same time to facilitate currency reform steps must be taken at the earliest moment to set up a [state] bank. Yet reform of the currency can only go hand in hand with a reorganization of foreign trade.' The message which Kalņiņš underlined was 'thrift in the whole economic life of the state', a policy calculated without reference to party-political interests.[92]

The prospect of more rigorous economic management did not in itself discourage German interest groups, as can be seen, for example, from the plea of the 'Union of official trade representations in East Prussia' later in the year. The German government was reminded that trade agreements with the border states were 'a matter of life and death for the economic life of East Prussia, cut off as it is from the Reich and in need of raw materials from the border states and export markets there'.[93] The pressure of such demands was confirmed by the German chargé in Latvia, Radowitz. Radowitz agreed with the idea, current in the Auswärtiges Amt, that the most effective means of pressurizing Latvia into a more amenable attitude on its agrarian and currency legislation would be to restrain the big financial groups in Germany who were ready to advance credit against the security of timber. Yet he was highly doubtful about economic sanctions, because they

constitute a double-edged weapon in the prevailing circumstances here ... Given the violent thrust of our finance, trade and industrial circles, large and small, towards the East, in anticipation of big business with Russia, a request to hold back will probably meet with mixed feelings. Apart from this, if the more responsible circles are restrained, the profiteer will still do his business, the goods which are needed here will still arrive. In the end only the worthier economic interests will suffer, whilst the action against Latvia would be as good as worthless.[94]

There was no question of the Reich's political leaders failing to recognize the force of arguments in favour of an active trade offensive. This was as true of Fehrenbach's administration as it was of Josef Wirth's first cabinet from May 1921. Yet the very existence of Soviet Russia gave an extremely sensitive political dimension to the whole question of extending economic relations in the East. In the summer of 1921 this consideration encouraged a less precipitate approach towards such matters than some of the Reich economic leaders desired. Vital domestic and international considerations dictated caution in the matter of Weimar–Soviet relations. Wirth's espousal of 'fulfilment' precluded immediately risking the loss of Allied goodwill by premature political ties with Russia in 1921, particularly since he was aiming for accommodation from the Western powers both on the key problem of reparations and on the future of Silesia. The figures within Germany most closely associated with a desire to deepen Weimar–Soviet relations were thus held in check, notwithstanding the modest beginnings of industrial collaboration with Russia for military purposes.[95] In the Auswärtiges Amt the anti-Bolshevik views of the leader of the Eastern Department, Behrendt, prevailed. The leader at the Russian desk, von Maltzan – a man closely associated with attempts to develop relations with the Soviets – was restrained to the point where his removal to the Athens embassy was being arranged. The priority given to achieving accommodation with the Western powers was also confirmed by the presence of Friedrich Rosen as Foreign Minister in Wirth's Cabinet. All this did not mean abandoning the negotiations with Russia, but rather an absence of immediate haste in resuming full relations.[96] The framework which Simons had outlined before being replaced by Rosen was preserved for the time being.

As long as I am at the helm I shall try to drive the Reich carriage further along the track on which it has moved, with much jolting and stumbling, for half a year: strict neutrality towards the East, holding the door open to Russia, a position of readiness for good or ill *vis-à-vis* Poland, economic understanding with the neutrals on the basis of reciprocity, most-favoured-nation treatment and the policy of trade agreements based on international law.[97]

Simons has been criticized for his failure to give German policy a clear lead in his pursuit of open-ended options, but this does insufficient justice to the complexity of the problems facing Germany.[98] In point of fact, the preparations for treaties with Latvia and Estonia contributed indirectly to the eventual stabilization of relations between Germany and Russia. For Simons, as for Behrendt and Rosen, however, the *fact* of such negotiations was the important point for the time being. They were not disposed to abandon their attempts to persuade Latvia and Estonia to modify their agrarian and currency legislation. It was made clear to the Riga government, when it renewed its requests for economic talks to begin, that any finalization of a trade agreeement would depend on satisfaction being given to Reich Germans damaged by the agrarian reforms and the currency law of 1920.[99] The Auswärtiges Amt's attempt to get the Latvians to modify what Wever called their 'robber's economy' was in one respect perfectly consistent with the desire to make the Baltic into a springboard.[100] After all, the survival of German communities in the border states was regarded within the *Auslandsdeutsche* movement and the German government as a pre-condition of such a goal (see above, chapter 2). Linking discussion of the status of the Reich German plaintiffs with the trade talks nonetheless worried the economic interests in the Reich since these were opposed to all obstacles in the way of an agreement with Latvia and, by this time, after a series of discussions between the main groups involved (the timber-dealers, bankers and industrialists), had drawn up a scheme for arranging credit for Latvians to buy German goods (cf. below, Chapter 4).[101]

One obvious means of pressing the Tallinn government was to make Estonia's accommodation towards German citizens affected by its emergency legislation a pre-condition of the Reich's recognition of Estonia as a state. (Such an option was not available in the case of Latvia, where, according to the German–Latvian agreement of 1920, Germany had automatically to give recognition once the Allied

Powers had done so.)[102] The idea was quickly rejected on wider political grounds, and instead Germany linked the issue of the treatment of Reich Germans in Estonia to the trade talks for which the new Päts government called in February 1921. In other respects the German government had learned from its experience with Latvia not to burden the negotiations with too many specific issues. Broad general principles were outlined in Berlin, including most-favoured-nation rights, free transit for German goods through Estonia and the securing of a supply of Estonian raw materials and German exports to Estonia. On this basis Henkel prepared a draft treaty in Tallinn in conjunction with the Estonians and taking account of written suggestions sent to him from the Deutsche Industrie und Handelstag. When the draft was passed to Berlin on 28 April 1921 most of the German desiderata had been secured.[103] Unlike the German–Latvian convention of 1920, the agreement made no provision for a German credit in Tallinn. In Estonia in any case a banking institution already existed in the form of the Scheel bank, which was more in favour of than against Reich German interests, and the branch of the Darlehnskasse Ost was still functioning.[104]

A further reason for caution on the part of Germany's political leaders in 1921 related to the interest of the Estonian and Latvian governments in successfully resolving their claims for war damages against the Reich. As in its convention with Latvia, so in the draft agreement with Estonia, the German government committed itself to settling damages through a separate agreement at a future date. At that stage it wanted the issue kept distinct from the talks for a trade agreement, for reasons which will be clear shortly. The precise opposite was true of the Baltic governments, who hoped to exploit the known interest of Weimar economic circles in Baltic trade to bring about an early settlement of war-damage claims at the same time as, if not before, the conclusion of a trade agreement. This was certainly felt to be true of the government of Zigfrids Meierovics, a national coalition coming into being on 19 June 1921 with a slogan of 'Latvia for the Latvians'. In the Auswärtiges Amt view, this reduced the prospect of accommodation from Riga over Reich German interests, since the new government proclaimed its intention of pushing on with agrarian reforms 'whereby outside influence will be reduced'.[105] The change of government would have sabotaged even the resumption of the German–Latvian talks scheduled to take place in Riga, had it not been for the efforts of the State Secretary in the Latvian Foreign

Office, Albats. To the relief at least of the Reich economic negotiators ready to leave for Riga, Albats promised to use his influence to get some satisfaction of the claims of Germans affected by the reforms of 1920, providing preliminary German–Latvian economic talks actually took place in Riga.[106]

It was felt by the German government that Meierovics was primarily concerned with achieving a foreign policy success to launch his new administration. The Auswärtiges Amt was prepared to acknowledge the economic pressures in Germany to the point of allowing such 'preliminary exchanges' to take place in Riga, even though it remained pessimistic. Once the German delegation reached Riga, however, the underlying tension between the Auswärtiges Amt and the Reich Ministry of Economics became overt. Crohn-Wolfgang and Sjöberg from the Ministry of Economics, Stepath and Scholz from the Reich Ministry of Transport and Hermann Eschenburg of the Lübeck Chamber of Commerce rapidly moved through the discussion of the proposed German credit and general economic relations. The outline of a provisional trade agreement began to emerge. Despite the uncertainty over Latvian customs and the restrictions imposed under the Versailles treaty on Germany's ability freely to regulate its own tariffs, a provisional agreement excluding customs could at least broaden existing private economic relations and give German firms and banking interests more confidence in investing in Latvia.[107] After setting up sub-committees with the Latvian negotiators, the German delegation conducted three sets of detailed talks covering general economic issues, matters concerning transport and, finally, the many legal problems arising from the proposed 'settlement and activity of German physical and juridical persons'.[108]

The failure of the German delegation to acknowledge the Auswärtiges Amt's political reservations caused Behrendt to remind the Reich Ministry of Economics that the issue of agrarian and currency reforms 'had not been mentioned by so much as a word, either on the German or on the Latvian side'. What upset Behrendt even more was the fact that Sjöberg and Crohn-Wolfgang were also planning to travel on to Tallinn in order to follow up the draft April agreement with Estonia. Scholz had actually returned to Berlin to finalize details on transport between Germany and the Baltic countries. Thus, although a good deal of preparatory work had been accomplished with the drafts of the German–Latvian agreement exchanged on 29 August 1921, the political brakes were applied in Berlin. Here there was concern about Latvia's expected insistence that the ultimate success of the economic talks depended on a 'satisfactory outcome' to Latvia's reparations claims against Germany. The German government's refusal to be lured into this particular situation effectively deadlocked the Riga exchanges. When Crohn-Wolfgang's team left Latvia it had to remain content for the time being with the formal request of the Meierovics government, that 'the path between Berlin and Riga be made shorter'.[109]

In the absence of a decisive commitment in the German government immediately to resume full relations with Russia, there was a certain logic in Behrendt's insistence that the pace of economic developments should not prejudice the solution of what, in the case of Latvian reparations claims, for example, were complex political issues with direct implications for German foreign policy at large. How could German–Latvian negotiations for war damages be squared with the provisions of articles 116 and 117 of the Versailles treaty? The former referred to 'all the territories which were part of the former Russian Empire', when reserving the rights of Russia 'to obtain from Germany restitution and reparations based on the principles of the present [peace] treaty'. The second article committed Germany to recognizing agreements which the Allies might make with 'the states now existing or coming into existence in future, in the whole or part of the former empire of Russia'. True, as Rathenau had argued in 1920 (see above, chapter 1), it was in Germany's best interests to make the sort of agreements with the 'territories of Russia' that would in fact help to determine the final stand taken by the Allied Powers on the Russian question as a whole. As the Reich Minister of Finance said when applying this doctrine to the specific problem of reparations, 'We can at least demand of the Entente that it does not simply disregard agreements which we make with Russia and the border states *after* the [Versailles] treaty comes into force.'[110] Yet this made it all the more important to exercise caution in drawing up such agreements. Any premature German–Latvian agreement on war damages might have set unwanted precedents. Indeed, the Soviet representative in Berlin, Viktor Kopp, had once suggested that the German–Latvian agreement of 1920 was an appropriate model for a treaty between Germany and Russia.[111] Further doubts were created by the idea that the Russo-Latvian peace treaty of 1920 established Latvia's right to claim a share of any reparations due to Russia insofar as they applied to Latvian territory. Admittedly, the provisions of articles 116 and 117 of the Versailles treaty had been drafted with an eye to a future non-Bolshevik Russia constituting itself. The Allied Powers could hardly be expected to press the reparations claims of a Communist Russia. Nevertheless, it was not easy for Germany to dismiss the political dangers, since from early 1919 the French President of the Allied Reparations Commission had been pressing for the rights of the border states in East Europe to reparations from Germany.[112] Any settlement of Weimar–Baltic war-damage claims threatened to have far more than local significance.

The impasse in Weimar–Baltic relations in the summer of 1921 serves as a reminder of the complex interaction of political and economic factors in the post-war resumption of Germany's trade drive towards Russia and the East European states. Behrendt rightly indicated that the regional Baltic alliance projects were a crucial factor in the obvious reluctance of Estonia and Latvia to finalize trade deals with Germany. 'Latvia and Estonia want to cooperate closely with each other in economic matters', Behrendt argued, 'yet the Germans are to be made to take the blame. We must oppose this tactic by remaining prepared to fulfil the obligations of our [1920 German–Latvian] agreement ... but cooperation with the Latvians beyond the terms of that convention does not seem appropriate.'[113] Behrendt's obvious frustration raises interesting questions about the problems posed for the 'great powers' by the 'small' countries of inter-war Europe. Crohn-Wolfgang showed perhaps more understanding, in the face of his disappointments in 1921, by writing: 'It is understandable that the foreign relations of the new states can only gradually become clearer ... To which side they can turn, wherein lies their own interest, only the future can show. The insecurity of their position determines that for the time being they probe and feel on all sides, and this cannot be reconciled with a decisive step in one direction.'[114]

Paradoxically, the difficulties in the way of Weimar–Baltic trade agreements did not in themselves prevent Germany from slowly recovering from its low point in the foreign trade of Estonia and Latvia in 1920 and thereafter successfully meeting the British and Allied economic challenge by the close of 1921. The reasons for this will be examined in the following chapter. Generally, the systematic discussion of Baltic problems fostered by the German government had provided the sort of supportive background for private enterprise penetration of the Baltic that was absent in Britain.[115] The fact that even draft trade agreements were drawn up between Germany and the Baltic countries in the summer of 1921 testifies to the 'power of economic facts' at a time when considerable ill-will existed towards Germany in Estonia and Latvia. Baltic leaders could not afford to ignore Germany's economic weight in relation to their own reconstruction, but this was tempered by the perception that trade agreements with the Weimar Republic would actively influence the overall political relationships of the region. For Germany to persuade the Baltic countries to take the 'decisive step', as Crohn-Wolfgang put it, required among other things a closer identity of political and economic leadership in Berlin than existed in 1921. This at least was provided with the formation of the second Wirth administration in October 1921. The revitalized German effort to reach agreement with the Baltic countries thereafter began to merge with the wider movement in Western Europe to resolve economic relations with Russia. Competition in the attempt to make the Baltic countries into springboards to Russia became more pronounced under those conditions and negotiations for trade treaties in the region were certain to become more politicized.

4

The politics of provisional trade treaties

Wirth's attempt to make more acceptable to German opinion the pursuit of his major policy goal, a reparations settlement with the Allied Powers, received a severe setback with the London Ultimatum of 5 May 1921 and the scale of payments which Germany had to accept. Later, in October, came the Allied decision to partition Upper Silesia; it was felt in the Reich that this favoured Poland, for which country Wirth had no love. The event increased the domestic opposition to Wirth's strategy of securing Allied concessions through fulfilling the terms of the peace treaty. By contrast, the crisis bringing down Wirth's first administration in October 1921 revealed beyond question the existence of a broad band of support in German public and private life for consolidation of relations with Russia. The political–economic basis of what has been termed the 'Rapallo lobby' spanned industry of all types and particularly heavy industry; it included self-evidently the parlimentary opposition to fulfilment, centring on the DVP and DNVP; it attracted military leaders like von Seeckt.[1] These groups shared a profound resentment of the Western powers. As an alternative to fulfilment they unrealistically preached the defiant use of contacts with Russia as an instrument of Weimar foreign policy. In this respect at least, the decision of Wirth's second administration, from October 1921, to put more emphasis on the pursuit of a political agreement with Russia, was assured of nationalist backing – an important consideration in view of the difficulties the Chancellor had experienced in holding his coalition together.[2]

Personnel changes in the Auswärtiges Amt clearly signalled the shift in priorities. Foreign Minister Rosen, who had wanted to restrict contacts with the Russians strictly to the economic field, was relieved of his office, which Wirth ran at first before handing it over to Walther Rathenau. Behrendt, the profoundly anti-Soviet head of the Eastern Department of the Auswärtiges Amt was replaced by Baron

Ago von Maltzan. Discussion of the 'red baron' in the historiography of Weimar–Soviet relations has invariably served to entrench the conspiracy view of the genesis of the Rapallo treaty. In the process the ideas of a so-called 'Easterner' like von Maltzan have been greatly over-simplified.[3] True, as his co-workers testified, he was a 'man of extraordinary intellect', who could 'think through large political issues from beginning to end'; a man who made sure that his subordinates 'always received clear instructions ... yet each individual was only kept fully informed about what was going on in his own sector'.[4] Nevertheless, von Maltzan was far removed from 'Easterners' like von Seeckt, for example, in his appreciation of the political realities in East Europe. Unlike Behrendt, who had said at the time of the German–Latvian agreement in July 1920, 'Thank God we have made peace with a part of Greater Russia', von Maltzan's commitment to improving German–Russian relations was coupled with an understanding of the problems of the new leaders in the Baltic States. He had personally been closely associated with the pressures inside the German establishment to abandon the 'policy of the Baltic Germans'.[5]

Von Maltzan's appointment, like that of the new German Ambassador to Latvia, Erich Wallroth, himself later head of the Eastern Department, was part of a deliberate attempt to inject new life into the stagnant atmosphere which had formed in Weimar–Baltic relations under Behrendt's direction in the summer of 1921.[6] In talks with the Estonian Ambassador to Berlin, Menning, and with the Latvian representative, Woit, on 13 and 5 November respectively, the German government reversed its previous line by declaring its willingness not to allow the disputes over the Baltic currency and agrarian legislation to hold up the negotiations for trade agreements, 'in the interests of a speedy settlement'.[7] In response, the government of Konstantin Päts in Tallinn used the excuse of current trade talks with Finland to continue prevaricating over the Berlin initiatives. The Estonians remained primarily concerned about the best way to secure their war-damage claims against Germany. As in the case of Latvia, the German experts continued meanwhile collating their own evidence. The strategy broadly agreed by the German treasury in November 1921 was to soften the Estonian government for a global agreement by impressing on them the extent of Germany's own legitimate demands, which in turn would create a favourable atmosphere for economic talks.[8] The Reich Trustee Company representative, currently at work in Riga on German–Latvian claims, was empowered to go on to Tallinn. Here he continued in the first half of 1922 to try to substantiate the Reich's claim to goods and materials abandoned by Germany in Estonia and for German improvements to roads and buildings.[9] It was on Latvia, therefore, that the Wirth administration concentrated its immediate attention. At the end of November 1921 the first of a series of meetings took place in the Auswärtiges Amt with the German chambers of commerce and economic interest groups, to work on the draft treaty which Crohn-Wolfgang's team had drawn up during its stay in Riga in the summer. The participants were left in no doubt that the Auswärtiges Amt and the Reich Economics Ministry were at last firmly at one in their belief that 'an economic agreement [with Latvia] is an absolute necessity for regulating our relations in the East'.[10]

The prospect of normalizing relations with Russia did not therefore lessen, but rather increased, the vigour of German negotiators in Baltic trade treaty talks. The considerable effort made to associate the Baltic countries with what Wallroth later called 'the new path taken in our *Ostpolitik* last November', is also, however, a reminder that the immediate concern of Wirth's administration remained the wider economic reconstruction of Russia and East Europe, with the attendant benefits for Germany.[11] It is this that secured for the government the more general support of the Centre Party and SPD for continuing talks with the Soviets, rather than the power, political advantages and leverage anticipated by nationalists and military circles. Wirth was not given carte blanche in the East in October 1921. However much the more aggressive Weimar revisionists might deny it, the central issue of German economic policy, reparations, continued to depend for its solution on the Western powers. After October 1921, as before, there was no necessary incompatibility between the development of Germany's Russian policy and the politics of fulfilment, at least in the sense that the Allied Powers also made renewed efforts to resolve their own relationship with Russia in the winter of 1921/1922. Indeed, historians of the Eastern bloc have seen fulfilment in terms of its part in diverting Western economic rivalry towards a consortium of capitalist powers to monopolize business with Russia.[12] At Cannes, in January 1922, Lloyd George coupled reparations problems with the wider task of reconstruction in Europe and expressly related Germany's incapacity to pay reparations to its failure as yet to build up its position in the economy of East Europe.[13]

When the British Foreign Secretary, Lord Curzon, argued in the course of further Anglo-French exchanges for the idea of a world economic conference including Germany and Russia, as a means of achieving a 'general detente which would facilitate the economic reconstruction of Europe', a useful platform was provided for the Wirth cabinet to pursue its wider strategy in East Europe. In Rathenau's opinion, that strategy was one of impressing on the other powers that Germany was 'an indispensable economic factor'.[14]

The fact that British policy once again helped to set the framework for Germany did not, however, lessen the commercial rivalry between the two powers. This alone ensured that any trade agreements concluded with the East European states would be heavily politicized. Political issues were further emphasized by Soviet initiatives early in 1922 to reduce the threat which they perceived in Lloyd George's idea of a united capitalist consortium at the planned world economic conference at Genoa. It was inevitable, and indeed understandable, that Soviet security fears should be heightened at the prospect of the Baltic countries functioning as the agents of Western business intervention, and that Lenin should respond by working for separate agreements with the individual powers.[15] It is the nature of this heightened intra-European rivalry that makes it more difficult to accept the habitual but one-sided condemnation of Germany's attempts to 'play the Russian card', since all powers were trying to do this to some extent in the early months of 1922, including the Baltic countries. By that time, however, some of the underlying structural advantages enjoyed by Germany in the competition for influence in East Europe were only too evident. A brief closer consideration of the reasons for Germany's success in meeting the Anglo-French challenge for business in the Baltic will confirm this.[16]

Being nearer, Germany had lower transport costs, which made it possible for German businessmen to send even small quantities of goods at a profit – a factor linked with the German ability to supply a much wider range of goods to the Baltic than could Britain.[17] Hardly irrelevant, either, was the fact that German goods were generally cheaper. For a period at least, German production costs were lower than those in Britain.[18] The depreciation of the German mark gave German exporters an edge over their British counterparts as the British governments pursued a policy of 'sound money' in the 1920s. One well-documented example of price competition between German and British exporters was provided by Telefunken's successful undercutting of the Marconi organization in a bid in November 1921 for a large wireless station in Estonia;[19] the pattern was repeated in other bids, with the Erich Hoth concern in Berlin also winning orders at the expense of British companies.[20] Such advantages were greater in view of the simultaneous depreciation of the Baltic and other East European currencies after 1918.[21] Significantly, in May 1920, Wirth's cabinet had decided to postpone the application to the East European states of the restrictions on German trade which had been designed to stimulate domestic production and exports in order to help meet the obligations imposed by the London ultimatum on reparations. 'Trade restrictions in relation to the East are to be held in abeyance, particularly in order to secure the necessary agricultural products from the countries with weak currencies.'[22]

The benefits to Germany of early gains in Baltic markets were increased by the fact that such business was consolidated through subsequent service and replacement contracts; this was particularly important in the case of machinery and factory equipment requiring installation and trainee schemes. British Foreign Office sources continued to receive reports confirming that the crucial first orders had too often been captured by German firms – an achievement not unconnected with such events as the opening early in 1922 of Germany's 'Economic Institute for Russia and the Border States' in Königsberg, with its own journal, *Der Osteuropa Markt*.[23]

It is not, however, sufficient to explain British business passivity exclusively in terms of the less quantifiable importance of the Baltic market in British trade as a whole.[24] To make such judgements is to forget how much contemporaries expected of commerce with Russia, disappointed as those hopes later turned out to be. Yet the numerical and qualitative superiority of German branches and agents of German firms in the Baltic by 1922 does, as we have already implied, say a good deal about the higher priority given by German governments to stimulating trade with Russia and the Baltic in the immediate post-war years. It is revealing to note that, in contrast to Germany, with its emphasis on the 'state tradition', British traders and governments alike were increasingly resentful and distrustful of the leading role of the state in Latvia and Estonia, particularly during the hectic legislative activity of 1921/1922, as Baltic leaders desperately sought to capitalize on their slender resources. According to one study, this helped significantly to explain the fact that British traders were still holding back early in 1922 from the Baltic States and the British Foreign Office advised British firms against investment in Estonia and Latvia before the conclusion of proper trade treaties.[25]

Reservations about the economic situation in the Baltic after 1918 had also been a factor in the repeated Treasury refusals to sanction loans for the Baltic countries in 1919, unless in conjunction with the Allies. Even this door closed on 25 June 1919, when the Supreme Council decided to give supplies but not financial aid.[26] Of course, Allied war materials might have been said to be in the nature of a loan, but difficulties experienced by Latvia and Estonia in repaying these sums even created reluctance in the Treasury to allow Baltic governments to raise money from British banks or from the London Money Market.[27] Here was a case where fiscal policy was at variance with the British government's proclaimed interest in trying to capture Baltic markets by facilitating credit for Latvia, Estonia and Lithuania; without such credit the Baltic countries could hardly 'buy British'.[28] When the Baltic states did manage to get their hands on Allied capital they were compelled to pay absurdly high interest rates for loans and credit.[29] True, in the long run such frustrations ensured that Latvia and Estonia did not have as large a burden of foreign indebtedness as other states in East Europe, but British trade was not helped in its competition with Germany.[30] As the abortive Tilden-Smith venture had demonstrated, British experts appreciated the importance of helping the Baltic leaders to rebuild their banking and financial systems, but there remained in Britain unwillingness to participate through capital investment in Baltic banks in 1921, precisely at the time when Latvian and Estonian governments struggled to stabilize their currencies and, in Latvia's case, to set up a state issuing bank in order to give the government greater control over the economic crisis.

The policies pursued by the Latvian Finance Minister (Kalniņš) to steer his country through its post-independence crisis were clearly likely to cause as much of a headache for German exporters as they did for the British and others. This is very evident in the analyses written about Latvia's economic affairs in 1921 by Schneemann and Wallroth. The former graphically outlined the frustrations experienced by foreign traders:

Latvia fails to exploit economically its natural riches, such as its agriculture, its wealth of woodland, its harbours and railways, or to pursue a policy of releasing the estates to the landlords; it refuses to accept concessions agreements and the management of its transit trade ... Instead, Latvia brusquely rejects such proposals and offers; although it has no alternative to find the necessary means, it imposes crippling restrictions on the trading and industrial ventures which are beginning to stir, with the result that trade and industry are virtually at a standstill in Latvia at the moment.

Schneemann admittedly saw a chink of light in Kalņińś' hard-headed policy package of austerity measures, his attempt to stabilize the currency and to establish a bank of issue, but he remained dismayed at the tight restrictions the Finance Minister wished to retain on foreign enterprise. On the proposed Latvian Bank, Kalņińś was expecting the capital to be one-third Latvian and two-thirds foreign, whilst the distribution of power on the managing board was to be the exact opposite of this. Schneemann felt that 'no capital in the world would join on this basis'.[31]

The proposal regarding the Latvian state bank illustrated the difficulty the Latvians had in containing and directing the influx of private foreign capital for private concerns in the Baltic. These were often more interested in trade with Russia than in the economic problems of Latvia as a newly independent state. It was Kalņińś' repeated assertion that his country's natural resources provided the best potential guarantee of Latvia's economic recovery. His attempts to restrict the printing of currency and to facilitate trade and exports from Latvia had to be seen in relation to the empty treasury he found on taking office, as he reminded the press attaché at the German embassy in Riga.[32] Yet Kalņińś' radical measures included as well extremely high taxation, which also attacked foreign business ventures. It was the latter aspect that Wallroth stressed in a lengthy analysis of Latvian economic problems written in late January 1922. Giving due credit to the way in which the policies of Kalņińś had balanced the Latvian budget by the end of the financial year 1921/1922, Wallroth affirmed that in the long run it would be impossible for a country with a population the size of Latvia's to sustain the three- to seven-fold increase in taxation which had taken place in 1921. Like Schneemann, Wallroth also commented on the detrimental effect of customs and tax policies on the foreign enterprises poised in Latvia in readiness for trade with Russia. Many of these concerns failed to renew their trade patents in December 1921 as a result of the fiscal burdens imposed under Kalņińś. Wallroth was equally critical of the policy of creating an artificially high level for the Latvian rouble. The rise in the value of currency did not lead to a fall in prices because of the exorbitantly high customs dues levied by Latvia in order to improve its balance of payments. 'Excessive' customs duties meant higher living costs. In spite of this, Wallroth expected domestic pressures ultimately to force a policy change, bringing with it a greater concern for production and improved East–West trade. In contrast to the gloomy response of British observers, Wallroth also stressed the value of Latvia's natural resources. The German Ambassador could talk of Latvia's 'teething problems' and he saw the current 'command economy' as the product of 'unbelievable difficulties in consolidating a new state created, as it were, from nothing'.[33]

At least Kalniņš' rigorous economic policy and the establishment of state monopolies in flax and timber meant that the Latvian state accumulated respectable exchange reserves. Together with savings from his restraints on, and cuts in, public expenditure, Kalniņš had at least created the basis for stabilizing the lat and ultimately for setting up the State Bank from Latvia's own resources at the end of 1922. A slow return to something like normal banking was already taking place in the second half of 1921. It would be more accurate to say normal in Baltic terms. Although highly developed before 1914, the centre of banking in Estonia and Latvia had been St Petersburg, and the numerous commercial banks in the provinces had their head offices in the Russian capital. Notwithstanding the destruction of records, the withdrawal of liquid assets from Baltic branches by the Russians in the war, even the disappearance of parent concerns, the commercial banks in the Baltic countries after 1919 were largely created out of the business of pre-war banks. The commercial banks remained, as before, largely concerned with foreign trade. It is difficult to exaggerate the importance of the fact that those Baltic banks which financed foreign trade were themselves chiefly financed by private foreign capital. Without this, foreign trade would certainly not have developed so rapidly, and, as the survey prepared by the Royal Institute of International Affairs commented, 'the interest of foreign capital in this type of bank is considerable. The United Kingdom and Germany have the greatest participation in the commercial banks of Estonia and Latvia.'[34] In fact this view was very much based on data for the later inter-war years; comparable figures for the early 1920s are not available. For this reason the point about the relative success of German financial penetration and the Weimar Republic's ability to compete against British pressures can best be made by examining specific examples of banking ventures in Latvia under German influence. It also demonstrates how quickly the

Germans responded to Vogl's plea in 1919 for a banking involvement in Latvia (see above, chapter 3).

One interesting case study is provided by Latvia's oldest, and one of its largest, commercial banks, the Riga Commercial Bank. Founded in 1871, the bank had been mainly supported by German capital and its shares had been handled on the Berlin Stock Exchange. In spite of wartime interruptions the bank was re-settled in Riga in 1918 during the German occupation. When peace came the bank managed to sort itself out financially with the aid of funds from the Dollar Trading Company in San Francisco, but its management remained largely in the hands of those of German origin. It had branches in Dünaberg, Libau, Mitau, Rositten and Windau, as well as a branch in Schaulen in Lithuania. Moreover, the Riga Commercial Bank retained a large share in its former branch in Tallinn, which after the war became the Estonian Industry and Trade Bank. The latter in turn had branches in Dorpat, Hapsal, Pernau and Walk. Its impressive network in the border states was completed through the stake which the Riga Commercial Bank retained in its former offices in Warsaw, known after the war as the Polish Commercial Stock Bank.[35] With a turnover in 1922 of 11 689 958 121 Latvian roubles, the Riga Commercial Bank was one of the most active in Riga, as Wallroth later confirmed. It represented above all the interests of the minorities in the Baltic states, especially German ones, and had almost the biggest clientele among the business community. Three on the four-man managing board were of German origin.[36]

It is significant that the source of the above information, the earliest attempt systematically to survey the banking system in Latvia, was commissioned by the German embassy in Riga from the economist and businessman, B. Siew.[37] Siew's review illustrated another aspect of Baltic banking, namely its degree of specialization. This resulted in an 'unusually clear distinction between the function of the commercial banks and that of other units in the system'.[38] In January 1920, according to Siew, there were 32 private credit institutions, including the commercial banks, as compared to 313 institutions which had existed in January 1914. By 1921/1922, as a result of a surge of new formations in the wake of Kalniņš' efforts, there existed 10 large banks, 25 mutual credit associations and 115 other institutions. Prominent were a number of relatively small joint stock banks; this was a reflection of the early rush of private foreign interests to set up speculative enterprises – a process which the Latvian government later discouraged. In comparison with pre-war times the overall scale of operations was far smaller, and yet the post-war demand for credit in trade and industry was enormous (see table 7).

How important it was to have a stake in Latvian banking is evident from the central role which the banks played not only in financing trade, but also in the eventual restructuring of Baltic industry (see below, chapter 7). Overall figures of German involvement are as we suggested, difficult to come by for the early phase, but an inkling of how active Germans were becoming by 1921/1922 can once more be gathered from individual examples. On 6 December 1921, Wallroth reported on the recent setting-up of a new joint stock bank at a meeting chaired by Siew in the building of the Riga Association for the Protection of Retail Trade and Industry. The managing board, of largely German origin, included a former director of Marconi in St Petersburg.[39] Other formations with a German or Baltic German stake included the Riga Credit Bank and the Riga International Bank, both founded in 1922.[40] Still more interesting was the registration of the statutes of the so-called Libau Bank on 31 January 1922.[41] The Libau Bank provides a more instructive illustration of the penetration of independent Latvia by German capital at a time when foreign capital was still by and large wary of the long-term political future of Latvia, and when, in Germany's case, the restriction on its financial management imposed as a result of reparations was added to the obstacles created by Latvian chauvinism. The development of the Libau Bank provides a much-needed glimpse of the earliest stages of foreign involvement in Latvia, to set against the rather general surveys of foreign capital in the Baltic in the 1930s.

The Libau Bank eventually became the fourth largest of Latvia's joint stock banks; it emerged after long negotiations between the former president of the Libau Exchange Association, Smit, and the German Darmstädter Banking Group. Essentially, the talks involved transforming the old Libau Exchange Bank – formerly belonging to the Libau Exchange Association – to a new private joint stock bank, the 'Libau Bank'. The older bank had insufficient credit abroad to function efficiently. In agreement with the Libau Exchange Association and the Darmstädter Bank, the new institution opened in spring 1922 with a share capital of 300 000 lats and acquired the assets of the former Libau Exchange Bank. Half of the share capital was taken up by the Libau Exchange Association; the other half was acquired by a group comprising the Darmstädter Bank in Berlin, the Northern

Trade Bank, also in Berlin, and the Lithuanian Bank, in Kovno. The Kovno organization and the Northern Trade Bank were in any case both financed by the Darmstädter Bank. Ultimately the latter planned, according to Wallroth, to found a domestic bank in Tallinn too, as it had in Kovno and Libau, and then to coordinate the overall management of its financial institutions in the border states through the Northern Trading Bank in Berlin. In Wallroth's words again: 'The extent of the original German participation is masked through the mutual collaboration of the Lithuanian, Estonian and Latvian banks.'[42] German involvement was further concealed by the composition of the board of directors of the Libau Bank. Although headed by Dr Fischer of the Darmstädter Bank, the board included native Baltic personalities and other foreign industrialists. As Dr Fischer later implied to Wever on his return from the bank's formal opening, the Libau Bank might prove to be the beginning of 'large-scale activity in the border states'. Significantly, neither Fischer nor the German representative in Latvia had been publicly present at the celebrations launching the Libau Bank.[43]

The outcome of the above development can be briefly traced at this point. When a Riga branch of the Libau Bank was opened, the business centre of gravity rapidly shifted from Libau, so that by 1923 its Riga 'branch' was responsible for about 90% of the turnover. By 1923 the Libau shareholders had sold out to a highly favourable offer from the Darmstädter Bank, effectively crippling the resistance of the Libau Exchange Association to the shift of power. The German Consul in Libau, Wilhelmlitten, rightly confirmed the way in which Riga, 'the economic heart of the country, draws all business to itself'.[44] The interesting feature of this episode is that the Latvian government turned a deaf ear to the pleas of the Libau Exchange Association to frustrate the shift of influence and business to Riga. By then the Latvian leaders had learned the lesson of not frightening foreign capital away as it had done in the immediate post-war months.[45] That this goodwill did not exist when the Libau Bank was founded, however, simply underlines the readiness of German capital to become involved, in spite of the risks and inconveniences of the early independence phase. Although the Latvian government continued to find it virtually impossible to attract finance for its planned state bank, Latvian private banking was beginning to settle in place in the critical period before the World Economic Conference at Genoa and German involvement was virtually unstoppable.[46]

This situation both attracted and repelled Latvian governments and leaders. That Latvia was in effect already relatively well pre-pared by private German traders as a 'springboard' is suggested by a German embassy report of 10 January 1922: 'In Latvia most of the larger German trade and industry concerns and firms orientated towards the East have local agents and consignment stocks destined for Russia.'[47] By this time, too, the factors which it has been suggested helped Germany had made a demonstrable impact on Britain's early post-war lead in Baltic trade. By the second half of 1921 Germany had overtaken the British position in exports to the Baltic, providing 40.7% of Estonian and 48.1% of Latvian imports (see table 2). Germany had also edged Great Britain out of its lead in the transit trade to Russia.[48] The figures are all the more revealing when the far greater extent of European competition for trade in the Baltic, in comparison with the years before 1914, is taken into account. Germany's success is well illustrated by the international trade fair which opened in Riga for the first time in 1921, an event specifically designed to foster Latvia's economic life and above all its trade with Russia. Dramatic proof was provided of how successfully German private enterprise had responded to the call of German governments for more active commercial penetration of the Baltic countries. Germany took 45% of the share of the exhibitions, Latvia 36%, whilst France and Britain could manage only 4% and 2% respectively. In some sections of the trade fair, notably that for agri-cultural machinery, the German presence was overwhelming. German firms presented 61% of agricultural machinery and 73% of dairy machinery. In the overall industrial sections of the fair the German share of 65% was an early reflection of the Weimar Republic's leading role as an exporter of industrial goods in Europe. It was possible to talk of German domination of the Latvian market.[49]

The Meierovics government could not ignore German pressures to consolidate an economic foothold through a trade agreement, as the resumption of German–Latvian economic talks in Berlin on 9 February 1922 confirmed. The re-opening of negotiations greatly pleased Wallroth, who regarded them as offering the chance of main-taining and developing Germany's route eastwards over the Latvian 'bridge.' In particular, Wallroth argued that only a quick settlement of outstanding disputes would give Germany the freedom for decisive political and economic activity in Latvia in the spring and summer.[50]

Although von Maltzan could not accept Wallroth's case for securing agreement by conceding Latvian damage claims for the entire war period, he was prepared to include German requisitions in the overall settlement of war damages in the concurrent Riga talks.[51] Additional grounds for German concern to achieve a timely agreement were provided early in February 1922, when the Russians allowed duty-free imports from Latvia, thus ensuring that the Estonian monopoly in transit trade would soon be ended. For Wallroth this development had great potential for the recovery of German industry in Latvia. He saw it as a prelude to greater Russian involvement with the border states and as a further sign of the expected return to pre-war trade patterns between Russia and the West through the Baltic.[52]

In reality the problem of the German–Latvian war-damage claims, although also the subject of talks in Riga from February 1922, was still no nearer resolution prior to Genoa, owing to the continuing uncertainty surrounding article 116. Other more general but more important considerations frustrated the Wirth administration's new emphasis on reaching speedy agreements with the Baltic countries so as to be in a strong position for the resumption of fuller trade with Russia. The first was the pervading fear in Latvia of the political problems which Western commercial penetration might bring in its wake. This was, of course, particularly acute in relation to the Weimar Republic. Given the presence and size of the German minority in both Estonia and Latvia, as well as the mounting evidence of Germany's leading role in Baltic imports by 1921/1922 (see table 2), the conclusion of trade treaties with Berlin remained a matter of keen controversy in Baltic public life. Anti-German sentiment was still strong, as ugly incidents in both countries confirmed in the late summer of 1921. The murder of Erzberger in that year provoked a series of scathing articles in the Baltic press examining the 'German character', and Hentig talked of a 'yawning gap' between our 'growing economic interests and [our] declining political power'.[53] Of course, economic aid from Germany remained indispensable; but, since the political loyalties of Baltic leaders lay with the Allied governments on the whole, the best option for Latvia and Estonia was, as Crohn-Wolfgang had recognized, to keep all options open for the time being, including the one of continuing talks with Germany. In addition, one obvious way to contain German, as indeed other foreign, influence was to foster competition between all the European powers interested in the Baltic. And here Wirth's government had to contend with the inflated expectations of Baltic opinion in the run-up to the World Economic Conference at Genoa, that the small countries would automatically derive benefit from the heightened international interest in Russia and its business.

TRADE AND REGIONAL ALLIANCE SYSTEMS

All the above considerations need to be set firmly in the context of regional political and economic alliance schemes. The interaction between these and the rival policies of the larger powers gives substance to the point made earlier about the way in which Baltic trade-treaty talks had become much more politicized by 1922. The nature of this interaction is invariably overlooked in writing on the Baltic alliance systems of the 1920s, whose history has been treated almost exclusively in terms of the obstacles to reaching overall agreement in the region.[54] The reality was that the schemes complicated enormously, by their very existence, the policy options facing Baltic leaders. The Polish seizure of Vilna in October 1920 certainly made it difficult for Lithuania to participate in any grouping of the border states in which Poland played a leading role; in itself this offered a measure of relief for Weimar *Ostpolitik*, by providing a setback to the prospects of achieving the five-power military defence agreement envisaged at the Balduri Conference of August 1920. It also checked Pilsudski's federal policy.[55] Yet it did not in itself simplify the policy choices in Tallinn and Riga. On one level the Vilna dispute tended to encourage efforts to bring about closer agreement between the three small Baltic states, as can be seen from the words of Latvia's Foreign Minister to the Latvian Assembly in 1921: 'In foreign policy the government is pursuing the goal of political and economic entente with the neighbouring states. In the first instance, the conclusion of economic and political conventions with Estonia, Lithuania and Finland, then the regularization and improvement of the situation with our more distant neighbour, Poland.'[56]

The policy outlined by Meierovics found expression in the exchanges between Latvia, Estonia and Lithuania in May and June 1921, under the immediate pressure of combating a feared threat from the Soviets. As a result, a Latvian–Estonian defensive agreement, directed against Russia, was concluded on 7 July 1921, and on 23 July the two Baltic states put forward plans for a common payments system, standardized measures and postage and transport

links – all pointing towards the declared ideal of a customs union.[57]
The significance of Meierovics' policy statement was that it left open
the future extension of the Baltic states agreement to both Poland and
Finland. The considerable early interest of the latter power in Baltic
alliance schemes has long been recognized, and it has even been
argued recently that until the end of 1920 at least attempts were
being made to divide the Baltic region into spheres of influence
between Poland and Finland.[58] Particularly strong grounds existed
for closer links between Finland and Estonia, since the Finns had
played a crucial role in the liberation of Estonia in 1919. The Finnish
Foreign Minister, Holsti, and his Centre Party were most actively in
favour of the Baltic bloc projects. Although facing considerable
opposition from the Finnish right, Holsti was helped by the general
concern in his country about Soviet intimidation in Karelia. That
Finnish opinion in general continued to be interested in Baltic bloc
schemes was of course confirmed by the choice of Helsinki for the
venue of the conference between Finland, Latvia, Estonia and
Poland between 25 and 29 July 1921.

If anything the policy choices in the Baltic states were more problematic from 1921, owing to the obvious tightening of Franco-Polish
ties. The inexorable shift in French policy towards underpinning a
strong Polish state was accelerated at the end of 1920 with the collapse of any lingering French hopes for a reconstituted Russia and the
recovery of the loans to the Tsarist government.[59] The Franco-Polish
alliance of February 1921 constituted a factor of the first importance
in Baltic bloc discussions. Manifestly, the sudden shift in French
policy towards finally encouraging Estonian and Latvian independence early in 1921 was linked to its policy towards Poland. The
recognition of Estonia and Latvia by Paris signalled France's commitment to a strong barrier of states in East Europe and logically
encouraged Poland to extend its political relationship with the Baltic
countries as well as with the 'Little Entente'. France's Baltic policy
was an integral part of its overall concept of altering the international
balance of power against Germany.[60] By September 1921, when
Estonia and Latvia were admitted to the League of Nations, France
demonstrated its interest in regional consolidation by even supporting the impractical proposal of the Belgian, Paul Hyman, for a
Polish–Lithuanian dual state held together by a military alliance and
enlarged by the addition of the port of Memel.[61]

The support of a major power behind Polish efforts to bring about a Baltic bloc actually increased rather than decreased the task of policy orientation in Baltic capitals. Their reservations about Poland's own hegemonic pretensions had always been a factor in the effort to consolidate at least the smaller unit of the three Baltic countries.[62] Yet they could hardly ignore the implications of French policy, in view of the continuing uncertainty in East Europe in 1921 and of the reluctance of British governments to match their political goodwill to the Baltic countries with physical support for them.[63] Baltic alliance projects were here seen to be interlinked with the wider problem of Anglo-French efforts to reach common ground over the post-war European order. In particular, French efforts to find an effective security substitute for the lapsed Anglo-American guarantee of 1919 touched directly on the concerns of the border states. According to the French Ambassador to Great Britain, Saint-Aulaire, in December 1921, the original guarantee was no longer felt to be adequate in Paris, because it did not cover the eventuality of an indirect attack on France through her Eastern allies.[64]

In further Anglo-French exchanges at the turn of 1921/1922, French Premier Briand tried to assure his British counterpart, Lloyd George, that it was a question not so much of military commitments as of grouping the countries of Central Europe about France and Britain. 'If the latter were in agreement, the others would follow'.[65] The British Foreign Office took a less rosy view of French motives by arguing later that France's Baltic policy was in fact aimed primarily at completing the encirclement and isolation of Germany. The judgement echoed that of the German Economics Ministry: that French trade policy in Eastern Europe aimed to remove Germany's rear cover and to prevent the recovery of German influence.[66] There was, however, little comfort here for Germany if it was hoped that Anglo-French differences were greater than their mutual concern over Germany. The latter point is, almost without exception, overlooked in a long literature on inter-war policy which exaggerates the rifts between London and Paris. The logic of Britain's own competitive commercial policies in the Baltic and East Europe was equally the curtailment of German political influence.[67] From such a vantage-point one might well question the judgement that Palmerston's policy of 'building long lines of circumvallation to confine the future extension of Russia' was the exception it has so often been seen as.[68] If it is argued that this expressed the anti-Russian strand in British policy, whereas the French were motivated in their Baltic policy above all by anti-German sentiments, there remained equal discomfort for Weimar–Baltic relations, as Wallroth had suggested when he had been Ambassador to Helsinki earlier in 1921: 'Border states policy, insofar as it tends beyond economic agreements and so forth towards a closer political grouping of the border states in the form of defensive alliance, means for its supporters here Entente policy'.[69]

In this interplay of the diplomatic interests of great and small powers the kernel of the alliance projects remained the determination of Baltic leaders to further their economic collaboration. Indeed, at the Baltic conference in Helsinki in the summer of 1921, it had been argued that the solution to intra-Baltic trade relations had to be seen as a pre-condition for the successful functioning of any future alliance system. How committed Baltic governments were to preparing for this can be seen from Latvia's insistence, in the draft terms which it had drawn up with Germany in August 1921, that any most-favoured-nation treatment it had agreed with Germany would not be allowed to prejudice rights and advantages which Latvia might concede to its 'neighbour states'. In the absence of the sort of general agreement on trade and tariffs which followed the Second World War, the use of such clauses in trade treaties after 1918 became a policy instrument of some effect. In this instance the so-called 'Baltic clause' reserved the right to offer preferential treatment in the matter of customs dues to the units of the putative Baltic bloc.[70] The Latvian negotiators insisted on this point yet again soon after their arrival in Berlin on 9 January 1922, because their government intended 'to enter into a close treaty relationship with Finland, Estonia and Lithuania'.

In the light of the earlier discussion about the interplay between the policies of the large and small states, it is not surprising that the German negotiators sharply countered the Latvian attempt to introduce limitations to the principle of most-favoured-nation treatment which had been agreed in the German–Latvian convention of July 1920. Although the question was eventually left open in Berlin as to whether or not Russia would be acceptable to the German side as a 'neighbour state', and although the German experts could accept the case for Finland, Estonia and Lithuania being so treated, opinion was unanimous amongst them 'that any possible demand by Latvia to include Poland in the neighbour states must be rejected under all circumstances'.[71] Continuing German–Latvian disagreement over war damages also affected the talks on the economic agreement going on in Berlin, but the Baltic clause and what it implied was identified as the major cause of the break in the trade negotiations between 21 February and the last week of March 1922. That much is evident from a memorandum prepared on 11 March for the Reichsrat Committee on Foreign Affairs:

The dispute is as follows. According to the binding provisions of the agreement of 15 July 1920, Germany enjoys unrestricted most-favoured-nation rights in Latvia. Now Latvia requires Germany to forgo this right in consideration of customs concessions accorded to Latvia's neighbour states. On our part, Latvian wishes were respected from the outset insofar as they concerned Estonia, Lithuania and Finland. After further negotiations, during which Latvia brought up the issue of its special position *vis-à-vis* Russia, we had agreed to forgo the customs concessions granted to the latter state by Latvia. Subsequently the Latvians sabotaged the conclusion of the agreement by rejecting every formulation which stated that Poland should not belong to those neighbour states to whom Latvia might grant special advantages not given to us on the basis of most-favoured-nation treatment.[72]

The link between political aims and economic policies was also to be seen in the way in which the Estonian government used the excuse of conducting trade talks with Finland in the autumn of 1921 in order to postpone discussions with Germany. Although the Estonian–Finnish agreement was concluded on 29 October 1921 – the date incidentally of the signature of the British–Estonian treaty[73] – the government of Konstantin Päts made no secret of its dislike of closer ties with Germany. This view was shared by the Estonian Foreign Minister, Antons Piip. Contemporary observers were not slow to read political motives into the success of France in negotiating substantial customs concessions for its wine exports to Estonia, as well as for its silks and luxury goods.[74] Indeed, the Estonian Trade Minister let Hentig know early in March 1922 that no progress was being made in the matter of a trade treaty with Germany, because Estonia was 'hampered by political ties with France'.[75] The remark gave substance to the independent report from the German representative in Bern, Mueller, about French attempts to extend the guarantee treaty it wanted with Britain to Poland, Latvia and Estonia.[76] Moreover, the suggestion that French policy was aimed at leading a bloc of border states at Genoa so as to strengthen its hand in relation to Britain and Italy was consistent with what Maltzan had heard from the Latvians; namely, that the French leader, Poincaré, had again been in communication with Poland, Latvia and Romania on the subject of their possible share in Russia's war debts. Once more the persistent idea was aired that France would allow Latvia the right accorded to Russia against Germany under the terms of article 116. Meierovics pointedly suggested to German sources that if Latvia followed the French line on this matter it would mean the growth of French influence in the border states; a refusal would increase France's isolation.[77]

Although the Baltic conference at Warsaw actually took place during the break in the German–Latvian talks, it would be incorrect to see it exclusively in terms of French alliance policies. The conference also expressed the renewed uneasiness in the Baltic states about Russia after the mobilization of Soviet troops on Finland's border late in 1921. According to the Russians, the proclamation by the Karelian Finns of a non-Bolshevik government on 21 November 1921 violated the 'autonomy' of eastern Karelia, which had been fixed in the Russo-Finnish peace treaty.[78] It seems likely that the French were indeed less enthusiastic by then about the prospect of a Polish–Finnish military alliance, but chiefly because of Foch's belief that it would divert Poland's energy against the Soviet Union and run counter to France's aim of frustrating a resurgence of German power in the region.[79] This goal was best achieved through an extension of the *political* alliance system in the border states, and closer ties between Poland and Finland were seen as a useful check to the feared orientation of Finland towards Germany, for the German army had played a crucial role in Finland's independence struggle in 1918.[80] French policy was thus hardly disadvantaged by the Warsaw conference between 13 and 17 March 1922. Meierovics' draft proposals brought to a climax a distinct phase of Baltic diplomacy first initiated by the resolutions of the Riga and Helsinki conferences of 1920 and 1921. At Warsaw, Poland, Latvia, Estonia and Finland re-affirmed their desire for peace in East Europe and the need for political and economic cooperation. Article 7 of the 'Accord' pledged the signatories to benevolent neutrality in the event of one of their number being attacked and committed them to immediate consultations on joint measures in such an event. Additionally, none of the states involved in the Warsaw Accord would conclude any treaty or agreement directed against any of the four members.[81]

The fact that Finland later refused to ratify the Accord and thus invalidated it must not obscure the relevance of the 'accord policy' for the policies and interests of the European powers then attempting to consolidate a stake in the Baltic area.[82] Many would have agreed at the very least with the analysis of the German Ambassador to Warsaw, Berndorff, who insisted that the Accord was 'considerably more important than one could have anticipated in view of the intimidation of the conference by Russian warnings and threats and in view of the ... strong stand of the Polish right-wing parties against the Baltic union as it is conceived by Pilsudski'.[83] Berndorff's point was that even the publicized principles of the Accord 'offer a basis on which to achieve wider aims'. That these would materially affect Weimar *Ostpolitik* was suggested by the interview given by Meierovics to the *Gazet Warszawska* immediately after the signing of the Accord. The Latvian leader spoke of two possible orientations to the policy of his small country:

One of these is to adapt to the policy of Russia and Germany, a horizontal orientation, as it were ... Yet we take into account that anything which serves the cause of a Russo-German understanding is a factor prejudicing peace, that we all long for peace and that therefore we cannot go along with these two states. This would be tantamount to hitching ourselves to a war wagon.

The 'vertical' orientation, by contrast, embraced the Baltic bloc, which Meierovics fervently hoped would in time include Lithuania and possibly Romania.[84]

Meierovics was a skilled diplomat, and his public statements, it is true, were to some extent the product of a situation where anti-German feeling remained strong in Latvia, where public opinion demanded of him support for the Baltic bloc, and where he could not too openly disclose his personal and continuing reservations about Polish policy.[85] Nonetheless, the Latvian leader's public postures perfectly illustrate the problems confronting a German government bent on committing the Latvians to a far-reaching trade agreement. The semantic athleticism shown by Baltic political figures – in professing their readiness to be an 'economic bridge' whilst also proclaiming their aversion to furthering political contacts between Russia and Germany – continued to present German governments with the sort of obstacle which had caused Behrendt and Rosen to dig their heels in throughout 1921. In 1922, however, the close identity between German economic and political interests which was achieved as a result of the Wirth administration's new emphasis made it possible for the Auswärtiges Amt to begin to reverse the line taken earlier. In-

stead of regional alliance schemes being allowed to constitute a check
to German efforts to secure trade agreements in the Baltic, the latter
were more likely increasingly to be regarded as instruments actively
to influence the political configuration of the region.

This strategy was already implicit in the German response to the
proposed Baltic clause but was first overtly stated in the Auswärtiges
Amt in March 1922, as the Warsaw conference loomed. The immediate occasion was provided by the sudden request from Estonia early
in March for the re-opening of talks with Germany. In Hentig's view
the overture came from Tallinn primarily because the regime was
hard-pressed by the Budget Commission of the Riigikogu and was
hoping to relieve some of the strain at home by making progress in
the matter of German–Estonian compensation claims.[86] Hentig's
scepticism was, however, discounted in the Auswärtiges Amt, where
it was fast becoming accepted wisdom that an earlier agreement over
what were expected to be relatively unproblematic compensation
negotiations with Estonia would provide leverage against Latvia.[87]
Because of difficulties with the latter state, which had now publicly
linked the compensation issue to the trade treaty talks,[88] and
'because of the political constellation in the East', the German
government was prepared to try to reach some general agreement in
principle over the war-damage issue. The decision was formally con-
veyed to Menning in Berlin on 16 March, the day before the Warsaw
Accord was made public.[89] On the day of that agreement von
Maltzan's private letter to Hentig set out the reasoning in the Auswärtiges Amt at greater length.

In this document it was argued that the prospect of an alliance of
border states, which at the very least would not be pro-German, had
increased. 'French policy appears to be behind this and in our negotiations with the border states we have not yet succeeded in clarifying
our relations by removing differences inherited from the past.' The
Latvians were 'delaying matters by every trick in the book', both
to await the outcome of the Warsaw conference and to watch the
progress of the German–Latvian talks on compensation in Riga. On
this subject Latvian demands had turned out to be 'spiralling, not to
say unconscionable'. By examining individual claims the German
government might be able to reduce the total Latvian demand to a
quarter of the total, but it was still not certain that even such a sum
could be found within the limits imposed by the Reich Ministry of
Finance.

If no agreement is reached on the question of damages and there is thus a likelihood of failing to conclude an economic agreement, then we shall have to acknowledge the fact that an anti-German mood has again set in in Latvia, and that in Riga all conceivable difficulties await our trade and transit to Russia.

Because Germany had also run into difficulties in its economic talks with Lithuania,

Estonia naturally assumes disproportionate importance for us. I work on the premise that we waged no real war in Estonia and that for this reason damages were not inflicted on buildings and land to the extent that they were in Lithuania and Latvia .... Inevitably, there are claims for measures taken by the occupation authorities, especially requisitions. Yet these do not so readily conjure up past war as do ruined buildings, and I think they can be more easily assessed on the basis of requisition bills and similar proofs .... We shall not therefore be daunted by our depressing experience with Lithuania and Latvia. With renewed hope we shall enter into the negotiations which the Estonians want ... Our firm aim will be to reach agreement with the Estonians in this matter ... Above and beyond the issue of war damages, we must now generally aspire to sit firmly in the saddle in Estonia, and as far as possible detach Estonia from the belt of border states.

Recognizing the obstacles to such a policy, not least the proposed Polish–Finnish military agreement, the letter continued:

For all that, we would have to try to direct Estonia towards its community with its Finnish neighbours, to stress the relationship to Scandinavia and to deepen the conviction in Estonia that it is not so much a member of the bloc of border states as a Scandinavian state in the broader sense.[90]

The German response therefore shifted as the regional alliance schemes reached a critical point. It has already been suggested that by the turn of 1921/1922, with German firms and banking institutions in place in Estonia and Latvia, a 'springboard' was in effect in place. It is thus less surprising that by the early months of 1922 Germany's policy of consolidating its economic foothold in the Baltic countries not only served the cause of German–Russian trade but was becoming more overtly directed against the Franco-Polish challenge in the Baltic area. In other words, political and economic goals were increasingly overlapping in Germany's case, very much to its advantage in terms of motivation and drive. The process offered a contrast both to Britain, where reluctance to assume direct political responsibilities reduced somewhat the impetus of the nation's own commercial policies, and to France, where a vital political involvement was not matched by a sufficiently powerful economic presence.

For the Baltic states themselves the uncomfortable clash of priorities, the inherent problem of squaring economic realities with political preferences, could best be solved through close association of Germany with the Western powers at the Genoa conference, followed by a combined Western assault on Russian markets. Although finally prepared to sign a provisional trade treaty with the Weimar Republic on 27 March 1922, the Latvians therefore had no urge to ratify it before a solution to the compensation talks or before the World Economic Conference, on which they continued to pin their hopes. To examine the text of the German–Latvian treaty is, however, to be clear, both in the implications it had for domestic legislation in Latvia and for the German minority there, as well as for Latvia's regional economic goals, that it was a multi-faceted instrument of Weimar *Ostpolitik*. It demonstrated the way in which the traditionally close link in Germany between government, finance and industry permitted a more flexible response to the Baltic problem to be forged in the Weimar Republic in the immediate post-war years.

In article 1 a series of provisions was formulated applying most-favoured-nation treatment to legislation affecting Reich Germans and Reich German firms operating in Latvia. The Latvian government expressly agreed to be accommodating as far as possible, within the framework of its current legislation, in the matter of Reich Germans or German firms acquiring property and immovables for industrial purposes. Both sides were manifestly aware of the link between such attempts to create favourable conditions for the restoration of business activity and the position of the German minority as a whole. Concerning imports and exports, article 3 contained the German promise to show particular goodwill in facilitating the export to Latvia of German semi-manufactured and manufactured goods, particularly if these were for agricultural needs or for the reconstruction and development of Latvian industry. The Latvians reciprocated with promises relating to timber and agricultural products. Free transit for German goods to Russia was agreed. What struck contemporaries as of particular significance (and this afforded a contrast to British approaches) was the fact that the German negotiators secured an undertaking from the Latvians that future economic legislation, notably where it concerned taxation and customs dues, would as far as possible be characterized by stability and continuity. The Latvian response here was not unrelated to the bait of a more generous credit action by Germany.

The article concerning the proposed credit for Latvia perfectly illustrated the difference between the *modus operandi* of the British and the German governments. In contrast to the former's *ad hoc* encouragement of trade with the Baltic, the German government affirmed in its agreement with Latvia: 'The bearers of credit are private German business circles, who are jointly to form one or more organizations. The German government will immediately convene representatives of the interests concerned and will assume direction of the efforts made to raise such credit.' The German organization or organizations thus offered security to the Latvian purchaser that the German seller would fulfil his contractual obligations. On the other side, the Latvian government was to provide the guarantee for the German suppliers that the Latvian purchasers would complete payments. When in individual cases both the German business organization and the Latvian government were prepared to stand surety, the relevant certificates of guarantee would be exchanged. Once the total involved in such transactions went beyond the proposed 500 million-mark credit, a new general agreement would have to be negotiated.[91] The direct involvement of the German government in this provision is all the more interesting in view of the difficulties it was currently pleading with the Allied powers in meeting the schedule of reparations payments. Although not itself providing finance, the support of the Berlin administration for the efforts of private German finance was of critical importance and must be seen too as generally strengthening the German banking interest in Latvia which has been remarked earlier.

The fact that the agreement was not ratified in the hectic weeks leading to the Genoa conference must not be allowed to obscure its fundamental importance for our understanding of Weimar *Ostpolitik*. It is a reminder that at the less glamorous level of day-to-day bargaining between Weimar officialdom and that of the smaller states of East Europe, German policy was already 'active' in many and diverse ways. The logic of the economic policy exemplified by the German–Latvian agreement of March 1922 was to exert continuing pressure on Latvia to commit itself to the prospect of developing Russo-German contacts which, even on the level of trade treaties, had unwelcome implications for Poland and for Franco-Polish political goals in the region. Such a conclusion might be taken simply as reinforcing the long-standing conviction of historians about the inherent threat to the border states of Russo-German relations. Without anticipating discussion of this central thesis of so many works on Weimar–Soviet relations, it will suffice here to point out that no concerted discussion on the subject of the Warsaw Accord took place between Berlin and Moscow, even though it manifestly worried both of them, and even though they were finalizing their agreement on the resumption of full economic and political relations. Wirth's government made no attempt even to respond helpfully to the unofficial hint of the Russian Chargé d'Affaires in Warsaw, Obelenski, who remarked to the *Berliner Tageblatt* representative that the Soviet government intended to 'spring open' the agreements reached by the border states at Warsaw. These were regarded in Moscow as evidence of French plans for a military alliance, according to Obelenski.[92] The German government received no official notification from the Soviets of their intentions, which became clear when the Russian delegation called in to meet Polish, Estonian and Latvian representatives in Riga, *en route* to the World Economic Conference at Genoa. The resulting 'Riga protocol' was in effect a swift response by Lenin to the Warsaw Accord. Apart from re-affirming the treaties of peace which the Russians had concluded with the border states in 1920, the protocol expressed a shared commitment to the economic reconstruction of East Europe and pledged a joint readiness to coordinate activities at the coming economic conference, 'taking [a] stand on the principle of respect for the political and economic sovereignty of their countries and on the need to resort to foreign credits for the reconstruction of the economic life of Eastern Europe'.[93]

It is difficult to see how the spirit of the Riga protocol was to be reconciled with that of the Warsaw Accord unless the persistent uncertainty in East Europe prior to the World Economic Conference is kept in mind. The two documents provide another illustration of the dilemma facing Baltic leaders. They also demonstrate the way in which Baltic diplomacy exploited what opportunities there were for movement between the major powers. When the press adviser to the Latvian and Estonian delegation to Genoa stopped over in Berlin on his journey to the economic summit to talk to von Maltzan, he had no hesitation in discussing recent events with the backing of both the Latvian and Estonian governments, but he warned that these 'must observe a certain reticence in view of the sensitivities of the Entente'. Von Maltzan was told that the Riga conference had not had the support of the French, which was hardly surprising, but that the border states were all vitally concerned with the economic and political consolidation of Russia. Von Maltzan's reply was to the effect that the two principles of Weimar *Ostpolitik* were independence for the border states, which constituted a bridge and transit area to Russia, and a friendly and understanding attitude towards the Soviets without interference in their internal politics. He was, therefore, 'delighted to hear that these two aims were now agreed on for us through the conference at Riga and he could assure [Ammende] that every action which assumed the restoration of Russia would have our liveliest sympathy'.[94]

Shortly thereafter this fact was demonstrated to the wider world with the unexpected conclusion of the agreement between Germany and Russia at Rapallo, during the World Economic Conference – an event which upset Allied plans and re-awakened French fears as well as those of its allies in East Europe. That the agreement marked an important stage in the development of German foreign policy after the Versailles treaty has never been disputed in the plethora of studies on the 'Rapallo relationship'. That those studies have nonetheless failed to do full justice to the range of functions of the Rapallo agreement in Weimar *Ostpolitik* I hope to demonstrate in the next part of this book.

5

Randstaatenpolitik

In recent times a growing understanding of the hesitant and erratic
development of early Weimar–Soviet relations has made it harder to
sustain the argument once advanced, above all in the works of British
and American historians, that the Rapallo treaty signified a
German–Russian 'community of fate' or 'unholy alliance'.[1] An
integral part of that explanation was the implicit threat seen in the
Rapallo 'partnership' to the very existence of the border states situated between the two powers.[2] Such a view was found particularly in
earlier studies of 'Poland between East and West', which analysed the
diplomacy of Weimar–Soviet relations almost exclusively in terms of
a dual pressure from the two great powers. Less attention was given
to the evidence suggesting that the relationship between Germany
and Russia continued to be problematic after, as before, Rapallo.[3]
To be fair, Germany's military and political leaders in the 1920s did
recognize with satisfaction that the Rapallo treaty heightened the
sense of insecurity of the Polish leaders, whose state's borders
remained a major target for Weimar revisionism.[4] The anti-Polish
invective in German public life after 1918 makes it possible to see at
first glance why historians were so tempted to draw parallels between
the Rapallo agreement and the Nazi–Soviet non-aggression pact of
1939. The manifest difference between the two treaties is, however,
that the latter was a prelude to a physical assault on Poland and the
Baltic. To infer by linking the two pacts that 1939 was the logical
outcome of 1922 is seriously to distort our understanding of the
nature of Weimar *Ostpolitik*.

By contrast, West German historical writing on the Rapallo treaty
has given less weight to the intangible 'spirit' of Rapallo informing

the above line of interpretation and rather more to the mundane text of the agreement, which, it will be known, was concerned with the re-establishment of political relations between Germany and Russia, the mutual rejection of war damages and a shared intention to build up and extend economic ties with each other. Such provisions were made alarming to the Western Powers by, if anything, their own suspicions and fears about the Soviet Union. This line of argument has echoes in East German historical writing, where the Rapallo agreement is invariably regarded as an early model of peaceful co-existence.[5] By and large, West German historians defended Germany's right to restore its international standing by pursuing what they felt to be an 'active' policy for the first time since 1919. In doing so, they played down the undeniable fact that military collaboration between the Reichswehr and the Russians was helped by the existence of the Rapallo treaty. They also emphasized that German policy towards Poland envisaged not war, but peaceful economic and political pressure to bring about the revision of Germany's eastern borders, as desired by all parties in the Weimar Republic.[6]

Hermann Graml's attempt to break with the West German interpretation of Rapallo contended that his fellow-countrymen had given insufficient attention to the long-standing hegemonic pretensions in German foreign policy, which Graml saw the German–Russian agreement as primarily serving. He further argued that historians in the Federal Republic failed to give sufficient weight to the fact that the Rapallo treaty increased the resentment of Poland and France towards Germany. The feeling of insecurity in Paris and Warsaw was heightened by the German–Russian agreement, and the fear was intensified that the two 'outcasts' of post-war Europe would take joint action against Poland. Such renewed anxieties about aggressive German revisionism, Graml contended, made it more, not less, difficult for Germany subsequently to regulate its relationship with the Western Powers.[7] Whilst Graml's work represents one of the surprisingly few attempts to relate Weimar foreign policy systematically to the debate on the 'continuity' of German policy aims between 1870 and 1945, it is flawed by a failure to appreciate that the Weimar Republic did not have a monopoly on nationalism in early twentieth-century Europe – a point which has been made indirectly in many of the newer writings on international relations in the post-war period and on French and British foreign policy.[8] In such a comparative context the possibility must at least be admitted that attempts were made by Weimar policy to strike a balance between the assertion of the Reich's national interests and those of Europe as a whole. More recently it has been argued, in what was in effect an updated defence of the West German tradition of historical writing on Weimar–Soviet relations, that even if the Soviet Union preserved its global aim of revolution and the German Reich's central preoccupation comprised foreign policy revisionism, the two states could become in the 1920s 'legitimate members of the international system, in that at that time they did not envisage changing the European status quo through war or fundamentally questioning the existing peaceful order'.[9]

The interesting point about the argument so briefly outlined above is that it has been conducted largely in the absence of any systematic new empirical study of the practical implications of the Rapallo agreement for the development and policies of the 'lands between' Germany and Russia, although central to all differences of opinion about the significance of the Weimar–Soviet pact are precisely those East European states. It is a major purpose of this chapter to redress the balance by analysing the impact of the German–Russian agreement on the Baltic countries and to use the findings to test some of the propositions advanced in the historiographical debate about Rapallo.

The prospect of a new phase beginning in Weimar *Ostpolitik* was marked by von Maltzan's telegram from Genoa on 21 April 1922: 'Unofficial contacts made with the Soviets concerning mutually benevolent handling of the border states problem'.[10] An attempt to take a more systematic overall approach towards the range of problems outstanding between the German and Baltic governments was also signalled by Blücher's planned visit to Baltic capitals immediately after the signature of the Rapallo treaty. The purpose was to orientate the German representatives in Riga, Tallinn and Kovno on the general political situation; this led to arrangements being made for the first ever conference of German government staff in the border states in May 1922.[11] In practice, there is little trace in the German files that any systematic discussion took place with the Soviets over Baltic problems in 1922/1923, particularly in the case of Estonia and Latvia.

By contrast, the German government appeared to have its hand strengthened through the psychological shock experienced by Baltic leaders as a result of the collapse of the Genoa conference, together with the disappearance of the enticing prospect of a greater role for the Baltic countries in East–West trade. Instead there remained the certainty of the German–Russian agreement. Politically unwelcome as this undoubtedly then was in the Baltic countries, they could hardly afford to ignore the professed intention in the Rapallo treaty that Germany and Russia would intensify economic relations. The delegates at Genoa from Estonia, Latvia and Lithuania not only hastily assured von Maltzan of their desire to resume trade talks with Germany, but also diplomatically stressed their growing awareness that, as a result of the German–Russian agreement, it seemed 'more than ever necessary to form a quite open and reliable bridge between Germany and Russia'.[12] Poland was notably absent from the exchanges, and neither the Baltic countries nor Finland joined Warsaw in signing the Allied protest against the Rapallo treaty. Haniel, in the Auswärtiges Amt, underlined the obvious when transmitting to Hentig in Tallinn the good news about the Baltic request to re-start talks: 'Intensive contacts resumed with the border states. Estonia, Lithuania and Latvia have met Finland without Poland. Warsaw conference thus probably illusory.'[13]

On this subject, Holsti's failure early in May 1922 to secure the ratification of the Warsaw Accord in the Finnish parliament, together with the no-confidence motion carried against him, reflected the conviction gaining ground in Finland that it should build on its friendship with Germany rather than rely on regional alliances. Indeed, it has been suggested that the more active Finnish interest in the Baltic bloc prior to 1922 resulted largely from Germany's apparent weakness in the post-Versailles order in Europe.[14] The Rapallo treaty thus at last seemed to many in Helsinki to offer a more practical route to security; as von Maltzan recorded at Genoa, the Finnish delegation was at pains 'to secure our friendly mediation with the Soviets in possible future disputes between Finland and Russia'.[15] Clearly, good relations with Finland would also contribute to the ultimate success of the strategy, which had been outlined in the Auswärtiges Amt prior to Genoa, of levering Estonia out of the 'girdle' of border states and strengthening its attachment to Scandinavia instead of to Poland.

Since that strategy had been predicated on the basis of successfully resolving the question of war-damage claims, the immediate attraction of the Rapallo agreement was the leverage provided not so much by its 'spirit' as by its terms. When von Blücher carried out his tour of the Baltic immediately after Rapallo, he believed that a major aspect of his brief was the need to popularize the idea that 'the understanding reached between Germany and Russia at Genoa raises the prospect of an agreement [with the Baltic states] on a similar basis: mutual renunciation of claims for war damages and the granting of most-favoured-nation principles'.[16] In fact this message echoed the wording of the German note to the Allied Powers at Genoa, justifying the Rapallo agreement as an opportunity 'to make a peace which excluded all long-term indebtedness and a chance to rebuild relations unburdened by the past'.[17] In this respect the Rapallo treaty could function not only to further the Weimar Republic's continuing general drive to revise the reparations settlement made with the Allies, but also to develop its tactic of gradually recovering the right to make its own terms of trade as far as possible, through treaties on a most-favoured-nation basis. Both developments promised the vital reduction of overall costs to the German economy.[18] The Rapallo agreement raised hopes in Berlin of similar package deals with the Baltic countries and the prospect beckoned of thereby creating links 'in the chain of treaties with the new states on the eastern and south-eastern frontiers of Germany'.[19]

Manifestly, after Rapallo it was possible to direct such activity in a more sustained fashion against French policy in East Europe. The German–Russian agreement also constituted a potential check to Poland's pretensions in the Baltic region – an aspect which is quite strikingly apparent in the meetings which the Latvian leader had with Rathenau, Wirth and von Maltzan in mid-June 1922, when following up the informal exchanges at Genoa. Meierovics heard, to his dismay in view of the immense public clamour in Latvia on the issue of war damages and the belief there in Germany's duty to pay them, that the Berlin government had been perfectly serious at Genoa. The Latvian leader was told by Rathenau and Wirth that: 'Corresponding to the procedure at Rapallo, a full settlement by mutual renunciation of both states' claims seemed perfectly acceptable.'[20] Among the incentives offered by the German government (interestingly enough in view of the Locarno settlement later) was an arbitration agreement on the lines of that concluded between Germany and Switzerland. Yet the conversations on Berlin were coloured by the known intention of Meierovics immediately after Rapallo to continue to explore contacts with France and Poland – a factor which the Latvian indeed deliberately exploited when he subsequently spoke with von Maltzan.[21] The latter was reminded that 'there were also anti-German combinations which would be uncomfortable for Germany. He [Meierovics] would regret it if Latvia was compelled to join such a combination.'

This was doubtless an indirect response to the earlier remark by Rathenau, that 'the possible degree of intimacy between their two countries' depended on the nature and extent of the ties between Latvia, Poland and France.[22] Characteristically, von Maltzan replied to Meierovics' scarcely veiled threat with a thrust of his own. Germany

could never blame Latvia for *Realpolitik*. No more had we blamed Finland when it entered into a very intimate relationship with Poland. The experience of Finland had shown, however, that that country had, on its own account, recognized the difficulties and ultimately uncomfortable problems attendant on that policy. I had the impression that at the moment a similar mood prevailed in Estonia and Lithuania. Tallinn and Kovno had been so far excellent transit posts for our economic traffic with the East. I had always hoped that Riga's much disrupted harbours would regain their earlier function as an entry point for the East.[23]

Given, however, the worries of Meierovics about the Rapallo agreement, and given the hostility of the Latvians towards any attempt by Germany to escape from its obligations to compensate Latvia, there was no immediate prospect of the Berlin negotiators avoiding yet another round of punishing talks on this particular issue. Consequently ratification of the German–Latvian provisional trade agreement was further postponed.[24]

Confirmation of the impasse with Latvia reinforced the strategy of working in the first instance for a settlement with Estonia. On 10 June 1922, the Tallinn government also followed up its contact with the German delegation in Genoa and formally confirmed its desire to re-open talks.[25] Once again the Auswärtiges Amt's justification in responding promptly was the need to counter French attempts to create 'as much economic and political influence as possible in the states neighbouring Germany and specifically to use the Baltic states as a barrier between Germany and Russia'.[26] Both governments agreed, however, on the value of a preliminary exchange of views before the final negotiations took place, precisely to avoid the damaging public impasse which the German–Latvian talks had reached. The German response to Tallinn on 6 July 1922 stressed the advantage of preliminary soundings in Berlin in terms of the Estonians having the opportunity to make contact with relevant German firms and industrial undertakings.[27] When the Estonians Wirgo and Küpparsepp arrived in Germany early in September to join their Ambassador in Berlin for the informal exchanges, the Auswärtiges Amt left no doubt that in the all-important matter of reparations the German claims would far outweigh those of Estonia. The figure ultimately presented by the Germans totalled 533 million gold marks, of which 446 million were state claims, 87 million those of private individuals and concerns; this compared with the Estonian demand for 250 million gold marks, comprising 225 million for the state and 25 million for private claims.

In reality the intention in Berlin was to convince Tallinn of the benefits of doing a deal à la Rapallo; the German figures were as much directed at conditioning public opinion in Estonia to be realistic in its expectations. That the Estonian government at least was becoming more amenable was indicated, it was believed in the Auswärtiges Amt, by the relatively small percentage of private claims in the overall Estonian total.[28] Whilst the Estonians still entertained a hope of holding out the inducement of an economic agreement as bait to move the reparations question towards a quicker solution, German negotiators now insisted on a package deal. Von Blücher reminded Menning on 13 September 1922 that his government shared the wish of the Estonian Foreign Minister, Piip, for a prompt resolution of the economic discussions and the issue of damages. 'But we don't want to settle one without the other.'[29] His message was underlined by von Maltzan when he met Wirgo after the latter's series of conversations with Stockhammern (of the Reich Ministry of Economics) on the trade agreement proposals. Of the assurances von Maltzan received from Wirgo – namely that the Estonian Finance Minister had come to appreciate the case for a mutual liquidation of respective war debts even if the general public had not – the 'red baron' remarked that the procedure was sound only if, 'as in the case of the Rapallo agreement, it is accompanied by the regulation of economic relations'.[30]

Attention did not waver from the goal of countering French policy in the Baltic region. During his conversations with Wirgo in Dresden, Stockhammern had considered both the British and the French positions in the matter of likely customs concessions. Wirgo heard that Germany 'could not endure a preferential position for France'. Additionally, Stockhammern continued to argue for strictly limiting

Estonian exemptions from most-favoured-nation principles to specific neighbour states on specific issues.[31] Once again von Maltzan strongly backed Stockhammern's effort. He told Wirgo 'repeatedly and pointedly', that the exceptions which Germany expected from the most-favoured-nation treatment could only be made for neighbour states. 'Herr Wirgo', von Maltzan later commented ironically to Stockhammern, 'took note of my remarks without so much as a mention of France'.[32] The attempt to persuade the Baltic countries to form an economic bloc with Germany and Russia could scarcely have been pressed harder as an alternative to the 'vertical' orientation of the Baltic bloc, to use the terminology of Meierovics.

How closely related the Weimar–Baltic and Weimar–Soviet trade-treaty negotiations were in the view of the Auswärtiges Amt and Economics Ministry was confirmed by Wallroth's secondment from his Riga post for three months in 1922, to work on the legal and economic aspects of the Rapallo treaty and its extension, as well as by von Maltzan's own careful monitoring of events in the border states. At the close of 1922 the latter was therefore particularly concerned, although the Rapallo agreement had been broadened to include the Ukraine in November, about the Cabinet crisis leading to the replacement of Wirth's administration by Cuno's. '*Ostpolitik*', von Maltzan wrote to Brockdorff-Rantzau in one of a series of exchanges, 'is much endangered by the new constellation'. He aired this anxiety at his first meeting with the new Foreign Minister, von Rosenberg and was able to reassure Brockdorff-Rantzau later that he had formed the impression that at least none of the political parties in the new coalition would directly attack 'our *Ostpolitik*'.[33]

Maltzan had even let it be known that he 'felt unable to carry on with Russian policy under a minister who did not support my line'.[34] Instead, his own influence was secured with his promotion to the State Secretaryship in the Auswärtiges Amt; this caused Brockdorff-Rantzau to observe, however, that von Maltzan could no longer so openly press 'for the line to the East'. Not surprisingly, at the same time the German Ambassador to Moscow expressed the hope that the 'hitherto regular exchange of views could be maintained'.[35] In reality, von Maltzan's concern that policy issues in the East might be short-changed as a result of the mounting preoccupation of the German government with Allied reparations carried considerable weight. 'My successor', von Maltzan was able to reassure Brockdorff-Rantzau on 22 December 1921, 'will probably be Wallroth. The latter will be replaced [in Riga] by Minister Köster. I have only taken this step in the firm conviction that I can thereby continue to serve our *Ostpolitik* politically. I most earnestly beg you not to regard this step as desertion.'[36]

A few weeks later came the crisis within the Weimar Republic after the Allied Reparations Commission declared Germany in default and French and Belgian troops moved into the Ruhr. Von Maltzan was given an unlooked for opportunity to reconcile his long-standing interest in *Ostpolitik* with his wider duties as State Secretary. Behind Poincaré's gamble in 1923 lay a determined French strategy to use the reparations crisis to inflict a severe blow on German heavy industry, thus bringing to an end the imbalance between France and the Weimar Republic.[37] If, however, this goal is seen as an integral part of French security policy, along with the attempt to restrain Germany's economic and political influence in East Europe, the intimate link between the Ruhr action and Weimar *Ostpolitik* is readily appreciated. Equally, an important consideration behind the German policy of passive resistance in the West was the determination of the Cabinet and the Reichswehr to forestall attacks on Germany's eastern borders or pressure from France's allies in the East. Stresemann was not alone in urging that 'it is not impossible that we shall be attacked from the East'.[38] Even the prospect of Poland and the border states participating in Allied sanctions provided a serious strategic challenge to the Reich and to its links with East Prussia. How impotent it was was demonstrated by the Lithuanian action in wresting Memel from League of Nations control during the Ruhr crisis. By sending troops into the Memel area, the Lithuanian government was effectively incorporating it into the state.[39] Poland's success in getting the Allied Powers to recognize its border with Russia on 15 March 1923 also deepened the gloom in Berlin during the 'trial of strength' between France and Germany.

Under these conditions the politicization of Weimar–Baltic trade treaties became more pronounced than ever. It was consistent with Auswärtiges Amt policy, and with von Maltzan's line in particular, that, in the face of considerable pressure from the Memellanders, the German government refused to let the Lithuanian coup in Memel interfere with the successful resolution of the economic talks with Lithuania which had resumed in Dresden in November 1922. This provided a good example of priority-setting in foreign policy. 'Germany', complained the German Consul in Memel, 'has sacrificed us on the altar of the German–Russian–Lithuanian friendship'.[40] For von Maltzan, however, the pending German–Lithuanian trade treaty was a sign that, at last, progress was being made slowly, 'step by step'.[41] The agreement at least added extra weight to Germany's consistent attempt after Rapallo to settle compensation claims without payment, even though priorities had been reversed through events, Estonia now falling into second place in the sequence of planned agreements with the border states. When Hentig was told on 10 February 1923 of the Auswärtiges Amt's readiness to open formal negotiations in Tallinn once agreement in principle over war damages looked likely, he was reminded of the overall strategy. Just as Lithuania's example was likely to influence Estonia, so the Auswärtiges Amt stressed the 'exceptional value' of a German–Estonian agreement not only in securing at least temporarily the most-favoured-nation treatment which German trade and industry was advancing as its minimum demand, but also in applying extra leverage to Latvia.[42]

Undoubtedly, Lithuania's agreement with Germany influenced the Estonian government. Its Foreign Minister, Hellat, although regarded as a nationalist and hostile to the Baltic Germans in Estonia, was also seen as a realist in the Auswärtiges Amt. There was felt to be little reason to disregard Hellat's claim that it was high time in any case for Estonia's trade-treaty situation to be regularized, a process which clearly had to include Germany in view of its dominant position in the small country's foreign trade. In addition, a note of urgency was introduced for Hellat by the fact that the elections due in late spring 1923 held in prospect a change of government in Tallinn.[43] Full weight should also be given, however, to the pressure which the German negotiators could apply by exploiting the uncertainty in Estonia about the full implications of the Rapallo treaty. At the end of January 1923, Menning was suddenly confronted with the idea that Germany might reserve the right to claim for the Estonian share of Russia's pre-war debt to Germany. 'MENNING: But Germany has forgone compensation claims against Russia in the Rapallo treaty. CRULL (Aus. Amt): Only in respect of those demands where Russia was the debtor, not in respect of those which under international law fall on Estonia. MENNING: This is a wholly new demand, which as yet no other foreign state had raised against Estonia. CRULL: But which, as far as I know, no state has so far explicitly ruled out'.[44]

Crull's shock tactics were of course merely part of the softening-up process directed against Estonian public opinion, to help sell the idea of a Rapallo-type agreement to Estonia, so that Germans and Estonians could begin 'drawing a line under the past and devoting our energies exclusively to reconstruction'.[45] Nevertheless, it is easy to see why matters moved so quickly at last. Once the Estonians had formally declared themselves ready for full negotiations on 20 February 1923, the German government immediately began preparing drafts for the planned mutual declaration on war damages.[46] The drafts had been exchanged by 4 April and Crull left for Reval on 15th of that month to finalize them before proceeding fairly smartly with the economic talks, the other part of the package. Here the German priority remained at the very least to secure most-favoured-nation treatment in all areas relating to the consolidation and expansion of Germany's economic policy in Estonia. The agreement was to underpin more securely the already considerable and growing private German economic presence in Estonia. The Tallinn talks between Crull, Hentig and Dr Jung on the one hand and the Estonians, M. Hurt (Trade and Industry), K. Rosendorff (Finance), Tofer and the Director of the legal section of the Estonian Foreign Office, A. E. Poom on the other culminated on 5 May in a protocol detailing the areas of agreement. General most-favoured treatment was fixed in mutual trade relations, covering transit and re-export and storage of German goods in Estonian ports, the right to acquire and own moveable and immoveable wealth and to have access to pursue trade, commerce and industry. These provisions applied for the private citizens of each state as well as for commercial concerns, including insurance companies.[47] Where the talks ran into difficulty, and where the political dimension of the trade-treaty talks was most in evidence, was over the question of extending the most-favoured-nation treatment to the area of customs and tariffs.

In spite of a degree of goodwill on both sides, in the last resort the very different conditions pertaining to the Estonian and German tariff systems respectively precluded agreement for the time being in this area. Central to Germany's predicament remained the fact that under the Versailles terms any concessions it made on trade to third parties automatically had to be extended to the Allied Powers. The German government could not therefore reciprocate for the most-favoured customs concessions it demanded of Estonia. Consistently with its overall strategy in the border states the German government was prepared to accept the limitations to most-favoured-nation treatment which Estonia had accorded to Finland in an earlier treaty. It was also prepared as ever to recognize as 'neighbour states' entitled to special concessions Latvia and Lithuania and, significantly, after Rapallo, though not before, Russia. The favoured position of Britain and France in Estonia's trade treaties with these states was altogether more serious. In return for tariff concessions to Britain, it is true, Estonia received no reciprocal privileges for its own exports. Yet the general absence of special tariffs in Great Britain gave Estonia advantages in selling goods there. This was certainly related to Britain's ability to maintain its position as the leading purchaser of Estonian goods, notwithstanding Germany's dominance of the Estonian import scene (see tables 2, 3 and 4).[48]

In the case of France, a list of specific items where tariff concessions would apply had been agreed on both sides. For France this included luxury goods, as well as some chemical and textiles goods and most groceries, whilst Estonia was given concession for its exports of flax and spirits and some foodstuffs. 'Which [country] comes off better doesn't bother Estonia, which in any event secured a privileged market for its goods in France.'[49] German interest groups were hardly likely to be contented with Estonian assurances that 'our treaty with France was made for political reasons. It will not last long because our trade relations with France are too slight.'[50] Something more tangible was needed. As Crull argued later in his report from Tallinn, Germany could not afford indefinitely to forgo most-favoured-nation treatment in customs too. 'We would thereby be put in an intolerable position, not only in relation to France, whose export to Estonia is minimal, but in respect of England, with whose textile products we have to compete here.'[51] Attempts were made to convince Tallinn that, in return for the tariff concessions it wanted, Germany would in practice deal favourably with Estonian exports by applying the extremely limited exceptions it made in its tariffs for 'states with weak currencies'. This was not enough to tempt the Estonians. Crull rightly argued that until Germany restructured its tariffs to a maximum and minimum scale it could never expect concessions for its products in those countries which operated a double tariff.[52]

In the end, therefore, the question of tariffs was excluded from the proposed agreement pending a later full-scale trade treaty. Yet the draft of the temporary trade treaty which German government departments considered in May, and which Wallroth was insistent 'had to be signed as soon as possible on compelling political grounds' (as it eventually was on 27 June 1923), at last secured the firmer legal base for German economic enterprise in Estonia. Another small brick fell into place in the edifice of German sovereignty over its foreign trade, the postponement of tariff agreements notwithstanding. The fact that the German–Lithuanian trade treaty was also signed on 31 May, as the Estonian–German talks moved towards a resolution, represented a breakthrough in Weimar trade policy in East Europe at a time when the political and strategic situation in the region looked its gloomiest. The coincidence was hardly fortuitous. The Weimar–Baltic trade agreements of 1923 were the fruit of the overall situation created by the Rapallo treaty and of Germany's redoubled effort in its 'year of crisis' in 'breaking through the girdle of border states placed round Russia'. The importance of the timing of the Baltic agreements was confirmed by the fact that shortly afterwards, in late June 1923, the German–Soviet economic negotiations were resumed.

Since, it has been argued, the 1923 crisis eventually strengthened Poland territorially and added new bonds between Warsaw and Paris,[53] the breakthrough achieved by the Weimar Republic in its trade policy towards the Baltic states provided a small but vital measure of relief. This was a more tangible, if limited, by-product of the Rapallo 'relationship' than the direct political pressure which, in most accounts, Germany and Russia are felt to have been able to bring to bear in the East against a feared Franco-Polish action in 1923. There is, by contrast, no substantial evidence in the German archive material relating to the Baltic countries that Moscow and Berlin made any progress towards carrying out the 'mutually benevolent' treatment of border states problems which had been proclaimed at Genoa – at least before 1925, by which time the situation had changed a great deal (see below, chapter 6). Certainly, Germany was given little indication, for example, of the thinking behind the Soviet diplomatic offensive in the Baltic area shortly after Genoa, which led to a disarmament conference in Moscow between 2 and 12 December 1922, with Poland and the Baltic states.

Undoubtedly, the Soviet Union's own feeling of insecurity in the face of Franco-Polish attempts to tighten the *cordon sanitaire* after Genoa lay behind Russia's public expressions of disappointment over the lack of attention given to disarmament during the World

Economic Conference. Lenin's government claimed with some justice that it wanted to concentrate its available resources on Russia's reconstruction.[54] In the event, the Poles were able to take the lead in the border states during the summer of 1922, to develop the theme of 'moral' before 'material' disarmament. In short, the border states maintained their insistence on Russia's signing collective security agreements with them before the question of arms reduction was raised.[55] What did emerge, however, was the beginning of a stronger relationship between Moscow and the Lithuanian government, which had sided separately with the Russians during the disarmament conference. On this matter, admittedly, the German government was at last brought more fully into the picture when Brockdorff-Rantzau was informed of the exchanges between the Soviets and the Lithuanian Ambassador to Moscow, Baltruṣaitis. It was entirely consistent with von Maltzan's conception of *Ostpolitik* that the idea should be encouraged in the Baltic countries of a three-way friendship between Germany, Lithuania and Russia. Yet both von Maltzan and Brockdorff-Rantzau were in agreement that when Baltruṣaitis was received in Berlin, it had to be made clear to him that, in spite of Germany's interest in developing its political and economic relations with Russia, 'we could not consider any specific alliance of a military tinge'.[56]

A rather different view of such an alliance was taken by the head of the Reichswehr, when in October 1923 the Lithuanians made separate contact with Wehrkreiskommando 1 in Königsberg. The suggestion was made of either an unofficial agreement between Lithuanian and German irregular forces or a formal defence agreement. Seeckt's view, presented to the German Chancellor, Stresemann, in the form of a memorandum, was that Lithuania's overtures arose from its need to maintain its new position in Memel. Little seemed to have changed for Seeckt since 1920.

The prospect of a German–Lithuanian agreement must always be considered in the first place with a view to our relationship with Russia. We have in times of war and peace a great interest in the railways running from East Prussia to Russia, through Lithuania, Latvia and Estonia … In its turn, Russia must place the greatest value on securing and maintaining these connections. For any war against Poland, though, … it will be of the utmost significance whether the border states are allied with [Russia] … or whether they stand under the political and military influence of Poland. Thus the interests of Germany and Russia in the border states problem run parallel.[57]

Whilst the Auswärtiges Amt certainly took the point that any German–Lithuanian alliance would need to be discussed with Moscow, as von Maltzan informed Rantzau in due course, the talks with Lithuania were 'platonic'.[58]

The suggestion raised between the German and Russian delegations at Genoa of Weimar–Soviet coordination of policies towards the Baltic countries remained, then, a vague aspiration rather than a policy throughout the rest of 1923, even though the signature of the Estonian–Latvian defence alliance on 1 November 1923 marked a distinct phase in the border states problem. The main provisions of the treaty covered mutual aid in the event of either state being attacked and re-affirmed the desire of each to live in peace with its immediate neighbours.[59] Since the Warsaw Accord had by then lapsed, owing to Finland's refusal to ratify it, the Tallinn agreement was a logical and more realistic step towards Latvia and Estonia preserving common interests.[60] Moreover, it immediately attracted the attention of France, and on 12 November 1923, Poincaré told Poland's representative in Paris, Zamoyski, soon to be Polish Foreign Minister, that the French government wanted Poland to adhere to the Latvian–Estonian agreement.[61] The event gave point to Seeckt's fears, and, together with the Memel coup, it certainly provided the starting-point for a notable increase in the range of files in the Auswärtiges Amt under the rubric *Randstaatenpolitik*, thus reflecting the more systematic discussion of overall policy towards the border states which had been urged by von Blücher immediately after the Rapallo agreement had been concluded. The trend was exemplified by the meeting of the German representatives to the Baltic countries, convened in Riga on 28–9 November 1923, to assess the importance and significance of the Estonian–Latvian defensive agreement in the light of overall developments in the border states.

The accounts of the conference of ambassadors, written by Adolf Köster (Riga), Wedding (Tallinn), Olshausen (Kovno) and Consul Thermann of the Auswärtiges Amt, shared the view that the alliance between Estonia and Latvia was 'just the beginning of a larger bloc of border states, as has been attempted for some time on the basis of a joint defence against Russia'.[62] In Köster's words, the Tallinn agreement had given the Baltic bloc projects 'tangible form'. The German ambassadors took note of the economic interest and activity of Britain, and indeed America, to the extent that the latter used its diplomatic and trade mission in Riga chiefly to monitor Russia's economic development, but attention was focussed above all on Franco-Polish policies in the region. Whilst Köster stressed the generally heightened French diplomacy in the border states as a whole, Thermann felt that the weight of effort was being concentrated on Tallinn, since the Latvian Foreign Minister, Meierovics, appeared once more to be actively working for a rapprochement between Poland and the Baltic countries. All the German representatives recognized the importance of Finland's key position in any plans for a regional grouping. The Finnish failure to ratify the Warsaw Accord of 1922 was rightly seen as reflecting Finland's growing interest in a policy orientation towards Scandinavia, but the latter's apparent determination to preserve its neutrality constituted an obstacle to Helsinki's effort to solve its security needs in that direction. Although a continuation of the Lithuanian–Polish quarrel was for the moment therefore one obvious desideratum for Weimar *Ostpolitik*, in that it continued to check Poland's overall attempt to secure dominant influence in the Baltic area, the question of a shared German–Russian response to *Randstaatenpolitik* inevitably became a central concern of the debate conducted by the German representatives.

The first point to stress here is the extent to which thinking in the Auswärtiges Amt continued to develop the distinction between Poland on the one hand, the Baltic countries on the other. In other words, if a threat was to be read into the Rapallo treaty, it applied to Poland rather than to the border states as a whole and was not a military one on the German side so much as one of isolating Warsaw in East Europe. The methods were all-important, however, and the fact that the Weimar Republic's trade-treaty policy towards the Baltic countries had political implications which could support its general attempt to revise the Versailles settlement should not be allowed to obscure the element of stability which German governments perceived in an economic bloc linking Germany and Russia via the border states. The overlap was described perfectly in Köster's account:

After what has been said, the German attitude to the border states problem can no longer be in any doubt. We have an exceptionally strong interest in the border states, who are excellent buyers of our goods. We have in the border states an economic outpost for exploiting the Russian market. Politically we have the greatest interest in the Baltic states keeping away from an alliance with Poland.

The twin German aims of economic influence in the Baltic countries and political resistance to Polish hegemony and to French attempts to restrict the German state in East Europe made good sense in Berlin; but to what extent could these be translated into closer collaboration with Russia over Baltic problems? This question, too, becomes much more insistent from 1923. From a purely diplomatic point of view (by far the most usual one in studies of Weimar–Soviet and Weimar–Polish studies of the 1920s), it is not difficult to see why historians wrote as if German–Soviet collaboration was orchestrated against the East European states after Rapallo. Von Seeckt's views were perhaps too readily equated with those of Weimar *Ostpolitik* as a whole precisely because his overt hostility towards Poland was widely echoed in political and public opinion in the Weimar Republic. Yet, as von Seeckt's analysis of the border states situation confirmed, he had made little progress in his grasp of the political realities of East Europe by 1923. His argument that Russo-German interests in the border states problem ran 'parallel' barely concealed a continuing indifference to the independent existence of the Baltic countries. By contrast, the shared concern of the German political leadership and the Auswärtiges Amt in late 1923 'that the main aim of German policy in the border states is to prevent an alliance which groups those states under Polish leadership against Russia' was affected and modified by wider economic and political commitment in the Baltic countries.

To appreciate this it only needs to be emphasized that the Baltic alliance systems, although complicated by the extension to the region of Western political and security interests, were chiefly motivated after 1919 by the belief in the need to plan for the eventuality of resurgent Russian threats against the border states.[63] That Russia, too, had to consider its own security as a result of newly independent states on its borders was given less weight perhaps than it should have been. From the Soviet viewpoint, the existence of the Baltic republics was made more threatening precisely because of their accessibility to Western economic and political influence. From this vantage-point, of course, ties with Germany had additional importance for the Soviets, in bringing the economically dominant partner in the Baltic countries into a better political relationship with Moscow. Yet for Germany the pursuit of economic influence in the Baltic countries required stable relations between Russia and the region to achieve maximum effect, and Germany's own economic policies were in effect contributing to the slow consolidation of independent Baltic states. A paradox thus existed at the heart of any attempted Weimar–Soviet coordination of policy in the border states.

This has certainly not been recognized in existing studies of the Baltic countries in the international system, where even closer economic relations between Germany and Russia after Rapallo have been seen as threatening Latvia and Estonia. In fact the choice of personnel for offices connected with the Baltic in 1922/1923 continued to reflect a belief in the likelihood of the Baltic countries consolidating their independent position.[64] Although von Maltzan's name will forever be associated with the 'Rapallo lobby', and although the oversimplified distinction between 'Easterners' and 'Westerners' in German foreign policy debates tended wrongly to put him amongst the ranks of those who pursued agreements with Russia at all costs, it is worth emphasizing again that von Maltzan's advocacy of German–Soviet cooperation was coupled with support for independent Baltic countries. His early resistance to annexationism, and his role in switching German policy in Latvia and Estonia from the Baltic Germans, have already been remarked.[65] Equal care was shown in Berlin over the selection of personnel to fill the Baltic posts after 1919. In Tallinn, as we saw earlier, Henkel began the slow, careful and exhausting task of rebuilding Germany's damaged standing. Otto von Hentig, who replaced Henkel in the summer of 1921, had urged in turn that 'influence is only possible through constant effort from a favourable position'. Von Maltzan was careful when Hentig left in 1923 to secure the posting of 'an older man [Wedding], knowledgeable on Russian and Scandinavian affairs'.[66] Still more revealing were the appointment of Köster to the Riga post in 1923 and that of Wallroth to the Eastern Department of the Auswärtiges Amt.

Adolf Köster, formerly Foreign Minister in Müller's first coalition in 1920, and Minister of the Interior under Wirth from October 1921 to November 1922, also had a considerable reputation as a man of letters and in general enjoyed the sort of political eminence which was calculated to impress on the Riga government how seriously the Weimar Republic took its policy of active friendship with the Baltic countries. A man who had long been interested in ties with the Latvian Social Democrats, Köster had written as early as October 1917 that 'an independent Courland with a German elite over it is impossible ... the aim of Germany cannot be to conserve that old

colonial relationship'.[67] Although Köster's arrival marked the beginning of more systematic financial support for the cultural position of
the Baltic German element in Latvia (see below, chapter 7), the new
German ambassador specifically supported Schiemann's concept of
active Baltic German collaboration with the Latvian state, even
though he was attacked for this by nationalist Reich German circles
in Riga and at home in the Reich.[68] How important it was to have
personalities in Tallinn and Riga who could keep firmly in the fore-
front the priorities of good Weimar–Baltic relations when handling
the Baltic German issue was also demonstrated by von Hentig's
earlier conversation with the Estonian Foreign Minister, Hellat.
According to the latter, 'the pure light of our [Germany's] relations
with Estonia was refracted by the Baltic Germandom like a prism ...
Baltic Germandom was not loyal and on account of this it was desirable to exclude it from state influence'. It was characteristic of von
Hentig's reply that he recognized that a number of Baltic Germans
had indeed opted for Germany and had gained Reich citizenship;
'but others had opted just as decisively for Estonia'. He reaffirmed
too, Germany's 'strong present and future interest in the existence of
an Estonian state'.[69]

Wallroth's arrival at the Eastern Department of the Auswärtiges
Amt reinforced this message. He categorically rejected any suggestion
that, in retaliation for the unfair Estonian treatment of German compared with other foreign landowners, Germany should dispossess
Estonians in the Reich without compensation. Any such ensuing
conflict between the countries

would in fact seriously damage German interests [in Estonia]. The already
hardly enviable position of the German minorities in cultural matters could
be made unendurable; the existence of German merchants and entrepreneurs
could be so affected by a worsening of conditions of settlement and residence
that they could pull out. The damages would also be incalculable to German
exports and transit goods to Estonia and Russia.

Although the German government continued to work for compensation for Reich German landowners who had been dispossessed by
agrarian legislation, Wallroth remained consistently opposed to
allowing the issue to damage Germany's overall economic relations
with the Baltic countries. And in 1923 the problem was not allowed
to interfere with the settlement of war-damage claims or provisional
trade treaties.[70]

Wallroth had a dislike in general for the way in which Baltic German emigré circles in the Reich appeared to be indifferent to the fate of the Baltic countries, whose qualities the German ambassador to Riga had always emphasized in a positive way. He had put the matter beyond all doubt in his analysis of 'German–Latvian prospects' in May 1922, when reviewing the impact of Rapallo. The document has a considerable interest in view of Wallroth's subsequent promotion to the Eastern Department of the Auswärtiges Amt. In his opinion the severe and traumatic setback to Latvia's expectations as a result of the Genoa conference would encourage those Baltic political circles who saw a 'dead end' in Latvian chauvinism. This would probably reduce the opportunities for Baltic German emigrés to make political capital in their constant criticism of Latvia, but Baltic Germans who had chosen patiently to work within the new Baltic republic would benefit, particularly those in the towns. The premise of the argument remained one of a later up-swing in East–West trade, but Wallroth's message was clear: 'The more the owners of this ship [i.e. Latvia] become convinced that in any foreseeable future there is no real German interest in replacing the Latvian captain with a Russian one, the more one can reckon on the German side to keep a hand on the tiller. For on the whole, after Genoa as before, time works for Germany.'[71] Wallroth's repeated advice on the paramount need to 'restore order to the troubled souls' of Baltic leaders, echoed von Hentig's argument that 'the weaker Estonia feels in relation to Russia, the more it will allow itself to be influenced by third parties to follow an anti-German line'.[72]

Such evidence throws serious doubt on the view that because the Rapallo treaty facilitated Weimar–Soviet contacts it constituted an automatic danger for Latvia and the other Baltic countries.[73] Economic considerations argue against the conventional suggestion that the Rapallo treaty lessened the German interest in the Baltic states, and run counter even to the assumption that Germany sanctioned Russian claims against their independence.[74] 'On the contrary', as Meierovics was assured, 'a secure and peaceful periphery opens up the prospect of joint [German–Baltic] activity in many different forms'.[75] It was precisely the message of Crohn-Wolfgang's book, also published in 1923, that Germany's economic advantages derived from activity in an independent Latvia on the edge of Russia.[76] In addition, political considerations – specifically, the desire to check Franco-Polish hegemony in the region – reinforced the distinction made in Weimar *Ostpolitik* between Poland on the one hand, the Baltic countries on the other.

The German government could well affirm in 1923 that the Weimar Republic no longer had an active interest, in contrast to 1918, in supporting a barrier against Russia, but it could not be unaware, even on purely domestic grounds, in 1923 of all years, of the potential advantages to be derived from the Baltic countries holding Communist influence at a respectable distance from the Reich's borders. This was pointed up by the mission in October 1923 of the prominent member of the Soviet Commissariat for Foreign Affairs, Viktor Kopp, when he conducted a series of soundings with Poland and the Baltic countries about the prospect of access to Germany in the event of the expected Communist uprising in that country and made a series of proposals for non-aggression treaties and neutrality pacts in November of the same year.[77]

In truth the overtures from Russia intensified the uneasiness in the border states and fuelled the ever-present fears of Soviet force being used against Baltic independence – thus keeping alive discussion about the most effective regional security grouping. It would be wrong to suggest that in the 1920s the Soviets planned actively to re-incorporate the Baltic countries, but they were never entirely happy with the prospect of an increasingly stable and flourishing group of capitalist 'small states' on their borders – a prospect viewed, by contrast, with no disfavour in the Auswärtiges Amt. Apprehension over Soviet intentions at the same time made for difficulties in creating stable economic relations between Germany and the border countries. For this reason more serious attention should perhaps be given to the idea expressed by the Finnish delegation at Genoa in 1922, that Germany should use its influence with Russia to persuade the latter country to provide a greater measure of security for the Baltic region. Even such a strategy required a greater measure of agreement between Germany and Russia than seemed feasible in 1923. As Wipert von Blücher argued later in a review of the whole question of neutrality in the Baltic area, 'The differences in the internal politics of both countries [Germany and Russia] will of course make a closer relationship difficult. Moreover, the foreign policy sympathies and interests of both countries cannot automatically be reduced to identical political tactics in the Baltic area' – a central reality which had profoundly important implications from 1924 onwards.[78]

It was also slowly becoming clear in 1923 that to the political differences between Germany and Russia in the Baltic area could increasingly be added different economic interests. Since this was only barely perceptible in 1923, a fuller analysis of this and its effects in the second half of the 1920s can be postponed (see below, chapter 7). In any case, a pre-condition of Germany consolidating more fully its economic and trade prospects in East Europe was its own recovery after the crisis of 1923. However, a brief indication is in order here. Notwithstanding the importance attached to the Baltic countries as transit areas to Russia, it was becoming impossible to conceal the fact that earlier Western assessments of a massive future up-swing in trade between East and West through the Baltic had been wildly optimistic. True, total transit trade to and from Russia passing through Estonia and Latvia continued to grow in actual terms from 1920, with Latvia increasingly assuming the first place in the transit figures from 1921 (see table 1), thus disposing of the lead which Estonia had briefly enjoyed in 1920 as a result of its earlier peace settlement with the Soviets. None of this was to be sneered at in a Germany anxious for any trade openings. Yet if one goes beyond the question of transit trade to the idea of the Baltic 'springboard', whereby Latvia and Estonia were to function as intermediaries in economic relations in general between Russia and the West, the evidence was accumulating by 1923 that such a path was likely to be, relatively speaking, a 'dead end'.[79] One reason for this was undoubtedly the sort of political friction between Russia and its Baltic neighbours that has been mentioned above, but it was not the only reason.

A more important cause of the disappointment of the springboard hope relates to the longer-term structural readjustments to Baltic economic life after the First World War, which had been partially concealed in the early post-war years of haste and emergency planning. The decline in the Baltic share of East–West trade when compared with the pre-war period was also a product of Russia's failure dramatically to expand its relations with the Western powers, and this accelerated the restructuring of Baltic industry. Earlier hopes for the recovery of the once large Baltic industries geared to supplying the needs of the Russian hinterland before 1914 were giving way to more realistic proposals by 1923. Attention was being given instead to encouraging the growth of newer small- and medium-scale industries, directed towards domestic and regional markets and especially towards newer markets in the West.

In sum, the German economic presence in the Baltic countries was increasingly likely to play a key role in integrating their economic life with that of the West (see below, chapter 7). Such economic perspectives, looming in outline in 1923, serve to reinforce the general criticisms made in this chapter about traditional interpretations of the Rapallo agreement. Far from leading to increased Weimar–Soviet collaboration in the Baltic area, its chief effect might have been to delay a long-term divergence of Weimar–Soviet interests in the region. These had been lost sight of by the earlier quest for an economic springboard. But the merging of that quest with the policy of using economic and political influence in the Baltic region to improve the Weimar Republic's strategic position overall was a feature of 1923, a year of transition in so many ways, and this raised issues above and beyond the relationship between Russia and Germany.

6

The politics of arbitration:
Locarno and the Baltic

———— ∼ ————

The events of 1923 proved beyond doubt the force of Wipert von Blücher's judgement, that 'the problem of the Baltic, because of the present allocation of its shores and the way in which this came about, is closely linked with the Versailles question and the Eastern question'.[1] The Baltic arena therefore also provides an opportunity to reconsider from another vantage-point the policies of Gustav Stresemann, a man whose name has frequently been used to describe an era of critical importance in European diplomacy. The immense literature on Germany's celebrated Foreign Minister has not fully resolved the central interpretative problem of his relationship to Hitler's foreign policy because the Weimar Republic's most famous personality died at the very time when Germany was lurching once more towards an overtly aggressive stance in Europe. What Stresemann might have done had he lived longer is a fascinating question, but the present chapter seeks to give due attention to the comparative international context in which Stresemann actually operated. This is not to revert to the simplistic notion of Stresemann as a 'good European'. Rather, it is to recognize that his impeccable nationalist pedigree and his record as an annexationist in the First World War did not preclude his developing more constructive policy initiatives with inherent promise for European stability.

It is not without interest that his own political career-path from wartime annexationist to *Vernunftrepublikaner* – a process where the 1923 crisis exercised a formative influence[2] – paralleled the development of Weimar–Baltic relations from intervention to collaboration. Stresemann's own convictions ultimately ensured that key elements of Weimar–Baltic relations after 1919 would be maintained and strengthened: namely, the need to give cultural and welfare support to German minorities, including those in Latvia and Estonia; the active encouragement of German economic penetration, and with it the growth of political influence in an important strategic region. Under Stresemann, moreover, it proved possible to weld these ingredients together more effectively and eventually to conduct a more systematic attempt to reduce the threat of a Franco-Polish alliance being extended to the Baltic countries.

The opportunity for the Auswärtiges Amt to develop the more systematic *Randstaatenpolitik* required by developments in the Baltic region in 1923 stemmed directly from the resolution of the Franco-German 'trial of strength' over the Ruhr. The fall of Poincaré in May 1924 and the election of the Cartel des Gauches pledged to a policy of international collaboration ensured, together with Britain's support, a favourable outcome to the London Conference on reparations in July and August 1924. The conference also provided Germany with the occasion to negotiate for the first time with the Allied Powers as a partner rather than as a subject. The ensuing Dawes plan vindicated Stresemann's earlier policy as Chancellor in 1923 of ending passive resistance in the Ruhr. In economic terms, the new reparations settlement opened the way for a resumption of large-scale capital movements and for a more systematic development of Germany's trade-treaty network, once the Versailles restrictions on the Weimar Republic's trade had ended in January 1925.[3]

The importance of this in the long run for Weimar *Ostpolitik* can hardly be exaggerated. For convenience the focus will remain for the moment largely on the political dimension to Stresemann's foreign policy, leaving the economic aspects to be followed in the next chapter. First, it must be recognized that the opportunities which Stresemann expected to arise as a result of his agreement with the Allies did not lessen the overt hostility of the German nationalists and public opinion in general towards the Versailles settlement. Not the least of Stresemann's achievements was the fact that he was able to secure a broad enough basis of domestic support in the Reichstag to sustain his policy of collaboration with the Western powers amidst so much criticism at home. Apart from the Centre Party, the Democrats and of course his own party (the DVP), the SPD at least backed his foreign policy from outside the government.[4] The political consensus was somewhat shaky at times but at least it relieved the Auswärtiges Amt of the extremes of direct political pressure which had often affected policy-making between 1919 and 1923. Such a relatively favoured position was a crucial pre-condition for orchestrating the Locarno strategy later.[5]

The attempt to foster more active *rapprochement* between Germany and the Allied Powers during the run-up to the Dawes plan could not, of course, immediately guarantee tangible improvements for Germany's position in East Europe and the Baltic. Here, anxiety over what the process of Franco-German reconciliation would entail for a still largely unsettled region of Europe was compounded by the death of Lenin and the ensuing speculation about Soviet policy, as well as by the public discussion of British and French recognition of the Soviet Union, eventually given by Britain in February and by France in October 1924. The instant rumours in Baltic capitals and in Warsaw, about France recalling its ambassadors from the border states as a prelude to disengagement there, were themselves symptomatic of great uneasiness.[6]

Such extreme pessimism was misplaced. Admittedly, just as the crisis of 1923 has been regarded as a climacteric to the French strategy of squeezing Germany on the Ruhr and encircling it in the East, so the French acceptance of the Ruhr evacuation has appeared to herald a slackening of the Franco-Polish alliance in practice.[7] This seemed especially likely after the victory of the Cartel in 1924. Franco-Polish collaboration had hitherto depended largely on the parties of the Right in France.[8] It would be more accurate to suggest, however, that the 'refoundation' of the post-war European order brought about as a result of the crisis of 1923 was an essential but insufficient pre-condition for a more systematic *Randstaatenpolitik* being carried out by the German government. Providing relief on Germany's western borders in effect placed a greater potential strain on France's Eastern allies, and precisely because of this the French remained determined not to give Germany a free hand in the East. The continuing efforts of France to maintain and strengthen the Polish position in the border states, as well as the conclusion of the Franco-Czech agreement of 1924, testified to this central concern. The Auswärtiges Amt rightly saw the treaty with Czechoslovakia as one of a series planned to maintain pressure on Germany after 1923.[9]

For such reasons Moscow retained a vital key to the diplomacy of the Baltic region, and Stresemann could no more escape the question of how far to cooperate with Russia over Baltic problems than previous foreign ministers of the Weimar Republic. Indeed, his task was more difficult in many respects. Merely by pursuing *rapprochement* with the Allied Powers Germany intensified Soviet fears that a hostile Western coalition lurked behind the projects for alliances in the border states. To calm those fears seemed to the officials of the Eastern Department of the Auswärtiges Amt an important, not to say fundamental, priority. As German Ambassador to Moscow, Brockdorff-Rantzau constantly stressed the urgent need for the German–Soviet collaboration over Baltic affairs. He even feared the danger of a French deal with the Russians following the recognition of the Soviet Union by Paris, on the grounds that in the long run it would be cheaper for France to drop Poland and 'the whole tribe of *Rand-und Schandstaaten*'.[10] His anxiety was echoed in the Auswärtiges Amt, which at the beginning of 1924 reaffirmed the priority of preventing a Polish-led group of border states directed against Russia.[11]

The question was, as ever, 'how?' The Dawes settlement and what it implied for the future development of German–Allied relations also greatly complicated the answer. Neither Stresemann nor his celebrated State Secretary at the Wilhelmstrasse, Schubert, could afford to overlook the Allied interest in the Baltic states. Any Weimar–Soviet collaboration over Baltic issues had at the very least to have points of reference with the policies of London and Paris after 1923 if the policy of *Verständigung* was to maintain its momentum. In practice, therefore, there was less mileage than has been assumed for Germany in exploiting differences between the Allied Powers over the Baltic and East Europe. Although the French had most actively and consistently supported the creation of a large, Polish-led Baltic bloc as part of its overall strategy for dealing with the German problem, a growing British concern about Sovietization in the region also resulted in indirect if fitful encouragement to Baltic alliance projects, at least as the picture presented itself to Berlin.

Britain's commercial interests in the Baltic countries had, of course, long since been recognized, as indeed had the fact that the British government was reluctant to commit itself to direct involvement, even after the Soviet-inspired but abortive Communist coup in Tallinn in December 1924. Yet the latter event actively stimulated all the British worries about Russia after the death of Lenin.[12] Throughout 1924 reports continued to come into Berlin regarding British advice on Latvian and Estonian defence systems, on the possibility of a British naval presence to bottle the Red Fleet into Kronstadt in the event of a Russian attack against the Baltic countries and on financial help to ensure war supplies.[13] British references to the Baltic as a *Mare liberum* were numerous. The comment made to Meierovics by Ramsay MacDonald's Under State Secretary, Ponsonby, in June

1924, that the 'prevention of Russian expansion to the Baltic was a vital issue' for London, convinced the German government that the absence of a direct British physical commitment did not signify London's disinterest.[14]

The Auswärtiges Amt certainly did not take literally the later suggestion by the then Foreign Office representative in Riga, E. H. Carr, 'an extraordinarily talented and purposeful personality', according to Riesser. The latter was told by the celebrated historian-to-be that 'not a single soul' in the Foreign Office in London was interested in the Baltic countries. Carr was known gleefully to re-count the tale about a health trip to Oesel made by the head of the British mission, Sir Tudor Vaughan, which had convinced the Russians that London had leased the island for a base.[15] Notwith-standing such frivolity, it was symptomatic of German Baltic policy under Stresemann that the Auswärtiges Amt tuned in more carefully to the signals from Britain. No serious belief was entertained in the German government as to British military involvement or as to Britain's conducting a sinister political game in the Baltic states.[16] Yet a recognition of a growing British hostility towards Russian activ-ities in the region necessarily became an element in Stresemann's policy. 'Obviously interested' but 'cautiously active', the description of London's response to the Helsinki conference of Baltic ministers in January 1925, in fact best encapsulated the Auswärtiges Amt's over-all view of Britain's Baltic policy in the second half of the 1920s.[17]

Britain's concern to see greater stability in the Baltic area at the very least was not, unlike French policy, clearly expressed in any systematic view of the various Baltic alliance projects in what proved to be their terminal phase in 1924–6. Even within the British Foreign Office advice fluctuated, as far as the German government could determine, between those like Gregory, chief of the Northern Section, who intimated that a Baltic bloc joined by Poland was the only way to hold Russia in check, and Ponsonby, who issued warnings to Latvia against attaching itself to the Franco-Polish alliance.[18] In its own undramatic way the awareness in Berlin that Britain found wholly unacceptable any preponderance of German–Russian power in the Baltic played its part in defining the limits to which Strese-mann and Schubert were prepared to go when working with Russia over Polish–Baltic problems, though they had to go some way.[19] Von Maltzan, too, kept this point firmly in mind. After considering in March 1924 a memorandum from the German Naval Command on

Russia's call for a 'neutral Baltic' at the recent League disarmament conference in Rome, the State Secretary merely advised Brockdorff-Rantzau to express Germany's sympathy. Privately he urged that the Soviet proposals to close the Baltic to the ships of non-riparian states had absolutely no prospect of success in view of Anglo-French determination to keep the Baltic as a free sea.[20]

True, Stresemann was obviously obliged to recognize that the link with Russia had become an article of faith with the German conservatives and with large sections of German public opinion since Rapallo. The fact remained that he had to calculate privately the parameters of Weimar–Soviet collaboration over the border states in the interests of maintaining his credibility with the West, particularly once the Locarno initiative had been taken in February 1925. At least the German government gave due consideration to what Riesser referred to as Russia's 'nightmare of alliances' in the Baltic states.[21] The Kopp proposals no longer had the rationale of preserving access through the Baltic countries in the event of revolution in Germany, but they continued to be discussed in the spring of 1924. More specifically, the proposed Soviet guarantee of the borders of the Baltic countries, which had been part of the original Kopp package, was briefly offered again to the states individually. Undoubtedly this was a direct response to the attempt of the strongly pro-French Polish Foreign Minister, Zamoyski, to orchestrate a collective response by the border states to the Moscow proposals, by arranging a conference in Warsaw for 16 and 17 February 1924.[22] A further factor was Poland's known interest in discussing its own attachment to the recently concluded Estonian–Latvian defence alliance, which confirmed all the fears in the Auswärtiges Amt on this score.[23] In the event, Zamoyski was only partially successful and the simultaneous proposals from the Riga and Kovno conferences underlined the considerable uncertainty in Baltic capitals about the best way to handle Kopp's offer.

The initiative by the Galvanauskas administration in Lithuania was potentially troublesome to Germany. The Kovno conference ending on 21 May 1924 would have been regarded in earlier years as a setback to Polish policy, for as usual Warsaw refused to take part in meetings with the Lithuanians. Superficially the agenda for the Kovno conference concentrated on 'economic' issues precisely because of the political problems still outstanding between the border states. From 1923, however, the formal incorporation of Memel by the Lithuanian government impelled it more actively to try to attach itself to the Estonian–Latvian defence alliance to avoid further isolation.[24] In short, it was difficult for Galvanauskas, on Lithuanian resources alone, to maintain his proclaimed goal of remaining firm over Memel whilst also keeping the Vilna issue alive.[25] Weimar policy towards Latvia and Estonia, with whom Germany had no territorial disputes, was therefore increasingly dogged by the Memel issue from 1923, a significant development in Weimar *Ostpolitik*. However remote the prospect of resolving the Polish–Lithuanian dispute appeared in 1924, the German government anxiously scoured reports from diverse sources about increased Allied pressure to find a compromise solution between Kovno and Warsaw – a development which it was felt in Berlin was likely to reinforce Poland's claim to leadership of a Baltic bloc.

The most significant initiative was the Allied signing of the Memel convention on 8 May 1924, whereby sovereignty over the Memel area was formally transferred to Lithuania.[26] A major purpose of this act was to bring more stability to the Baltic region, and the note from the Allied Conference of Ambassadors to the Lithuanian government on 2 June 1924 linked the Memel settlement with the pronounced expression of interest in a Lithuanian–Polish compromise.[27] In this matter the British government took more than a passing interest.[28] The new Lithuanian government from 18 June 1924, under Tumenas, continued to give 'a certain anxiety' to Maltzan, as he confessed to Brockdorff-Rantzau, because it did not keep its promises regarding the treatment of Germans in Memel and 'is obviously flirting with Poland'.[29] It was made clear to the Lithuanians that, in view of Germany's tolerance over the Memel question, the idea of a Polish–Lithuanian *rapprochement* would not be understood in Berlin.[30]

On the one hand, such steady psychological pressure clearly acted in effect as a complement to Soviet diplomacy over the Baltic bloc schemes. Up to a point the Germans could appreciate that Russian encouragement of divine unrest in the Baltic states complicated attempts to set up a Baltic alliance system, which, if not automatically aimed against Russia, could be so influenced. Berlin could also comprehend Soviet fears, in view of the memory of Allied intervention and civil war and in view of Russia's internal traumas after Lenin's death. Yet a 'Baltic bloc' was less likely to be directed against the Weimar Republic once the process of *Verständigung* got underway, and increasingly, for Stresemann's purposes, Soviet diplomacy constituted too blunt a weapon – or, rather, it was a double-edged weapon. It encouraged as much as it discouraged regional security initiatives, with its constant mixture of half-promise and half-threat. It did not, however, offer any long-term basis for constructive development in the Baltic region. No doubt this also had much to do with the inherent pull between the office of Narkomindel (the nearest thing the Russians had to a foreign office), which in effect developed more traditional bureaucratic and diplomatic practices, and the Comintern, which existed primarily to promote revolution.[31] A perfect illustration of this process was provided by the abortive Communist coup at Tallinn in December 1924, which achieved the considerable feat of re-activating Finland's interest in the Baltic bloc, to the extent of hosting the conference of Baltic foreign ministers at Helsinki in January 1925.[32]

The significance of the Helsinki conference between Poland, Finland, Estonia and Latvia was *not* simply that ultimately 'only' an arbitration treaty was signed, 'with the usual generalities',[33] but also that it provided the Poles with the *opportunity*, however briefly, of trying to revive the Warsaw Accord policy of 1922; all this in spite of the growing distrust towards Poland being shown by Latvian foreign policy under the direction of Zigfrids Meierovics.[34] In short, Soviet-inspired unrest increased the freedom of movement for Franco-Polish diplomacy, and this was the very opposite of what the German security initiative required once it had been launched at the beginning of 1925. Stresemann needed to hold Poland sufficiently in check to sell the Locarno concept to his noisy domestic enemies, but without endangering the priority of a Franco-German settlement in the West through overt threats to Poland. Stresemann thus had a pronounced interest in the Baltic countries' feeling more, rather than less, secure. The incentives for Latvia, Estonia and Lithuania to join a regional scheme with Poland had to be reduced still further by reassuring the Baltic states over their security fears. How big a task this was for Stresemann even at home may be gauged fom an article in the *Deutsche Zeitung* on the Tallinn coup; this argued that 'the small, insignificant border states had simply reaped what they had sown'.[35] Undeterred, Stresemann set about giving a more positive twist to the task of checking Polish influence in the Baltic, which was ultimately certain to affect the nature of Weimar–Soviet relations.

Here the principle of arbitration was invaluable. It has been a feature of the long historiographical debate on Stresemann's foreign policy that doubt has frequently been thrown on the value of the treaties of arbitration which Germany offered to Poland and Czechoslovakia in 1925. Because the treaties excluded political and territorial disputes they have been largely seen as a cynical device used to preserve the option of revising Germany's eastern borders at a more convenient date.[36] Much of this criticism has tended to overlook Stresemann's need to sell the idea of arbitration to his domestic critics.[37] Yet in the broader context of European security after the First World War the concept of arbitration represented a useful and valuable extension to the work of the League of Nations. It was notable that the Helsinki arbitration agreement of January 1925 also excluded territorial disputes, partly because, as in the case of Germany and Poland and of Germany and Czechoslovakia, there was also an unresolved territorial dispute between Poland and Latvia over Latgale.[38] Moreover, the Helsinki conference reaffirmed the principle of arbitration in conjunction with the attempts of Poland and the Baltic countries to agree on a collective approach to League issues, particularly those raised by the Geneva protocol on European security.[39]

The initial reaction of France and her Eastern allies to the German offer of arbitration treaties instead of the desired guarantee of the German–Czech and German–Polish borders was fiercely adverse. Anger had abated somewhat by April 1925, but both Stresemann and von Schubert were anxious to reinforce their case. The Baltic countries offered an obvious means to this end, particularly since the cause of good Weimar–Baltic relations would also be advanced through arbitration agreements. The Estonian Foreign Minister, Pusta, had already discussed such a treaty with von Schubert in Berlin in late March, as well as the Helsinki agreement. Early in the following month the State Secretary confirmed to the German embassy in Tallinn that, 'sharp criticism has given way to more reasoned judgement' but that 'we nonetheless constantly have a great interest in strengthening the argument that such [arbitration] treaties are a suitable means for securing peaceful relations between countries. For this reason I should value it if the negotiations with Estonia ... were to begin and to be concluded as soon as possible.'[40] On 15 April Wallroth also re-opened the idea of a German–Latvian arbitration treaty in a talk with the Latvian ambassador to Berlin, Woit.[41]

The German offer of arbitration agreements was explained to Moscow as part of the general attempt to keep Russia from feeling alarmed throughout 1925 at the prospect of a Western security agreement and of Germany's possible participation as a future member of the League of Nations in any sanctions against Russia. The emphasis in the Auswärtiges Amt's explanation to Moscow of the offer of arbitration to Poland and Czechoslovakia was on the fact that the procedure made it easier for the Quai d'Orsay to drop its demands to have Poland included in the security pact.[42] The Russians were not so easily placated, however, particularly since their own attempt to conclude a new economic and political agreement with Berlin met with a dilatory response at that stage.[43] Under these circumstances, the Eastern Department officials of the Auswärtiges Amt, notably Dirksen, greatly valued the opportunity to demonstrate Germany's continuing goodwill towards Russia by showing more interest in collaborating over Baltic problems. How far this was possible in 1925 remains to be seen.

Germany's pursuit of arbitration agreements with the Baltic countries also served, as has been suggested, the familiar cause of trying to resolve the troublesome issues of wartime damages and compensation for the dispossessed Reich German landowners. Even the Latvian press suggested that arbitration represented the 'summit' of such disputes.[44] Although it was therefore ostensibly the Weimar Republic's interest in keeping open the issue of its Eastern borders that prompted it to offer arbitration agreements, their very propagation also pulled German foreign policy along a more positive and constructive route to the settlement of disputes in post-war Europe. Indeed, Soviet anxiety itself confirmed this. Moscow was correct in fearing that its relationship with Germany would change as a result of the German security initiative. It is not without irony, and it is certainly no coincidence, that the first real effort to give meaning to the principle, expressed after Rapallo, of Weimar–Soviet collaboration over Baltic affairs, took place under a German Foreign Minister whose major priority was to reach agreement with the West. Whilst German efforts to work with Russia in the Baltic region were intended to augment the pressure which the Republic could apply to Poland through the security initiative, in practice the Soviets were also likely to be pulled towards the more constructive line inexorably being drawn by Stresemann's *Ostpolitik*.

The idea of actively launching a more positive German initiative over the Baltic alliance schemes, one which went beyond the purely negative resistance to any project involving Poland, was actually brought into play by the influential German Ambassador to Latvia, Adolf Köster. In April 1925 he proposed a joint guarantee of the Baltic countries by Germany and Russia as by far the most appropriate vehicle for frustrating Franco-Polish diplomacy in the Baltic. Two factors need to be kept in mind here. The first is that someone of Köster's stature should have judged the time appropriate to propose the concept of a joint guarantee, and the second is that the Austwärtiges Amt should have given it such an extensive airing at the very time that Germany was proclaiming that it could not make any guarantees over its eastern borders. The debate in itself is almost as significant as the final outcome of the Köster proposal, as an illustration of the constantly evolving concept of revisionism in the Weimar Republic.

The immediate cause for Köster's alarm had been the news that members of the French military mission in Warsaw had visited Riga at the end of March 1925 for talks with Estonian, Polish and Romanian military representatives, the Finnish government sending observers.[45] Hans Eduard Riesser, the Legation Secretary at the Riga embassy, shared Köster's concern over the talks, particularly when these were taken in conjunction with Polish–Lithuanian discussions under Britain's auspices concerning the timber flow on the Njemen. Whilst not underestimating the still considerable obstacles to a Polish–Lithuanian compromise, Riesser argued that even an agreed stand on League issues by the two countries would mean that 'the large border states bloc is again afoot'. Riesser, like Köster, combined a belief in the pact with the West with a conviction that Germany had a 'bitter need' of Russian support over *Ostpolitik*.[46]

At the end of March 1925, in the first significant exchange with a Baltic leader over Stresemann's security initiative, Köster had already been at pains to counter the anxiety of Meierovics about Latvia being left 'hanging in mid-air' as a result of the proposed Western pact. For Latvia, Meierovics argued, the choice was between joining the Franco-Polish combination or the 'West bloc' which the security pact negotiations seemed to portend, comprising France, Great Britain, Belgium and Germany. In reply the German Ambassador invited Meierovics to think about possible combinations 'which included Russia, Germany and the three northern border states without Poland'.[47] The suggestion was all the more pointed in that the German–Latvian negotiations over a trade agreement seemed set at last to make a breakthrough (see below, chapter 7).

What Köster had in mind became clearer when he went to Berlin in the second half of April for talks in the Austwärtiges Amt, where he duly presented his memorandum, 'On prevailing political tendencies in the border states'.[48]

The document was a direct response to the challenge of Poland's 'redoubled' effort 'here in the North', which in turn resulted from Polish fears about the Allied recognition of Russia and the implications of Stresemann's Western pact initiative. In Köster's view, a joint Weimar–Soviet guarantee pact would cost Germany 'virtually nothing', at least in relation to Estonia and Latvia, since talks for arbitration agreements were in any case already underway. As the memorandum admitted, Russia would have to pay a somewhat higher price since the guarantee 'would mean Russia finally abandoning these countries'. The gains for Moscow would be that the action, 'promised to secure for all time Russia's right flank in the event of a military clash with the West'. Further, Köster urged the advantages for Germany of its status being enhanced in the border states, as well as a much-needed improvement in relations between Berlin and Moscow at a critical time for Weimar foreign policy. As *Izvestia* was to comment in May, 'It goes without saying that for the Soviet Union, Germany's choice of a definitely Western orientation and entry into the League of Nations can objectively only lead to the deterioration of relations between Germany and the Soviet Republics.'[49]

The general thrust of Köster's argument was broadly accepted in the memorandum drawn up by Dirksen on 24 April. In the pact's favour were the politically desirable cooperation with Russia and the splitting of Poland from the Baltic countries. A serious reservation, which Dirksen felt applied at the very least whilst the Western pact negotiations were in progress, was that such a guarantee would probably lead to increased Franco-Polish pressure to have similar agreements made with Warsaw and Prague. Secondly, the shadow of the Memel dispute now fell on Germany's relations with Latvia and Estonia. Memel posed the problem of finding a form of guarantee which could apply equally to all three Baltic states. The significant point was that no objection could be seen to actually beginning *talks* with the Russians on the whole question, even whilst the security pact negotiations were in progress.[50] Since Soviet policy had made clear its aversion to collective agreements with the border states, Dirksen's suggestion, at least to start talking with Moscow, amounted to increasing pressure on the Russians to follow a line most in accord with Germany's best interests.

It is notable that Stresemann's advice to Köster gave a further positive twist to the discussion. Meierovics had to be made aware that his idea of a 'Western bloc' emerging from the security pact talks was premature and that it implied the isolation of Russia. Since Germany's more limited aim of bringing security to its Western borders did not preclude a sound relationship with Russia, Köster was instructed to draw parallels between German policy *vis-à-vis* the Soviets and that of Latvia. Stresemann advised Latvia 'irrespective of a friendly relationship with the Western powers, to maintain contact with Russia too ... Any understanding between Latvia and Russia which goes beyond the present status quo will ... be greeted in Germany as an element in the pacification of the East.' In such an eventuality, Köster was to make it clear, Germany could offer further incentives in the form of greater German accommodation over Latvia's wishes during the current German–Latvian economic talks (see below, chapter 7).[51] It was left to Brockdorff-Rantzau's discretion to find a suitable moment to raise the matter of a joint guarantee in Moscow. Yet the German government at once systematically and deliberately fostered the idea in Riga, Tallinn and Kovno that it was actively preparing to use its friendly relationship with Russia to persuade Moscow to guarantee the Baltic countries, thus further indirectly increasing the pressure on the Soviet leaders to adopt a more positive line over Baltic problems.[52]

In June the situation in the border states was deemed to justify a further general appraisal. It was a gloomy month in view of the French note of 16 June refusing Germany's request to be exempt from League sanctions against Russia when the Weimar Republic became a member of the League of Nations. It also insisted on a German guarantee of Poland. The Auswärtiges Amt memorandum of June not surprisingly again emphasized the advantage of a Russian–German guarantee of the Baltic countries, not only because it would prevent the further political and economic separation of Russia from Germany, but because it would lessen the strategic threat to Germany's borders. In addition, it would forestall an increase in the number of Poland's 'clients' in the League of Nations. On this occasion the Auswärtiges Amt gave more attention to the practical implications of Weimar–Soviet collaboration and distinguished between 'large' and 'small' means of keeping Polish influence to a minimum in the Baltic countries: in other words, between the guarantee pact itself on one hand and, on the other, a range of economic incentives and greater German accommodation over Baltic war-damage claims. Once more, the implied pressure on Russia to facilitate Germany's security action was evident. The element of arbitration which Köster's original proposition had included, and which the Soviets had refused to include in their earlier talks with the Baltic countries, was emphasized in the Auswärtiges Amt memorandum explicitly because it would bring Russia nearer to the Western system.[53]

In practice, the major attempt to capitalize on the idea that Germany was actively fostering initiatives to reduce Baltic insecurity was concentrated on Latvia in 1925. That was appropriate in view of Köster's presence there and of Latvia's central role in Weimar–Baltic economic relations after 1919. Apart from these considerations, Meierovics had now developed serious reservations about Franco–Polish policy in the border states. His stand contrasted sharply with that of the Estonian government, which was working actively for a conference in Tallinn in the summer to coordinate policy towards the German security pact overtures.[54] It was wholly consistent with the spirit of those negotiations that Stresemann and von Schubert attached importance to giving as full an explanation as possible of Germany's intentions in a further talk between von Schubert and Woit in Berlin on 23 June 1925. Here the Germans took the opportunity to act at least in the spirit of Köster's idea if, again, the onus was placed on Russia. Woit was told: 'in the matter of relations between Germany and the border states on the one hand and between Russia and the border states on the other, we attached the greatest value to achieving clarity and agreement between the three parties concerned'. When Woit voiced his worries about Russia's part in this scenario, von Schubert disclosed, 'requesting utmost secrecy, that we were prepared to influence the Russians to give certain guarantees to the border states, especially Latvia, in respect of their independence' and that Brockdorff-Rantzau had been given instructions on this point.[55]

Schubert was quite frank about the distinction being made between Poland on the one hand, the Baltic countries on the other, when Meierovics again met with him in Berlin on his tour of West European capitals in July 1925. In a long conversation dwelling on the advantages of an arbitration treaty between Germany and Latvia and of the proposed economic talks for a full-scale trade agreement in

the autumn, von Schubert implicitly contrasted this favoured position with that of Poland. The need for a revision of the Polish–
German border 'would prove itself' in time. If there had been any
doubt in the mind of the Latvian, it was removed by von Schubert
repeating the news about Brockdorff-Rantzau's instructions to raise
the question of possible Russian guarantees of the border states.
Meierovics revealed how his views had changed since his earlier
hostile references to the menace of German–Soviet collaboration in
1922, by voicing the opinion that a combination of the border states
with their large neighbours would provide a 'good basis'. What was
interesting about von Schubert's comments, although Meierovics had
no way of knowing this, was the way in which the matter of a joint
German–Soviet guarantee had already given way to the tactic of
working primarily to get *Russia* to commit itself to the security of the
Baltic republics.[56] The formal German offer to the Baltic countries
remained that of an arbitration agreement and a full-scale trade
treaty.

Meierovics' subsequent trip to London and Paris left him in no
doubt that Britain had more understanding than the French of
Latvia's need to reach agreement with both Russia and Germany.[57]
Pusta's experience was similar during his own visit to the West in
August – a journey which had originally formed part of his plan to
prepare the ground for a full-scale discussion of Germany's security
action amongst the border states at a conference to be held in
Tallinn.[58] Pusta had already been subject to considerable opposition
at home, where his domestic critics charged him with conducting an
anti-Russian foreign policy.[59] The fact that Pusta signed the arbitration agreement with Germany on 10 August during his stay in Berlin
was helpful to Weimar *Randstaatenpolitik* in 1925 precisely because of
Estonia's known support of Poland in the regional alliance discussions. The Estonian decision was realistic. From the middle of the
summer the signs were unmistakable that the British government
would not support France in insisting on German guarantees to
Poland and Czechoslovakia. Furthermore, London was also sympa-
thetic towards the German government's reservations about being
involved in future League sanctions against Russia on the basis of
article 16 of the League covenant. Briand virtually admitted to the
German Ambassador in Paris that Germany and Poland would have
to work out their own differences by direct agreement.[60]

Such favourable omens made it possible for Stresemann to main-

tain his original line of offering arbitration agreements only on
Germany's eastern borders. Under these circumstances there was
markedly less inclination in the Auswärtiges Amt actively to pursue
the matter of a joint German–Russian initiative to guarantee the
border states. One of the original reasons for the proposal, the need to
maintain a dialogue with the Soviet Union during the Western pact
negotiations, became less urgent from June 1925, when the German
government was contending in any case with pressure from Moscow
to negotiate a new international basis for German–Russian relations.[61] Moreover, the dismal failure of Pusta's diplomacy in the
summer of 1925 made depressing news for Poland. Köster had a
distinct impression from talking with his Latvian Foreign Office contacts that the plans for a Baltic league had been 'put back in the files'
and the then Finnish Foreign Minister, Idmann, also confirmed that
'the [Warsaw] Accord policy is losing ground rapidly and there is no
reason for its revival'.[62] Instead of the annual Baltic Foreign Ministers' conference taking place in Tallinn in 1925, it materialized at the
League session of September 1925. As it turned out, the meeting
became the last of the regular series in the 1920s. The fact that it
came only weeks after the death in a car crash of one of the most
significant Baltic leaders, Zigfrids Meierovics, contributed to the
impression of an era ending.

The death of Meierovics in any case effectively 'ripped a large
hole' in the Auswärtiges Amt's scheme for German–Latvian–Soviet
collaboration.[63] This disappointment was more than offset by the
fact that the Locarno agreements greatly increased Germany's attraction for the Baltic countries. The domestic attacks which Pusta
had to face in Estonia, the visible shift which Meierovics had initiated
before his death towards settling disputes with Germany and, finally,
the pressing effort of the Lithuanians to engage the Weimar Republic
in a far-reaching political dialogue, all these were symptomatic of the
changed reality for German policy which Stresemann's efforts had
done so much to create.[64] The harsh fact for Poland was that however appropriate the policy of the Warsaw Accord had been in 1922,
it was no longer so in 1925. The Accord policy had been predicated
not only on the fear of Russia, but also on a confrontation between
Germany and France. The success of Stresemann's diplomacy – more
accurately, the use Stressemann was able to make of the changed
international context after the 1923 crisis – made the Accord policy
seem hopelessly anachronistic.

At the same time, this would not have been the case had it not been for the consistent and patient effort made by German governments since 1919 to develop a basis of trust with the new Baltic governments. From the vantage-point of such long-term efforts to draw a line under past conflicts between Germany and the Baltic peoples, Köster's idea for a guarantee pact emphatically cannot be considered as simply another example of the devious intent on the part of Germany and Russia to keep East Europe and the Baltic in their shared grip at all costs. It seems odd indeed to deduce a threat to Baltic independence from the evidence of a guarantee proposal, even if it ultimately failed to materialize in its original form.[65] The most revealing feature of the discussion in the Auswärtiges Amt and between German and Baltic officials, on the subject of improving Baltic security, is this: Germany obviously intended, in spite of the often proclaimed interest not to upset Russia over Baltic affairs, to bring Russia's Baltic policy more into line with its own, not the other way round. This became more than ever necessary after Locarno. Once the Weimar Republic had fully engaged in the policy of *rapprochement* with the West, with all this entailed after the Dawes settlement in terms of intra-European trade, there was even less question of any exclusive German–Soviet relationship than there had been earlier.

In Brockdorff-Rantzau's view *Ostpolitik* could not even be made as such after the Locarno treaties, but such an opinion was an extreme reaction of disappointment from a man who, as Foreign Minister in 1919, had been traumatized by the Versailles experience into the belief that Germany's future lay in working largely with Russia.[66] His ideas did, however, show an awareness that the British and French were unlikely to allow relief for Germany on the Rhine simply to give Stresemann the chance to re-open the settlement in the East in the immediate future. For this very reason Stresemann continued to be emphatically interested in continuing *stability* in the Baltic in order to maintain the political and economic containment of Poland. This had the advantage of being both beneficial to Germany's own economic presence in Latvia, Estonia and Lithuania and of being consistent with Britain's interest in stable Baltic relations as a result of its own worsening relations with the Soviets from 1925 onwards.[67] To repeat: this indicated not the need, let alone the possibility, of Germany playing Russia off against the West, or *vice versa*, but the need to involve the Soviet leaders too in the maintenance of peace and security in the Baltic countries. The advantage of Germany preserving a working relationship with Moscow was that this could also help in its own way to contain the predictable flurry of Polish–Baltic diplomacy and the understandable effort of the Baltic countries to see an 'Eastern Locarno'.

The idea of an Eastern Locarno took various forms. The main schemes identified by the Auswärtiges Amt involved a proposed agreement, embracing the Scandinavian states, the Baltic countries and Russia, put forward by the former Finnish Foreign Minister, Professor Erich; a Baltic entente which would include the three Baltic states and Germany and Russia and, finally, guarantee or non-aggression treaties between Russia and the Baltic republics. All these were interlinked with Polish-inspired projects ranging from a revival of the Warsaw Accord idea to what Stresemann described as a 'fantastic combination', which it was hoped would include Sweden, Finland, Poland and Russia.[68] For Köster, the most effective way to frustrate the Polish *Ostlocarno* plans remained a joint German–Russian guarantee of the Baltic countries.[69] His opinions were coloured by the knowledge that Meierovics' successor at the Latvian Foreign Office, Hermanis Albats, wanted actively to continue the policy line, taken from the summer of 1925, of consolidating relations with Russia and Germany.[70] Welcome as this was in Berlin, neither Stresemann nor Schubert was likely to be convinced of the necessity for a joint guarantee at this stage of play. The Locarno treaty had, after all, vindicated Germany's policy of offering arbitration agreements rather than firm territorial guarantees in East Europe. Equally important, neither Britain nor France would have welcomed the obvious imbalance of power which an explicit German–Russian guarantee of the Baltic countries would have signified. Allied hostility was far too high a price for Germany to pay for securing the link between Russia and Germany. In Stresemann's world-view the Western powers continued to hold the key to the major problems of reparations and the occupied Rhineland.[71]

In a situation where *Westpolitik* commanded so much of Stresemann's energies, a German–Russian guarantee of the Baltic countries threatened to make Germany too dependent on the whims of Russia's Baltic policies. The best way of reducing the continuing turbulence in the region therefore remained to persuade Russia itself to move further towards a genuine system of support for Estonia, Latvia and Lithuania. This again became a possibility when at the end of March 1926 the Soviet leaders re-opened talks with the border states for neutrality and non-aggression treaties. A residual fear in Berlin, that the Soviet reaction against Locarno might prompt the Russians to reach agreement with Poland too, receded rapidly when Poland renewed its alliance with Romania on 26 March. Thereafter Polish–Soviet relations were additionally burdened with the unresolved quarrel between Russia and Romania over Bessarabia.[72] In Dirksen's words, it also 'solved for Germany the dilemma of making the conclusion of our treaty with Russia [Treaty of Berlin] dependent on the breakdown of the Polish–Soviet talks'.[73]

Precisely the prospect of a renewed agreement with Russia offered Stresemann the chance both to reinforce the idea of a Soviet contribution to Baltic security and finally to put to rest Köster's idea of a joint guarantee of Latvia, Estonia and Lithuania. In deliberate contrast to his warnings to Krestinsky, the Soviet Ambassador in Berlin, against any Soviet guarantee of Poland, Stresemann offered every encouragement to the improvement of Soviet–Baltic relations through the medium of non-aggression treaties – a point which Schubert reinforced three days later, on 30 March. The State Secretary informed Krestinsky:

we had had reports from our Ambassadors in the border states, who are all on good terms with their Russian colleagues, that the Russians intended to conclude guarantee pacts with the three border states and perhaps also with Finland, either separately or collectively. Naturally, this matter interests us very much and I would be grateful if the Ambassador could keep me informed about the course of these negotiations.

Köster's hope for a joint Russo-German guarantee was finally ended with Schubert's admission to Krestinsky that the idea of an Eastern pact 'must ripen somewhat'.[74] Privately, Köster was duly informed that no plans existed to develop the idea of a joint Weimar–Soviet guarantee of the Baltic countries before 'a degree of clarity had been reached in Baltic–Soviet negotiations'.[75] The burden was where Stresemann had wanted it, with Russia.

What did this mean? That the whole episode had been a cynical device designed by the Wilhelmsstrasse simply to hold Poland in check until the Locarno treaty was safely in the bag? There were no doubt many in German military circles and in nationalist groups who subjugated all aspects of the 'Lilliput' states to the overriding concern of preparing a later revision of the Polish borders, confined as they were for the foreseeable future to playing war games featuring Poland

and the Baltic countries.[76] It remains highly misleading to think of Germany's Baltic policy primarily in terms of deliberate manipulation, not least because this does no justice to the very great difficulty of persuading the small states to take a predictable course in foreign policy in 1925/1926, as before and after. Nor could the Germans fail to react to and to counter the extension of French interests through the border states, since, apart from anything else, this presented a severe strategic headache for the defence of East Prussia. Such considerations spoke in favour of Germany's preference for more settled Baltic affairs. That was also the surest way to help supplement the policy of *Verständigung* with the Allies. Unrest in East Europe could always disturb Franco-German relations. The virtue of Locarno was that by imposing a degree of mutual restraint on France and Germany it also impelled both powers towards the search for a measure of accommodation over East European problems. The significant feature of the Baltic guarantee project is not that in the end Stresemann could not accept the risks for Weimar revisionism, but that it existed in the first place and that ultimately, through further Weimar–Soviet exchanges, the *effect* which Köster had wanted was more or less achieved, as we shall see.

The talks between Germany and Russia leading to the Treaty of Berlin on 24 April 1926 devoted considerable attention to Baltic problems, in stark contrast to the months prior to the Rapallo treaty in April 1922. This was not surprising. The form of the Berlin agreement was chosen further to reduce Soviet apprehensions about Germany's membership of the League of Nations. The geographical location of the Baltic countries naturally made them of central concern to the discussion of possible League sanctions through the application of article 16 of the League covenant. It was not by chance that the Soviets were considering non-aggression treaties with the Baltic countries as well as the treaty with Germany in 1926. Understandably, the Soviets wanted to use their relationship with Germany to help prevent Peter the Great's Baltic window to the West becoming an all-too-convenient doorway to the East. Had Stresemann merely wanted to retain Russia's goodwill in the interests of a 'balance' between East and West after Locarno, he could have indicated a disinclination to become involved in Baltic affairs in the Bismarckian tradition. At the very least he could have signified that Germany would do nothing actively to prevent the future reabsorption by Russia of the Baltic countries.

The avoidance of such a fate was, however, the absolute priority for the Baltic states, and the pursuit by Weimar governments of good relations with the Baltic countries had, as we have shown in this book, produced not only sympathy for Baltic independence, but also an economic engagement by German finance and commerce, which materially supported the new states (see below, chapter 7). Thus, in trying to involve the Soviets in giving greater security to the border states, the Auswärtiges Amt under Stresemann gave a decidedly positive impetus to a line of Weimar Baltic policy established since the spring of 1919 at the latest. Under the influence of Germany's security initiative, the principle of 'mutually benevolent' Weimar–Soviet cooperation over border-states problems was interpreted as meaning Germany's 'friendly mediation' in Soviet–Baltic relations. This also allowed the German government to keep an eye firmly on its relations with the Allies. What was the implication of this if not that the German government was unwilling in the last resort to give the Russians a free hand in the Baltic?

This was wholly consistent with the doctrine propagated under Stresemann's tenure of the Wilhelmstrasse that the Weimar Republic eschewed the use of force to achieve its ends in East Europe; this was no mere device but a central component of Weimar *Ostpolitik*. It was because the Locarno settlement gave extra weight to the idea that the German government was not interested in forceful change in Europe that its pursuit of active and friendly collaboration with the Baltic peoples became all the more credible. It was perfectly logical also for Germany to present the agreement with Russia in April 1926 as yet another contribution to the stability of the Baltic region. Even in Estonia, where commitment to Poland remained far stronger than it was in Latvia, the Berlin treaty seemed 'interesting and valuable' in view of the current Russian–Baltic negotiations for non-aggression treaties. The Lithuanian government even went so far as to express a wish that Germany and Lithuania conclude an agreement on the lines of the Berlin Treaty.[77]

As to Latvia, where at last rapid progress was made in the solution of the trade treaty talks in the wake of the Berlin treaty, the *Rigasche Rundschau* shrewdly observed that the German–Russian agreement would also reduce the Soviet need to conduct an anti-League policy, by soothing Russian fears of German involvement in any possible League sanctions. 'If such an agreement is reached, whereby the League ideal as well as peace in the East is secured, then every effort must be made for us to participate in the arrangement.'[78] In general there was 'little sign in the press of the uproar that arose a couple of years ago when the two large neighbours seemed to be getting too intimate with each other', as Köster reported. In his view this was because in the current Soviet–Latvian non-aggression talks Riga was also searching, like the Weimar Republic, for a formula 'combining the maximum of neutrality towards Russia with full loyalty to the League'. The Berlin treaty demonstrated that the German government 'considers good German–Latvian relations to be wholly compatible with good German–Russian relations'.[79]

The Russo-German Berlin agreement of April 1926 was therefore, like Rapallo, represented by the German government not as a threat, but as an inducement for the border states to reach similar agreements with the Soviet Union. From the point of view of Stresemann's *Ostpolitik*, if the Russian and Baltic peoples could be encouraged to make non-aggression treaties this would admirably complement the slowly but steadily improving relationship between Germany and the Baltic republics – as exemplified above all by the conclusion of the Latvian–German trade treaty and compensation agreement in June 1926 (see below, chapter 7). It proved impossible in the 1920s, in spite of German encouragement, for the Soviet Union to conclude a non-aggression treaty with Latvia, not least because of Moscow's refusal to make any collective guarantees of the border states. Its determination to make only separate treaties has been somewhat bluntly described as giving Russia 'a free hand to deal with potential victims one by one'.[80] The judgement presupposes, like so much writing on the Baltic in the 1920s, that the Soviets actually had plans to attack the region in the immediate future. In the eyes of many Western observers, the danger was much more from the possible Sovietization of the Baltic. Be that as it may, the fitful discussion between the Russians and Latvians in 1926 and 1927 did not produce the sort of watertight guarantee of Baltic independence that the Riga administration wanted.

The talks did, however, indirectly contribute towards the Soviet–Latvian economic agreement of June 1927. Although the performance of Russia in Latvian economic life proved disappointing (see below, chapter 7), the political significance of the 1927 treaty was undeniable. Taken in conjunction with the German–Latvian economic agreement and the successful resolution of the long and bitter wrangling between Riga and Berlin over the legacy of the First

World War, it can be argued that the outline was beginning to emerge of a bloc, comprising Russia, Germany and Latvia, towards which Meierovics had been moving in the last weeks of his life. The Latvian Foreign Minister and socialist, Cielēns, thus continued the work of Meierovics, deliberately giving priority to maintaining cordial relations with Germany and Russia between 1926 and 1928. In Cielēns' view, 'Mr Meierovics did not have time to carry this plan into effect and it has fallen to my lot to do so'.[81] Such a development was virtually a substitute for the sort of guarantee that Köster had envisaged, at least in the sense that it also effectively provided a major obstruction to a large Baltic bloc embracing Poland. It was fitting that Latvia, the centrepiece of Wilhelmine Germany's Baltic occupation policy and the chief target for a Baltic springboard in the first post-war years, should also have become a cornerstone of Weimar *Ostpolitik* under Stresemann.

Whilst Latvia's action was not without its effect on Estonia, in view of the determination of the two small states at least to preserve their 1923 pact, the other significant check to the regional alliance schemes for the remainder of the 1920s was finally provided by the German–Lithuanian–Soviet discussions of 1925/1926 and by the conclusion of a Soviet–Lithuanian non-aggression treaty in September 1926. Here at last, in the months after Locarno, the Russians and Germans for the first time actually got round to a more systematic exchange of views on Baltic problems, some four years after the German–Soviet delegates at Genoa had pledged mutually benevolent treatment of border states issues. For Stresemann, the German–Soviet treaty of April 1926 aroused the expectation of a 'continuing, confidential exchange and mutual understanding of issues of interest to both countries'.[82] Lithuania provided an example of what this could mean, for in 1926, apart from the Soviet talks with Kovno on a non-aggression treaty, the German government was also engaged in discussions on a possible economic and political agreement on a large scale as a result of a Lithuanian initiative.[83]

As to the latter, the government of Bistras expressed a desire to 'orientate its policy wholly towards Germany' shortly after the Locarno conference. The overture was immediately interpreted in the Auswärtiges Amt as a manifestation of extreme anxiety, stemming not only from the twin burden imposed on Kovno by the disputes over Vilna and Memel, but also from Lithuania's serious economic difficulties and its abiding fear of isolation. This condition Stresemann was interested in alleviating in view of the overall policy of minimizing the prospects of the Polish-led Baltic league.[84] An interesting possibility which was discussed internally by the German government was to provide a framework for German–Lithuanian collaboration in the form of a customs union; this became at least theoretically possible once Germany had regained control of its foreign trade in January 1925. Dirksen's memorandum on the subject was notable for its concentration on the political implications. Self-evidently, it would constitute another decisive check to a Baltic bloc with Poland. Of more immediate importance, Dirksen considered that a customs union would effectively 'incorporate' Memel in Germany through the extension of the German customs frontier. In such a context the earlier objections to a guarantee of the three Baltic countries would disappear. At a stroke, too, it would be possible to accommodate a long-standing British interest in regulating the timber flow along the Njemen – an issue originally seen in Berlin as providing London with an unwelcome opportunity to influence a Polish–Lithuanian compromise.[85]

Within the Auswärtiges Amt, Wallroth was particularly keen on the customs union and actively advocated, as he had earlier in Latvia, the use of economic means to achieve political goals.[86] Impetus was given by the ratification of the German–Lithuanian trade agreement in May 1926, and Wallroth rejected the idea that a hard line should be taken towards Lithuania over its failure to keep its word to give equitable treatment to Reich Germans in the Memel-land. He argued instead that negotiations were the only way to achieve German goals and to make the Kovno administration more amenable.[87] In fact, the economic argument was used to deflect the much more insistent Lithuanian demands for political agreement from June 1926 onwards. These requests resulted from a transformation of the Lithuanian political scene when a long period of Democratic rule was brought to a close by a coalition government of People's Socialists and Social Democrats under Sleževičius.[88] Schubert argued that the political collaboration with Germany suggested by the Lithuanians would in any case require 'economic underpinning' – a formula enabling Berlin to delay a detailed response to the political proposals until after the further economic discussions scheduled for the autumn. As von Schubert reminded Gaus, the trick was to encourage Kovno without being lured into a 'Lithuanian adventure'.[89]

Indeed, both Stresemann and von Schubert shunned a direct political deal with Lithuania for fear of prejudicing the Memel question and from a desire to avoid reawakening the ever-present Allied uneasiness about German political influence in the Baltic. The Foreign Minister and his State Secretary responded to the active Lithuanian diplomacy by simultaneously encouraging Kovno to make progress in the talks it was concurrently having with Moscow for a non-aggression treaty. Once again, Germany preferred to use economic influence, what Dirksen had misleadingly called 'small means', rather than direct political interference in the Baltic region. Simultaneously, the Lithuanians were kept interested by references to a German–Lithuanian arbitration treaty which might have a long preamble on political issues.[90] Meanwhile, Schubert kept Moscow informed at least of the generality of the exchanges with Lithuania, in order to calm Soviet suspicions about Russian interests being damaged.

The German government was, however, able to exploit its relationship with the Soviets to ensure an acceptable formula for the Lithuanian–Russian non-aggression treaty. In a long talk with Krestinsky on 10 May 1926, Stresemann put the German objections to the wording originally proposed by Moscow for its treaty with Lithuania; that the Russians would not take the initiative to raise the matter of the dispute between Germany and Lithuania over the status of Memel. The phrase, according to Stresemann, 'must at the very least appear as a lack of interest in the Memel question', though this was not compatible with the spirit of the Berlin treaty.[91] In the last resort, however, it was accepted that the omission of all references to Memel in the Lithuanian–Soviet non-aggression treaty would best serve the German desire to preserve the option of future revision.[92] As Gaus argued, the mere mention of Memel in the Lithuanian–Russian agreement would arouse a suspicion amongst the Allied Powers that the pact was a direct product of the Treaty of Berlin, thus reawakening once more Western fears of Weimar–Soviet dominance of the Baltic countries.[93] As a result of Stresemann's objections, the Lithuanian attempt to have the Memel settlement underpinned by the pact with Russia was deflected. The text of the agreement made no reference to Memel.[94] With the conclusion of this treaty a final nail was placed in the coffin of the Baltic bloc schemes of the 1920s, particularly after the rightist–nationalist coups taking place in Poland in May 1926 under Pilsudski and in Lithuania in December of the same year.

According to Litvinov, the form of the Soviet–Lithuanian treaty had been directed at achieving precisely the demise of the Baltic bloc.[95] The Soviets, Wallroth also recorded, 'were whooping like schoolboys' because they had 'thrown another large rock into the League pool'.[96] His reaction indicated the mixed blessing for Germany of collaborating with the Russians over *Ostpolitik*. For one thing the Lithuanian–Soviet agreement made it possible for the Germans to deflect Lithuanian pressure for a full-scale political agreement with Berlin, and even for an arbitration treaty with a lengthy political preamble, on the grounds that coming so soon after the Lithuanian–Soviet treaty it would inevitably provoke Allied resistance.[97] The Lithuanian–Russian agreement, in providing an effective immediate bar to any wider Baltic–Polish agreement, also marked the end of the discussion of a specific German guarantee of the Baltic countries. Effectively, however, the Weimar Republic's 'guarantee' was provided by German economic activity in the three Baltic republics, by Germany's League membership and by Stresemann's further pursuit of agreement with the Allied powers.

Clearly, the relationship between Germany and Russia, fitful as it was, did help to limit Poland's political and economic influence in the Baltic countries, although the highly active diplomacy of the border states themselves played its own important part in gradually defining the policy options which were available. The intensive Lithuanian lobbying in both Berlin and Moscow in 1926 was a reminder of the way in which Baltic governments sought to capitalize on slender resources. The fact remains, however, that Seeckt's diagnosis about German and Russian interests in the Baltic 'running parallel' turned out to be incorrect. Had there been a close identity of interest between Moscow and Berlin over Baltic problems, it would have been only too easy to create a joint German–Russian guarantee of Estonia, Latvia and Lithuania. In fact, in spite of all the effort on the Soviet side, it was impossible for the Russians to extend the Rapallo treaty or that of Berlin to achieve a common policy with the Weimar Republic towards the Baltic states. Since that was the case, it is difficult to see how the Weimar–Soviet relationship could ever have achieved the goal to which Brockdorff-Rantzau and others aspired, and which historians of Weimar–Soviet relations have reported *ad nauseam*, of pushing Poland back to its ethnic frontiers.[98]

From the vantage-point of Weimar–Baltic relations, it can only be concluded that at the very least the use of force by Germany was pushed into a highly remote future. It is more likely that it was excluded as an instrument of *Ostpolitik* by Stresemann altogether. True, his containment of Poland in the Baltic area was more effective than that of previous German foreign ministers, but it is unrealistic to see Weimar–Baltic relations as a mere offshoot of revisionism. Alternatively, if it is insisted that Weimar–Baltic relations were, like all aspects of Weimar policy, related to 'revisionism', then it says something about the nature of that concept. In the case of Latvia and Estonia, where there were no territorial disputes, it was comparatively easy for an overtly constructive line of policy to evolve after the end of the war, but even in the case of Lithuania the Memel dispute, which increasingly affected German policy to the other two Baltic states after 1923, was not allowed at any stage actively to damage relations between Kovno and Berlin. In 1927 Wallroth was able to assure Köster: 'our standing effort here, as in Kovno, is to bring the Lithuanians over to us through economic concessions'. Problems were being made for Berlin through the 'thickheadedness of our friend Voldemaras', even though the Memellanders had been told over and over again by the Auswärtiges Amt: 'there are broader aspects to our *Ostpolitik* than that offered by the Memel perspective'.[99] It is not satisfactory to comment on the degree of support effectively given by German policy to the Baltic countries, only to dismiss it by reference to its role in 'revisionist' goals against Poland.[100] The Baltic countries together comprised a not insignificant power factor, and even to forge a policy maintaining the status quo there, for whatever reason, was to contribute towards a *modus vivendi* in East Europe which could hardly be easily reversed.

Holding open issues like the German–Polish borders or the Memel problem was necessary to German governments if they were to sell the idea at home of any policy geared to collaborating with the Western powers. Because of the immense resentment against Versailles within the Weimar Republic, it was essential to present policy in terms of a purposeful move towards ultimate change in Germany's favour. As von Schubert realized, however, in the context of discussing the Memel issue, dilatory treatment of Eastern issues could not go on for ever. 'We will have to be clear too about the specifics of our *Ostpolitik* and must set out a definite, logical path.'[101] In short, the longer the status quo continued, the more likely it was to resist change. Although it is outside the terms of reference of the present study, much recent work has emphasized the way in which, in spite of the fact that Stresemann continued to play to the public gallery at home by a firm insistence on German territorial claims against Poland at the 'high policy' level, at the lower, less glamorous, but perhaps more important, level day-to-day negotiations went on for the easing of minority disputes and economic issues in the last half of the 1920s, notwithstanding the Polish–German customs war.[102]

Certainly, it is the constructive aspect of Germany's presence in East Europe that is finally most striking in the Weimar Republic's brief history of relations with the Baltic countries. If we turn finally to an examination of the eventual outcome 'on the ground' of German economic policies and of its protection of minorities, the contrast is marked between the relative standing of Russia and Germany in the independent Baltic states. This manifestly had much to do with Stresemann's attempt to align German policy with the Western powers. Weimar–Soviet relations were increasingly subjugated to this larger goal in the second half of the 1920s. Whilst Russia's policy had played its part in preventing the appearance of a Baltic bloc, it had failed to align the small neighbouring countries as a whole on its side or fully to gain their confidence. However unfair it was to the Soviet leaders in the 1920s, who had more than enough domestic problems on their plates, they failed to convince the Baltic states that there was no Russian threat to their independence. Admittedly, as we have indicated at various stages in this study, there were many in Germany who contemplated Russia's recovery of the Baltic states with relish, but they never had any serious impact on the policy of the German government. And, as an Auswärtiges Amt memorandum pointed out in the middle of the 1920s, the many opponents of the 'common border with Russia' school of thought valued the opportunities in the cultural and economic fields which independent Baltic countries presented to Germany. They argued: 'At the very least we can have no interest in accelerating the disappearance of the Baltic states or even help out in this direction if we don't wish to violate the supreme principle of our own continental policy, self-determination.'[103]

7

Trade, minorities and *Ostpolitik*

———— ⁓ ————

The pursuit of trade agreements and the care of the *Auslandsdeutsche* had been interdependent objectives of Weimar governments from the end of the war. The attraction of these goals derived from their potential leverage against the restraints placed on a weakened Germany by the Versailles treaty. In that respect they were not really a substitute for foreign policy, but *constituted* foreign policy, enabling German governments to be 'active' on the international scene far earlier than was once assumed. The provisional trade agreements made between the Weimar Republic and the Baltic countries were a small but important part of a wider effort by Germany *de facto* to offset the one-sided restrictions imposed on its foreign trade for the first five years of peace. A series of bilateral temporary trade agreements in East Europe represented a substantial challenge to French, and indeed British, efforts to prevent a resurgence of German economic and political dominance in the 'lands between' Germany and Russia.

In the Baltic area Weimar policy had successfully 'broken through' the ring of border states round Russia by 1923, but the greatest opportunity to consolidate Germany's economic and political presence in the region came after 1924. It arose in the first instance from the Dawes plan. The new reparations scheme led to a resumption of large-scale capital movements in Europe, and in Germany it intensified the pressure for a trade expansion following the traumatic crisis of 1923. There was, it has been suggested, a 'national necessity' to export.[1] It was, of course, recognized above all by Stresemann and his own party, the DVP, which has been described as the 'spokesman of light industry'.[2] Secondly, the German government was permitted

171

to make its own terms of trade from 10 January 1925; this meant that the Republic's network of trade treaties could be rebuilt on a more permanent basis and could include agreements over customs. There was admittedly a cloud on the horizon in the shape of the opposition, above all in German agriculture and heavy industry, to Stresemann's policy of maximising foreign sales for the sake of Germany's more dynamic export-orientated industries, particularly the electro-chemical industries. As a result of domestic pressures, the so-called 'small tariff revision' of August 1925 re-instated protective tariffs for agriculture and heavy industry, although at much lower levels than those fixed in 1902. An import licence scheme was also re-introduced on 9 September 1925. The domestic compromise over tariff levels boded ill in the event of a return to depression, but for the moment modest agricultural protection seemed a tolerable price to pay to achieve enduring trade treaties.[3] What was in effect a qualified victory for German export industries signified the Weimar Republic's involvement in world trade, with reservations.[4] At least Germany's foreign trade could be secured on the basis of new, full most-favoured-nation treaties after January 1925.

The pacific expansion of full trade treaties was therefore virtually a counterpart to the Locarno policy, an essential complement to Germany's security initiative. Admittedly, the argument that *only* from 1925 was it possible for the Republic to capitalize fully on its economic and political weight in its trade-treaty negotiations has to be qualified in the light of what has been argued throughout this present study and of what had already been achieved in the Baltic through purely temporary trade agreements.[5] This is not to deny that the freedom of the German government at last to negotiate customs agreements on its own terms was significant. Above all, Germany could more effectively exploit its tremendous capacity as a consumer of the cheaper products of East Europe, particularly food-stuffs.[6] Equally, however, due account has to be taken of the whole range of German exports to the Baltic countries, not least because the expansion of German–Baltic trade was directly related to the well-being of the German element as a whole in Estonia and Latvia. An additional important feature of the Weimar Republic's trade-treaty network in the second half of the 1920s was the opportunity it provided further to secure the *Auslandsdeutsche*. In the Baltic countries this could be seen in the reversal of Berlin's earlier tactical decision in 1922/1923 to give the *provisional* trade agreements with the Baltic states priority over the active defence of the rights of the dispossessed Reich German landowners of Latvia and Estonia. From 1924, in the case of both states, the solution to agrarian disputes became the *sine qua non* for the conclusion of *full-scale* trade agreements.[7] This issue needs to be followed in some detail before the wider economic links between Germany and the Baltic in the late 1920s are analysed, because of its symbolic importance as an indicator of good Weimar–Baltic relations.

The number of landowners was relatively small, some 42 in Latvia and about 130 in Estonia; in the latter only a small percentage had been Reich Germans before 1918 and most, the so-called 'new Reich Germans', had taken German citizenship between 1920 and April 1926, when the Estonian law for compensating dispossessed landlords came into force.[8] The figures themselves were less significant than the connection between German landholdings and the survival and well-being of the German communities as a whole – a point which Wallroth underlined at the end of 1925 when rejecting Baron Lerchenfeld's suggestion of reprisals against Estonian property in the Reich:

Even if I do not accept that we need Estonia more than it needs us, reprisals would undoubtedly do exceptional damage to German interests. I am thinking only of the position of the German minorities and the fate of German merchants and businessmen in Estonia. The reprisals you mention, suspension of dealing in the Estonian mark on the Berlin stock exchange, terminating the provisional trade treaty and other trade policy measures would undoubtedly affect German as much as Estonian commerce.

In any event, as Wallroth argued more generally, 'now is not the appropriate time to take forceful action and to increase the circle of our enemies in view of our still extremely difficult foreign policy position'. A firm line was needed, but only through collaboration with Baltic governments, not in opposition to them.[9]

Contrary to all previous expectations in Berlin, compromise first became possible in the case of Latvia. On 30 April 1924, legislation was passed in Riga against state compensation for dispossessed Latvian citizens (thus including the German Balts) whilst it permitted direct negotiations to take place over foreign landowners between the Latvian government and the powers concerned.[10] The procedure was partly designed to stifle criticism in the League of Nations about the treatment of foreign landowners.[11] What made the matter promising to Berlin was that shortly afterwards, in July 1924, Riga intimated that the compensation of the Reich German landowners might be solved in conjunction with the hitherto intractable German–Latvian dispute over war-damage claims arising from article 5 of the 1920 treaty.[12] The breakthrough was important because the reparations issue had technically prevented the ratification of the temporary trade agreement of March 1922. It was all the more welcome in that an earlier hopeful proposal by Crohn-Wolfgang, to solve the war damages dispute in conjunction with a credit to Latvia to buy German goods, had foundered on Riga's objection that it could meet neither the initial cash payments nor the short term of repayment.[13]

Latvia's readiness to contemplate a general settlement of mutual reparations claims was also due to Germany's success in negotiating similar package deals with Estonia and Lithuania in 1923.[14] When those treaties had been safely ratified in 1924, and once the Dawes plan had given Germany more freedom to regulate its financial affairs, two further considerations required immediate attention.[15] The first was the need to pre-empt organized domestic political resistance to the proposed package deal in both Germany and Latvia. That particular objective was eventually accomplished by treating the settlement as a purely formal execution of article 5 of the 1920 agreement between Germany and Latvia, thereby obviating the need for detailed debate by the legislatures of both countries.[16] The second and related consideration concerned the insistence of the dispossessed Reich Germans that any general settlement agreed between the German and Latvian governments should not prejudice their legal right to any future or increased compensation which the Latvian government might grant to foreign landowners.[17]

Only on this basis was the German government able to conduct parallel talks with the organization representing the German landowners, the Schutzstelle für Reichsdeutschen Besitz in den Randstaaten, originally formed in May 1921 under the guidance of Graf Medem and A. Schwarz.[18] The rate of compensation eventually agreed was 25 marks per hectare, a bare 3% of the real value of the property involved. Even so, the German government was concerned to avoid public discussion of the fact that payment was to be made from Reich funds in order to prevent the landowners concerned submitting 'sky-high' claims, as well as to avoid further pressure from the *Auslandsdeutsche* organizations for increased direct aid to Germans abroad.[19] How successful the Auswärtiges Amt was in this respect may be seen from the final wording of the protocol eventually accompanying the German–Latvian trade agreement of 1926. Both countries renounced all further claims (à la Rapallo) to reparations, and the Reich government agreed to make no future demands for the dispossessed Reich German landowners, providing Riga did not compensate other foreigners above the agreed price of 25 marks per hectare. The six million marks which the German government had earmarked for Latvia's reparations claims was drawn on to help the German landowners. Technically, the Latvian government met the cost; in reality payment was ultimately made by Berlin on the basis of a series of separate agreements between the landowners and the Schutzstelle für Reichsdeutschen Besitz. When it is compared with the original Latvian reparations claims of some 130 million marks, there can be little doubt that the final settlement was relatively favourable for the Reich government, even allowing for the fact that a topping-up action took place in 1928 to the tune of 753 000 marks.[20]

Although a domestic political crisis in Latvia had threatened the final deal in December 1925, the new Ulmanis administration was able to deflect the opposition of the Social Democrats in the Foreign Affairs committee of the Saiema to the wording of the protocol. As Ulmanis had remarked to Paul Schiemann, the Weimar Republic's foreign policy situation seemed different after Locarno, and Latvian social democracy too would come round to accepting the need for a settlement of relations with Germany.[21] To the international considerations favouring a closer working relationship between Germany and Latvia before and after Locarno (see above, chapter 6) were added, however, economic pressures in both states. The prospect of the compensations dispute being settled removed the block to the trade talks, which, the Auswärtiges Amt had decided in a series of departmental meetings between 2 and 4 July 1925, should, to save time, be based as far as possible on the text of the 1922 agreements.[22] The new German tariffs on agricultural imports could be exploited to underline the disadvantages for Latvia of holding up a full trade agreement.[23] At the same time, the Riga government was also considering the introduction of a double tariff, involving a higher rate of charges for states which had not yet signed trade treaties with Latvia.[24]

Appropriately, the German faction in the Saiema managed to delay the introduction of the proposed double tariff by threatening to withdraw its support for the Ulmanis coalition in February 1926.[25]

The Auswärtiges Amt, in stressing how 'intolerable' such tariffs would be to German economic interests, affirmed that 'in this office the greatest value must be attached to bringing about the signing of the trade agreement as quickly as ever possible'.[26] Such mutual economic concerns, coupled with increasing disappointment in Latvia with the Baltic bloc and the impression left by the series of German diplomatic overtures which had culminated in the Locarno and Berlin treaties, tended to reduce the wrangling between German and Latvian experts to a largely academic level. The final text of the trade treaty was wrestled out in the spring and summer of 1926 and was signed on 28 June 1926, together with the protocol on the compensation question.[27] Wallroth wrote with massive understatement to Köster: 'I, too, have greatly rejoiced that our tedious Latvian treaty saga has finally come to an end.'[28]

Although the provisional German–Estonian trade treaty of 1923 provided the working basis for German economic activity in Estonia, the dispute over the German landlords continued to frustrate the signing of a full trade agreement for a further wearisome three years – an illustration of the enormous sensitivity remaining in key areas of Weimar–Baltic relations. German reprisals against Estonian property were ruled out, as we have seen. The 'Latvian option' of linking the question of agrarian compensation with that of war damages was excluded, since the latter had already been settled in the 1923 agreement between Germany and Estonia. The only route remained that of persuading the Estonians to compromise within the talks for a full trade treaty. The portents were not nearly so favourable as they had been with Latvia. Initially, in 1920, the German government had made joint representations with other foreign governments whose citizens had been deprived of land by Estonian agrarian reforms, notably Finland, Great Britain, Italy, Denmark and Norway. Yet it had rapidly become apparent that by far the greater number of German landowners was being more shabbily treated than other foreigners, in spite of Estonia's formal promise to Berlin on 30 June 1921 to grant most-favoured-nation treatment. Unlike other foreign landlords, the Reich Germans were often in practice prevented from continuing to work their property. Even in the face of a steady stream of complaints from these landowners the German government resolutely maintained a low profile over the issue in 1922/1923 in order to secure the provisional agreement on trade with Estonia.[29] Only when this agreement was ratified by the

Reichstag on 28 June 1924 did the Auswärtiges Amt reverse its policy line, as was formally required by the Reichstag at the instigation of the right-wing deputies, Graf Reventlow, Professor Freytag-Loringhoven and Professor Hoetzsch. These successfully moved that future economic negotiations between the two countries should be made dependent on the Estonian government keeping its promise to give most-favoured-nation treatment to the German landowners.[30] In short, Germans were to be no worse treated than other foreign landlords in Estonia. [31] On 4 July 1924, the Auswärtiges Amt duly instructed the German embassy in Tallinn to represent Reich German agrarian claims with 'greater energy and special attention'.[32]

Nevertheless, the priority for Weimar *Ostpolitik* remained to secure overall agreement with Estonia. Fair compensation, not a reversal of the agrarian legislation, was the immediate target of the Auswärtiges Amt. This in turn required taking due account of the current financial difficulties in Estonia in the last part of 1924, these being largely caused by a run on the Eesti Pank reserves. Realistically, the Auswärtiges Amt thought it unlikely that the individual Reich German landowners would receive large cash compensations, particularly since a still hostile Estonian opinion did not bother to draw fine distinctions between 'Reich German' and 'Baltic German' landowners. Under the influence of its current dealings with Latvia, the Auswärtiges Amt therefore also developed a broader strategy from September 1924 onwards; this favoured a more general deal between Estonia and Germany rather than the continuation of the immensely protracted and complicated representation of each individual case of dispossession. Such a strategy required among other things a clearer ordering of priorities, for example the giving of preference to those Germans who intended to continue working the land in Estonia and to those in more dire need, namely the aged and poorer landowners. Inevitably, the Auswärtiges Amt proposed in November 1924 that the German landowners from Estonia should also form an organization to coordinate strategy with the German government.[33]

The organization duly emerged in April 1925 in the form of the Verband der in Estland enteigneten Reichsdeutschen Gutbesitzer. Largely representing the interests of the 'old Reich Germans', it was directed by Baron Lerchenfeld.[34] In 1925 the German government had first to await the outcome of the compensation law being drafted by the Estonians before pressing harder on behalf of the Reich German landowners – quite apart from the desire in Berlin not to upset the talks with Latvia. How closely the proposed deal with Estonia was likely to compare with the German–Latvian arrangement may be seen from the remarks of Crull in May 1925, when he sketched out the likely cost to the Reich if it also advanced loans to the German landowners in Estonia. Crull specifically argued that the latter could not expect more than the 25 marks per hectare offered to their compatriots in Latvia; this on Crull's rough calculation amounted to 1 300 000 gold marks. 'This sum is so small that I believe we could raise it without bringing in trade and industry circles. The only problem seems to me, the guise in which the Reich Finance Minister can dress this aid, in order to avoid the attention of the [Allied] Reparations commission and the public.'[35] On this basis Lerchenfeld's organization evolved with the German government a limited scheme of loans. They were in effect advances made against what the Estonian government would eventually pay under the terms of its legislation, an initial sum of 600 000 marks being set aside.[36] On 10 June 1926 a specially appointed commission in Berlin held the first of its meetings to apportion funds according to a list compiled by Lerchenfeld and his colleagues.[37]

Throughout the ensuing phase of the dispute the Auswärtiges Amt remained determined, as with Latvia earlier, not to let its defence of Reich German landowners damage the overall German economic and political interest in Estonia. By 1927 the direct talks on compensation between the Tallinn government and German landowners were well underway, and, on the grounds that in practice the Estonians were fulfilling their promise to give most-favoured-nation treatment, the German government dissolved the link imposed by the Reichstag between the agrarian issue and the trade-treaty talks.[38] In addition the continuing financial crisis in Estonia, which required a League of Nations loan in 1927, made clear the resurgence of West European, notably British, interest in preserving Estonia as a bulwark against Sovietization. Such considerations made the Germans all the more anxious to avoid a customs war with Estonia when Tallinn in turn declared its plans for a double tariff. In any case by 1928 most of the 'old' Reich Germans had received their limited cash compensation from the Estonian government. The 'new' Reich Germans had to make do with debenture bonds in view of the financial constraints imposed on Estonia as a condition of the League loan.[39] Under these circumstances the Auswärtiges Amt remained determined not to let the few compensation cases still outstanding hold up the trade treaty.[40] It shared the concern of the Reich Association for Overseas Trading in March 1929 (the month when the trade agreement was finally concluded) 'that the business, so painstakingly built up in Estonia, threatens to dry up completely if the treaty is not put into force very soon'.[41] To the Association's relief the Reichstag ratified the German–Estonian trade treaty in the summer of 1929, leaving the last few cases of Reich German agrarian compensation claims to linger on until 1931/1932.[42]

The trade treaties with Latvia in 1926 and with Estonia in 1929 finally broke the chain of petty discriminations which German businessmen had been forced to endure in the early post-war years. The detailed regulations in the treaties concerning the activity of Germans living and working in the Baltic countries finally vindicated the immense patience of the Weimar Republic's negotiators. The treaty with Latvia above all confirmed the paramount importance of Germany's economic presence in the border states. In the words of the Latvian Economic Ministry's own journal, the 1926 trade agreement with Germany was a turning-point in Latvia's economic development.[43] More than anything else the event testified to the 'power of economic facts' only six years after contemporary writers had registered the 'current against all things German'.[44] Those economic realities are well worth reviewing for the second half of the Weimar Republic's life, for they provide an important and virtually neglected key to interpreting the political relationships in the region after the peace settlement of 1919–21.

If the foreign trade of the Baltic countries is taken as a whole the combined importance of Britain and Germany – self-proclaimed commercial rivals in 1919 – is immediately noticeable throughout the second half of the 1920s. Taking a high total from 1923, the two powers provided for example almost 71% of Estonian imports and accounted for the purchase of almost 45% of that small country's exports (see table 2).[45] It is instructive to probe further into the way in which Britain headed Germany in purchasing Estonian and Latvian exports, whilst Germany easily maintained the lead in sales to the Baltic countries which it had gained by the beginning of 1922. Germany's share of the total imports of both states was invariably more than twice that of Great Britain, frequently even higher after 1924 (see table 4).[46] The proportion of imports coming from Germany never fell below 39% in Latvia between 1921 and 1930, and often rose above 40% whilst the Weimar Republic supplied as much as 54.7% of the goods to Estonia in 1922/1923, its share falling in 1927 to a relative low of 26.4%.[47]

Apart from the natural geographical advantages which Germany enjoyed in relation to the Baltic countries and its more enterprising business salesmanship, as well as the existence of a German sales organization network (see above, chapter 4), other factors help to explain the relative drop in British exports after 1924. When the Reichsmark and the pound sterling were stabilized, the comparatively high level set for the pound meant that German goods were cheaper to import into East Europe; this in itself also enabled a far greater range of goods and services to be provided to the Baltic states than the British could manage.[48] In British eyes, even the misfortunes of Germany between 1918 and 1923, involving the destruction of German credit and business capital, had its advantages. It meant that the national and municipal debt, along with war loans and most of industry's obligations, were cancelled, thereby enabling reconstruction and re-equipment to take place, free of the relics of the past still persisting in Britain.[49]

It was felt by some British sources that, provided peace continued, Germany would long remain the major industrial exporter to Europe, particularly in the metal and machine industries, in chemicals and manufactured products, whilst in the Baltic Britain resumed its pre-war trading role as an importer of raw materials rather than as a supplier of manufactured goods.[50] Certainly, the statistics bear out this general idea. Germany never provided less than 47% of manufactured goods to Latvia between 1924 and 1928, and its share of that country's imports of raw materials and semi-manufactured goods did not fall below 41%.[51] Taking finished goods in the metal industries for the three years 1925–8, German suppliers met 63.1% of Latvia's needs, and their lowest tally was still as much as 53.5%; for Estonia, the high and low were respectively, 58.4% and 42.6%. These compared with a British contribution in this sphere of between 4.9% and 7.7% in Latvia and between 12.8% and 19.6% in Estonia. The pattern was repeated elsewhere in the manufacturing industries (see tables 5 and 6).[52] As an earlier economic study commented succinctly, 'the position of Germany in providing the Baltic states with industrial machines and instruments proved exceptionally strong and robust'.[53]

This is not to deny Britain's contribution to Baltic imports, particularly in comparison with the other trading partners of these states, notably Belgium and the Scandinavian countries (see tables 3 and 4). In textiles, for example, proportionally more of the needs of Latvia and Estonia were met by Britain.[54] Nevertheless, the relatively scarce studies of British commerce in the Baltic have emphasized the fact that Britain was the major recipient of Baltic exports, which of course were mainly agrarian.[55] This is slightly misleading if the comparative figures are examined over the period from 1920 to 1927 or so. After a poor start in 1920 the German percentage share of Baltic exports rose steadily. From a position in the early 1920s where Germany lagged behind Britain in Estonia's exports by as much as 45%, it had narrowed the gap to a mere 1.6% by 1927. In the case of Latvia, Britain's lead was cut from 66.3% to 7.6% in the same period.[56] Moreover, in this general picture of Baltic exports it should be emphasized that the Weimar Republic continued to be the chief consumer of Baltic dairy products, taking, for example, 80% of Latvian butter by the close of the 1920s.[57]

Such a market was of very great significance to both Estonia and Latvia. To appreciate this it has to be remembered that the upheavals caused by agrarian reform initially produced a considerable drop in agricultural production as the larger estates disappeared. Many of the new small farmers had little experience and were relatively unaware of new techniques. Partly to offset the effects of this, there took place a remarkable development of the cooperative associations in both countries. These increased in Estonia, for example, from 60 to 331 between 1918 and 1939. In neither country was the development wholly new, since before the war the cooperative movement had functioned to assist savings or to buy machinery. Yet after 1919 the cooperative principle became the basis of an organizational network for the collection and processing of produce and helped to stimulate the post-war specialization in the Baltic countries in dairy and high-quality meat products. Cooperative marketing associations were then able to find ready outlets in the West, notably Britain and Germany. Because Baltic agricultural exports formed the backbone of the foreign trade of Estonia, Latvia and Lithuania, it was clearly a relief that the German tariff levels of 1925 were not high enough to prevent the German market from absorbing its due share of Baltic dairy products.[58]

If the total foreign trade of both Latvia and Estonia is considered, both exports and imports, then after 1923 the German share was always well ahead of that of Great Britain.[59] In this very basic respect alone, the proclaimed British aim in 1919, namely to curtail Germany's influence in the region, had not been achieved. Still less was it possible to talk of French success in consolidating its political goals against Germany in the Baltic countries. The French were never able to match their considerable political stake in the Baltic region with a sufficiently strong economic presence (see tables 3, 4, 8 and 9), although French policy, far more than that of Britain, sought to encircle and contain Germany in the border states.[60] As to Britain, it has been suggested that its Baltic policy was formed largely in respect of its Russian policy; also, that its commercial interest in the region was primarily a reflection of its concern to see it develop as a transit zone to Russia. In some respects this is a promising line for explaining why, as the prospect of opening up the Russian market grew more remote following Lenin's death in 1924, and as Russian transit trade through the Baltic countries failed to live up to the fabulous predictions of 1919, the British interest faded in actively competing for Baltic markets.[61] Certainly, as we have seen in this study, Russia by contrast assumed a greater significance for the Weimar Republic's political and economic goals in the region. Moreover the maintenance of a suitable working relationship with Russia was profoundly necessary for the Weimar Republic in terms of its domestic politics, where a range of opinion from right to centre valued the link, where, in spite of disappointment with the pace of Russo-German trade, important German business interests still lived in hope, and where military-strategic interests dictated friendly relations with the Soviet Union.[62] This was indeed very different from the British case. Apart from the brief exception provided by the short-lived administration of Ramsay MacDonald, London's conservative governments continued to nourish a profound distrust of the Soviet regime.

Such important differences, together with the Weimar Republic's primary political goal of preventing a Polish-led Baltic bloc, ensured that a much closer, or perhaps more obvious, relationship existed between German commercial and political interests in the region than was the case with its main economic adversary, Britain, or its main political opponent, France. The previous chapters of this book have shown too that German governments gave far more systematic encouragement to German private business enterprise in the region than British administrations did. For all this, it remains difficult to accept without reservations the argument that Britain lost interest in the Baltic countries after 1924. Britain's aversion to and distrust of the Soviet Union, which were heartily reciprocated it must be said, continued to give it an interest at least in the survival of independent border states, even if British public opinion did not tolerate the idea of overt commitment to the defence of far-away countries about which it knew nothing. That British governments were not indifferent to the prospect of a joint German–Soviet action threatening Baltic independence was recognized by Stresemann and duly calculated in his *Ostpolitik* (see above, chapter 6). The reluctance of German governments after Locarno fully to develop a joint policy with Moscow towards the Baltic countries necessarily reduced to nil the prospects of any serious German–Russian attempt to push Poland back to its ethnic borders. This was a perfectly logical outcome to the well-established preference in the Auswärtiges Amt for peaceful and constructive political and economic relations with the Baltic countries to restrict Poland's freedom of movement. German 'revisionism' as *practised* here between 1919 and 1929 at least employed the methods of trade treaties and minority support, which if they admittedly derived initially from Germany's weakness in international politics, progressively consolidated the status quo in the Baltic area. This was hardly unwelcome for British policy.

The implication of the present study is that such realities materially helped towards the conclusion of German–Baltic trade treaties, since a pronounced aim of Baltic leaders had been to bring the political and economic interests of their states into conjunction.[63] The fact that the Locarno treaties furthered such a desirable end by bringing Latvia's chief economic partner, Germany, into a better relationship with Riga's most important political friend, Britain, no doubt influenced the signing of the German–Latvian trade treaty in 1926 more than did the Berlin treaty. More significantly, Germany's economic policy was in effect helping to pull the Baltic countries into the Western orbit, particularly after 1922; this provides another perspective from which to extend the comparisons between German and British Baltic policy.

In this connection it needs to be emphasized again that Germany no less than Britain was disappointed by the relative setback to earlier hopes about the role of the Baltic in East–West trade. Transit trade admittedly continued to be important, if not of the order of magnitude which had encouraged the mushrooming of foreign trading concerns in Latvia and Estonia in 1919/1920. The total transit trade to and from Russia through Estonia reached a high point in 1922 and thereafter declined in volume. There was more or less a steady rise in the total tonnage passing through Latvia between 1921 and 1930, apart from two hiccups in 1923 and 1925. Here above all the greater importance of the Soviet Union as a market for the German economy was manifest. Whereas the percentage share of Britain and Germany of total transit through Latvia to the Soviet Union was roughly comparable in 1921, at respectively 29.3% and 29.7% each, after 1924 the British share dwindled quite dramatically to 0.9% in 1926, a year when, partly owing to the German–Latvian agreement, Germany's quota was as high as 84.9% (see table 1).[64]

In terms, however, of the overall trade between the Baltic countries and the Soviet Union in the 1920s, the situation was still more depressing than the proponents of the 'Baltic springboard' had anticipated. The proportion of Estonia's foreign trade going to the Soviet Union declined from 25% in 1922 to a mere 3% by 1935. In the case of Latvia, a brief resurgence of trade from 2% to 15% between 1927 and 1929, as a result of the Soviet–Latvian trade treaty of 1927, was not sustained. By 1933 the figure had dropped to 1%.[65] When such figures are compared with those given earlier for the Weimar Republic's trade with the Baltic countries, and when the impact of the German–Latvian trade treaty of 1926 is compared with that of the Russian–Latvian agreement of 1927, the observer can have no doubt about the answer to a question posed by an economist in the 1920s: 'Latvia and Russia, or Latvia and Germany. This question of economic *rapprochement* is posed by the pressures of economic and geographical realities. Its solution can only be achieved within the overall framework of Latvia's foreign policy.'[66]

Whilst this reality may not have squared at all well with the professed intention of Weimar governments not to upset Russia over Baltic affairs, it *did* parallel Stresemann's political *rapprochement* with West Europe. Above all, it was a *necessary* outcome of Russia's own failure to re-activate its pre-war economic relationship with its lost provinces. This condemned to frustration all the earlier hopes invested in Estonia and Latvia for the resumption of those pre-war large industries which had once functioned to service the insatiable markets of Tsarist Russia and which in this respect distinguished Estonia and Latvia sharply from Lithuania. After 1918 the different economic and social organizations of respectively Russia and the Baltic states – in short, the failure of a 'restored' Russia to re-emerge as many had hoped and expected in the West – virtually closed one of the two main routes for the development of the economic life of the three small border states. The alternative was to look towards newer markets in the region, but especially in the West. The first route might have saved large-scale Baltic industries, always assuming that Russia had made good its wartime depletion of the big Baltic factories, particularly in the bustling pre-war industrial centres of Tallinn and Riga.[67]

The second route meant, as economic relations between major industrial states and underdeveloped areas were then conceived, embracing the role of an agrarian country, purchasing finished goods and machinery from the West and paying for this with agrarian exports, the 'backbone of Baltic trade'. The inevitable aspirations of the newly independent border states nonetheless to develop other sectors of their economies thereafter had to be confined to the development of newer, small-scale and medium-sized industries, geared to supplying local needs and, to a much more limited extent, filling small gaps in the demand of the Scandinavian and Western powers. Notable examples of this trend were the new plywood and furniture factories of Estonia and the woodworking industries of Latvia, the opening-up of oil-shale workings in Estonia and its export of oil, petroleum and asphalt, notably to Germany.[68] These were all industries, in other words, which no longer relied primarily on expensive imports of raw materials which had once been finished for the Russian market.[69]

Of course, something of the larger concerns remained, notably the Krainholm mills, if operating on a much reduced scale by the mid-1920s.[70] There were also large complexes such as the sugar refinery at Jelgava and the power station at Keggum. In general, however, the 'restructuring' of the Baltic economies which took place after the war involved the growth of smaller-scale concerns. That this restructuring made significant progress can be seen from the example of Latvia, where between 1920 and the later 1930s the number of small undertakings rose from 1 430 to 5 700, whilst the labour force employed in them increased almost fourfold.[71] Moreover industry remained concentrated largely in Tallinn and Riga, with the notable exception of the Narva textiles concerns and of Libau, the one centre of industry saved by the earlier German occupation from the ravages of Tsarist evacuation policies in the provinces.[72] It has been argued with some justice that the economic realities which made the Baltic countries areas of small- and medium-scale industry were reinforced by a socio-political factor – namely, the fear that the amount of foreign capital needed to regenerate the large pre-war concerns would be too great and would carry the risk of foreign interference. In addition, the dominant agrarian interests and parties were not enthusiastic about the prospect of a large industrial proletariat. The Baltic countries were therefore likely to remain 'peasant republics', as the figures for 1930 confirmed. By then only 17.4% of the population of Estonia and 13.5% of that of Latvia were engaged in industry.[73]

If this development checked plans for the expansion of East–West trade through the Baltic countries, one significant feature of the whole process was the way in which Weimar policy adapted to, and indeed contributed to, the restructuring of the Baltic economies. The newer pattern did not become fully clear until almost half-way through the 1920s, certainly not before 1923/1924, which was roughly when Britain's exporters began to lose their initial enthusiasm more rapidly but when Germany's interest continued to develop apace and its patient strategies to begin to pay dividends in terms of political influence. It was ironical in this respect that the preference of the agrarian nationalist-dominated assemblies of Latvia and Estonia for agrarian development rather than large-scale industrialization, should have been partly motivated by an interest in avoiding too great a foreign influence through capital involvement. Yet German capital still played a major part, even when the original schemes for rebuilding the large, once German-dominated industrial concerns in the Baltic countries gradually gave way to smaller-scale but more varied operations. Here was yet one more measure of the durability and resilience of Germany's economic and political interest in the Baltic countries.

Detailed studies of foreign investments in the Baltic countries for the 1920s are notable for their absence,[74] but the general picture confirms the growing German presence throughout the range of Baltic enterprise and in particular in the large centres of Tallinn and Riga, where German minorities were at their most numerous and concentrated. The patchiness of the evidence available for Estonia, or indeed Lithuania, makes it desirable to treat Latvia as a case study. If the general figures of foreign share capital in Latvia are taken as of 1 January 1932, the general pattern of Anglo-German dominance is repeated. Yet although Britain, through capital participation, had the edge over Germany in the textiles industries, the German share of investment overall was more than twice that of Great Britain and was spread throughout the entire range of trade and manufactures, particularly the textiles, ceramic, wood and metal industries (see table 9).[75] Of a total share capital of 195.2 million lats, 104.7 million, or 53.7%, was of foreign origin.[76] Germany's share of all foreign capital was no less than 15%. 'A whole series of industrial undertakings as well as three of the biggest banks functioned to a considerable extent with German working capital.' The latter point is noteworthy in view of the enormously important role of the banks in the Baltic countries in financing commercial and industrial ventures (cf. above, chapter 4).

Whilst it is true that the extent of other foreign capital involvement in the Baltic countries makes it impossible to equate Germany's share with 'control' (see table 8), there is a significant relationship between German financial participation and the numbers of Reich Germans actively working in Estonia and Latvia, leaving to one side for the moment the role of the Baltic German element as a whole. In this respect the position of the Reich Germans working in Latvia differed from that of other foreign citizens active there, notably Lithuanians, Poles, Russians and Estonians. The 4 355 Reich Germans working in Latvia at the end of the 1920s cannot be seen as casual labour, as the Lithuanians and Poles tended to be, for example. The fact that the Reich Germans were in Latvia as functionaries of German banking, trading concerns and industrial corporations barely concealed their intrinsic importance to the very existence of the still young and inexperienced Latvian economy. That so many Reich Germans worked in Latvia was an unavoidable consequence of the state's determination to build up its economic foundations. The German presence in Riga and elsewhere was in turn an expression of the close financial interrelationship between their motherland and Latvia; qualitatively, their functions could not easily, if at all, be taken over by Latvian citizens. At the time there simply was not enough native expertise available for the task in hand. The extent of Germany's multi-faceted involvement in relation to that of Britain can be gauged from comparing the figure for Reich Germans working in Latvia with that for British agents and functionaries, of which there were 500 by 1930.[77]

To revert briefly to the wider international aspects of Germany's economic role in the Baltic, it is not wholly satisfactory in the light of the foregoing analysis to treat Anglo-German trade rivalry in the area too exclusively in terms of wholly opposed foreign policy ends, though this has tended to happen in the relatively few studies of British commercial involvement in the newly independent states of East Europe.[78] Of course, British and German policies had been incompatible during the last stages of the war. The post-war situation was very different, however, and, although Germany was able to establish and maintain a dominant presence in the Baltic republics, it is misleading to reduce this to a crude struggle for political influence with the British for the remainder of the 1920s; for this can only be done by exaggerating the different foreign policy positions of the two powers and overlooking some interesting points of contact in the Baltic countries.

This is obviously not to deny the central importance of the German revisionist aims against Poland. Warsaw's political influence in the region was substantially contained not only by Stresemann's Locarno strategy, but also by the ability of Germany to offer more economic advantages to the Baltic countries than could ever be derived from a regional economic bloc (see tables 3 and 4). Significant advances in the latter direction were precluded not only by the political conflicts which have been examined in this study, but by the similarity in economic structure of the border states – although the ideal of a closer economic and political collaboration between Estonia and Latvia was kept alive by their project for a customs union in 1927.[79] The Soviet–Latvian trade treaty of 1927 was felt in Berlin at the time to be helpful because it provided a further obstacle to Poland's plans, but equally important to the Auswärtiges Amt and Reich Economics Ministry was the hope that Latvian–Soviet economic relations would be revitalized, with all the attendant benefits for Germany's economic presence in the Baltic states.[80] That this scenario failed to materialize merely underlines, by contrast, how much more fruitful was the contribution of the German–Latvian trade treaty of 1926.

Such a positive contribution becomes as interesting for the historian of Weimar foreign policy as the end which it purported to serve, namely to prevent the Baltic states from coming under Polish control. Although the British reacted against France's obsession with a fixed alliance system keeping Germany encircled in the East, they did share with the Weimar Republic an interest in stable relations in the Baltic countries in the second half of the 1920s. And Britain's continuing hostility towards the Soviet Union makes it difficult to accept, as we have already argued, the equation of Britain's declining share of Baltic imports with British indifference to the fate of the small states.[81] It is always risky in any case to deduce from a small percentage of given business that the business itself was unimportant. Baltic foreign trade showed a steady increase in value in the inter-war period, apart from the slump, and by 1938 the Baltic states together were exporting half as much as the Soviet Union.[82] A small percentage of any trade is preferable to none, to most businessmen at least. Moreover, if Germany's economic activity in the Baltic is taken in conjunction with Stresemann's success in restraining the more virulent form of Weimar revisionism, and if full weight is given to the *rapprochement* between Germany and the Western powers after 1924, then it is even possible to argue that the most important aspect of Anglo-German trade rivalry, in the 1920s at least, was the way it benefited the Baltic countries themselves. Britain's role as a major purchaser of Baltic exports after all provided a good deal of the foreign currency reserves on which Latvia and Estonia drew to pay for the import of machinery and manufacturing goods, which came overwhelmingly from Germany.

Whilst this may not have been entirely pleasing to British businessmen, both Britain and Germany *in effect* helped to pull the Baltic states into the orbit of Western economic and political life and away from Russia. It is notable in this context that the German–Lithuanian trade agreement merely reserved to Lithuania the right to make special concessions to Estonia and Latvia and made no mention of either Poland or Russia – a significant gain for Germany's longer-term attempt to restrict the 'Baltic clause'. For the duration of the five-year agreement there was neither the possibility of a three-power Baltic economic bloc nor a *rapprochement* with Russia. The German Foreign Minister, Curtius, could therefore say with some justice to his Estonian counterpart, at a meeting in Geneva in 1931, that Germany had tried 'to encourage the independence of the Baltic states, since we were hardly keen to see them becoming dependent on Russia or joining a Polish-led bloc'.[83] Such a sentiment would not have been out of place in the British Foreign Office. German influence as such in the Baltic region was not intolerable to British policy in the 1920s. By contrast, when the National Socialist regime came into power London attempted a more sustained, if belated, counter-thrust to German economic hegemony through the pursuit of bilateral trade agreements between Britain and the Baltic republics.[84]

It is not therefore satisfactory to argue that Weimar *Ostpolitik* accepted Baltic independence largely as a result of its revisionist aims against Poland, for such a judgement fails to attach anything like enough weight to the constructive implications of Weimar Baltic policy.[85] This brings us back to the Baltic Germans. The Reich's defence of the German element as a whole in the Baltic countries, along with direct political involvement in the region and a substantial economic stake, formed a trilogy of concerns which comprised an increasingly positive interest of Weimar policy, as conceived and practised by Stresemann, in independent Baltic countries. Stresemann's arrival at the Auswärtiges Amt was in itself a guarantee that the German minority in the Baltic would continue to receive substantial aid in the field of cultural policy. The initial, somewhat sporadic, sums of money provided by the Reich in 1919/1920 for supporting German schooling in the border states (see above, chapter 2) continued to be paid. Yet in retrospect 1923 provides, as in so many other spheres of German policy, a dividing line, for after that year more systematic provision was made. Estimates for funding German schooling alone between 1927 and 1933/1934 vary between 30 to 35 thousand marks per annum in Latvia and, for Estonia, about 20 thousand marks yearly. Between 1921 and 1928 as much as a quarter of the German school budget deficit in Latvia was made good by the Reich, as well as a third of the cost of maintaining the Herder Institute in Riga and some two-thirds of the grants to German students studying there. In addition, the running costs of the organization in Latvia looking after the cultural and social welfare interests of the Baltic Germans were heavily subsidized by the German government – not to mention support for the German theatre in Riga and the German language press in Latvia.[86]

Small as such sums were in terms of the Reich's total budget, they often made a crucial difference to the Baltic Germans. In Latvia, the development of more systematic funding was associated with the arrival of Dr Köster as German Ambassador in 1923 and was accompanied by the necessary restructuring of the Baltic German organizational network. On the initiative of the Committee of the German Balt Political Parties (see above, chapter 2), an association was set up of the various Baltic German cultural, social and welfare bodies. This 'Zentrale Deutsch–Baltischer Arbeit', functioning initially as a section of the 'Committee', took over the vital coordinating tasks for the 'non-political' cultural and welfare work. It comprised, apart from the parliamentary delegation, representatives of Baltic

German economic life, of the welfare and educational administration of the German community as well as of church, youth and student societies.[87] Once this rationalization had taken place a new procedure was developed to replace the earlier, somewhat *ad hoc* distribution of funds. Thereafter, Köster was given a 'claim budget' before the start of each financial year; this listed the contributions from the Baltic German community as well as the sums expected from the Reich, and gave an indication of the eventual distribution of resources to the different branches of German activity in Latvia.[88] The contribution expected of the *Auslandsdeutsche* to his own survival (see above, chapter 2) was made in the Baltic German community of Latvia through the introduction in 1926 of self-taxation on a sliding scale of 0.5 to 3.0% of monthly income. It was administered by the Zentrale, which in the same year became independent from the 'Committee'. By 1928 the organization of the Baltic German community was rounded off with the setting-up of the Deutsch–Baltischer Volksgemeinschaft.[89]

The twice-yearly collections which had taken place within the Baltic German community before the introduction of self-taxation in 1926 had already yielded between two and six million Latvian roubles per annum, and the accumulation of such funds was clearly crucial to the work of the political fraction in developing the possibilities inherent in the Latvian School Law of 1919. Unlike Estonia, where a comparable process of social care and welfare took place,[90] and where the law on cultural autonomy was passed in February 1925, in Latvia the Baltic Germans had to be content with defending their culture through the educational structure. Once the 'Administration for German Culture' had become an autonomous authority within the Latvian Ministry of Culture, in accordance with the School Law, progress really depended on the nature of the collaboration between the head of the German school system in Latvia and the current Latvian Education Minister.[91] In this overall context, too, the founding of the Herder Institute in Riga in 1921, with the initial support of Riga's Great Guild, and its recognition by the Latvian government as a private German *Hochschule*, was a critically important development.[92]

The 1925 cultural autonomy law in Estonia, possibly stimulated at least in part by the abortive Communist putsch in Tallinn in December 1924, was regarded at the time as an object lesson for minorities throughout Europe. It epitomized the positive collaboration between German and Baltic nationalities which was the professed goal of much of the *Auslandsdeutsche* organization and of such men as Paul Schiemann. Control of German schools and cultural activities passed to a self-elected association of Baltic Germans, the Council for Culture (*Kulturrat*), which had the power to levy taxes on its community – a development which made obsolete the Deutsche Schulhilfe, first founded in 1919.[93] Recognized by even the more chauvinistic sector of the Estonian press as opening the way for 'a more significant collaboration of the German element in public life',[94] the new body ultimately enabled the Deutsch–Baltische Partei to disburden itself somewhat and to concentrate more exclusively on its political activity in the Rigiikogu.[95] The demarcation clash between the new cultural administration and the organization set up in 1920, the Verband deutscher Vereine in Estland, needed to be resolved. This was eventually achieved by concentrating under the latter's umbrella all those aspects of Baltic German life not falling within the legal remit of the German Council for Culture: that is to say, welfare care, the encouragement of business and the economy, professional training and the very important task of looking after the relations between the Baltic German community and the *Auslandsdeutsche* movement.[96]

The development of the organizational network briefly outlined above constituted an advance in itself, at least in light of the upheavals of 1918/1919. Its fundamental premise remained, however, that of peaceful co-existence with the new Baltic leaders and was tolerated by the dominant nationality because of this. The Auswärtiges Amt, through its ambassadors, exploited every opportunity to reinforce the policy of Weimar–Baltic collaboration. The fact that this was intended to serve the wider interests of Weimar *Ostpolitik* was undeniable; so, equally, was the determination to avoid irredentism and to calm Baltic fears about the German element being a fifth column. That this concern permeated even the cultural sphere is apparent from Köster's stand, fully endorsed by the Auswärtiges Amt, in 1927, against the efforts of the director of the Herder Institute to have his institution elevated to university status, thus constituting an unwelcome rival to the Latvian state university.

The aim of the Reich's policy towards the border states is so to integrate these states between Germany and Russia that, economically and politically, they become a substitute for the border between Germany and Russia which disappeared with the Versailles Treaty. In other words, they are to be links and bridges between Germany and Russia. In practice it cannot be expected that the German element in Latvia, comprising three and a third per cent of the population, will ever again attain its pre-war mastery. Thus Germany cannot achieve its goal without the decisive collaboration of the Latvians. There has been success in so arranging relations between Germany and Latvia ... that, economically and politically, Germany has now become the most important factor for Latvia. The Reich's cultural policy cannot follow a different route. We must try to be the most important supplier for the Latvian people in cultural policy too ... As in the economic and political sphere, so in that of cultural policy, we must maintain the closest possible relations to the Latvian state and its institutions.[97]

That this policy aroused considerable resistance from Reich German circles in the Baltic countries and from nationalist circles inside the Weimar Republic, that it earned the continuing dislike of the Baltic German emigrés in Germany, was a measure of the progress being made by the sort of policy line detailed by Köster. Such can also be said of the personal abuse of Köster by the same political circles. As the German ambassador correctly argued, there was a link between the success of the responsible *Auslandsdeutsche* policy pursued in Latvia and Estonia and the strength of the republican tradition in Germany itself, both equally under pressure in the later 1920s.[98]

An important measure of the German government's progress in its aim to preserve the German element in the post-war era was the fact that by 1928 the political basis of the German element in Latvia was stronger than that of any German minority in Europe or abroad.[99] As in Estonia, it is impossible to conceive of a successful policy of Weimar–Baltic collaboration without the continuing effort of the most influential Baltic German leaders to work within the political framework of the new Baltic countries. In both Estonia and Latvia, the discipline and organization of the Baltic German politicians enabled them to exercise influence in a context notable for an exceptionally large number of extremely small parties. Predictably, much of this work concerned the well-being of the Baltic Germans themselves.[100] Obvious political manoeuvres by the Baltic Germans to help Weimar policy were largely precluded by the basic requirement of maintaining and developing cooperation between Germany and the Baltic states. An interesting because rare example of direct Baltic German action to support Reich policy concerned the Soviet–Latvian trade agreement of 1927. In giving critically important coalition support to the Latvian SPD administration over this, the Baltic German 'Party' went against its tendency to collaborate with the bourgeois groups in Latvia, which were relatively unsevere on the question of agrarian compensation. In this instance Wallroth's approval was justified because it was a case 'of an acutely important foreign policy question ... where the proper interests of the German Balts and the Latvians coincided so closely with the foreign policy aims of the Reich'. Notably, however, any suggestion of trying to commit the German fraction to a *general* political line towards the Skujenieks government was rejected precisely because nothing could be more damaging than the charge that the Baltic Germans were acting on behalf of the Reich. Its prime function had to be to defend the autonomy and overall position of the German element.[101]

The political line maintained by the Baltic German leadership in Latvia and Estonia, notwithstanding noticeable resistance in the late 1920s from the younger element in the German community, was a direct expression of a wider involvement in the public and economic life of the states. The relatively high proportion of Baltic Germans in the free professions and public service was itself another indicator of the slow if still painful process of coexistence between German and Baltic peoples. In Latvia especially, by the late 1920s, Baltic Germans were playing a prominent role once more on the numerous commissions set up by the Latvian government.[102] Admittedly, this needs to be seen constantly against the overall decline suffered by the Baltic German element. On Maydell's earlier calculations, between 1897 and 1922 the German element in Estonia suffered a yearly loss through emigration of 1.9% a year, and from 1922 to 1934 of 0.9% a year. In Latvia the annual loss rate was 1.4% between 1897 and 1925 and 1.2% between 1925 and 1935.[103] Such figures help to account for the generally gloomy note in much Baltic German historiography. Yet what of the wider concern of Weimar policy? How far had the situation been saved in comparison with the outlook in 1918/1919, and how successfully had Weimar–Baltic collaboration achieved one of the fundamental aims of the *Auslandsdeutsche* movement, namely to sustain the economic basis of the German minority through interaction with German–Baltic economic relations?

In terms of maintaining a foothold in the Baltic countries, the most dramatic economic change had taken place on the land, as we saw earlier. In the area comprising Latvia before the war, of the 880 *Rittergüter*, each with an average of 2520 hectares, and of all German farms and church holdings, only 1170 German holdings were left by the 1930s, with an average of 56 hectares. In Estonia, only 350 concerns were functioning by 1934, with an average of 86 hectares.[104] True, the agrarian reforms had the effect of increasing the number of German small farmers in the 1920s. After 1925 in particular, the German government began to give more attention to their plight, having for so long been preoccupied mainly with the position of the once large estate-holders. The sums available were nonetheless extremely limited. A notable example was the 300 000 marks to help resettle German farmers in Latvia in 1927.[105] Stresemann's own attempt to provide more systematic support after 1925 for compact settlements of Germans abroad also included those in the Baltic countries. The 30 million marks' relief credit programme announced to help the *Auslandsdeutsche* generally in 1926, and disbursed through the Deutsche Stiftung, represented the first really substantial funding by the German government for German minorities. As well as the German element in Latvia and Estonia, however, the money had to support Germans in North Schleswig, Eupen-Malmédy, the Volga Republic of Russia, Lithuania, Memel and, of course, Poland.[106]

Although such activity has been interpreted almost exclusively in terms of preserving the basis for later revisionist claims, the inclusion of the Baltic Germans alone throws some doubt on this.[107] Also, as has been argued elsewhere, Stresemann's policy towards the *Auslandsdeutsche* embraced the doctrine of 'self-help' by the minority concerned; in the conditions of the 1920s, this was necessarily best realised by collaboration with the host country. General foreign policy grounds, particularly after Locarno, argued in favour of a steady improvement of relations between German minorities and their host countries, difficult as it was for Stresemann and the Auswärtiges Amt to persuade rightists in Germany and some of the Deutschtum leaders of this central reality. As in other areas of Stresemann's policy, it is increasingly necessary to set his public rhetoric against the *actuality* of his response to the German minority problem. It is noticeable that Stresemann's known concern for the *Auslandsdeutsche* was not permitted to disrupt the wider policy strategy. At the 'lower level' of everyday activity, away from the public glare of revisionist politics, the emphasis remained firmly on taking the heat out of the minority conflicts in East Europe which so disadvantaged the German element after 1918.[108]

The Baltic Germans were no exception to this rule. It was significant that the 30 million mark credit action of 1926 specifically excluded help in restoring the industrial and commercial concerns of Germans abroad, where the emphasis remained on self-help and where, in Latvia and Estonia, the German element could hope to derive some benefit in the long run from the inexorable drift towards the major industrial and commercial centres in Riga, Tallinn and other towns. Here above all was the test of the policy of making the *Auslandsdeutsche* the agent and beneficiary of Germany's economic recovery in East Europe. By the 1930s, no less than 22.6% of the German element in Latvia was self-employed, 19.2% being the corresponding figure for Estonia.[109] The extent of the stake which the German element as a whole had managed to secure in the restructured Baltic economies may be seen from the fact that 57% of the Germans in Latvia, 52.1% of those in Estonia, were engaged in trade, transport and industry by the end of the 1920s.[110] Further detail is provided by a report of the Reichsstelle für Aussenhandel which reviewed the overall wealth of the German element in the Baltic states at the end of the 1930s. By this time the German minority in Estonia may have owned as much as a fifth of the state's total wealth, although comprising only 1.5% of the population. Of the 1500 large trading concerns in Estonia by the mid-1930s, 8.5% was German-owned.[111]

A spectacular example of how German-owned institutions could help to sustain Germany's leading position in the economic life of the north-east was provided by the Scheel bank. It financed directly most of the large and important industrial undertakings in Estonia and had shares in others. Of purely German-owned undertakings in trade and industry, nine-tenths had share or credit links with the Scheel bank. Since a high proportion of Estonian big business was German-owned, the greater part of the Estonian economy was influenced by the Scheel concern. The fundamental importance of such a banking presence for the economic existence of the German element made it relatively cheap for the Reich to help out financially when the banking crisis eventually hit the border states at the end of the 1920s.[112] Equally, contemporary reports in the 1930s testified to the fact that the Baltic Germans remained the wealthiest sector and that they were able to conduct their business 'peacefully and undisturbed' as late as 1934.[113]

To catalogue such a presence exhaustively would be pointless in this present study. The rising nationalist mood in Germany and in the Baltic countries after 1929 was not able in itself to alter immediately the main outlines of Weimar–Baltic relations. That the developments of the 1920s would be affected in due course was beyond doubt. The capacity of the Reich to absorb Baltic agricultural products would be reduced by the growing mood of protectionism in Germany; the impatience of elements within the Baltic

German camp with the Schiemann concept of peaceful coexistence would grow under the influence of Hitler's Reich. Then, indeed, with a very different political ideology informing the policy of the Reich, those very elements of German influence which had been preserved in the Baltic countries by the patient policy of collaboration could be used and exploited to refashion an instrument of expansion which would recall the days of Brest–Litovsk. The National Socialist view of a *Grossraumwirtschaft*, with its emphasis on bilateral trade treaties and its impatience with the liberal, most-favoured-nation agreements of the 1920s, through which Weimar–Baltic trade had linked East and West, would transform the concept of the *Auslandsdeutsche* as Stresemann had understood it. For Hitler, as for Wilhelm II, 'the whole Baltic area must become Reich territory'.[114]

History has heard much about the 'Baltic German mentors' of Adolf Hitler and his movement, but our present study has been concerned among other things with that other Baltic German tradition epitomized by Paul Schiemann and by the international collaborative minority work furthered by the Baltic-German-inspired Nationality Congress from 1925. The Weimar Republic's policy of active collaboration with the Baltic countries depended for its success on the Schiemann line. That this policy line also prevented Polish hegemony in the Baltic was in fact consistent with the revisionist foreign policy practised by all Weimar governments. To focus only on this, however, and to ignore the constructive offshoots of Germany's determination to maintain its political and economic presence in the Baltic region, would be further to condone the still-current obsession with tracing unbroken lines between Wilhelmine and Hitlerian foreign policy. Economic progress was the acid test of survival for the new Baltic states. Economically, a closed regional system would have been disastrous for them in the long run because of their predominantly agrarian structures. Germany's contribution to their survival should not be underestimated. The fact that Weimar–Baltic economic relations helped to sustain the independence of the Baltic countries from Russia in the formative stages of independence suggests, too, that we should fundamentally reassess the ingrained habit of regarding Weimar–Soviet relations as threatening to European security in the 1920s. The trilogy of political, economic and minority interests which the Weimar Republic's Baltic policy served had a considerable potential for East–West relations and for small states which it is unwise to ignore in our understandable interest in explaining Hitler's policy in this century.

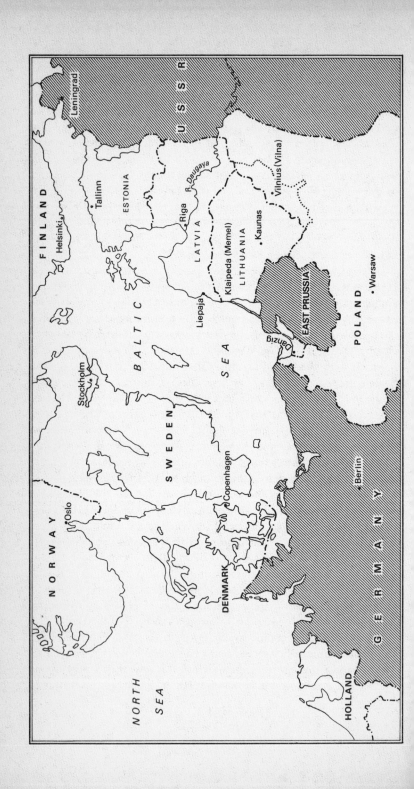

Tables

—— ~ ——

Table 1 *Comparison of German and British share of transit to and from Soviet Russia through Latvia*

	Germany to Russia (tonnage)	As % of total transit	British %	Russia to Germany (tonnage)	As % of total transit	British %
1921	21 703	29.7	(29.3)	916	10.9	(61.0)
1922	111 930	34.2	(19.7)	5699	12.1	(56.1)
1923	21 028	29.4	(11.6)	30 905	18.2	(43.9)
1924	6421	20.7	(38.5)	22 936	7.4	(46.0)
1925	4235	19.3	(7.5)	29 865	15.4	(47.1)
1926	98 011	84.9	(0.9)	82 149	35.4	(31.6)

Based on Hinkkanen-Lievonen, pp. 279–80.

Table 2 *Germany's percentage share of the foreign trade of Estonia and Latvia[a]*

	Estonia				Latvia			
	Imports		Exports		Imports		Exports	
1920	29.9	(26.2)	3.9	(45.2)	18.6	(20.7)	1.2	(67.5)
1921	40.2	(27.9)	3.9	(39.6)	48.1	(14.3)	17.9	(35.6)
1922	54.7	(14.9)	12.7	(22.2)	42.6	(18.7)	13.0	(40.3)
1923	51.0	(19.7)	10.8	(34.1)	45.2	(17.0)	7.6	(46.3)
1924	36.6	(14.0)	22.6	(33.5)	39.0	(16.2)	16.4	(41.5)
1925	29.4	(12.3)	31.2	(25.0)	41.5	(13.8)	22.6	(34.6)
1926	29.1	(12.1)	23.1	(28.8)	39.9	(9.9)	24.3	(34.0)
1927	26.4	(14.3)	29.8	(31.4)	40.6	(10.6)	26.4	(34.0)

[a]British percentage share in brackets for comparison.
Based on Hinkkanen-Lievonen, pp. 282–3. (Figures for 1920/1921 are for weight.)

Table 3   Distribution of the foreign trade of the Baltic countries: exports as percentage of the total value

To:	Estonia			Latvia			Lithuania		
	1923	1927	1930	1923	1927	1930	1923	1927	1930
Germany	10.8	29.8	30.1	7.6	26.4	26.6	43.3	51.6	59.9
UK	34.1	31.4	32.3	46.3	34.1	28.4	26.9	24.8	19.5
Belgium	9.0	5.4	1.9	19.7	10.8	6.4	1.8	2.0	2.0
Holland	0.7	2.7	2.2	2.8	5.9	6.0	1.4	1.7	2.0
France	1.5	1.2	4.2	6.6	2.2	5.2	1.2	1.1	0.7
Estonia	–	–	–	1.4	*	1.4	*	*	0.1
Latvia	8.0	5.2	1.7	–	–	–	15.9	8.8	6.9
Lithuania	*	*	*	1.7	*	2.7	–	–	–
Sweden	10.0	4.4	4.0	1.4	1.4	1.1	*	1.6	1.2
Norway	0.4	1.6	1.1	*	0.4	*	*	0.1	*
Denmark	6.2	3.5	7.7	3.2	1.9	1.6	2.5	0.3	1.3
USSR	6.7	6.3	4.5	3.7	1.7	14.1	*	0.5	1.6
Finland	8.5	4.8	2.7	0.3	1.2	0.7	*	0.2	*
Poland	*	*	*	0.8	4.0	1.1	*	0.1	*
Danzig	1.2	0.3	1.2	0.2	**	0.1	*	*	*
Austria	*	*	*	*	0.5	0.2	*	*	*
Czechoslovakia	*	*	*	0.5	0.2	0.4	*	1.5	0.1
Italy	*	*	*	*	0.1	0.2	*	0.1	0.1
Switzerland	*	*	*	0.1	0.1	0.2	*	*	0.2
USA	1.3	1.2	2.0	2.4	2.5	1.0	1.8	1.8	0.8
Other countries	1.6	2.2	4.4	1.3	6.6	2.6	5.2	3.9	3.6
TOTAL	100.0	100.0	100.0	100.0	100.0	100.0	100.0	100.0	100.0

* = Included in 'Other countries'. ** = Included in Poland.
Source: *The Baltic states*, p. 126.

Table 4 *Distribution of the foreign trade of the Baltic countries: imports as percentage of the total value*

From:	Estonia 1923	Estonia 1927	Estonia 1930	Latvia 1923	Latvia 1927	Latvia 1929	Lithuania 1923	Lithuania 1927	Lithuania 1929
Germany	51.0	26.5	28.3	45.2	40.6	37.2	80.9	53.2	48.5
UK	19.7	14.3	8.6	17.0	10.6	8.5	5.3	6.7	7.7
Belgium	2.3	1.9	1.9	2.4	1.8	1.9	*	1.2	2.4
Holland	1.0	1.6	1.7	4.9	3.0	1.9	0.6	3.4	3.2
France	0.6	3.5	4.2	1.4	2.3	3.2	0.3	1.3	3.0
Estonia	–	–	–	2.4	*	1.3	*	*	1.1
Latvia	3.8	3.1	2.7	–	–	–	3.3	*	4.3
Lithuania	*	*	*	5.4	–	3.1	–	–	–
Sweden	3.2	5.1	4.8	2.4	4.2	3.0	0.2	1.9	2.4
Norway	0.1	0.3	0.1	*	0.1	*	0.3	0.4	
Denmark	3.1	1.7	2.1	3.1	6.7	1.9	0.1	1.1	1.7
USSR	4.0	9.1	9.3	3.6	7.3	5.9	*	2.4	4.4
Finland	3.2	2.2	2.2	0.4	0.7	0.8	0.5	0.7	
Poland	*	*	*	3.9	8.0	10.5	*	7.8	3.3
Danzig	4.1	0.2	8.5	2.1	*	0.8	1.0	**	**
Austria	*	*	*	*	0.8	0.8	*	0.5	0.5
Czechoslovakia	*	*	*	1.2	2.7	3.7	3.3	5.2	5.8
Italy	*	*	*	*	0.4	1.1	*	0.8	2.0
Switzerland	*	*	*	0.8	1.3	1.8	*	0.9	1.2
USA	3.7	14.2	12.7	2.9	2.8	5.2	2.1	5.5	4.7
Other countries	0.2	16.3	12.9	0.9	6.7	7.3	2.9	7.3	2.7
TOTAL	100.0	100.0	100.0	100.0	100.0	100.0	100.0	100.0	100.0

* = Included in 'Other countries'. ** = Included in Poland.
Source: *The Baltic states*, p. 126.

Table 5   *Germany's percentage share of Baltic imports in finished goods*

	(a) Total value of finished imports (in millions of marks)	(b) German share (in millions of marks)	(b) as % of (a)
Latvia			
1925	105.9	51.8	48.9
1926	105.2	49.5	47.1
1927	91.2	40.9	44.8
1928	106.6	50.2	47.1
Estonia			
1925	42.4	19.5	46.9
1926	45.3	20.3	44.6
1927	56.2	21.3	37.1
1928	71.0	26.5	37.3

Germany's percentage share of Lithuania's finished goods imports: 1925, 76.4; 1926, 70.1; 1927, 68.6; 1928, 62.2.
Total value of German finished goods imports to Baltic countries in millions of marks: 1925, 114.0; 1926, 107.0; 1927, 103.9; 1928, 119.4.
Based on Brenneisen, *Aussenhandel und Aussenhandelspolitik*, p. 378.

Table 6   *German share in Baltic finished textile imports*

	Total value of imports (in millions of marks)	Value of German share (in millions of marks)	German % share	British % share (for comparison)
Latvia				
1924	37.36	15.04	40.3	(21.8)
1926	40.48	15.52	38.3	(17.9)
1927	33.06	10.58	32.0	(19.8)
1928	42.25	13.92	33.0	(18.2)
Estonia				
1924		3.65	53.3	(25.2)
1926		4.45	43.0	(18.8)
1927		4.48	36.3	(19.2)
1928		5.64	32.0	(18.0)
Lithuania	(for comparison)			
1924			77.7	
1926			68.4	
1927			66.4	
1928			56.8	

Based on Brenneisen, *Aussenhandel und Aussenhandelspolitik*, pp. 378–9.

Table 7   *Private credit to Latvia, 1914–23*

	Balance of credit institutions (in millions of gold franks)		Number of credit institutions	
	1 Jan. 1914	1 Jan. 1920	1 Jan. 1914	1 Jan. 1920
Banks	509.21	2.92	13	5
Mutual credit societies	211.91	0.67	41	10
Loan and saving banks	177.27	0.21	259	17
TOTAL	898.39	3.80	313	32

	Balances at 1 Jan. (in millions of roubles)			
	1920	1921	1922	1923
Banks	146.30	330.85	514.61	1733.75
Mutual credit societies	33.63	88.90	170.01	366.61
Loan and saving banks	14.6	41.14	94.47	181.80

	Number of credit institutions			
	1920	1921	1922	1923
Banks	5	9	10	13
Mutual credit associations	10	22	25	28
Loan and saving banks	17	72	115	156
TOTAL	32	103	150	197

Source: Siew, Lettlands privat Kreditanstalten: DZA, 64562.

Table 8   *Latvia's foreign indebtedness at the end of 1930[a]*

	Millions of Swiss francs
Germany	25.7
Great Britain	16.1
Sweden	11.8
Netherlands	8.4
Belgium	7.3
Tsarist Russia	7.1
Estonia	6.6
USA	5.3
Others	16.5

[a]Distribution by creditor countries of nominal (paid up) participation in Latvian joint stock companies at the end of 1930.
Source: *The Baltic states*, p. 137.

Table 9 *German capital participation in branches of Latvian industry at the end of 1931 (in thousands of lats)*

	Germany	Britain (for comparison)
Ceramics	185	1221
Metal industries	2726	–
Chemical industries	4312	6
Leather industries	519	–
Textiles	3725	5278
Timber industries	1368	2386
Paper industries	1969	847
Printing	725	–
Semi-luxury industries	925	1760
Clothing industry	131	1
Building industry	200	–
Gas and electricity industries	25	–
Commerce	1148	1628
Shipping	250	–
Art/Sport	–	–
Real estate	1328	119
Transport	285	439
Insurance	911	–
Banking	4826	2390
TOTAL[a]	25 558	16 075

[a]Cf. France's total of 1660 (Bilmanis, *Latvijas Werdegang*, pp. 130–1).

Abbreviations

BAK   Bundesarchiv, Koblenz

DZA   Deutsches Zentralarchiv, Potsdam

FO   Foreign Office Library, London (microfilm of German archives)

PAB   Politisches Archiv des Auswärtigen Amtes, Bonn

PRO   Public Record Office, London

StA   Staatliches Archivlager, Göttingen

Notes

INTRODUCTION

1. F. Fischer, *Griff nach der Weltmacht. Die Kriegszielpolitik des kaiserlichen Deutschland 1914-18*, Düsseldorf, 1961; W. Baumgart, *Deutsche Ostpolitik 1918. Von Brest–Litovsk bis zum Ende des Ersten Weltkrieges*, Vienna–Munich, 1966; W. Basler, *Deutschlands Annexionspolitik in Polen und im Baltikum 1914–1918*, E. Berlin, 1962; B. Mann, *Die baltischen Länder in der deutschen Kriegszielpublizistik 1914–1918*, Tübingen, 1965; H.-E. Volkmann, *Die deutsche Baltikumpolitik zwischen Brest–Litovsk und Compiègne*, Cologne–Vienna, 1970.
2. Cf. the interesting re-interpretations of P. Krüger, *Die Aussenpolitik der Republik von Weimar*, Darmstadt, 1985.
3. Cf. W. Ruge, 'Die Aussenpolitik der Weimarer Republik und das Problem der europäischen Sicherheit 1925–1932', *Zeitschrift für Geschichtswissenschaft*, 22, 1974, pp. 276, 290.
4. F. W. Pick, *The Baltic nations*, London, 1945, p. 67.
5. Cf. H. Graml, 'Die Rapallo-Politik im Urteil der westdeutschen Forschung', *Vierteljahrshefte für Zeitgeschichte*, 18, 1970, pp. 366–91.
6. The exceptions tend to be found in works from the Eastern block. Cf. G. Rosenfeld, *Sowjetrussland und Deutschland 1917–1922*, E. Berlin, 1960.
7. D. Kirby, 'A great opportunity lost? Aspects of British commercial policy towards the Baltic States 1920–1924,' *Journal of Baltic Studies*, 5:4, 1974, pp. 362–8; M.-L. Hinkkanen-Lievonen, *British trade and enterprise in the Baltic states 1919–1925*, Helsinki, 1984.
8. Of K. Hovi's works (see bibliography) particular interest has been derived for my study from his *Interessensphären im Baltikum. Finnland im Rahmen der Ostpolitik Polens 1919–1922*, Helsinki, 1984; see also O. Hovi, *The Baltic area in British policy 1918–1926. From the Compiègne armistice to the implementation of the Versailles treaty*, Helsinki, 1980; cf. T. Polvinen, 'Zur Erforschung der jüngeren politischen Geschichte Finnlands', *Jahrbücher für Geschichte Osteuropas*, 13:2, 1965, pp. 231–46.
9. K.-H. Grundmann, *Deutschtumspolitik zur Zeit der Weimarer Republik. Eine Studie am Beispiel der deutsch–baltischen Minderheit in Estland und Lettland*, Hanover–Döhren, 1977.

10. For example, R. Frommelt, *Paneuropa oder Mitteleuropa. Einigungsbestrebungen im Kalkül deutscher Wirtschaft und Politik 1925–33*, Stuttgart, 1977, has virtually nothing on the detailed economic relations between Germany and East Europe.

I THE POLITICS OF PEACEMAKING 1919–20

1. Grundmann, *Deutschtumspolitik*, p. 63; R. Müller-Sternberg, *Deutsche Ostsiedlung. Eine Bilanz für Europa*, Bielefeld, 1969, p. 56

2. K. Maydell, 'Die Baltendeutschen vor ihrer Umsiedlung', *Jomsburg*, 4, 1940, p. 72; cf. R. Wittram's essay, 'Das ständische Gefüge und die Nationalität. Zum Strukturwandel in den baltischen Adelslandschaften im Neunzehnjahrhundert', in his *Das Nationale als Europäisches Problem*, Göttingen, 1954, pp. 158–9.

3. Cf. U. Germanis, 'Die Autonomie – und Unabhängigkeitsstrebungen der Letten', in J. von Hehn *et al.*, eds., *Von den baltischen Provinzen zu den baltischen Staaten*, Marburg, 1971, pp. 205ff.

4. Grundmann, *Deutschtumspolitik*, p. 73; W. Conze, 'Nationalstaat oder Mitteleuropa?', in W. Conze, ed., *Deutschland und Europa*, 1951, pp. 205ff.

5. Cf. H. Rothfels, 'The Baltic provinces. Some historical aspects and perspectives', *Journal of Central European Affairs*, 4:2, 1944, pp. 117–46 (pp. 131ff.).

6. R. Wittram, *Baltische Geschichte. Die Ostseelände Livland, Estland, Kurland 1180–1918*, Munich, 1954, pp. 236–7; Grundmann, *Deutschtumspolitik*, p. 78.

7. D. Sweet, 'The Baltic in British diplomacy before the First World War', *Historical Journal*, 13:3, 1970, pp. 489ff.

8. K.-H. Janssen, 'Die baltische Okkupationspolitik des deutschen Reiches', in Hehn *et al.*, eds., *Von den baltischen Provinzen*, p. 220; Mann, *Die baltischen Länder*; Basler, *Deutschlands Annexionspolitik*. Cf. Rüdiger von der Goltz, 'Die Früchten deutschen Siegen', 2.10.1917: BAK, Bundesarchiv–Militärarchiv, Nachlass Franz Joseph Isenburg-Birnstein (H O8–82/12–17, Bd 12).

9. Cited in Grundmann, *Deutschtumspolitik*, p. 86; cf. A. von Taube, 'Die baltisch–deutsche Führungspolitik und die Loslösung Livlands und Estlands von Russland 1916–1918', in Hehn *et al.*, eds., *Von den baltischen Provinzen*, p. 101.

10. Volkmann, *Baltikumpolitik*, pp. 226–9.

11. Grundmann, *Deutschtumspolitik*, p. 95, is virtually alone in arguing that the OHL had lost interest in the Baltic in 1918. Cf. Volkmann, *Baltikumpolitik*, p. 187.

12. R. Stupperich, 'Siedlungspläne im Gebiet des Oberbefehlshabers Ost', *Jomsburg*, 5, 1941, pp. 348–67.

13. Cf. Volkmann, *Baltikumpolitik*, pp. 92ff.

14. Cf. H. Rolnik, *Die baltischen Staaten Litauen, Lettland und Estland und ihre Verfassungsrecht*, Leipzig, 1927, p. 21.

15. On the Auswärtiges Amt, see A. von Taube, 'Das Auswärtige Amt und die Estnische Frage 1917–1918', *Jahrbücher für Geschichte Osteuropas*, 17, 1969, pp. 371–3; on Kühlmann, see Janssen, 'Okkupationspolitik', pp. 236–7 and Volkmann, *Baltikumpolitik*, p. 163; on Hintze, see Volkmann, *Baltikumpolitik*, p. 179.

16. L. Lewerenz, *Die deutsche Politik im Baltikum*, Hamburg, 1958, pp. 125ff.; Fischer, *Griff nach der Weltmacht*, p. 604.

17. Fischer, *Griff nach der Weltmacht*, p. 805.

18. Janssen, 'Okkupationspolitik', p. 253.

19. *Ibid.*, p. 241; cf. Rolnik, *Die baltischen Staaten*, pp. 18–19; Baumgart, *Deutsche Ostpolitik*, p. 370.

20. G. von Rauch, *The Baltic states. The years of independence, 1917–1940*, London, 1974, p. 25.

21. Cited Janssen, 'Okkupationspolitik', p. 225.

22. Wrangell, 'Ausschnitte aus der estnischen Politik 1918–1920', *Baltische Monatsschrift*, 1930, p. 529.

23. Cf. Volkmann, *Baltikumpolitik*, pp. 195–6.

24. PRO, Cabinet Office, WC 314/Appendix 4, January 1918; cf. M. W. Graham, *The diplomatic recognition of the Baltic States*, vol. 3, Los Angeles, 1939, p. 407.

25. E. Anderson, 'British policy towards the Baltic states 1918–1920', *Journal of Central European Affairs*, 19, 1959, p. 276.

26. Rolnik, *Die baltischen Staaten*, pp. 25–6; cf. memorandum by the Political Intelligence Dept on the Baltic provinces, 17, 1918, PRO, CAB 24/33.

27. W. Ribhegge, *August Winnig – eine historische Persönlichkeitsanalyse*, Bonn, 1973, p. 125; cf. D. Unfug, 'The Baltic policy of Prince Max of Baden', *Journal of Central European Affairs*, 23, 1963, pp. 152–65.

28. Cited in P. Borowsky, 'Die bolschewistische Gefahr und die Ostpolitik der Volksbeauftragten in der Revolution', *Industrielle Gesellschaft und politisches System*, Bonn, 1978, pp. 391–2.

29. Cf. Krüger, *Aussenpolitik*, pp. 23ff.

30. Both quotations from Ribhegge, *August Winnig*, p. 128.

31. BAK, Auswärtiges Amt, Akten betreffend Wiederaufnahme des Warenaustausches, Frieden II Wirtschaftliches, Baltenland Nr 4, Bd 1.

32. Rauch, *The Baltic states*, p. 62.

33. In general, K. Hovi, *Alliance de Revers. Stabilisation of France's alliance policies in East Central Europe 1919–1921*, Turku, 1984; *Cordon sanitaire or Barrière de l'Est? The emergence of the new French Eastern Europe alliance policy 1917–1919*, Turku, 1975, pp. 142ff.

34. P. Scheibert, 'Zur Intervention der Westmächte in Nordrussland', *Jomsburg*, 4, 1940, pp. 91–101.

35. Cf. L. Haupts, 'Zur deutschen und britischen Friedenspolitik in der Krise der Pariser Friedenskonferenz. Britisch–deutsche Separatverhandlungen im April/Mai 1919?', *Historische Zeitschrift*, 217, 1973, pp. 54–98, for the limits to such a strategy. See also U. Wengst, *Graf Brockdorff–Rantzau und die aussenpolitische Anfänge der Weimarer Republik*, Berne–Frankfurt a.M., 1973, p. 90.

36. In general, E. Matthias, *Die deutsche Sozialdemokratie und der Osten*, Cologne, 1954; E. Kolb, *Die Arbeiterräte in der deutschen Innenpolitik*, Düsseldorf, 1962.

37. Cited F. L. Carsten, *Reichswehr und Politik*, Cologne–Berlin, 1964, p. 21.

38. G. Noske, *Von Kiel bis Kapp*, Berlin, 1920, p. 178.

39. J. D. Gregory, *On the edge of diplomacy*, London, 1928, p. 187; A. Winnig, *Heimkehr*, Hamburg, 1935, p. 178.

40. Winnig, *Heimkehr*, pp. 14, 54, 58; *idem, Am Ausgang der deutschen Ostpolitik*, Berlin, 1921, p. 37. Text of treaty in *Heimkehr*, p. 88; undated letter of Winnig: PAB, Gesandtschaftsakten, betreffend des Beauftragten Mitau, 25 Geheim; for a Latvian viewpoint, see A. Blodnieks, *The undefeated nation*, New York 1960, pp. 152–3.

41. Cf. W. Elben, *Das Problem der Kontinuität in der deutschen Revolution*, Düsseldorf, 1965, p. 108.

42. Cf. H.-E. Volkmann, *Die russische Emigration in Deutschland 1919–1929*, Würzburg, 1966, pp. 61ff.

43. G. Rosenfeld, *Sowjetrussland und Deutschland 1917–1922*, E. Berlin, 1960, pp. 61ff. For a graphic account of the Freikorps mentality, see E. von Salomon, *Die Geächteten*, Gutersloh, 1930; J. Bischoff, *Die letzte Front. Geschichte der Eisernen Division im Baltikum 1919*, Berlin, 1935, p. 6: 'At no time did we recognize the November government.'

44. Ribhegge, *August Winnig*, pp. 129ff.

45. Cf. Carsten, *Reichswehr und Politik*, pp. 74ff.

46. BAK, Nachlass Reinhardt, Bdle 18 (HO 8/82 12–17): memorandum of 2.10.1917.

47. Cf. his letter from Mitau of 8.7.1919: PAB, Gesandtschaftsakten, betreffend des Beauftragten Mitau, 25 Geheim.

48. W. Duranty, *I write as I please*, London, 1935, p. 38.

49. Wipert von Blücher, *Deutschlands Weg nach Rapallo*, Wiesbaden, 1951, p. 49.

50. Rüdiger von der Goltz, *Meine Sendung in Finnland und im Baltikum*, Leipzig, 1920, pp. 134ff.

51. Cf. *ibid.*, pp. 173, 177–181; G. von Rauch, *Baltic countries*, pp. 60–1; Grundmann, *Deutschtumspolitik*, p. 102; H. Bosse, A. von Taube, *Baltische Köpfe*, Bovenden, 1953, pp. 148–9.

52. Goltz, *Meine Sendung*, p. 181; cf. his *Als politischer General im Osten*, Leipzig, 1936, p. 112; Baron von Manteuffel Katzdangen, *Deutschland und der Osten*, Munich, 1926, p. 10.

53. Film in Foreign Office Library, London: FO, Alte Reichskanzlei, Akten betreffend Kabinett Protokolle, vol. 1 (3438/D742105–7).

54. *Ibid.*

55. Ribhegge, *August Winnig*, p. 131.

56. FO, Alte Reichskanzlei, Akten betreffend Kabinett Protokolle, vol. 2, 8.5.1919 (3438/D742196–8).

57. *Ibid.*

58. H. G. Linke, *Deutsch–sowjetische Beziehungen bis Rapallo*, Cologne, 1970, p. 74.

59. Goltz, *Meine Sendung*, p. 190; Linke, *Deutsch–sowjetische Beziehungen*, p. 73.

60. Cf. Noske's statement to the Cabinet on 28.4.1919: FO, Alte Reichskanzlei, Akten betreffend Kabinett Protokolle, vol. 1 (3438/D742158); and vol. 2, 11.5.1919 (3438/742205–7).

61. Goltz, *Meine Sendung*, pp. 190–1.

62. Blücher, *Deutschlands Weg*, p. 74.

63. Goltz, *Meine Sendung*, pp. 190ff., 195; cf. the memorandum of Admiral Fremantle on the necessity for a policy towards the Baltic provinces, 11.3.1919: PRO, CAB 24/76.

64. Rauch, *Baltic states*, p. 62.

65. In general, Linke, *Deutsch–sowjetische Beziehungen*.

66. *Documents on British Foreign Policy (DBFP)* Series I, vol. 3, pp. 9ff.

67. H. de la Poer Gough, *Soldiering on*, London, 1954, p. 191; cf. Anderson, 'British policy', p. 191; cf. memoranda on Gough's, mission 20.8.1919, 3.9.1919: PRO, CAB 24/88.

68. Cited in Wrangell, *Ausschnitte*, p. 530.

69. Page, *The formation of the Baltic states*, p. 147. On the relative ignorance in Western government circles on what was going on in the Baltic, see S. Tallents, *Man and boy*, London, 1943, pp. 267, 313.

70. BAK, Nachlass von Schleicher, Akten betreffend Umdrucke des Grossen Generalstabes, Abteilung Fremde Heere und Fremde Heere Ost; cf. W. Lenz, 'Zur britischen Politik gegenüber den baltischen Deutschen 1918–1919', von Thadden, ed., *Das Vergangene und die Geschichte*, p. 276; Goltz, *Meine Sendung*, p. 207. For the idea that the Latvians were using the Allies to wage an anti-German policy, see J. von Hehn, 'Der Kampf gegen den Bolschewismus und der baltischen Ostfront', *Deutsches Archiv für Landes und Volksforschung*, 6, 1942, p. 699.

71. Cited G. Freund, *Unholy alliance. Russian–German relations from the Treaty of Brest–Litovsk to the Treaty of Berlin*, London, 1957, p. 40.

72. P. M. Awalov-Bermondt, *Im kampf gegen den Bolschewismus*, Hamburg, 1925, pp. 120, 124–5, 130–1, 164.

73. Groener's remark in FO, Alte Reichskanzlei, Akten betreffend Kabinett Protokolle, vol. 2 (3438/D742314–5); on the question of finance for September, vol. 3 (3438/D742984–5) and Goltz, *Meine Sendung*, pp. 227–8.

74. BAK, Depot Stülpnägel, Briefwechsel der Sp. Gen. d. Inf. Joachim von Stülpnägel in Kolberg und Hannover (H O 8 5/8); see also BAK, General oberst von Fritsch, Akten betreffend Baltikum-Kommission und General Kommando des VI. Reserve Korps, 1919–1920 (H O8–33/2).

75. Cf. *DBFP*, Series I, vol. 3, memo of 15.11.1919.

76. Goltz, *Meine Sendung*.

77. *DBFP*, Series I, vol. 3 pp. 225–6.

78. Cited Linke, *Deutsch–sowjetische Beziehungen*, p. 77. Cf. Müller's repeated stress in the Cabinet on the need to obey the Allied demands for evacuation; FO, Alte Reichskanzlei, Akten betreffend Kabinett Protokolle, vol. 3 (3438/D742829–30); and vol. 4 (3438/D743012–3).

79. *Ibid.*, vol. 4, (3438/D743123–4); cf. H. Niessel, *L'évacuation des Pays Baltiques par les Allemands*, Paris, 1935, p. 184.

80. *DBFP*, Series I, vol. 3, p. 173.

81. Report of 17.7.1919: PAB, Gesandtschaftsakten betreffend des Beauftragten Mitau, 25 Geheim, Packet Nr. 198.

82. FO, Auswärtiges Amt, Akten betreffend politische Beziehungen Estland zu Russland, Politik 3, vol. 1 (K249/K076313–4).

83. Anderson, 'British policy', pp. 285–6; J. von Hehn, *Die Entstehung der Staaten Lettland und Estland. Der Bolschewismus und die Grossmächte*, Berlin, 1956, p. 198.

84. Cf. G. Rutenberg, *Die baltischen Staaten und das Volkerrecht*, Riga, 1928, p. 73.

85. K. Pusta, 'Die Baltenstaaten im europäischen Staatenbund', *Baltisches Handbuch* (Danzig), 1930, p. 102.

86. Vaclovas Sidzikauskas, 'Our tradition of cooperation', *Baltic Review*, 1, 1953, p. 35.

87. Cited M. Watson Graham, *Diplomatic recognition*, p. 409. Cf. opening sections of K. Hovi, *Interessensphäre im Baltikum. Finnland im Rahmen der Ostpolitik Polens*, Helsinki, 1984.

88. Hinkkanen-Lievonen, *British trade and enterprise*, p. 75.

89. M. K. Dziewanowski, 'Pilsudski's federal policy 1919–1921', *Journal of Central European Affairs*, 10, 1950, pp. 118, 120; Sepols, *Za kulisami*, pp. 211–12.

90. *DBFP*, Series I, vol. 11, p. 211; cf. Lt-Col. Du Parquet, *Der Drang nach Osten. L'Aventure Allemande en Lettonie*, Paris, 1926, p. 278; R. Vanlande, *Avec le Général Niessel en Prusse et en Lithuanie*, Paris, 1922, pp. 174–5.

91. H. Rodgers, *Search for security. A study of Baltic diplomacy 1920–1934*, Hamden, Conn., 1975, pp. 16–17.

92. FO, Alte Reichskanzlei, Akten betreffend Kabinett Protokolle, vol. 5 (3438/D74351).
93. Goltz, *Meine Sendung*, p. 259; Carsten, *Reichswehr und Politik*, pp. 76–9.
94. Carsten, *Reichswehr und Politik*, p. 78.
95. *Akten der Reichskanzlei. Das Kabinett Müller I*, ed. M. Vogt, Boppard, 1971, meeting of 3.5.1920, No 77.
96. FO, Auswärtiges Amt, Akten betreffend Verhandlung mit Sowjetrussland (K281/K095854–5).
97. Aide-mémoire of the Auswärtiges Amt: FO, Auswärtiges Amt, Akten betreffend Verhandlungen mit Sowjetrussland (K281/K095960–2). On the likely effect of Soviet victory for the Baltic, see A. Dennis, *The foreign policy of Soviet Russia*, London, 1924, p. 115; A. Tarnowski, *Two Polish attempts to bring about a Central East European organization*, London, 1943, p. 4; *DBFP*, Series I, vol. 11, p. 375.
98. FO, Auswärtiges Amt, Akten betreffend Verhandlungen mit Sowjetrussland (K281/K095945–50).
99. *DBFP*, Series I, vol. 11, pp. 200–1, 211.
100. Note of 20.4.1920: FO, Auswärtiges Amt, Akten betreffend politische Beziehungen Deutschland zu Lettland, vol. 1; and memorandum of Blücher, 17.5.1920: Akten betreffend allgemeine auswärtige Politik (Reichsratsausschuss für auswärtige Angelegenheiten) Reichstag, vol. 1 (L1757/L512034–6).
101. BAK, Auswärtiges Amt, Akten betreffend Wiederaufnahme des Warenaustausches, Frieden II Wirtschaftliches, Baltenland Nr 4, vol. 3.
102. *Ibid.*
103. Meetings of 16, 17 and 20.4.1920: FO, Auswärtiges Amt, Akten betreffend politische Beziehungen Deutschland zu Lettland (K2330/K663471, K663472–82).
104. DZA, Büro des Reichspräsident, Akten betreffend Russland (708/2).
105. Cf. J. W. Hiden, 'The Baltic problem', in V. R. Berghahn and M. Kitchen, eds., *Germany in the age of total war*, London, 1981, pp. 154–5.

2 THE BALTIC GERMANS AS *AUSLANDSDEUTSCHE*

1. Köster to Auswärtiges Amt, 9.3.1923: DZA, Reichsministerium des Innern, Akten betreffend Nachrichten über politische Vorgänge. Lettland (16628).
2. Rauch, *Baltic states*, p. 87; Axel de Vries, *Das Deutschtum in Estland*, Taschenbuch des Grenz- und Auslandsdeutschtums, No. 21, Berlin, 1927, pp. 7–8.
3. Hehn, *Entstehung*, p. 21.
4. Cf. Wrangell, 'Auschnitte', pp. 531–2, citing comments of Estonian socialist Martna to British Foreign Office.

5. Hehn, *Entstehung*, p. 21; cf. W. Görlitz, *Die Nordostdeutschen. Füʰrungsschichten und ihre Umwandlungen seit dem Ersten Weltkrieg*, Hamburg, 1963; G. Bruns, *Gesammelte Schriften zur Minderheitenfrage*, Berlin, 1933, pp 253.

6. Hehn, *Entstehung*, p. 21.

7. Cf. E. Fromme, *Die Republik Estland und das Privateigentum*, Berlin, 1922, pp. 4ff., on the impact of the law on mortgage holders and creditors; Baron A. Heyking, *The main issues confronting the minorities of Latvia and Estonia*, London, 1922, pp. 36–7.

8. Stavenhagen, *Das Deutschtum in Lettland*, Taschenbuch des Grenz- und Auslandsdeutschtums, No. 20, Berlin, 1927, p. 4; cf. C. A. Macartney, *National states and national minorities*, London, 1934, p. 510.

9. J. von Hehn, 'Vom baltischen Deutschtum in den letzten 20 Jahren', *Deutsches Archiv für Landes- und Volksforschung*, 5, 1941, p. 219.

10. Schiemann's article is in W. Wachtsmuth, *Von deutscher Arbeit in Lettland*, Vol. 3, Cologne, 1953, pp. 5–9; cf. W. von Knorre, 'Vom Wirtschaftsleben des baltischen Deutschtums', in M. H. Boehm and H. Weiss, eds., *Wir Balten*, Salzburg–Munich, 1951, pp. 112–16.

11. See O. Boelitz, *Das Grenz- und Auslandsdeutschtum. Seine Geschichte und seine Bedeutung*, Munich–Berlin, 1926.

12. Letter of 2.2.1919: BAK, Reichskanzlei, Akten betreffend Baltische Staaten, Bd 1 (R4 31/47).

13. Cf. the speech of Baron Stackelberg-Kuerkull to the Estonian National Assembly on the first reading of the agrarian law, 26.6.1919: DZA, Auswärtiges Amt, Akten betreffend die Agrarreform in Estland und die aus derselben entstandenen Reklamationen, Bd 1 (66954).

14. M. Valters, *Baltengedanken und Baltenpolitik*, Paris, 1926, p. 256.

15. See also the Handbook of the Historical Section of the Foreign Office, No. 57 (*Courland, Livonia, Estonia*): PRO, FO, 373/10.

16. Memorandum of 6.6.1921: FO, Auswärtiges Amt, Akten betreffend politische Beziehungen der Randstaaten zu Deutschland, Politik 2 Baltikum (K1752/K429126–9).

17. Letter from 'Ostexport', 22.4.1920; cited Grundmann, *Deutschtumspolitik*, p. 245.

18. Von Maltzan to Wedding, 12.7.1923: FO, Auswärtiges Amt, Akten betreffend politische Beziehungen Estland zu Deutschland, vol. 1 (K246/K075748–9).

19. Memorandum of 6.6.1921: FO, Auswärtiges Amt, Akten betreffend politische Beziehungen der Randstaaten zu Deutschland, vol. 1 (K1752/K429126–9).

20. Wrangell to von Maltzan, 21.2.1920: PAB, Auswärtiges Amt, Akten betreffend Deutschtum im Ausland, Lettland, Bd 1 (Politik 25,Lettland).

21. Von Blücher to Wrangell, 21.12.1920: *ibid.* Cf. von Maltzan's scribbled note on a letter of the Deutsch–Russischer Verein of 13.5.1921: DZA,

Auswärtiges Amt, Akten betreffend Austauschgeschäfte Wirtschaftsabkommen, Estland, Bd 1 (66339).

22. W. von Rüdiger, *Aus dem letzten Kapitel deutsch–baltischer Geschichte in Lettland, 1919–1939*, Hanover–Wülfel, 1955, p. 35.

23. Wever report of 11.3.1921: FO, Auswärtiges Amt, Akten betreffend politische Beziehungen Deutschland zu Lettland, Politik 2 Lettland, vol. 2 (K2331/K663781–2).

24. Cited Grundmann, *Deutschtumspolitik*, p. 49.

25. J. W. Hiden, 'The Weimar Republic and the problem of the Auslandsdeutsche', *Journal of Contemporary History*, 12, 1977, p. 273.

26. J. von Hehn, *Die Umsiedlung der baltischen Deutschen. Das letzte Kapitel baltisch–deutscher Geschichte*, Marburg, 1982, p. 23.

27. Pamphlet of the 'Volkspende für die verbliebenen Auslandsdeutschen' in letter to the Reich Minister for Reconstruction, 8.12.1920: BAK, Reichsfinanzministerium, Akten betreffend die vereinigte Fürsorge für das Auslandsdeutschtum, Schaden 7 Generalia, Bd 1 (R2/Zg.29/1959/ 1013).

28. Heilbron to Reich Ministry of the Interior, 8.2.1922: BAK, Reichskanzlei, Akten betreffend Auslandsdeutschtum, Auswärtige Angelegenheiten, Bd 4 (R431/545).

29. Auswärtiges Amt to Bund der Auslandsdeutschen, 18.4.1922: *ibid.*

30. Memorandum on the different organizations, 4.10.1922: *ibid.*

31. Cf. N. Krekeler, *Revisionsanspruch und geheime Ostpolitik der Weimarer Republik. Die Subventionierung der deutschen Minderheit in Polen 1919–1933*, Stuttgart, 1973, pp. 13–20; Grundmann, *Deutschtumspolitik*, p. 136.

32. Hiden, 'Auslandsdeutsche problem', pp. 274–7; Grundmann, *Deutschtumspolitik*, 136.

33. Krekeler, *Revisionsanspruch*, p. 149; Z. A. Zeman, *Nazi propaganda*, London, 1964, p. 102.

34. Cited in K. Düwell, *Deutschlands auswärtige Kulturpolitik 1918–1932*, Cologne–Vienna, 1976, p. 79.

35. Cf. Hehn, *Umsiedlung*, p. 24.

36. 26.7.1920: BAK, Reichsfinanzministerium, Akten betreffend die Geschäftsberichte des Bundes der Auslandsdeutschen, Schaden 3b Generalia, Bd 1 (R2/Zg 29/1959/874).

37. Walter Dauch, 'Die Bedeutung der Auslandsdeutsche. Amtlicher Bericht über den Kongress der Auslandsdeutschen': BAK, Reichskanzlei, Akten betreffend Auslandsdeutschtum, Auswärtige Angelegenheiten, Bd 1 (R431/542).

38. Speech of Dr Walter Lessing: *ibid.*

39. Letter to Auswärtiges Amt of 19.12.1919: BAK, Reichsfinanzministerium, Akten betreffend Bund der Auslandsdeutschen und Andere, Schaden 3b Generalia, Bd 1 (R2/Zg 29/1959/870).

40. Letter from von Medem, 20.1.1920: BAK, Auswärtiges Amt, Akten betreffend Friedensverhandlungen. Allgemeines Material, Frieden II Wirtschaftliches, Baltenland Nr 1 (R4/31/49). For Bach's ideas, see his memorandum of 28.6.1920: DZA, Auswärtiges Amt, Akten betreffend Schadenersatz-Kommissions (64746/1).

41. Reichsbank letter, 19.2.1919: BAK, Answärtiges Amt, Akten betreffend Finanz, Bank- und Wirtschaftsfragen, Frieden II Wirtschaftliches, Baltenland Nr 9; cf. Burchard's authorization for Viktor von Stackelberg to provide care for refugees from the Baltic in Copenhagen, 12.12.1919: BAK, Auswärtiges Amt, Akten betreffend Friedensverhandlungen. Allgemeines Material. Frieden II Wirtschafltiches, Baltenland Nr 1.

42. Volkspende für die vertriebenen Auslandsdeutschen to Reich Minister of Reconstruction: BAK, Reichsfinanzministerium, Akten betreffend die vereinigte Fürsörge für das Auslandsdeutschtum, Schaden 7 Generalia, Bd 1 (R2/Zg 29/1959/1013); cf. Reich Minister of Reconstruction to the Deutsche Auslands Institut, 6.12.1920: BAK, Reichsfinanzministerium, Akten betreffend Schadensförderungen der Auslandsdeutschen, Generalia, Bd 2 (R2/Zg 29/1959/868).

43. Text in BAK, Reichsfinanzministerium, Akten betreffend Gründung einer Rückwandererfonds Kommission bei den Darlehnskassen, Schaden 7, Generalia, Bd 1 (R2/Zg 29/1959/1011).

44. Entstehung und Grundgedanken der Gesetzgebung über die Entschädigung der von Deutschen im Auslande erlittenen Kriegsschäden, 31.12.1920: BAK, Reichsfinanzministerium, Akten betreffend Schadensförderungen der Auslandsdeutschen, Generalia, Bd 2 (R2/Zg 29/1959/868).

45. Memorandum of December 1919 by Professor Walther Schücking: *ibid.* Bd 1 (R2/Zg 29/1959/867).

46. Reich Ministry of Reconstruction to Stresemann, 4.2.1920, and note of 3.8.1920 from Reich Ministry of Economics: *ibid.*

47. Note of 5.4.1921: BAK, Reichsfinanzministerium, Akten betreffend Gründung einer Rückwandererfonds kommission bei den Darlehnskassen, Schaden 7, Generalia, Bd 1 (R2/Zg 29/1959/1011).

48. Report dated 26.7.1926: BAK Reichsfinanzministerium, Akten betreffend die Geschäftsberichte des Bundes der Auslandsdeutschen, Schaden 3b, Generalia (R2/Zg 29/1959).

49. Account of the talk 11.2.1921: DZA, Auswärtiges Amt, Akten betreffend Schadenersatz-Kommissions (6474671).

50. Cf. 13.5.1921: DZA, Reichsjustizministerium, Akten betreffend Wirtschaftsabkommen mit dem Ausland, Lettland, 1921–6 (8096).

51. Henkel report, end of June 1920: FO, Auswärtiges Amt, Akten betreffend politische Beziehungen Estland zu Deutschland, vol. 1 (K2325/K663535–K663546).

52. For Hieckmann's view, see BAK, Auswärtiges Amt, Akten betreffend Reichseignen Güter in Lettland und Litauen, Entschädigung I, Frieden II, Wirtschaftliches, Baltenland Nr 4a.

53. Fischer to Auswärtiges Amt, 25.2.1920: ibid.

54. Behrendt letter, 4.5.1920: DZA, Reichsministerium des Innern, Akten betreffend Verhandlung mit Lettland und Estland 1920–1 (19323).

55. By 18.5.1925, between 800 and 900 claims involving German Balts had been processed and a total of 37 596 833 marks paid out. Report 17.7.1925: DZA, Auswärtiges Amt, Akten betreffend Schadenersatz-Kommissions, Handel Lettland II, Nr 3 (64746/1).

56. Reich Ministry for Reconstruction, 20.10.1920: BAK, Reichsfinanzministerium, Akten betreffend die Entschädigung von Deutschbalten auf Grund des Deutsch–Lettischen Abkommen, REK Generalia Nr 4, Bd 1 (R2/Zg 29/1959/675).

57. Meeting of departments in the Treasury, 10.1.1921: DZA, Auswärtiges Amt, Akten betreffend Schadenersatz-Kommissions (64746/1).

58. 'Das Vereinsleben. Mitteilungsblatt des Deutschen Schutzbundes', report of 1920 sent to the Auswärtiges Amt on 30.3.1921: BAK, Reichskanzlei, Akten betreffend Auslandsdeutschtum, Auswärtiges Angelegenheiten, Bd 3 (R431/545).

59. Memo of 17.5.1920: FO, Auswärtiges Amt, Akten betreffend Reichsratsausschuss für auswärtige Angelegenheiten, vol. 1 (L1757/512034–6).

60. Rüdiger, *Aus dem Letzten Kapital*, p. 35.

61. *The Baltic States. A survey of the political and economic structure and the foreign relations of Estonia, Latvia and Lithuania*, Royal Institute of International Affairs, London. 1938, pp. 33, 36.

62. Heyking, *Main issues*, p. 20.

63. R. Wittram, 'Die Schulautonomie in Lettland', *Zeitschrift für Ostforschung*, 1, 1952, pp. 259ff.; O. Bertling, 'Das Deutschtum im freien Lettland', *Baltisches Jahrbuch*, 1930, pp. 218–19. On Estonia, see H. Weiss, 'Das Volksgruppenrecht in Estland vor dem zweiten Weltkriege', *Zeitschrift für Ostforschung*, 1, 1952, pp. 253–5; F. Wertheimar, *Deutschland, die Minderheiten und der Völkerbund*, Berlin, 1926, pp. 97–8; K. Aun, *On the spirit of the Estonian minorities law*, Stockholm, 1950, pp. 240–1; C. Peterson, P. H. Ruth and H. Schwalm, eds. *Handwörterbuch des Grenz- und Auslandsdeutschtums*, vol. 2, Breslau, 1938, p. 152.

64. Bruns, *Gesammelte Schriften*, pp. 11–12; Heyking, *The main issues*, pp. 26–30; Wertheimar, *Deutschland, Minderheiten*, pp. 46, 142; Macartney, *National states*, pp. 261–3.

65. Wittram, 'Schulautonomie', p. 256.

66. For these points in order: J. von Hehn, *Die baltischen Lande. Geschichte und Schicksal der baltischen Deutschen*, Klozingen am Main, 1951, p. 22; Wittram, 'Wendepunkte der baltischen Geschichte. Gegebenheiten

und Betrachtungen', in *Wir Balten*, pp. 46–7; Rothfels, 'Perspectives', p. 137.

67. W. Wachtsmuth, *Wege, Umwege, Weggenossen*, Munich, 1954, p. 222.
68. Hehn, *Umsiedlung*, p. 25.
69. VDA letter of 1.10.1920 and meeting of 8.2.1921: both in DZA, Reichsministerium des Innern, Akten betreffend Unterstützung der Deutschbalten (Brüderhilfe), Bd 1, 1920–6 (5955); cf. tables in Grundmann, *Deutschtumspolitik*, p. 606.
70. DZA, Reichsministerium des Innern, Spezialbüro Koch, Nr 1 (13091).
71. Wachtsmuth, *Wege, Umwege*, p. 188. On VDA funds, see Wanner (Deutsche Auslandsinstitut) to Auswärtiges Amt, 8.11.1921: BAK, Reichskanzlei, Akten betreffend Baltische Staaten, Bd 4 (R431/50).
72. Cf. letter of Professor Dr R. Eucken in 1922 on his recent lecture tour of Latvia: 'It would be very important if the term spent at the Herder Institute in Riga could be counted as part of the period of study in Germany. This would be a considerable gain and would bring the German Balt still closer to the Reich German.' (BAK, Auswärtiges Amt, Akten betreffend Auslandsdeutschen, Auswärtige Angelegenheiten (R432/545)).
73. On the role of the Embassy, see Rüdiger, *Aus dem Letzten Kapitel*, p. 35. On the Reich German Association, see the Radowitz' circular of 10.5.1921 and that of Consul Wilhelm Litten: PAB, Gesandtschaftsakten, betreffend Reichsdeutsche Kolonie, Riga, Packet No. 39 (Gg.16).
74. Köster to Auswärtiges Amt: PAB, Auswärtiges Amt, Akten betreffend Deutschtum in Ausland, Lettland, (Politik 25, Lettland).
75. Grundmann, *Deutschtumspolitik*, pp. 150–1; Hehn, *Umsiedlung*, p. 26.
76. Cited Grundmann, *Deutschtumspolitik*, p. 201.
77. Wertheimar *Deutschland, Minderheiten*.
78. Walters, *Baltengedanke*, p. 259.
79. Wachtsmuth, *Von deutscher Arbeit*, vol. 3, pp. 42–4.
80. On the old route to politics in the Baltic provinces, see H. von Rimscha, 'Paul Schiemann als Minderheitenpolitiker', *Vierteljahrshefte für Zeitgeschichte*, 4, 1966, pp. 46–7.
81. Rothfels, 'Perspectives', pp. 122–3; de Vries, 'Das Deutschtum in Estland'; Hehn, *Vom baltischen Deutschtum*, p. 219.
82. Wittram, 'Wendepunkte'.
83. *Handwörterbuch*, vol. 2, p. 152. Cf. A. von Taube, 'Landespolitik', pp. 26–7; M. H. Boehm, 'Werner Haselblatt. Dem Andenken an diesen Kämpfer für das Recht der deutschen Minderheiten', *Jahrbuch des baltischen Deutschtums*, 1959, pp. 73–4. Cf. M. Garleff, *Deutschbaltische Politik zwischen den Weltkriegen*, Bonn, 1976, p. 15.
84. Wachtsmuth, *Von deutscher Arbeit*, vol. 3, pp. 37–8.
85. Rüdiger, *Aus dem letzten Kapitel*, p. 161; Wachtsmuth, *Von deutscher Arbeit*, pp. 42–4, 88.

86. Rüdiger, *Aus dem letzten Kapitel*, p. 5; H. von Rimscha, *Die Staatswerdung Lettlands und das baltische Deutschtum*, Riga, 1939, p. 162.
87. H. von Rimscha, 'Die Politik Paul Schiemanns während der Begründung der baltischen Staaten im Herbst 1918', *Zeitschrift für Ostforschung*, 5, 1956, pp. 68–9; also Rimscha's 'Paul Schiemann als Minderheitenpolitiker', *Vierteljahrshefte für Zeitgeschichte*, 4, 1966, p. 46; D. Unfug, 'The Baltic policy of Prince Max of Baden', *Journal of Central European Affairs*, 23, 1963, pp. 152–65.
88. E. von Rosenberg, *Für Deutschtum und Fortschritt in Lettland. Erinnerungen und Betrachtungen*, Riga, 1928, pp. 36, 65.
89. Rimscha, *Staatswerdung*, p. 162; Wachtsmuth, *Von deutscher Arbeit*, vol. 3, p. 83.
90. Wachtsmuth, *Von deutscher Arbeit*, vol. 3, p. 41; Rimscha, 'Paul Schiemann', p. 51.
91. Rauch, *Baltic states*, p. 77.
92. *Ibid.*, pp. 92–5. In general, Garleff, *Deutschbaltische Politik*.
93. Paul Schiemann, *Ein europäisches Problem. Unabhängige Betrachtungen zur Minderheitenfrage*, Vienna–Leipzig, 1937, p. 9; Salts, *Politische Parteien*, pp. 38–9.
94. *Handwörterbuch*, vol. 2, p. 162.
95. Schiemann's guidelines are cited in Rüdiger, *Aus dem letzten Kapitel*, pp. 22–3, and in Wachtsmuth, *Von deutscher Arbeit*, vol. 3, pp. 107ff.

3 THE SPRINGBOARD CONCEPT

1. *DBFP*, Series 1, vol. 3, p. 227.
2. D. Groener-Geyer, *General Groener. Soldat und Staatsmann*, Frankfurt, 1959, p. 288.
3. G. Stresemann, *Vermächtnis*, vol. 1, Berlin, 1932, p. 64.
4. H. Müller-Werth, *Friedrich Rosen. Aus einem diplomatischen Wanderleben*, Wiesbaden, 1959, p. 288.
5. For a discussion of the reforms, see Krüger, *Aussenpolitik*, pp. 27–8.
6. H.-J. Schröder, 'Zur politischen Bedeutung der deutschen Handelspolitik nach dem Ersten Weltkrieg', in G. Feldman *et al.*, eds., *Die deutsche Inflation. Eine Zwischenbilanz*, Berlin–New York, 1982, p. 236.
7. Krüger, *Aussenpolitik*, p. 125.
8. In general, Schröder, 'Zur politischen Bedeutung'.
9. Cf. J. Bariéty, 'Die französische Politik in der Ruhrkrise', in K. Schwabe, ed., *Die Ruhrkrise 1923*, Paderborn, 1985, pp. 11–27.
10. E. Anderson, 'The USSR trades with Latvia. The treaty of 1927', *American Slavic and East European Review*, 21, 1962, p. 296.
11. H. F. Crohn-Wolfgang, 'Die baltischen Randstaaten und ihre handelspolitische Bedeutung', in *Schmollers Jahrbuch*, 45: 1, Munich–Leipzig, 1921, p. 212.

12. H. F. Crohn-Wolfgang, 'Die Republik Lettland und ihre wirtschaftliche Zukunft', *Jahrbücher für Nationalökonomie und Statistik*, 1:118, 1922, p. 424.

13. Anderson, 'USSR trades', pp. 296–7.

14. Crohn-Wolfgang, 'Die Republik Lettland', p. 424.

15. Anderson, 'USSR trades ', p. 297.

16. Cf. A. Hesse, *Die Wirkungen des Friedens von Versailles auf die Wirtschaft des deutschen Ostens*, Jena, 1930.

17. See the report of B. Siew, dated 22.12.1922, 'Lettlands private Kreditanstaltung': DZA, Auswärtiges Amt, Akten betreffend Bank- und Sparkassenwesen in Lettland, Bd 1, 1920–1 (645162).

18. A. Blodnieks, *The undefeated nation*, New York, 1960, p. 183; A. McCullum Scott, *Beyond the Baltic*, London, 1925, pp. 146–7; Ilja Romas, *Die wirtschaftliche Struktur der baltischen Staaten und die Idee einer Zollunion*, Rytas, 1934, pp. 129–30; U. Kaur, *Wirtschaftsstruktur und Wirtschaftspolitik des Freistaates Estland 1918–1940*, Bonn, 1962, pp. 42–3; A. Bilmanis, *Latvijas Werdegang*, Leipzig, 1934, p. 62.

19. In general, see C. Zacchia, 'International trade and capital movements 1920–1970', in *Fontana Economic History of Europe*, vol. 5, No. 2, London, 1976, pp. 509ff.

20. D. Kirby, 'A great opportunity lost? Aspects of British commercial policy towards the Baltic states 1920–1924', *Journal of Baltic Studies*, 5:4, 1974, p. 363; H. Rolnik, *Die baltischen Staaten Litauen, Lettland und Estland und ihre Verfassungsrecht*, Leipzig, 1927, p. 26.

21. E. Anderson, 'British policy towards the Baltic states 1918–1920', *Journal of Central European Affairs*, 19, 1959, p. 288. On the relevance of the British fleet for British trade prospects, cf. PRO, Cab 23/20 (meeting of 31.2.1920) and Cab 8(19) (meeting of 1.11.1919). Cf. S. Tallents, *Man and boy*, London, 1943, pp. 373–6; Duranty, *I write as I please*, p. 39.

22. Duranty, *I write as I please*, p. 37; *DBFP*, Series 1, vol. 3, pp. 60–5; A. Grant-Watson, *An account of a mission to the Baltic states in 1919*, London, 1957, pp. 45–8.

23. Du Parquet, *Der Drang nach Osten*, pp. 129–31, 248.

24. *Ibid.*, p. 38. More generally on Anglo–French rivalry, see K. Hovi, *Alliance de Revers. Stabilization of France's alliance policies in East Central Europe 1919–1921*, Turku, 1984, p. 68.

25. Cf. O. Hovi, *The Baltic area in British policy 1918–1921*, vol. 1, Helsinki, 1980, p. 202.

26. BAK, Auswärtiges Amt, Akten betreffend Wiederaufnahme des Warenaustausches, Frieden II Wirtschaftliches, Baltenland Nr 4, Bd 2.

27. Erdmansdorff (Riga) to Auswärtiges Amt: BAK, Auswärtiges Amt, Akten betreffend Finanz, Bank- und Wirtschaftsfragen, Frieden II Wirtschaftliches, Baltenland Nr 9.

28. Henkel report, 28.6.1920: DZA, Auswärtiges Amt, Akten betreffend Handelsbeziehungen zwischen England und Estland, Handel 12, Bd 1 (66216).

29. Kirby, 'A great opportunity lost', p. 364; Hinkkanen-Lievonen, *British trade and enterprise*, pp. 116, 188.

30. See above, n. 26.

31. Report of 12.6.1919: BAK, Auswärtiges Amt, Akten betreffend Wiederaufnahme des Warenaustausches, Frieden II Wirtschaftliches, Baltenland Nr 4, Bd 2.

32. *Ibid.*

33. Report of 2.8.1919: *ibid.*

34. DZA, Auswärtiges Amt, Akten betreffend die Handelsverhältnisse mit den baltischen Provinzen (5124).

35. PAB, Gesandtschaftsakten, betreffend des Beauftragten Mitau, 25 Geheim, Packet Nr 198.

36. Schneemann to Auswärtiges Amt, 2.8.1919: see above, n. 33.

37. Kaur, *Wirtschaftsstruktur*, p. 139.

38. R. Brenneisen, *Lettland. Das Werden und Wesen einer neuen Volkswirtschaft*, Berlin, 1936, p. 64; Romas, *Wirtschaftliche Struktur*, p. 41.

39. Crohn-Wolfgang, *Lettlands Bedeutung*, p. 56.

40. Letter of 20.2.1919: BAK, Auswärtiges Amt, Akten betreffend Wiederaufnahme des Warenaustausches, Frieden II Wirtschaftliches, Baltenland Nr 4, Bd 1.

41. Feldmühle letter of 5.8.1919 and Meissner letter of 2.9.1919: both *ibid.*

42. See above, n. 26.

43. Hovi, *The Baltic area*, p. 202.

44. Cf. letters of 29.8.1919 and 11.9.1919 (Frankfurt am Main Chamber of Commerce): BAK, Auswärtiges Amt, Akten betreffend Finanz, Bank- und Wirtschaftsfragen, Baltenland Nr 9, Bd 1.

45. See O. Lehnich, *Währung und Wirtschaft in Polen, Litauen, Lettland und Estland*, Berlin, 1923, p. 222.

46. *Ibid.*, pp. 223, 251.

47. Crohn-Wolfgang, 'Baltische Randstaaten', p. 214.

48. Report of Vögl: BAK, Auswärtiges Amt, Akten betreffend Finanz, Bank- und Wirtschaftsfragen, Baltenland Nr 9.

49. *Ibid.*

50. Reichsbank to Auswärtiges Amt, 24.8.1919: *ibid.*

51. Reich Ministry of Economics to Auswärtiges Amt, 19.8.1919: *ibid.*

52. Darlehnskasse Ost (Berlin) to Tallinn branch, 25.10.1919: *ibid.*, Bd 2.

53. Report of Schneemann, 2.5.1921: DZA, Auswärtiges Amt, Akten betreffend Staatsfinanzen Lettlands im Allgemeinen (63895).

54. BAK, Reichsfinanzministerium, Akten betreffend internationale Steuerrecht. Verträge mit Lettland, Bd 1 (R2 Zg 1955ff 370).

55. Hinkkanen-Lievonen, *British trade and enterprise*, pp. 120ff.; L. Fischer, *The Soviets in world affairs*, New York, 1960, p. 251.

56. Cf. Siew, *Lettlands Volks- und Staatswirtschaft*, pp. 168, 169–80, on the situation after the signing of the Soviet–Latvian peace.

57. PRO, Cab 23/20, p. 68; *DBFP*, Series I, vol. 7, pp. 326–9.

58. *DBFP*, Series I, vol. 2, p. 748; vol. 7, pp. 326–9.

59. On Baltic–Soviet peace terms, see A. N. Tarulis, *Soviet policy towards the Baltic states 1918–1940*, Notre Dame Ind. 1959, pp. 56–7; R. von Freymann, 'Die lettländische–russische Friedensvertrag und seine Verwirklichung', *Rigasche Zeitschrift für Rechtswissenschaft*, 1:4, 1926/7.

60. Note in FO, Auswärtiges Amt, Akten betreffend Verhandlungen mit Sowjetrussland (Graf Mirbach) Ostschutz (K281/K095960–2).

61. Tarulis, *Soviet policy*, p. 56.

62. Henkel reports, 3 and 30.3.1920: FO, Auswärtiges Amt, Akten betreffend politische Beziehungen Estland zu Russland, vol. 1 (K249/K076223–9).

63. Henkel report of 3.3.1920: *ibid.*

64. *Ibid.*

65. H. F. Crohn-Wolfgang, *Lettlands Bedeutung für die östliche Frage*, Berlin–Leipzig, 1923; *idem*, 'Die Republik Lettland und ihre wirtschaftliche Zukunft', *Jahrbücher für Nationalökonomie und Statistik* (Jena), 1:108, 1922, pp. 420–31; *idem*, 'Die baltische Randstaaten und ihre handelspolitische Bedeutung', *Schmollers Jahrbuch* (Munich–Leipzig), 45.1, 1921, pp. 207–35.

66. Crohn-Wolfgang, *Lettlands Bedeutung*, p. 10.

67. Crohn-Wolfgang, 'Republik Lettland', p. 427.

68. For the drafts and note exchanges of 16 and 17.4.1920, see FO, Auswärtiges Amt, Akten betreffend politische Beziehungen Deutschland zu Lettland, vol. 1 (K2330/K663471–2, K663476–82).

69. FO, Auswärtiges Amt, Akten betreffend allgemeine auswärtige Politik (Reichsratsausschuss für auswärtige Angelegenheiten) Reichstag, vol. 1 (L1757/L512034–6).

70. Voluminous material on the Abwicklungsbehörde is in Potsdam (DZA). Cf the report of Swiejkowski on 12.11.1919 and the meeting in the German treasury on 15.11.1919: BAK, Auswärtiges Amt, Akten betreffend Reichseignen Güter in Lettland und Litauen, Entschädigung. Frieden II Wirtschaftliches, Baltenland Nr 4a, Bd 1. For a copy of the Treasury agreement, 15.1.1920 report: DZA, Reichsministerium des Innern, Akten betreffend Verhandlungen mit Lettland und Estland, Bd 1 (19323).

71. Simons' memorandum on the Latvian–German convention: DZA, Auswärtiges Amt, Akten betreffend Schadenersatz-Kommissions (64746/1).

72. M. Walters, *Lettland. Seine Entwicklung zum Staat und die baltischen Fragen*, Rome, 1923, p. 400.

73. O'Malley minute of 20.10.1920: PRO, FO, 371/5376, pp. 89ff.; *DBFP*, Series I, vol. 2, p. 230; cf. Crohn-Wolfgang, 'Baltische Randstaaten', pp. 15–16.

74. Cf. Hinkkanen-Lievonen, *British trade and enterprise*, pp. 153ff., 164, 167.

75. Meeting of 27.8.1920: DZA, Auswärtiges Amt, Akten betreffend Schadenersatz-Kommissions (647461/1); cf. Dr Frentzel to Auswärtiges Amt, 20.9.1920: ibid.

76. Meeting of 13.11.1920: *ibid.*

77. See comments of the Berlin representative of the Tallinn purchasing cooperative to the Auswärtiges Amt, 2.10.1920: DZA, Auswärtiges Amt, Akten betreffend Austauschgeschäfte Wirtschaftsabkommen, Bd 1 (66339); cf. Meierovics' discussion of English offers of aid with the German Foreign Minister, Simons, on 6.2.1921: FO, Auswärtiges Amt, Akten betreffend politische Beziehungen Deutschland zu Lettland, vol. 2 (K2331/ K663735–9).

78. The figures come from the meeting of 13.11.1920: see above, n. 76. Cf. Siew, *Lettlands Volks- und Staatswirtschaft*, pp. 122–3; Romas, *Wirtschaftliche Struktur*, pp. 167–8.

79. T. Pärming, *The collapse of liberal democracy and the rise of authoritarianism in Estonia*, London, 1975, p. 30; Grundmann, *Deutschtumspolitik*, pp. 695–6.

80. Report of 15.9.1920: FO, Auswärtiges Amt, Akten betreffend politische Beziehungen Deutschland zu Estland, vol. 1 (K2325/K661993); report of 'Waba Maa', 3.10.1925: DZA, Auswärtiges Amt, Akten betreffend Bank- und Sparkassenwesen in Estland, Finanzwesen 20, Estland, Bd 1 (65648).

81. Reichsbank directorate letter of 27.9.1919: BAK, Auswärtiges Amt, Akten betreffend Wiederaufnahme des Warenaustausches, Baltenland Nr 4.

82. Meeting of 2.12.1920: DZA, Auswärtiges Amt, Akten betreffend Schadenersatz-Kommissions (647461/1).

83. Meeting of 16.12.1920: *ibid.*

84. Lecture: *ibid.* Cf. DZA, Reichswirtschaftsministerium, Akten betreffend Russland, Polen, Estland, Finnland usw, Wirtschaftsabkommen, Bd 1 (8133). For Bach's memorandum, originally dated 28.6.1920, see *ibid.*

85. Cf. *Akten der Reichskanzlei. Die Kabinette Wirth I*, Boppard, 1973, pp. xxxv, 4, 12, 13; E. Laubach, *Die Politik der Kabinette Wirth 1921/22*, Lübeck–Hamburg, 1968, pp. 13ff.

86. G. Rosenfeld, *Sowjetrussland und Deutschland 1917–1922*, E. Berlin, 1960, p. 333.

87. Cf. Wever to Auswärtiges Amt, citing report of Simons' speech in the

Jaunakas Sinas: FO, Auswärtiges Amt, Akten betreffend politische Beziehungen Deutschland zu Lettland, vol. 2 (K2331/K663749–51); Henkel report of 31.1.1921, with resumé of Estonian press reaction: FO, Auswärtiges Amt, Akten betreffend politische Beziehungen Deutschland zu Estland, vol. 1 (K2325/K662023ff.).

88. Cf. Hinkkanen-Lievonen, *British trade and enterprise*, p. 136.

89. Crohn-Wolfgang, *Lettlands Bedeutung.*

90. Cf. Henkel to the firm of W. Klingelnberg & Sons: DZA, Auswärtiges Amt, Akten betreffend Austausgeschäfte, Wirtschaftsabkommen, Bd 1 (66339); Kaur, *Wirtschaftsstruktur*, pp. 124–5.

91. Wever letter, 1.4.1921: DZA, Auswärtiges Amt, Akten betreffend Staatsfinanzen Lettlands im Allgemeinen (63895).

92. Siew, *Lettlands Volks- und Staatswirtschaft*, pp. 45ff.

93. Memorandum: St. A, Akten des Oberpräsidiums von Ostpreussen, Akten betreffend Wirtschaftsnachrichten, Randstaaten (2087).

94. Radowitz to Berlin, 1.7.1921: FO, Auswärtiges Amt, Akten betreffend politische Beziehungen Deutschland zu Lettland (K2331/K663817–23).

95. Cf. Carsten, *Reichswehr*; H. Pogge von Strandmann, 'Grossindustrie und Rapallopolitik. Deutsch–sowjetische Handelsbeziehungen in der Weimarer Republik', *Historische Zeitschrift*, 222, 1976, pp. 265–341.

96. Cf. Laubach, *Politik der Kabinette Wirth*; Linke, *Deutsch–sowjetische Beziehungen.* pp. 110–11. On the historiography of Weimar–Soviet relations, see Hiden, *Germany and Europe 1919–1939*, pp. 86ff; K. Hildebrand, *Das Deutsche Reich und die Sowjetunion im internationalen System 1918–1932. Legitimät oder Revolution?*, Wiesbaden, 1977.

97. FO, Nachlass Brockdorff-Rantzau, Packet 9, No. 5 (9105H/H2236850–3).

98. Krüger, *Aussenpolitik*, pp. 122f.

99. Behrendt circular of 3.3.1921; BAK, Reichsfinanzministerium, Akten betreffend internationale Steuerrecht, Verträge mit Estland, Bd 1, (R2 Zg 1955ff.349).

100. Wever report, 1.4.1921: DZA, Auswärtiges Amt, Akten betreffend Staatsfinanzen Lettlands im Allgemeinen, Bd 1 (63895).

101. Meeting under Crohn-Wolfgang, 23.2.1921: DZA, Auswärtiges Amt, Akten betreffend Schadenersatz-Kommissions (64746/1).

102. Henkel's closing report: FO, Auswärtiges Amt, Akten betreffend politische Beziehungen Deutschland zu Estland, vol. 1 (K23225/K662066–73). Cf. O. W. Hentig, *Mein Leben. Eine Dienstreise*, Göttingen, 1962, p. 224; Graham, *Diplomatic recognition, Estonia*, p. 295.

103. Text in FO, Auswärtiges Amt, Akten betreffend politische Beziehungen Deutschland zu Estland, vol. 1 (K2325/K662036–41).

104. Cf. German Foreign Office letter of 27.4.1921: DZA, Auswärtiges Amt,

Akten betreffend Austauschgeschäfte Wirtschaftsabkommen, Estland, Bd 1 (66339); cf. Königsberg Chamber of Commerce to Henkel, 15.3.1921, and Deutsche Industrie- und Handelstag letter of 14.4.1921, both in BAK, Reichsfinanzministerium, Akten betreffend Kriegsschäden Deutschen in Estland, Bd 1 (R2/Zg 29/1959/742).

105. Crohn-Wolfgang, *Lettlands Bedeutung*, p. 40; memorandum of 11.11.1921; FO, Auswärtiges Amt, Akten betreffend politische Beziehungen der Randstaaten zu Deutschland (K1752/K429130–2). Kalŋiń's policy also doomed the Tilden-Smith venture.

106. Memorandum by Behrendt, 13.8.1921: DZA, Reichswirtschaftsministerium, Akten betreffend Wirtschaftsabkommen und Austauschangelegenheiten mit Lettland, Bd 2 (2403/3).

107. Crohn-Wolfgang, *Lettlands Bedeutung*, pp. 44–5.

108. Commission reports from Riga, 21 and 27.7.1921: DZA, Reichswirtschaftsministerium, Akten betreffend Wirtschaftsabkommen und Austauschangelegenheiten mit Lettland, Bd 2 (2403/3).

109. Behrendt memorandum: see above n. 106; cf. Crohn-Wolfgang, *Lettlands Bedeutung*, p. 5.

110. Note of 30.6.1920: DZA, Reichsministerium des Innern, Akten betreffend Verhandlungen mit Lettland und Estland 1920/1, Bd 1 (19323).

111. Kopp/von Maltzan conversation, 12.8.1920: FO, Auswärtiges Amt, Akten betreffend Verhandlung mit Sowjetrussland (K281/K095945–50).

112. F. Epstein, 'Zur Interpretation des Versailler Vertrages. Der von Polen 1919–1922 erhobene Reparationsanspruch', *Jahrbücher für Geschichte Osteuropas*, 5, 1957, pp. 315–35.

113. See above, n. 106.

114. Crohn-Wolfgang, 'Die baltische Randstaaten', p. 217.

115. Cf. Hinkkanen-Lievonen, *British trade and enterprise*, pp. 141ff.

4 THE POLITICS OF PROVISIONAL TRADE TREATIES

1. T. Schieder, 'Die Entstehungsgeschichte des Rapallo-vertrags', *Historische Zeitschrift*, 204:3, 1967, pp. 551ff.; H. Graml, 'Die Rapallo-Politik im Urteil der westdeutschen Forschung', *Vierteljahrshefte für Zeitgeschichte*, 18, 1970, pp. 366–91.

2. Ernst Laubach, *Die Politik der Kabinette Wirth 1921/1922*, Lübeck–Hamburg, 1968, pp. 110–11.

3. Cf. the discussion in J. W. Hiden, *Germany and Europe 1919–1939*, London, 1977, pp. 86ff.

4. Blücher, *Deutschlands Weg*, pp. 95–6.

5. J. W. Hiden, 'The Baltic Germans and German policy towards Latvia after 1918', *The Historical Journal*, 13:2, 1970, p. 305.

6. Cf. Wallroth to the Auswärtiges Amt on his interview in the Latvian press, 18.11.1921: FO, Auswärtiges Amt, Akten betreffend politische Beziehungen Deutschland zu Lettland, vol. 2 (K2331/K663864–5).

7. Blücher memorandum on talks with the Estonians, 11.11.1921: DZA, Auswärtiges Amt, Akten betreffend Wirtschaftsabkommen, Estland. Wünsche, Bd 1 (66301); von Maltzan to Wallroth, 11.11.1921, on talks with Woit: DZA, Auswärtiges Amt, Akten betreffend die Agrarreform in Lettland, Bd 2 (65797).

8. Cf. Lindenburg to Hentig on treasury talks, 1.11.1921: DZA, Reichsschatzministerium, Akten betreffend Estland, Bd 1 (7174).

9. Reichstreuhandelgesellschaft to Auswärtiges Amt, 16.12.1922: *ibid.*

10. Cf. report in BAK, Reichsfinanzministerium, Akten betreffend die Vereinigte Fürsorge für das Auslandsdeutschtum, Bd 1 (R2/Zg 29/1959/1013).

11. Wallroth to Auswärtiges Amt, 14.1.1922: FO, Auswärtiges Amt, Akten betreffend politische Beziehungen Deutschland zu Lettland, Bd 2 (K2331/K663875–8). On economic aspects, see Hilger, *Incompatible allies*, 166ff.

12. Rosenfeld, *Sowjetrussland und Deutschland*, pp. 361ff.

13. Laubach, *Politik der Kabinette Wirth*, p. 141.

14. Jules Laroche, *Au Quai d'Orsay avec Briand et Poincaré*, Paris, 1957, pp. 148–50. For Rathenau's remark, see Wirth, *Kabinette*, vol. 2, p. 676.

15. Cf. Chicherin's report to the Central Executive Committee on the subject of the invitation to the World Economic Conference: J. Degras, ed., *Documents on Soviet Foreign Policy*, vol. 1, London, 1951, pp. 289–92.

16. Cf. the pre-war situation: R. J. S. Hoffman, *Great Britain and the German trade rivalry 1875–1914*, New York, 1964, pp. 21ff., 80ff.

17. Hinkkanen-Lievonen, *British trade and enterprise*, p. 220.

18. *Ibid.*, p. 222.

19. *Ibid.*, p. 233; cf. Schröder, 'Zur politischen Bedeutung', p. 244.

20. Hinkkanen-Lievonen, *British trade and enterprise*, p. 223.

21. *The Baltic states*, pp. 130ff.

22. Wirth, *Kabinette*, vol. 1, p. 13.

23. Report of 19.1.1922: StA, Akten des (Königlichen) Ober-Präsidiums von Ostpreussen betreffend Wirtschaftsinstitut für Russland und die Randstaaten in Königsberg 1921–9 (2082(1)).

24. Hinkkanen-Lievonen, *British trade and enterprise*, p. 227.

25. *Ibid.*, p. 204. See also M.-L. Hinkkanen-Lievonen, 'Exploited by Britain? The problem of British financial presence in the Baltic states after the First World War', *Journal of Baltic Studies*, 14:4, 1983, pp. 331, 334.

26. Hinkkanen-Lievonen, *British trade and enterprise*, pp. 235–6.

27. *Ibid.*, p. 236.

28. *Ibid.*. p. 245.

29. *Ibid.*, p. 246.

30. *The Baltic states. A survey of the political and economic structure and the foreign relations of Estonia, Latvia and Lithuania*, Royal Institute of International Affairs, London, 1938, pp. 131, 134.

31. Report of 2.5.1921: DZA, Auswärtiges Amt, Akten betreffend Staatsfinanzen Lettlands im Allgemeinen, Bd 1 (63895).

32. Radowitz report of 1.7.1921: *ibid.*

33. Wallroth report of 20.1.1922: *ibid.*

34. *The Baltic states*, p. 141.

35. See above, n. 37.

36. Wallroth report of 21.4.1922: DZA, Auswärtiges Amt, Akten betreffend Bank- und Sparkassenwesen in Lettland, Bd 1 (64562).

37. Completed by December 1923, Siew's report was entitled 'Lettlands privat Kreditanstalten': see *ibid.*

38. Cf. *The Baltic states*, p. 140.

39. DZA, Auswärtiges Amt, Akten betreffend Bank- und Sparkassenswesen in Lettland, Bd 1 (64562). There are other reports in this file listing German-influenced banking institutions from 1921/1922.

40. Siew report (see above, no. 37), section 4. Cf. the efforts late in 1921 of the Memel Bank to open offices in Reval and Riga (Memel Bank to Hentig, 17.9.1921: PAB, Gesandtschaftsakten, betreffend Estland, wirtschaftlich, politisch (Geheim 2b, Packe 21. Reval).

41. Wallroth report of 8.2.1922: DZA, Auswärtiges Amt, Akten betreffend Bank- und Sparkassenswesen in Lettland, Bd 1 (64562).

42. Wallroth report of 15.5.1922: *ibid.*

43. Wever report of 20.6.1922: *ibid.*

44. Report of 1.11.1923: *ibid.*

45. *Ibid.*

46. Cf. Wallroth's further reports on German involvement of 14.3.1922 and 3.4.1922: *ibid.*

47. PAB, Gesandtschaftsakten, betreffend Estland, wirtschaftlich, politisch (Geheim 2b, packet 21. Reval).

48. Hinkkanen-Lievonen, *British trade and enterprise*, p. 279; for transit figures, see *Baltic states*, pp. 125ff.

49. Lehnich, *Währung und Wirtschaft*, p. 251.

50. See above, n. 12.

51. *Ibid.*

52. FO, Büro des Reichsministers, Akten betreffend Aufzeichnungen über die auswärtige Lage, vol. 1 (3177H/D686065–7).

53. Hentig to Auswärtiges Amt: FO, Auswärtiges Amt, Akten betreffend politische Beziehungen Deutschland zu Estland, vol. 1 (K2325/K662111–4).

54. H. I. Rodgers, *Search for security. A study in Baltic diplomacy 1920–1934*, Hamden, Conn., 1975, is a good example of this trend.

55. Cf. Dziewanowski, *Pilsudski's Federal policy*, pp. 284–5; Hovi, *Interessensphären*; C. J. Höltje, *Die Weimarer Republik und das Ostlocarno Problem*, Würzburg, 1958.

56. Cited in *La Lettonie en 1921*, published by the Ministre des Affaires Étrangères de Lettonie, Paris, 1922, pp. 23–4.

57. Viktor Bruns, *Politische Verträge. Eine Sammlung von Urkunden*, Bd 1, Berlin, 1936, p. 52; Siew, *Lettlands Volks- und Staatswirtschaft*, p. 207.

58. Hovi, *Interessensphären*.

59. In general, see Wandycz, *France and her eastern allies*, p. 215; Hovi, *Alliance de revers*.

60. Graham, *Diplomatic recognition, Estonia*, p. 289; G. von Rauch, 'Die baltischen Staaten und Sowjetrussland 1919–1939', *Europa Archiv*, 1954, p. 6862.

61. Müller (Berne) to Auswärtiges Amt, 27.10.1921: FO, Büro des Reichsministers, Akten betreffend Aufzeichnungen über die auswärtige Lage, vol. 1 (3177H/D685817).

62. Hovi, *Interessensphären*, pp. 145ff.; *DBFP*, Series I, vol. 11, p. 668; Rodgers, *Search for security*, p. 19.

63. Cf. the sensible comments of D. Kirby, 'A great opportunity lost? Aspects of British commercial policy towards the Baltic States 1920–1924', *Journal of Baltic Studies*, 4, 1974, pp. 364–5.

64. Laroche, *Quai d'Orsay*, pp. 148–50.

65. *Ibid.*

66. PRO, FO, 371/10376, p. 153; cf. Schröder, 'Zur politischen Bedeutung', p. 245.

67. Cf. Hinkkanen-Lievonen, *British trade and enterprise*, p. 272.

68. See Sweet, 'The Baltic in British diplomacy'.

69. Wallroth to Auswärtiges Amt, 10.5.1921: FO, Auswärtiges Amt, Akten betreffend Neutralisierung der Ostsee, vol. 1 (K154/K017299).

70. For general consideration of the problem, see I. Romas, *Die wirtschaftliche Struktur der baltischen Staaten und die Idee einer Zollunion*, Rytas, 1934.

71. Reich Finance Ministry note on the Auswärtiges Amt, memo of 10.1.1922: BAK, Reichsfinanzministerium, Akten betreffend die vereinigte Fürsorge für das Auslandsdeutschtum, Bd 1 (R2/Zg 29/1959/1013).

72. FO, Auswärtiges Amt, Akten betreffend allgemeine auswärtige Politik, Reichsratsausschuss für auswärtige Angelegenheiten, vol. 3 (L1757/L512303–5).

73. Memo for German–Estonian talks, 3.7.1922: DZA, Auswärtiges Amt, Akten betreffend Austauschgeschäfte Wirtschaftsabkommen, Bd 2 (65343).

74. Lehnich, *Währung und Wirtschaft*, p. 296.

75. See above, n. 73.

76. Müller report of 24.1.1922: FO, Auswärtiges Amt, Büro des Reichs-

228 *Notes to pages 111–19*

ministers, Akten betreffend Aufzeichnungen über die auswärtige Lage, vol. 1 (3177H/D68048).

77. Von Maltzan memo of 21.2.1922: FO, Auswärtiges Amt, Akten betreffend politische Beziehungen Deutschland zu Lettland, vol. 2 (K2331/K663884–7).
78. Hovi, *Interessensphären*, pp. 158–9.
79. *Ibid.*, pp. 162–3.
80. Cf. T. Polvinen, 'Zur Erforschung der jüngeren politischen Geschichte Finnlands', *Jahrbücher für Geschichte Osteuropas*, 13:2, 1965, pp. 231–46.
81. Text in Bruns, *Politische Verträge*, vol. 1. pp. 105–7; cf. K. Skirmunt, *Polens Aussenpolitik*, pp. 17ff.
82. Cf. Hovi, *Interessensphären*, p. 163; Rodgers, *Search for security*, p. 23.
83. Berndorf, 18.3.1922: FO, Auswärtiges Amt, Akten betreffend Aufzeichnungen über die auswärtige Lage, vol. 1 (3177H/D686179).
84. Report of interview in *Gazet Warszawska*: *ibid.*; Berndorf, 22.3.1922.
85. Rodgers, *Search for security*, pp. 21ff.
86. Hentig, 1.3.1922: DZA, Reichsschatzministerium, Akten betreffend Estland, Bd 1 (7174); 12.3.1922 and 13.3.1922: DZA, Auswärtiges Amt, Akten betreffend Austauschgeschäfte Wirtschaftsabkommen, Bd 2 (65343).
87. Hentig, 4.3.1922: DZA, Auswärtiges Amt, Akten betreffend Austauschgeschäfte Wirtschaftsabkommen, Bd 2 (65343).
88. Meierovics interview, *Gazeta Porarna*, Berndorf letter: see above, n. 84.
89. Crull's account, 16.3.1922: DZA, Auswärtiges Amt, Akten betreffend Handelsbeziehungen Deutschlands zu Estland (64091).
90. FO, Auswärtiges Amt, Akten betreffend politische Beziehungen Deutschland zu Estland, vol. 1 (K2325/K662143–7).
91. Text in BAK, Reichskanzlei, Akten betreffend baltische Staaten, Bd 4 (R4 31/50); cf. Lehnich, *Währung und Wirtschaft*, pp. 252–4.
92. Berndorf, 19.3.1922: FO, Auswärtiges Amt, Büro des Reichsministers, Akten betreffend Russland, vol. 4 (2860/D552400).
93. Text in Degras, *Documents on Soviet policy*, vol. 1, pp. 296–8; cf. von Maltzan circular seeking information on Russian aims from the German representatives in the border states: FO, Auswärtiges Amt, Akten betreffend politische Beziehungen zwischen den Randstaaten und Russland, vol. 1 (K1967/K510450).
94. Ibid.

5 RANDSTAATENPOLITIK

1. See Hiden, *Germany and Europe 1919–1939*, pp. 86ff.
2. Cf. Arnold Spekke, *A History of Latvia*, Stockholm, 1957, p. 361; E. Loennroth, 'The diplomacy of Osten Unden', in *The Diplomats*, p. 93; H. I. Rodgers, *Search for security*, pp. 26ff.

3. J. Korbel, *Poland between East and West*, Princeton, NJ, 1963, pp. 116–17.

4. Rabenau, *Seeckt*, vol. 2, p. 313; H. Helbig, *Die Träger der Rapallo-Politik*, Göttingen, 1958, p. 306.

5. Cf. T. Schieder, 'Die Entstehungsgeschichte des Rapallo-Vertrags', *Historische Zeitschrift*, 204:3, 1967, pp. 551ff., with G. Rosenfeld, *Sowjetrussland und Deutschland 1917–1922*, E. Berlin, 1960, pp. 260–2.

6. For a discussion which incorporates this argument in an overall re-interpretation of Weimar policy, see P. Krüger, *Die Aussenpolitik der Republik von Weimar*, Darmstadt, 1985, pp. 132ff.

7. H. Graml, 'Die Rapallo-Politik im Urteil der westdeutschen Forschung', *Vierteljahrshefte für Zeitgeschichte*, 18, 1970, pp. 366–91.

8. For an intelligent discussion of these, see J. Jacobson, 'Is there a new international history of the 1920s?', *American Historical Review*, 88, 1983, pp. 617–45.

9. K. Hildebrand, *Das Deutsche Reich und die Sowjetunion im internationalen System*, Wiesbaden, 1977, p. 38; cf. P. Krüger, 'Friedensicherung und deutsche Revisionspolitik. Die deutsche Aussenpolitik und die Verhandlungen über den Kellog-Pakt', *Vierteljahrshefte für Zeitgeschichte*, 22, 1974, p. 232.

10. FO, Auswärtiges Amt, Akten betreffend politische Beziehungen der Randstaaten zu Deutschland (K1752/K429137).

11. Wallroth to Auswärtiges Amt, 27.4.1922: *ibid.* (K429144).

12. Von Maltzan to Auswärtiges Amt, 27.4.1922: *ibid.* (K429148–9).

13. Auswärtiges Amt to Tallin, 28.4.1922: *ibid.* (K429143).

14. Cf. Tuomo Polvinen, 'Zur Erforschung', pp. 240–3.

15. Von Maltzan to Auswärtiges Amt, 28.4.1922: FO, Auswärtiges Amt, Akten betreffend politische Beziehungen der Randstaaten zu Deutschland (K1752/K429142).

16. Blücher to von Maltzan, 19.4.1922: *ibid.* (K429136).

17. Cited in A. Anderle, ed., *Rapallo und die friedliche Koexistenz*, E. Berlin, 1963, p. 93.

18. In general, H.-J. Schröder, 'Zur politischen Bedeutung', pp. 235–51.

19. Memo on the German treaty with Lithuania, May 1923: DZA, Büro des Reichspräsident, Akten betreffend das Baltikum, Litauen, 1919–1923 (713).

20. FO, Auswärtiges Amt, Akten betreffend Lettland (3015/K596311–2).

21. Von Maltzan's account dated 14.6.1922: *ibid.* For reports on Meierovics' visit to Paris, 21.6.1922, see Riga to Berlin: FO, Auswärtiges Amt, Akten betreffend politische Beziehungen zwischen den Randstaaten und Russland, vol. 1 (K1957/K510487–8).

22. See above, n. 20.

23. Von Maltzan's account (see above, n. 21).

24. Von Maltzan to Wallroth: FO, Auswärtiges Amt, Akten betreffend poli-

tische Beziehungen Deutschlands zu Lettland, vol. 2 (K2331/ K663940–2). For the announcement associating Latvia with the Franco–Polish military convention, see Benndorf (Warsaw) to Auswärtiges Amt, citing *Kurjer Warszawski* of 28.6.1922: FO, Büro des Reichsministers, Akten betreffend Aufzeichnungen uber die auswärtigen Lage (3177H/ D686423–4).

25. See Blücher's memo of 13.4.1922: DZA, Auswärtiges Amt, Akten betreffend Austauschgeschäfte Wirtschaftsabkommen, Bd 2 (65343); also Hentig to Auswärtiges Amt: *ibid.*

26. 4.7.1922: BAK, Auswärtiges Amt, Akten betreffend Kriegsschäden Deutschen in Estland, Bd 1 (R2/Zg 29/1959/742).

27. German note, 6.7.1922: FO, Auswärtiges Amt, Akten betreffend politische Beziehungen Deutschlands zu Estland, vol. 2 (K2325/ K662163–4).

28. German–Estonian meeting in Berlin, 28.9.1922: DZA, Reichsschatzministerium, Akten betreffend Estland (7174).

29. Blücher/Menning conversation, 12.9.1922, reported 13.9.1922: DZA, Auswärtiges Amt, Akten betreffend Austauschgeschäfte, Bd 2 (65343).

30. Von Maltzan memo of 4.10.1922: DZA, Reichsschatzministerium, Akten betreffend Estland (7174).

31. Guidelines for German–Estonian trade agreement, 3.10.1922: DZA Auswärtiges Amt, Akten betreffend Austauschgeschäfte, Bd 2 (65343).

32. *Ibid.*

33. Von Maltzan to Brockdorff-Rantzau, 9.12.1922: FO, Nachlass Brockdorff-Rantzau, Packet 14, No. 1 (9101H/H225089–91).

34. Von Maltzan to Brockdorff-Rantzau, 17.11.1922: *ibid.* (H225169).

35. Brockdorff-Rantzau to von Maltzan, 29.12.1922: *ibid.* (H225066–70); von Maltzan to Brockdorff-Rantzau, 15.12.1922: *ibid.* (H225085–8).

36. *Ibid.* (H225049–51).

37. Cf Bariéty, 'Die französische Politik', pp. 17ff.

38. FO, Nachlass Stresemann (7113H/H145064); cf. C. Höltje, *Die Weimarer Republik und das Ostlocarno Problem*, Würzburg, 1958; Krüger, *Aussenpolitik*, pp. 199ff.

39. In general, E. A. Plieg, *Das Memelland 1920–1939*, Würzburg, 1962.

40. *Ibid.* p. 26.

41. Von Maltzan to Brockdorff-Rantzau, 31.5.1923: FO, Nachlass Brockdorff-Rantzau, packet 14, No. 2, (9101H/H225582–6).

42. Crull to Hentig, 10.2.1923: DZA, Auswärtiges Amt, Akten betreffend Austauschgeschäfte (65343).

43. Hentig report of 22.2.1923: *ibid.*

44. Crull/Menning talk, 30.1.1923: *ibid.*

45. *Ibid.*

46. Crull to Reich Treasury, 28.2.1923, Hentig note to Estonian government, 7.4.1923: both in DZA, Reichsschatzministerium, Akten betreffend Estland, Bd 2 (7175).

47. Protocol ending the talks and details of meetings from 19.4.1923: DZA, Auswärtiges Amt, Akten betreffend Austauschgeschäfte (65343).

48. Hinkkanen-Lievonen, *British trade and enterprise*, pp. 282–3.

49. Account of negotiations on customs duties, 3.8.1923: DZA, Auswärtiges Amt, Akten betreffend Austauschgeschäfte, Bd 3 (64320).

50. Crull/Menning talk: *ibid.*, Bd. 2 (65343).

51. Crull report from Tallinn: *ibid.*, Bd. 3 (64320).

52. Report from Tallinn: *ibid.*

53. Wandycz, *France and her Eastern allies*, pp. 272–4.

54. Degras, *Documents on Soviet policy*, vol. 1, pp. 318–22; Brockdorff-Rantzau, 1.12.1922: FO, Büro des Reichsministers, Akten betreffend Russland, vol. 3 (2860/D552340).

55. Cf. *Conférence de Moscou pour limitation des armaments*. Édition du Commissariat des peuples aux affaires étrangères, Moscow, 1923, pp. 5–7; A. Barmine, *One who survived. Memoirs of a soviet diplomat*, London, 1938, p. 170.

56. Brockdorff-Rantzau to von Maltzan, 17.12.1922: FO, Nachlass Brockdorff-Rantzau, Packet 14, No. 1 (9101H/H225071–4); von Maltzan to Brockdorff-Rantzau, 23.12.1923: *ibid.* (H225047–8).

57. Cited Carsten, *Reichswehr*, p.155.

58. FO, Nachlass Brockdorff-Rantzau, Packet 14, No. 2 (9101H/H225265–6); cf. Post *Civil–Military fabric*, pp. 108ff.

59. Text in Albat, *Récueil des principaux traités*, pp. 77–9; V. Bruns, *Politische Verträge. Eine Sammlung von Urkunden*, vol. 1, Berlin, 1936, pp. 135–7.

60. Cf. von Rauch, 'Die baltische Staaten und Sowjetrussland', p. 6863.

61. Wandycz, *France and her Eastern allies*, p. 290.

62. Thermann memo, 7.12.1923: FO, Auswärtiges Amt, Akten betreffend Probleme (Randstaatenbund, einschliesslich Finnland und Polen), vol. 2 (K243/K071349–56); Köster's memo, 8.12.1923: *ibid.* (K071364–76); Olshausen's account, 8.12.1923: *ibid.* (K071380–7).

63. In general, Hovi, *Interessensphären*; Marti Turtola, 'The Baltic countries in the defence plans of Sweden and Finland 1923–1939', in *Proceedings of the Eighth Conference on Baltic Studies in Scandinavia*, Stockholm, 1985.

64. See Thermann's report: see above, n. 62.

65. cf. Krüger on von Maltzan's support for Schubert: *Aussenpolitik*, pp. 270–1.

66. Von Maltzan to Brockdorff-Rantzau, 24.5.1923: FO, Nachlass Brockdorff-Rantzau, Packet 14, No. 2 (9101H/H225587–91); W. O. Hentig, *Mein Leben. Eine Dienstreise*, Göttingen, 1965, p. 225.

67. Cited in B. Mann, *Die baltischen Länder in der deutschen Kriegszielpublizistik*, Tübingen, 1965, p. 127.

68. Grundmann, *Deutschtumspolitik*, pp. 258–64. Cf. FO, Nachlass Brockdorff-Rantzau, Packet 14, No. 2 (9101H/H225573–81).
69. Hentig letter of 12.12.1922: FO, Auswärtiges Amt, Akten betreffend politische Beziehungen Deutschland zu Estland, vol. 2 (K2325/ K662182–7).
70. Wallroth to Tallinn, 16.2.1923: *ibid.* (K662191–4).
71. Wallroth's assessment is dated 23.5.1923: FO, Auswärtiges Amt, Akten betreffend Beziehungen zwischen Lettland und Russland, vol. 2 (K253/K076955–62).
72. Hentig letter of 21.6.1922: FO, Auswärtiges Amt, Akten betreffend politische Beziehungen Estland zu Russland, vol. 1 (K249/K076365–6).
73. Rodgers, *Search for security*, p. 26.
74. For a rare exception, see Krüger, *Aussenpolitik*, p. 225.
75. Wallroth's account of talk with Meierovics, 9.9.1922: FO, Auswärtiges Amt, Akten betreffend politische Beziehungen Deutschland zu Lettland, vol. 3 (K2331/K663986).
76. Crohn-Wolfgang, *Lettlands Bedeutung*, p. 46.
77. This can be followed in Korbel, *Poland between East and West*, pp. 140–1; E. H. Carr, *The interregnum 1923–4*, London, 1969, pp. 226–7; see Wallroth to Rantzau, 7.11.1923: FO, Nachlass von Maltzan, Bdle 2, 10a (L794/L223078–83).
78. FO, Auswärtiges Amt, Akten betreffend Neutralisierung der Ostsee, vol. 1 (K154/K017379–97).
79. Blücher, *Deutschlands Weg*, p. 115.

6 THE POLITICS OF ARBITRATION: LOCARNO AND THE BALTIC

1. FO, Auswärtiges Amt, Akten betreffend Neutralisierung der Ostsee, vol. 1 (K154/K071379–97).
2. It is impossible to survey the Stresemann literature here. Important recent contributions to the discussion include Krüger, *Aussenpolitik*, pp. 207ff; M. J. Enssle, 'Stresemann's diplomacy. Fifty years after Locarno. Some recent perspectives', *Historical Journal*, 20, 1977, pp. 937–48; R. Grathwol, 'Stresemann revisited', *European Studies Review*, 7, 1977, pp. 341–52; M. Salewski, 'Zur deutschen Sicherheitspolitik in der Spätzeit der Weimarer Republik', *Vierteljahrshefte für Zeitgeschichte*, 22:2, 1974, pp. 121–47; for an East German perspective, W. Ruge, 'Die Aussenpolitik der Weimarer Republik und das Problem der europäischen Sicherheit 1925–32', *Geschichtswissenschaft*, 22:3, 1974, pp. 273–90.
3. For what this meant for France, see S. A. Schuker, *The end of French predominance in Europe. The financial crisis of 1924 and the adoption of the Dawes plan*, Chapel Hill, NC, 1976, pp. 179ff.; Jacobson, 'New international history', pp. 639ff.

4. M. Stürmer, *Koalition und Opposition in der Weimarer Republik 1924–1928*, Düsseldorf, 1967, pp. 248ff.

5. On Locarno, see J. Jacobson, *Locarno Diplomacy*, Princeton, NJ, 1972.

6. Wedding (Tallinn), 9.1.1924: FO, Büro von Staatsekretär von Schubert, Akten betreffend Russland–Polen–Randstaaten, vol. 1 (4556/E148460); Hoesch (Paris): *ibid.*(E148117).

7. Cf. Wandycz, *France and her Eastern allies*, pp. 271ff.; Bariéty, in K. Schwabe, ed., *Ruhrkrise*, pp. 24–5.

8. Wandycz, *France and her Eastern allies*, pp. 312ff.

9. Memo of 14.1.1924: FO, Auswärtiges Amt, Akten betreffend Probleme (Randstaatenbund), vol. 2 (K243/K071470–81); Laroche, *Quai d'Orsay*, pp. 185–6.

10. Brockdorff-Rantzau, 1.12.1924, on his talk with Chicherin: FO, Auswärtiges Amt, Akten betreffend Russland–Polen–Danzig, vol. 2 (4556/E148639–42).

11. Memo of 14.1.1924: FO, Auswärtiges Amt, Akten betreffend Probleme (Randstaatenbund).

12. Dittmar(Tallinn), 18.12.1924: FO, Auswärtiges Amt, Akten betreffend Sozialismus, Bolschewismus, Kommunism. Randstaaten, vol. 1 (K2171/K601588–924).

13. Wedding on Major Gooden's activities in Riga and Tallinn, 31.5.1924: FO, Auswärtiges Amt, Akten betreffend Militärangelegenheiten (Estland) (K250/K076543–4); on General Laidoner's visit to London, Wedding, 27.8.1924: DZA, Auswärtiges Amt, Akten betreffend Est. Anleihe usw, Bd 1 (64310).

14. Köster, 7.1.1925: FO, Auswärtiges Amt, Akten betreffend Russland–Polen–Danzig, vol. 2; Riesser/Meierovics talk, 28.6.1924: FO, Auswärtiges Amt, Akten betreffend politische Beziehungen zwischen England und die Randstaaten, vol. 1 (K2361/K668770–3). Cf. M. Howard on the relationship between Britain's 'continental commitment' and East Europe: *The continental commitment. The dilemma of British defence policy in the era of the two World Wars*, Harmondsworth, 1974, pp. 94, 133; cf. P. W. Schroeder, 'Munich and the British tradition', *Historical Journal*, 19:1, 1976, p. 239.

15. Riesser/Carr talk: FO, Auswärtiges Amt, Akten betreffend politische Beziehungen zwischen England und die Randstaaten(K2361/K668779–81).

16. *Ibid.*

17. Völker (Helsinki), 19.1.1925: FO, Büro des RAM, Akten betreffend Finnland, vol. 1 (3015/D594290): cf. in general, British Foreign Office memo on British policy towards the Baltic states, 19.11.1928: PRO, CAB 24/198.

18. Riesser, 28.6.1924, FO, Akten betreffend Beziehung England, Randstaaten, etc. (K2361/K668770–3).

19. Krüger, *Aussenpolitik*, pp. 281–2. 302–3.
20. Von Maltzan to Brockdorff-Rantzau, enclosing memo: FO, Auswärtiges Amt, Büro von Staatssekretär von Schubert, Akten betreffend Russland–Polen–Randstaaten, vol. 1 (4556/E148358).
21. See above, n. 15.
22. Köster, 19.1.1924: FO, Auswärtiges Amt, Akten betreffend Probleme, vol. 1 (K243/K071451–8); cf. Rauscher's report: *ibid.* (K071524–7);Anderle, *Friedliche Koexistenz*, pp. 84–5; on Zamoyski, see Wandycz, *France and her Eastern allies*, p. 315.
23. On Riga conference proposal, Köster, 15.1.1924: FO, Auswärtiges Amt, Akten betreffend Probleme (K071451–8).
24. Olshausen (Kovno), 12.1.1924: *ibid.* (K071418–20); 21.1.1924: *ibid.* (K071488).
25. A. E. Senn, *The great powers, Lithuania and the Vilna question 1920–1928*, Leiden, 1966, pp. 122–3.
26. Plieg, *Memelland*, p. 32.
27. A. Bregman, *La politique de la Pologne dans la Société des Nations*, Paris, 1932, p. 166.
28. On the Baldwin government's interest, Köster, 11.6.1925, FO, Auswärtiges Amt, Büro von Staatssekretär von Schubert, Akten betreffend politische Beziehungen zu den Randstaaten, vol. 1 (4561/E153708–10); cf. Chicherin/Rantzau talk. 12.1.1924: FO, Auswärtiges Amt, Büro von Staatssekretär von Schubert, Akten betreffend Russland–Polen–Danzig, vol. 2 (4556/E143645).
29. FO, Nachlass Brockdorff-Rantzau, Packet 14, No. 3 (9101H/H223739–45).
30. FO, Auswärtiges Amt, Akten betreffend politische Beziehungen Litauen zu Deutschland, Geheimakten, vol. 1 (K261/K081635).
31. Cf. W. Eichwede, in D. Geyer, ed., *Osteuropa Handbuch. Sowjetunion Aussenpolitik*, Cologne–Vienna, 1972, pp. 167ff.; cf. T. H. von Laue, 'Soviet diplomacy. G. V. Chicherin, People's Commissar for foreign affairs', in Craig and Gilbert, eds., *The diplomats*, pp. 234–81.
32. On the Tallinn coup, see Rauch, *Baltic states*, pp. 116–17; Rodgers, *Search for security*, p. 36. On Helsinki, see Tarulis, *Soviet policy*, p. 73.
33. Rodgers, *Search for security*, p. 36. This useful book is prone to oversimplifying the relationship between Germany and Russia.
34. *Ibid.*, p. 36.
35. 5.12.1924: FO, Auswärtiges Amt, Akten betreffend Sozialismus, Bolschewismus, Kommunism. Randstaaten, vol. 1 (K2171/K601617).
36. Rodgers, *Search for security*, p. 37.
37. Cf. Krüger, *Aussenpolitik*, pp. 269ff.
38. Rauscher, 17.1.1925: FO, Auswärtiges Amt, Akten betreffend Probleme (Randstaatenbund), vol. 4 (K243/K071781).

39. *Ibid.* (K071806–10).
40. FO, Büro des Reichsministers, Akten betreffend Estland (3015/D594776–7).
41. Wallroth memo, 17.4.1925: FO, Büro von Staatssekretär von Schubert, Akten betreffend Ostprobleme, vol. 4 (4456/E149832–3).
42. Schubert to Brockdorff-Rantzau: FO, Büro von Staatssekretär von Schubert, Akten betreffend Rückwirkungen der Garantiepaktverhandlungen auf die deutsch–russische Beziehungen(4562/E155072–3).
43. H. W. Gatske, 'Von Rapallo nach Berlin. Stresemann und die deutsche Russland-Politik', *Vierteljahrshefte für Zeitgeschichte*, 4:1, 1956, p. 8.
44. *Jaunakas Sinas*, of 7.2.1925; cf. BAK, Reichsfinanzministerium, Akten betreffend Kriegsschäden Deutschen in Estland, Bd. 1 (R2/Zg29/1959/742).
45. Cf. H. von Rimscha, 'Die Baltikumpolitik der Grossmächte', *Historische Zeitschrift*, 177, 1954, p. 284; cf. Köster, 28.3.1925: FO, Büro des Reichsministers, Akten betreffend Lettland, vol. 1 (3015/D596359); also Schubert to London and Paris, 6.4.1925: *ibid.* (D596370).
46. Riesser, 1.4.1925: FO, Auswärtiges Amt, Akten betreffend Probleme (Randstaatenbund), vol. 4 (K243/K072045–7).
47. FO, Büro von Staatssekretär von Schubert, Akten betreffend politische Beziehungen zu den Randstaaten, vol. 1 (4561/E153887–8).
48. *Ibid.*(E153689–93).
49. Cited in G. Freund, *The unholy alliance. Russian–German relations from the treaty of Brest–Litovsk to the treaty of Berlin*, London, 1957, p. 223.
50. 24.4.1925: FO, Auswärtiges Amt, Akten betreffend Probleme (Randstaatenbund), vol. 4(K243/K072089).
51. Stresemann to Köster, 2.5.1925: *ibid.*(K072090–3).
52. Copy of Stresemann letter and memo from Dirksen to Brockdorff-Rantzau: *ibid.*(K072089).
53. The memo is *ibid.*(K072191–3).
54. Cf. Rodgers, *Search for security*, pp. 44ff. Memo on Pusta: FO, Auswärtiges Amt, Akten betreffend politische Beziehungen Deutschland zu Estland, vol. 2 (K2325/K662338–9).
55. Account of talk of 23.6.1925: FO, Büro von Staatsekretär von Schubert, Akten betreffend politische Beziehungen zu den Randstaaten, vol. 1 (4561/E153741–3).
56. *Ibid.* (E153749–54).
57. FO, Auswärtiges Amt, Akten betreffend politische Beziehungen Deutschland zu Lettland, vol. 4 (K2331/K664204–5).
58. Hauschild, 20.7.1925: FO, Auswärtiges Amt, Akten betreffend Probleme (Randstaatenbund), vol. 5 (K243/K072292–3).
59. Cf. Köster, 17.8.1925: FO, Auswärtiges Amt, Akten betreffend Beziehungen zwischen Lettland und Russland, vol. 2 (K253/K077133);

also memo by von Schubert: FO, Büro von Staatssekretär von Schubert, Akten betreffend politische Beziehungen zu den Randstaaten, vol. 1 (4561/E153776).

60. Wandycz, *France and her Eastern allies*, pp. 353–4.
61. Wallroth note, 17.7.1925: FO, Auswärtiges Amt, Akten betreffend Probleme (Randstaatenbund), vol. 5 (K243/K072309–10).
62. Köster, 21.9.1925: *ibid.*(K072449–51); Hauschild, 25.8.1925: *ibid.* (K072348–9).
63. Cf. FO, Auswärtiges Amt, Akten betreffend Beziehungen zwischen Lettland und Russland, vol. 2 (K253/K077135–6).
64. Hiden, 'Baltic problem', p. 161.
65. Rodgers, *Search for security*, pp. 49ff.
66. Cf. Krüger, *Aussenpolitik*, pp. 384–6.
67. Cf. W. N. Medlicott, *British foreign policy since Versailles 1919–1963*, London, 1968, pp. 83–7; Cf. Memo on Russia and Locarno, 24.1.1928: PRO, CAB 24/192.
68. Auswärtiges Amt memo, 8.2.1926: FO, Büro von Staatssekretär von Schubert, Akten betreffend politische Beziehungen zu den Randstaaten, vol. 1 (4561/E153883–5); Stresemann memo: *Akten zur deutschen auswärtigen Politik*, Series B, vol. 2:1, pp. 177–9.
69. Köster, 6.2.1926: FO, Büro von Staatssekretär von Schubert, Akten betreffend politische Beziehungen zu den Randstaaten, vol. 1 (4561/E153890–1).
70. Rodgers, *Search for security*, pp. 48–9.
71. In general, Krüger, *Aussenpolitik*, pp. 335ff.; M. Walsdorff, *Westorientierung und Ostpolitik. Stresemanns Russlandpolitik in der Locarno-Ära*, Bremen, 1971.
72. Cf. Wandycz, *France and her Eastern allies*, p. 201.
73. Cited Korbel, *Poland*, p. 195. Cf. Schubert memo, 1.4.1926: FO, Büro von Staatssekretär von Schubert, Akten betreffend politische Beziehungen zu den Randstaaten, vol. 2 (4561/E153976–7).
74. Schubert/Krestinksy talk, 30.3.1926: FO, Büro von Staatssekretär von Schubert, Akten betreffend Rückwirkungen der Garantiepaktverhandlungen auf die deutsch–russische Beziehungen, vol. 7 (4562/E156735–9).
75. Von Schubert to Riga, *Akten zur deutschen auswärtigen Politik*, Series B, vol. 2:1, pp. 7651–2.
76. In general, G. Post Jr, *The civil–military fabric of Weimar foreign policy*, Princeton, NJ, 1973.
77. *Akten zur deutschen auswärtigen Politik*, Series B, vol. 2:1, pp. 424–7. On Estonia, Frank to Berlin, 8.5.1926: FO, Auswärtiges Amt, Akten betreffend politische Beziehungen zur Randstaaten und Russland, vol. 3 (976H/E686592–4).
78. 18.4.1926:FO, Büro von Staatssekretär von Schubert, Akten betreffend

Rückwirkungen der Garantiepakt verhandlungen auf die deutsch-russische Beziehungen, vol. 5 (4562/E156334–5).

79. 3.5.1926: FO, Auswärtiges Amt, Akten betreffend politische Beziehungen Deutschland zu Lettland, vol. 4 (K2331/K664223–6).

80. Rodgers, *Search for security*, p. 52.

81. *Ibid.*, p. 58.

82. Stresemann to Brockdorff-Rantzau: FO, Auswärtiges Amt, Akten betreffend Sicherheitspakt (Nord–Ost–Locarno, Ostsee Entente), vol. 1 (K244/K073052–3).

83. Cf. memo by von Schubert, 20.11.1925: FO, Büro von Staatssekretär von Schubert, Akten betreffend politische Beziehungen zu den Randstaaten, vol. 1 (4561/E153666–8).

84. *Ibid.*

85. *Akten zur deutschen auswärtigen Politik*, Series B, vol. 2:1, pp. 1–5.

86. On Wallroth's preferences, see his exchange with Gaus on 4.7.1926: FO, Büro von Staatssekretär von Schubert, Akten betreffend Deutsch–Litauische Beziehungen, vol. 1 (4560/E152182).

87. Wallroth memo, 20.1.1926: FO, Büro von Staatssekretär von Schubert, Akten betreffend politische Beziehungen zu den Randstaaten, vol. 1,(4561/E53864–8).

88. Rauch, *Baltic states*, pp. 117–18.

89. See above, n. 86.

90. Also mentioned in von Schubert/Gaus talk: see above, n. 86.

91. *Akten zur deutschen auswärtigen Politik*, Series B, 2:1, pp. 459–60.

92. Von Schubert/Brodowsky talk of 4.8.1926: FO, Büro von Staatssekretär von Schubert, Akten betreffend Deutsch–Litauische Beziehungen, vol. 1 (4560/E152227–8); and 7.8.1926: *ibid*, vol. 2 (E152288–300).

93. FO, Auswärtiges Amt, Akten betreffend Sicherheitspakt (Nord–Ost–Locarno, Ostsee Entente), vol. 2 (K244/K073052–3).

94. Cf. von Schubert/Krestinsky talk, 30.9.1926: *Akten zur deutschen auswärtigen Politik*, Series B, 2:2, pp. 288–9.

95. Von Schubert/Litvinov talk, 5.8.1926: FO, Büro von Staatssekretär von Schubert, Akten betreffend Deutsch–Litauisch Beziehungen, vol. 2 (45460/E152288–94). For text of the Soviet–Lithuanian treaty, see Bruns, *Politische Verträge*, pp. 204–5.

96. Von Schubert/Sidzikauskas talk, 30.9.1926: FO, Wallroth Handakten, betreffend Lettland (5265H/E319747–8).

97. Gaus/Sidzikauskas talk, 18.10.1926: FO, Auswärtiges Amt, Akten betreffend politische Beziehungen Litauen zu Deutschland, vol. 1 (K261/K081783–7).

98. Cf. Korbel, *Poland*, p. 176. Cf. the salutary remarks in C. Kimmich, 'The Weimar Republic and the German–Polish borders', In T. von

Gromada, ed., *Essays on Poland's Foreign Policy 1918–1939*, New York, 1970, pp. 37–8.

99. FO, Wallroth Handakten, betreffend Lettland (5265H/E319715–6).
100. Cf. Grundmann, *Deutschtumspolitik*, pp. 224ff.
101. See above, n. 86.
102. In general, H. von Rieckhoff, *German–Polish relations 1918–1933*, Baltimore–London, 1971. Cf. H. Lippelt, '"Politische Sanierung" – Zur deutschen Politik gegenüber Polen', *Vierteljahrshefte für Zeitgeschichte*, 19, 1971, p. 330; cf. Post, *Civil–military fabric*, pp. 38–9.
103. Seiler memo, 9.12.1925: FO, Büro von Staatssekretär von Schubert, Akten betreffend politische Beziehungen zu den Randstaaten, vol. 1 (4561/E153669–74).

7 TRADE, MINORITIES AND *OSTPOLITIK*

1. D. Abraham, *The collapse of the Weimar Republic. Political economy and crisis*, Princeton, NJ, 1981, p. 159.
2. M. Stürmer, 'Parliamentary government in Weimar Germany 1924–1928', in A. Nicholls and E. Matthias, eds., *German democracy and the triumph of Hitler. Essays in recent German history*, London, 1971, p. 67.
3. D. Gessner, 'The dilemma of German agriculture during the Weimar Republic', in R. Bessel and L. Feuchtwanger, eds., *Social change and political development in Weimar Germany*, London, 1981, p. 141.
4. Cf. Schröder, 'Zur politischen Bedeutung', pp. 247ff.
5. *Ibid.*, p. 248.
6. In general, D.Stegmann, 'Deutsche-Zoll und Handelspolitik, 1924/5–1929, unter besonderer Berücksichtigung agrarischer und industrieller Interessen', in H. Mommsen *et al.*, eds., *Industrielles System und politische Entwicklung in der Weimarer Republik*, Düsseldorf, 1974, pp. 499–513.
7. Cf. Wedding(Tallinn), 30.9.1924: DZA, Auswärtiges Amt, Akten betreffend die Agrarreform in Estland und die aus derselben entstandenen Reklamationen, Bd. 2 (64431).
8. Memo of June 1929: BAK, Reichskanzlei, Akten betreffend baltische Staaten, Bd. 4 (R4 31/50).
9. Wallroth to Lerchenfeld, 7.12.1925: DZA, Auswärtiges Amt, Akten betreffend Agrarreform in Estland, Bd. 4 (65001).
10. Rauch, *Baltic states*, pp. 87ff.
11. Cf. memo of July 1925 on Meierovics' visit to Berlin: FO, Büro von Staatssekretär von Schubert, Akten betreffend politische Beziehungen zu den Randstaaten, vol. 1 (4561/E153746–8).
12. Note of talk in Reich Finance Ministry: FO, Wallroth Handakten, betreffend Lettland (5265H/E319815–6).
13. Wallroth to Thermann, 1.8.1924: *ibid.* (E319808–12).

14. *Jaunakas Sinas*, No.30, cited FO, Auswärtiges Amt, Akten betreffend politische Beziehungen Deutschland zu Lettland, vol. 4 (K2331/ K664159–63).

15. Cf. Wallroth to Thermann, 1.8.1924: FO, Wallroth Handakten, betreffend Lettland (5265H/E319808–12).

16. See above, n. 11.

17. Von Schubert/Woit talk, 17.4.1925: FO, Büro von Staatssekretär von Schubert, Akten betreffend Ostprobleme (4556/E149832–4).

18. Cf. Hiden, 'The Baltic problem', p. 160.

19. FO, Wallroth Handakten, betreffend Lettland (5265H/E319799–801); cf. Küchler (German Foreign Office) to Robert Held, solicitor to Baron Carlos Lieven, 3.8.1926: DZA, Auswärtiges Amt, Akten betreffend Agrarreform Lettland, Bd. 5a (65081).

20. Von Schubert to Reichskanzlei, 26.8.1926: BAK, Reichskanzlei, Akten betreffend baltische Staaten, Bd. 4 (R4 31/50); Reich Finance Ministry talks, 5.1.1928: FO, Wallroth Handakten, betreffend Lettland (5265H/ E319670–1).

21. Riesser, 23.12.1925: FO, Büro von Staatssekretaär von Schubert, Akten betreffend politische Beziehungen zu den Randstaaten, vol. 1 (4561/ E13856).

22. Record of talks: BAK, Reichsfinanzministerium, Akten betreffend die vereinigte Fürsorge für das Auslandsdeutschtum, Bd. 1 (R2/Zg 29/1959/1013).

23. Köster to Wallroth, 29.6.1925: FO, Büro von Staatssekretär von Schubert, Akten betreffend politische Beziehungen zu den Randstaaten, vol. 1 (4561/ E153741–3).

24. Küchler to Reich Ministry of Finance, 19.2.1926: PAB, Handakten Ritter, Lettland, Bd. 1.

25. Köster to Wallroth, 10.2.1926: *ibid*.

26. 16.2.1926: BAK, Reichsfinanzministerium, Akten betreffend vereinigte Fürsorge, Bd. 1 (R2/Zg 29/1059/1013).

27. Text in Albat, *Récueil*, pp. 359–73.

28. 13.7.1926: FO, Wallroth Handakten, betreffend Lettland (5265H/ E319758–9).

29. Cf. the survey made in 1926 summarizing steps taken by the German government from 1920: DZA, Auswärtiges Amt, Akten betreffend Agrarreform Estland, Bd. 5 (65956).

30. Auswärtiges Amt memo of 30.4.1928, to the 'Association of Saxon industrialists in Dresden'(DZA, 66069).

31. Sittings of 24 and 26.6.1924: DZA, Auswärtiges Amt, Akten betreffend Austauschgeschäfte, Wirtschaftsabkommen, Bd. 5 (64320).

32. DZA, Auswärtiges Amt, Akten betreffend Agrarreform Estland, Bd. 3 (66372).

33. Crull to Wedding (Tallinn), 24.11.1924: *ibid.*
34. Grundmann, *Deutschtumspolitik*, p. 236.
35. Crull to Frank, 15.5.1925: DZA, Auswärtiges Amt, Akten betreffend Agrarreform Estland, Bd. 3 (66372).
36. Lerchenfeld to Dittmar, 20.2.1926: *ibid.*, vol. 5 (65956); Reich Ministry of Finance, 28.5.1926: BAK, Reichsfinanzministerium, Akten betreffend Kriegsschäden Deutschen in Estland, Bd. 1 (R2/Zg 29/1959/742).
37. *Ibid.*
38. Memo of 10.2.1928: FO, Wallroth Handakten, betreffend Estland.
39. Grundmann, *Deutschtumspolitik*, p. 238.
40. Auswärtiges Amt memo, 5.6.1928; BAK, Reichskanzlei, Akten betreffend Handelsverträge mit den baltischen Staaten, Bd. 1 (R431/1122).
41. 4.3.1929: DZA, Auswärtiges Amt, Akten betreffend Handelsverhältnis Deutschland zu Estland, Bd. 6 (64086).
42. Grundmann, *Deutschtumspolitik*, pp. 238ff.
43. B. Gernet, 'Lettlands auswärtige Handelsbeziehungen', in J. Bokalders, ed., *Lettlands ökonomist*, Riga, 1929, p. 108.
44. Walters, *Baltengedanken*, p. 426.
45. Cf. *The Baltic states*, pp. 125ff.
46. M.-L. Hinkkanen-Lievonen, manuscript on Britain as Germany's commercial rival in the Baltic states.
47. *Ibid.*
48. *The Baltic states*, p. 127; cf. the memo of 12.2.1924 on trade prospects and the problem of credit: PRO, CAB 24/165.
49. *DBFP*, Series Ia, vol. 5, 1973, p. 399.
50. Kirby, 'A great opportunity lost', p.365.
51. Gernet, 'Lettlands auswärtige Handelsbeziehungen', pp. 27ff.
52. Brenneisen, *Aussenhandelspolitik*, pp. 373, 380.
53. *Ibid.*,p. 381.
54. Cf. Bilmanis, *Latvijas Werdegang*.
55. Hinkkanen-Lievonen, *British trade and enterprise*, pp.274ff.
56. *Ibid.*, p. 282.
57. Gernet, 'Lettlands auswärtige Handelsbeziehungen', pp. 27–31.
58. *The Baltic states*, pp. 107–8.
59. Hinkkanen-Lievonen, *British trade and enterprise*, p. 282.
60. In general, Hovi, *Alliance de revers*.
61. Cf. Hinkkanen-Lievonen, *British trade and enterprise*, pp. 218ff.; see also memo on effects on British/Russian trade relations of the Anglo–Soviet dispute, 28.1.1927: PRO, CAB 24/184.
62. See the general literature on Stresemann, above, chapter 6.
63. Brenneisen, *Lettland*, p. 130.

64. Cf. tables in Hinkkanen-Lievonen, *British trade and enterprise*.
65. *The Baltic states*, pp. 126–7.
66. Brenneisen, *Lettland*, p. 130.
67. Cf. Romas, *Wirtschaftliche Struktur*, pp. 131ff.
68. Rauch, *Baltic states*, p. 124.
69. Siew, *Lettands Volks- und Staatswirtschaft*, pp. 264–5; Kaur, *Wirtschaftsstruktur und Wirtschaftspolitik des Freistaates Estland*, pp. 60ff.
70. Romas, *Wirtschaftliche Struktur*, p. 125.
71. Rauch, *Baltic states*, pp. 123–5.
72. *Ibid.*, p. 124.
73. *Ibid.*, p. 124; cf. Kirby, 'A great opportunity lost', p. 371.
74. Cf. the sensible comment of Hinkkanen-Lievonen, *British trade and enterprise*, pp. 263ff.
75. Bilmanis, *Latvijas Werdegang*, pp. 130–1; Gernet, 'Lettlands auswärtige Handelsbeziehungen', p. 25.
76. Brenneisen, *Aussenhandelspolitik*, p. 362; cf. Romas, *Wirtschaftliche Struktur*, pp. 134–9.
77. Brenneisen, *Aussenhandelspolitik*, p. 358.
78. Cf. Hinkkanen-Lievonen, *British trade and enterprise*, pp. 275–7.
79. Brenneisen, *Aussenhandelspolitik*, pp. 384–5.
80. Cf. Köster to Berlin, 4.11.1927: FO, Wallroth Handakten, Akten betreffend Lettland (5265H/E319679–84).
81. Cf. Hinkkanen-Lievonen, p. 133.
82. Rauch, *Baltic states*, p. 126.
83. W. Hubatsch, 'Die aussenpolitischen Beziehungen des deutschen Reiches zu Lettland und Estland', *Deutsche Studien*, 13, 1975, pp. 308–9.
84. Hinkkanen-Lievonen manuscript.
85. Cf. the negative view of Grundmann, *Deutschtumspolitik*, pp. 450ff.
86. Hehn, *Umsiedlung*, pp. 25–6; cf. Wachtsmuth, *Von deutscher Arbeit*, vol. I, p. 418.
87. Grundmann, *Deutschtumspolitik*, pp. 108–9.
88. Rüdiger, *Aus dem letzten Kapitel*, p. 35; Wachtsmuth, *Wege, Unwege*, pp. 229–33; cf. Hiden, 'Baltic Germans and German policy to Latvia', pp. 312–14.
89. Grundmann, *Deutschtumspolitik*, p. 109.
90. *Ibid*, pp. 109–13.
91. Wittram, 'Schulautonomie', p. 52.
92. Grundmann, *Deutschtumspolitik*, pp. 501ff.; cf. K. R. Küpffer, 'Über die Herdergesellschaft', *Jahrbuch des baltischen Deutschtums*, 1927, pp. 29–33.
93. In general, H. Weiss, 'Das Volksgruppenrecht in Estland vor dem zweiten Weltkrieg', *Zeitschrift für Ostforschung*, 1, 1952, pp. 254ff.
94. Wedding to Berlin, citing the *Postimes*: BAK, Reichskanzlei, Akten betreffend baltische Staaten, Bd 4 (R4 31/50).

95. De Vries, *Deutschtum in Estland*, pp. 11–13.

96. Grundmann, *Deutschtumspolitik*, p. 112.

97. *Ibid.*, pp. 521–22.

98. Köster to Berlin, 10.1.1925: PAB, Auswärtiges Amt, Akten betreffend Deutschtum in Ausland. Lettland 1, Politik, 25 Geheim; cf. Hiden, 'Baltic Germans', pp. 306–9.

99. Grundmann, *Deutschtumspolitik*, p. 528.

100. In general, Garleff, *Deutschbaltische Politik*.

101. Wallroth to Köster, 9.11.1927: FO, Handakten Wallroth, Akten betreffend Lettland (5265H/E369679–84); memo of 19.12.1927: *ibid.* (E319672–3).

102. Cf. Schiemann, 'Innenpolitische Jahresübersicht', pp. 24, 26; Brenneisen, *Lettland*, p. 56.

103. Kurt Baron von Maydell, 'Die Baltendeutschen vor ihrer Umsiedlung. Ein statistischer Rückblick', *Jomsburg*, 4, 1940, p. 79.

104. *Ibid.*, pp. 71–2.

105. Cf. conversation between Wallroth and Harry Koch, President of the German cultural council in Estonia, 30.5.1927: FO, Wallroth Handakten, Akten betreffend Estland (5265H/E319583–5).

106. Krekeler, *Revisionsanspruch*, p. 109.

107. *Ibid* pp.109ff.

108. Cf. Hiden, 'Auslandsdeutsche problem', pp. 285–6.

109. Maydell, 'Baltendeutschen', p. 87.

110. *Ibid.*, p. 86.

111. Grundmann, *Deutschtumspolitik*, pp. 726ff.

112. *Ibid.*, p. 698.

113. *Ibid.*, p. 727.

114. H.-E. Volkmann, 'Ökonomie und Machtpolitik. Lettland und Estland im politisch–ökonomischen Kalkül des Dritten Reiches, 1933–40', *Geschichte und Gesellschaft*, 2, 1976, pp. 471–500.

Bibliography

UNPUBLISHED PRIMARY SOURCES

BUNDESARCHIV, KOBLENZ

Reichskanzlei, Akten betreffend baltische Staaten (Estland, Livland, Lettland und Kurland) (R4 31/47–R4 31/50).
Akten betreffend Handelsverträge mit den baltischen Staaten (R 431/1122).
Akten betreffend Auslandsdeutschtum, Auswärtige Angelegenheiten (R 431/542–R 431/546).
Auswärtiges Amt, Akten betreffend Friedensverhandlungen. Allgemeines Material. Frieden II Wirtschaftliches, Baltenland Nr 1.
Akten betreffend Friedensverhandlungen. Vorbereitung des Verträges mit Kurland und Litauen (Lettland). Frieden II Wirtschaftliches, Baltenland Nr 2.
Akten betreffend Reichseignen Güter in Lettland und Litauen. Entschädigung. Frieden II Wirtschaftliches, Baltenland Nr 4a.
Akten betreffend Finanz, Bank- und Wirtschaftsfragen. Frieden II Wirtschaftliches, Baltenland Nr 9.
Akten betreffend Wiederaufnahme des Warenaustausches. Frieden II Wirtschaftliches, Baltenland Nr 4.
Reichsfinanzministerium, Akten betreffend internationale Steuerrecht. Verträge mit Estland (R2 Zg.1955 ff 349/50).
Akten betreffend Kriegsschäden Deutschen in Estland (R2/Zg 29/1959/867–869).
Akten betreffend die Geschäftsberichte des Bundes der Auslandsdeutschen (R2/Zg 29/1959/874).
Akten betreffend Bund der Auslandsdeutschen und Andere (R2/Zg 29/1959/850–872).
Akten betreffend die Vereinigte Fürsorge fur das Auslandsdeutschtum (R2/Zg 29/1959/1013).
Akten betreffend Gründung einer Rückwandererfonds Kommission bei den Darlehnskassen (R2 Zg 29/1959/1011).

Akten betreffend die Übersicht über die Lage des deutschen Eigentums im Auslande. Generalia (R2/Zg 29/1959/1039/40).

Akten betreffend die Zusammenfassung der gesamten Pflege der Grenz- und Auslandsdeutschtums (R2/Zg 29/1959/1059).

Akten betreffend die Entschädigung von Deutsch–Balten auf Grund des Deutsch–Lettischen Abkommen (R2/Zg 29/1959/675).

BUNDESARCHIV–MILITÄRARCHIV

Nachlass of Franz Joseph Isenburg–Birstein (H 08–82/12–17, Bd 12).

Nachlass of Generaloberst Werner Freiherr von Fritsch, Akten betreffend Baltikum-Kommission und General Kommando des VI. Reserve Korps, 1919–1920 (H 08–33/2).

Manuskript des Generalleutnant von Erberhardt, 'Meine Tätigkeit im Baltikum 1919' (H 08–33/3).

Korrespondenz mit Generalleutnant von Eberhardt (H 08–33/4).

Nachlass of Walter Reinhardt, Die Ereignisse im Osten–Baltikum, Polen und Oberschlesien, 1919–20 (H 08–86).

Nachlass of Kurt von Schleicher, Akten betreffend Umdrucke des Grossen Generalstabes, Abteilung Fremde Heere und Fremde Heere Ost. Monats- und Wochenberichte, Feindlagen usw.

Depot Stülpnägel, Briefwechsel der Sp. Gen. d. Inf. Joachim von Stülpnägel in Kolberg und Hannover (H 08–5/8).

DEUTSCHES ZENTRALARCHIV, POTSDAM

Auswärtiges Amt. Akten betreffend die Handelsverhältnisse mit den baltischen Provinzen, April 1918 – November 1919 (5134).

Akten betreffend Wünsche zum Zolltariff, Bd 1 (63842).

Akten betreffend Staatsfinanzen Lettlands im Allgemeinen, Bd 1 (63895).

Akten betreffend Handelsverhältnis Deutschlands zu Estland, Bd 1 (66142), Bd 2 (63967), Bd 3 (66325), Bd 4 (63968), Bd 5 (64169), Bd 6 (64086), Bd 7 (64032).

Akten betreffend Handelsbeziehungen Deutschlands zu Estland. Wirtschaftsabkommen-Schadenersatzforderungen, Bd 1 (64091)

Akten betreffend Handelsbeziehungen zwischen England und Estland, Bd 1 (66216).

Akten betreffend Handelsverhältnis Estlands zu Deutschland, Ein- Aus- und Durchfuhr (64021).

Akten betreffend Handelsbeziehungen Estland zu Deutschland, April 1920 – December 1933, Bd 1 (66028).

Akten betreffend finanzielle Beziehungen Estland zu Deutschland, Bd 1 (64164).

Akten betreffend Bank- und Sparkassenwesen in Estland. Finanzweswen 20 Estland, Bd 1 (65648).

Akten betreffend Est. Anleihe usw, Bd 1 (64310).

Akten betreffend Austauschgeschäfte Wirtschaftsabkommen. Estland, Bd 1(66339), Bd 2 (65343), Bd 3(64320), Bd 4(66074).

Akten betreffend Wirtschaftsabkommen. Estland, Wünsche, Bd 1 (66301).

Akten betreffend deutsche Zollbeschwerde gegen Estland, Bd 1 (65533).

Akten betreffend Umgestaltung des deutschen Zolltarifs in Estland, August 1927, Bd 1 (65379).

Akten betreffend Wünsche zum Zolltarif. Estland, Bd 1 (67299).

Akten betreffend Steuerbeziehungen Estland zu Deutschland, Bd 1 (68532).

Akten betreffend Beschwerden und Forderungen, Entschädigungs Ansprüche aus Deutschland gegen Estland, Bd 1 (66950).

Akten betreffend deutsche Zolltarifwünschen gegen Lettland, Bd 1 (64120).

Akten betreffend Zollbeziehungen zwischen Estland und Lettland, 1921–7 (65574).

Akten betreffend Bescherwerden und Forderungen, Entschädigungs Ansprüche aus Deutschland gegen Lettland (65974).

Akten betreffend Steuerbeziehungen Lettlands zu Deutschland, Bd 1 (66211).

Akten betreffend Anfragen über Zolltarife, Bd 1 (67299).

Akten betreffend Vertretung deutscher Firmen in Estland, Bd 1 (66220).

Akten betreffend Schadenersatz-Kommissions (64746/1).

Akten betreffend die Agrarreform in Lettland und die aus derselben entstandenen Reklamationen, Bd 1 (65781), Bd 2 (65787), Bd 3 (65080), Bd 4 (65125), Bd 5 (64099), Bd 5a (65081).

Akten betreffend die Agrarreform in Estland und die aus derselben entstandenen Reklamationen, Bd 1 (66954), Bd 2 (64431), Bd 3 (66372), Bd 4 (65001), Bd 5 (65956), Bd 6 (66955).

Akten betreffend deutsche Darlehne und die anlässlich der estnischen Agrarreform enteigneten deutschen Grossgrundbesitzer, Bd 1 (67145).

Büro des Reichspräsident, Akten betreffend das Baltikum. Litauen 1919–23 (713).

Akten betreffend Russland (708/2).

Reichsarbeitsministerium, Akten betreffend Auswanderung nach Kurland, Finland, Bd 1 (738).

Reichsjustizministerium, Akten betreffend Wirtschaftsabkommen mit dem Ausland. Estland, 1923–34 (8094).

Akten betreffend Wirtschaftsabkommen mit dem Ausland. Lettland, 1921–6 (8096).

Reichsministerium des Innern, Akten betreffend Unterstützung der Deutschbalten (Bruderhilfe), Bd 1, 1920–6 (5955).

Akten betreffend Verhandlungen mit Lettland und Estland 1920/1921, Bd 1 (19323).

Akten betreffend Auswanderung nach Lettland (1804).

Akten betreffend Auswanderung nach Estland (1766).

Akten betreffend politische Lage in den Ostseerandstaaten, 1920–5 (13379).

Akten betreffend Nachrichten über politische Vorgänge. Estland (16617). Spezialbüro Koch, Nr 1 (13091).

Reichsschatzministerium, Akten betreffend Estland, Bd 1 (7174), Bd 2 (7175).

Akten betreffend Lettland, Bd 1 (7182).

Reichswirtschaftsministerium, Akten betreffend Wirtschaftsabkommen und Austauschangelegenheiten mit Lettland, Bd 1 (2403/2), Bd 2 (2403/3).

Akten betreffend Beziehungen mit Litauen, Lettland (5173).

Akten betreffend Estland und Lettland (3948).

Akten betreffend finanzielle Beziehungen zu Estland (19568).

Akten betreffend Wirtschaftsabkommen mit Estland, Bd 1 & 2 (8091).

Akten betreffend Wirtschaftsabkommen mit Lettland (8099).

Reichswirtschaftsministerium, Akten betreffend Russland, Polen, Estland, Finnland usw. Wirtschaftsabkommen, Bd 1 (8133).

POLITISCHES ARCHIV DES AUSWÄRTIGEN AMTES, BONN

Auswärtiges Amt, Akten betreffend zwischenstaatliche Probleme. Interalliierte Baltikum-Kommission, Bd 3, Politik 4, Baltikum.

Akten betreffend Deutschtum im Ausland. Lettland, Bd 1 (Politik 25, Lettland).

Akten betreffend rechtliche Beziehungen Lettlands zu Deutschland (Rechtswesen 6, Lettland).

Akten betreffend Ausweisung von Deutschen zu den Randstaaten, Bd 1 (V.W.12).

Gesandtschaftsakten, betreffend des Beauftragten Mitau. Geheimakten der deutschen Gesandtschaft (Geheim 25, Riga, Packet Nr 198)

betreffend Reichsdeutsche Kolonie, 1920–41 (Gg.16, Packet 39).

betreffend Reichsdeutsche Verein Riga 1924–37 (Gg.16–1, Packet 39).

betreffend Deutscher Wohltätigkeitsverein, Bund der Reichsdeutschen, Verband der Reichsdeutschen in Estland (n.18.e Reval, Packet 75).

betreffend deutsch–russische Randstaaten 1923–36 (Wi 52.245, Riga).

betreffend Beihilfen für reichsdeutsche Schule (Geheim 16–2, Packet 195).

betreffend Estland, wirtschaftlich, politisch, 1919–22 (Geheim 2b, Reval, Packet 21).

betreffend Handelsbeziehungen Deutschland–Lettland (H.1. Riga, Packet 111).

Handakten Hauschildt. Randstaaten, Polen, Finnland (a.11.3).
Handakten Ritter, Estland, Bd 1, and Lettland, Bd 1 and 2 (Ha.Pol.Min.
Dir. Ritter).

STAATLICHES ARCHIVLAGER, GÖTTINGEN

Akten des (Königlichen) Ober-präsidiums von Ostpreussen betreffend Wirtschaftsinstitut für Russland und die Randstaaten in Königsberg 1921–9
(2082 (1)).
betreffend Handelsverbindungen mit Russland (2084 (3)).
betreffend Wirtschaftsnachrichten, Randstaaten (2087).
betreffend Heimatschutz, 1919–27 (4294 (2)).

FOREIGN OFFICE LIBRARY, LONDON

Auswärtiges Amt, Akten betreffend allgemeine auswärtige Politik und
deutsche Aussenpolitik, vols.1 and 2 (L756/L224502–566).
Akten betreffend allgemeine auswärtige Politik (Reichsratsausschuss für
auswärtige Angelegenheiten) Reichstag, vols.1–4 (L1757/L512005–481).
Akten betreffend politische Beziehungen Deutschland zu Lettland, Politik
2 Lettland, vol. 1 (K2330/K663458–668), vols. 2–4 (K2331/663689–4393).
Akten betreffend politische Beziehungen Deutschland zu Estland, vols. 1
and 2 (K2325/K661972–2541).
Akten betreffend politische Beziehungen der Randstaaten zu Deutschland,
Politik 2 Baltikum (K1752/K429125–181).
Akten betreffend politische Beziehungen Estland zu Deutschland, Politik 2
Geheim, vol. 1 (K246/K075747–753).
Akten betreffend politische Beziehungen Litauen zu Deutschland (K261/
K081586–802).
Akten betreffend Verhandlungen mit Sowjetrussland (Graf Mirbach) Ost-
schutz, vol. 1 (K281/K095838–6121).
Akten betreffend politische Beziehungen zwischen den Randstaaten und
Russland, vols. 1 and 2 (K1967/K510427–663).
Akten betreffend politische Beziehungen Finnland zu Lettland, Politik 3
Finnland/Lettland, vol. 1 (L280/L086398–441).
Akten betreffend politische Beziehungen Estland zu England, Politik 3
(K247/K075755–868).
Akten betreffend Beziehungen zwischen Lettland und Russland, Politik 3,
vol. 1 (K1969/K510723–67), vol. 2 (K253/K076891–7196).
Akten betreffend politische Beziehungen Estland zu Russland, Politik 3,
vol. 1 (K249/K076159–525), vol. 3 (K1968/K510661–722).
Akten betreffend politische Beziehungen Estland zu Polen. Randstaaten,
Estland, Politik 3, vol. 1 (K248/K075869–6158).

Akten betreffend das Ostseeproblem, Politik 4 Ostsee (L798/L235027–039).

Akten betreffend Neutralisierung der Ostsee. Allgemein, Politik 4, vol. 1 (K154/K017257–591).

Akten betreffend Sicherheitspact (Nord–Ost–Locarno, Ostsee Entente), Politik 4, vols. 1 and 2 (K244/K072486–3132).

Akten betreffend Probleme (Randstaatenbund einschliesslich Finnland und Polen), vols. 2–5 (K243/K071316–485).

Akten betreffend Agenten und Spionagewesen. Randstaaten, Estland, Politik 15 Geheim (K252/K076772–890).

Akten betreffend Agenten und Spionagewesen. Randstaaten, Lettland, Politik 15 Geheim, vol. 1 (K255/K077210–529).

Akten betreffend Sozialismus, Bolschewismus, Kommunism. Randstaaten, Politik 19 Geheim vol 1 (K2171/K601588–924).

Akten betreffend Forderung des Deutschtums in den Randstaaten. Randstaaten Allgemein, Politik 25 Geheim (K245/K075395–745).

Büro des Reichsministers, Akten betreffend Russland (9), vols. 1–13 (2860/D551563–5649).

Akten betreffend Lettland (72), vol. 1 (3015/D596310–540).

Akten betreffend Estland (86) (3015/D594748–947).

Akten betreffend Auslandsdeutsche (3177H/D684410–615).

Akten betreffend Aufzeichnungen über die auswärtige Lage, vols. 1 and 2 (3177H/D685759–788).

Büro von Staatssekretär von Schubert, Akten betreffend Russland–Polen–Randstaaten, vol. 1 (4556/E148046–442).

Akten betreffend Russland–Polen–Danzig, vol. 2 (4556/E148443–E1488612).

Akten betreffend Rückwirkungen der Garantiepaktverhandlungen auf die deutsch–russische Beziehungen, vols. 1–7 (4562/E154825–6748).

Akten betreffend Russland, vol. 3 (4556/E148863–9222).

Akten betreffend Ostprobleme, vols. 4–6 (4556/E149223–50031).

Akten betreffend politische Beziehungen zu den Randstaaten, vol. 1 (4561/E153665–900).

Akten betreffend Randstaaten, insbesondere Garantiepaktverhandlungen der Randstaaten mit Russland, vol. 2 (4561/E153901–4164).

Nachlass Ulrich Graf von Brockdorff-Rantzau, Packet 9, Nos.2–5 (9105/H236261–7045), Packet 14 (9101H/H224802–6027), Packet 15, No.1 (9101/H226183–772).

Nachlass Gustav Stresemann, Allgemeine Akten (7161H/H153872–5015).

Handakten Erich Wallroth, betreffend Estland (5265H/E319527–665).

betreffend Lettland (5265H/E319666–828).

betreffend Paktfragen (5265H/E319439–526).

PUBLIC RECORD OFFICE, LONDON

Cabinet Office: Cab 23 Cabinet Minutes.
Cab 24 Cabinet Memoranda.

PUBLISHED PRIMARY SOURCES

Akten der Reichskanzlei, Weimarer Republik, 1968–82.
Akten zur deutschen auswärtigen Politik 1918–1945, Series A: 1918–1925, vols. I and 2, Göttingen, 1982–4.
Series B: 1925–1933, vols. 1–21, Göttingen, 1966–83.
Albat, G., *Récueil des principaux traités conclus par la Lettonie avec les pays étrangères, 1918–1928,* Riga, 1928.
Berber, F., *Das Diktat von Versailles. Eine Darstellung in Dokumenten,* Berlin, 1939.
Bilmanis, A., *Latvian–Russian relations,* Washington DC, 1944.
Bruns, V., *Politische Verträge. Eine Sammlung von Urkunden,* Berlin, 1936.
Commisariat des Peuples aux Affaires Étrangères, *Conférence de Moscou pour limitation des armaments,* Moscow, 1923.
Degras, J, ed., *Documents on Soviet foreign policy,* vols. 1 and 2, London 1951–2.
Documents on British foreign policy, Series I, London, 1947–00; Series 1a, London, 1966–00.
Latvian Legation, *Minutes of the Baltic conference held at Balduri in Latvia in 1920,* Washington DC, 1960.
Papers relating to the Foreign Relations of the United States. The Paris Peace Conference 1919, Washington DC, 1942–7.
Quellen zur Geschichte des Parlamentarismus und der politischen Parteien, Series 1, vol. 2 (E. Matthias and R. Morsey, eds., *Die Regierung des Prinzen Max von Baden,* Düsseldorf, 1962), vol. 6:1–2 (S. Miller, ed., *Die Regierung der Volksbeauftragten, 1918/1919,* Düsseldorf, 1969).
Russian Liberation Committee, *Memorandum on the Baltic provinces question,* Paris, 1919.
Shapiro, L., ed., *Soviet treaty series,* vol. 1: 1917–1924, Washington DC, 1950.
Skirmunt, K., 'Polens Aussenpolitik zwischen Versailles und Locarno', *Berliner Monatshefte,* 18, 1940, pp. 18–23.
Volkmann, H. E., 'Das Bericht des Generalleutnants Walter von Eberhardt. Meine Tätigkeit im Baltikum', *Zeitschrift für Ostforschung,* 13, 1964, §§728–33.

MEMOIRS

Avalov-Bermondt, P. M., *Im kampf gegen den Bolschewismus,* Hamburg, 1925.
Barmine, A., *One who survived. Memoirs of a Soviet diplomat,* London, 1938.

Berndorff, H. R., *General zwischen Ost und West*, Hamburg, 1951.

Bessedovsky, G., *Revelations of a Soviet diplomat*, London, 1931.

Bischoff, J., *Die letzte Front. Geschichte der eisernen Division im Baltikum 1919*, Berlin, 1935.

Blodnieks, A., *The undefeated nation*, New York, 1960.

Blücher, Wipert von, *Deutschlands Weg nach Rapallo*, Wiesbaden, 1951.

Blum, O., *Russische Köpfe*, Berlin, 1923.

Crozier, F. P., *Impressions and recollections*, London, 1930.

D'Abernon, Viscount, *Ambassador of peace*, 3 vols., London, 1924–30.

Dirksen, H. von, *Moskau, Tokio, London. Erinnerungen und Betrachtungen zu 20 Jahren deutscher Aussenpolitik 1919–1939*, Stuttgart, 1949.

Du Parquet, Lt Col., *Der Drang nach Osten. L'aventure allemande en Lettonie*, Paris, 1926.

Duranty, W., *I write as I please*, London, 1935.

Goltz, Rüdiger von der, *Meine Sendung in Finnland und im Baltikum*, Leipzig, 1920.

Als politischer General im Osten 1918–1919, Leipzig, 1936.

Gough, H. de la Poer, *Soldiering on*, London, 1954.

Grant-Watson, A., *An account of a mission to the Baltic States in 1919*, London, 1957.

The Latvian Republic. The struggle for freedom, London, 1965.

Gregory, J. D., *On the edge of diplomacy. Rambles and reflections*, London, 1928

Hentig, W. O., *Mein Leben. Eine Dienstreise*, Göttingen, 1962.

Hilger, G. and Meyer, A. G., *The incompatible allies*, New York, 1953.

Kennedy, A. L., *Old diplomacy and new, 1876–1922*, London, 1922.

Kessler, Harry Graf, *Aus den Tagebüchern, 1918–1937*, Munich, 1965.

Laroche, J., *Au Quai d'Orsay avec Briand et Poincaré, 1913–1926*, Paris, 1957.

Nadolny, R., *Mein Beitrag*, Wiesbaden, 1955.

Niessel, H., *L'évacuation des Pays Baltiques par les Allemands*, Paris, 1935.

Noske, G., *Von Kiel bis Kapp. Zur Geschichte der deutschen Revolution*, Berlin, 1920.

Erlebtes aus Aufstieg und Niedergang. Der deutschen Sozialdemokratie, Zurich, 1947.

Powell, E. A., *Embattled borders*, New York, 1928.

Riesser, H. E., *Von Versailles zur Uno*, Bonn, 1962.

Rosen, F., *Aus einem diplomatischen Wanderleben*, Wiesbaden, 1959.

Rosenberg, Baron Ed von, *Für Deutschtum und Fortschritt in Lettland. Erinnerungen und Betrachtungen*, Riga, 1928.

Rüdiger, W. von, *Aus dem letzten Kapitel deutsch–baltischer Geschichte in Lettland, 1919–1939*, Hanover–Wülfel, 1955.

Scott, A. McCullum, *Beyond the Baltic*, London, 1925.

Stegman, H., 'Aus meinen Erinnerungen', *Baltische Hefte*, 7, 1960, pp. 91–113, 156–79.

Stresemann, G., *Vermächtnis*, 3 vols. ed. H. Bernhard, Berlin, 1922.

Tallents, Sir Stephen, *Man and boy*, London, 1943.

Vanlande, R., *Avec le Général Niessel en Prusse et en Lithuanie. La dernière défaite allemande*, Paris, 1922.

Wachtsmuth, W., *Wege, Umwege, Weggenossen*, Munich, 1954.

Von deutscher Arbeit in Lettland, 1918–1934. Ein Tätigkeitsbericht. Materialen zur Geschichte des baltischen Deutschtums, 3 vols., Cologne, 1951–3.

Winnig, A., *400 Tage Ostpreussen*, Dresden, 1927.

Am Ausgang der deutschen Ostpolitik. Persönliche Erlebnisse und Erinnerungen, Berlin, 1927.

Heimkehr, Berlin, 1935.

BOOKS AND ARTICLES

Anderle, A., *Die deutsche Rapallo-Politik. Deutsch–sowjetische Beziehungen 1922–1929*, E. Berlin, 1962.

ed., *Rapallo und die friedliche Koexistenz*, E. Berlin, 1963.

Anderson, E., 'An undeclared naval war. The British–Soviet naval struggle in the Baltic, 1918–1920', *Journal of Central European Affairs*, 22:3, 1962.

'British policy towards the Baltic states 1918–1920', *Journal of Central European Affairs*, 19, 1959, pp. 276–89.

'Die baltische Frage und die Internationale Politik der Allierten und Assoziierten Mächte bis zum November 1918': see H. von Rimscha and H. Weiss, eds., *Von den baltischen Provinzen zu den baltischen Staaten*, vol. 1.

'Die baltische Frage und die Internationale Politik der Allierten Assoziierten Mächte 1918–1921': see *Von den baltischen Provinzen zu den baltischen Staaten*, vol. 2.

'Die baltischen Staaten im Völkerbundsrat': see J. von Helm and C. J. Kenez, eds., *Reval und die baltischen Länder*.

'The USSR trades with Latvia. The treaty of 1927', *American Slavic and East European Review*, 21, 1962, pp. 296–321.

Angelus, O., 'Esten und Deutschen', *Baltische Hefte*, 14, 1968, pp. 108–34.

Arnot, R. P., *Soviet Russia and her neighbours*, New York, 1927.

Artoud, D., *La question des dettes interalliés et la reconstruction de l'Europe, 1917–1929*, Lille–Paris, 1978.

Ast, K., 'Estonia's struggle for independence', *Baltic Review*, 13, 1958, pp. 40–57.

Aun, K., *On the spirit of the Estonian minorities law*, Stockholm, 1950.

Bainville, J., *La Russie et la barrière de l'est*, Paris, 1920.

Baltic states, The. A survey of the political and economic structure and the foreign relations of Estonia, Latvia and Lithuania, Royal Institute of International Affairs, London–New York, 1938.

Bardoux, J., *De Paris à Spa*, Paris, 1921.

Basler, W., *Deutschlands Annexionspolitik in Polen und im Balitkum 1914–1918*, E. Berlin, 1962.

Baumgart, W., *Deutsche Ostpolitik 1918. Von Brest–Litovsk bis zum Ende des Ersten Weltkrieges*, Vienna–Munich, 1966.

Berg, A., *Latvia and Russia*, London–Toronto, 1920.

Berzins-Valdess, R., V. D. Bergs, *Lettonie. Vingt années d'indépendence*, Riga, 1938.

Bilmanis, A., *The Baltic states and the problem of the freedom of the Baltic sea*, Washington, 1943.

A history of Latvia, Princeton, NJ, 1951.

Latvijas Werdegang vom Bischofsstaat Terra Mariana bis zur freien Volksrepublik, Leipzig, 1934.

'The legend of the Baltic barrier states', *Journal of Central European Affairs*, 6, 1964–7, pp. 126–46.

'Lettland und das baltische Problem', in *Baltisches Handbuch*, Danzig, 1930, pp. 115–35.

Boehm, M. H., *et al.*, eds., *Wir Balten*, Salzburg–Munich, 1951.

Boelitz, O., *Das Grenz- und Auslansdeutschtum. Seine Geschichte und seine Bedeutung*, Munich–Berlin, 1926.

Bokalders, J., *Lettlands Oekonomist*, Riga, 1929.

Bonsal, S., *Suitors and suppliants. The little nations at Versailles*, New York, 1946.

Borowsky, P., 'Die "bolschewistische Gefahr" und die Ostpolitik der Volks beauftragten in der Revolution', in *Industrielle Gesellschaft und politisches System*, Bonn, 1978.

Bougoin, E., 'Pour un Locarno nord–oriental. La problème de Vilna', in *Révue des vivants (Paris)*, 1928, pp. 1134–53.

Bournazel, R., *Rapallo: Naissance d'un mythe. La politique de peur dans la France du bloc national*, Paris, 1974.

Bradley, J. F. N., *Civil war in Russia 1917–1920*, London, 1975.

Bregman, A., *La politique de la Pologne dans la Société des Nations*, Paris, 1932.

Brenneisen, R., 'Aussenhandel und Aussenhandelspolitik der baltischen Staaten mit besonderer Berücksichtigung der Beziehungen zu Deutschland', *Weltwirtschaftliches Archiv*, 30, 1929, pp. 366–87.

'Gewerbliche Sonderstellung der Ausländern in Lettland', in *Die Ostwirtschaft. Zeitschrift zur Förderung der wirtschaftlichen Beziehungen Deutschlands mit der Union der S. S. R., Polen, Finnland, Estland, Lettland, Litauen*, 16:1, 1927, pp. 11–13.

Lettland. Das Werden und Wesen einer neuen Volkswirtschaft, Berlin, 1936.

Bretton, H. L., *Stresemann and the revision of Versailles*, Stanford, Calif., 1953.

Bruns, G., *Gesammelte Schriften zur Minderheitenfrage*, Berlin, 1933.

Čakste, M., 'Latvia and the Soviet Union', *Journal of Central European Affairs*, 9, 1949, pp. 31–60, 173–211.

Carley, M. J., 'The politics of anti-bolshevism. The French government and the Russo–Polish war, December 1919 to May 1920', *Historical Journal*, 19:1, 1976, pp. 163–89.

Carr, E. H., *Conditions of peace*, London, 1942.

'Die historischen Grundlagen der sowjetischen Aussenpolitik', *Forschungen zur Osteuropäischen Geschichte*, 1, 1954, pp. 239–49.

German–Soviet relations between the two wars, Baltimore, Md, 1951.

A history of Soviet Russia. The Bolshevik revolution, 1917–1923, vol. 3, London, 1953.

The interregnum, 1923–1924, London, 1954.

The Russian revolution from Lenin to Stalin, London, 1979.

Carroll, E. M., *Soviet Communism and Western opinion 1919–1921*, Durham, NC, 1965.

Carsten, F.L., *Reichswehr und Politik*, Cologne–Berlin, 1964.

Castellan, G., 'Reichswehr und Armée Rouge 1920–1939', in *Les relations Germano-soviétique de 1933 à 1939*, Paris, 1954.

Cathala, J., *Portrait de l'Estonie*, Paris, 1937.

Coates, W. P. and Z., *A history of Anglo–Soviet relations*, 2 vols., London, 1943.

Russia, Finnland and the Baltic, London, 1940.

Cobban, A., *The nation state and national self-determination*, London, 1969.

Crohn-Wolfgang, H. F., 'Die baltischen Randstaaten und ihre handelspolitische Bedeutung', *Schmollers Jahrbuch* (Munich–Leipzig), 45:1, 1921, pp. 207–35.

Lettlands Bedeutung für die östliche Frage, Berlin–Leipzig, 1923.

'Die Republik Lettland und ihre wirtschaftliche Zukunft', *Jahrbücher für Nationalökonomie und Statistik* (Jena), 118:1, 1922, pp. 420–31.

D'Abernon, Lord, *The 18th decisive battle of the world*, London, 1921.

Debicki, R., *The foreign policy of Poland*, New York, 1962.

Dellinghausen, Baron von, 'Die baltischen Landestaaten unter russischer Herrschaft 1710–1918 und die gegenwärtige Lage im Baltikum', *Friedrich Manns Paedogogisches Magazin* (Berlin), 1080, 1926.

Dennis, A., *The foreign policy of Soviet Russia*, London, 1924.

Die kämpfe im Baltikum nach der zweiten Einnahme von Riga, Juni bis Dezember 1919. Darstellungen aus der Nachkriegskämpfen deutscher Truppen und Freikorps, Bd. 3, Berlin, 1938.

Dockrill, M. J., and Goold, D., *Peace without promise. Britain and the peace conferences 1919–1923*, London, 1981.

Dopkewitsch, H., 'Zur englischen Politik im Baltikum 1918–1919', *Deutsches Archiv für Landes und Volksforschung*, 6, 1942, pp. 119–47.

Doss, K., *Das deutsche Auswärtige Amt im übergang vom Kaiserreich zur Weimarer Republik. Die Schülerische Reform*, Düsseldorf, 1977.

Düwell, K., *Deutschlands auswärtige Kulturpolitik, 1918–1932. Grundlinien und Dokumente*, Cologne–Vienna, 1976.

Dyck, H. L., *Weimar Germany and Soviet Russia, 1926–33. A study in diplomatic instability*, London, 1966.

Dziewanowski, M. K., *Joseph Pilsudski. A European federalist, 1918–1922*, Stanford, Calif., 1969.

'Pilsudski's federal policy 1919–1921', *Journal of Central European Affairs*, 10, 1950, pp. 113–28, 271–87.

Elben, W., *Das probleme der Kontinuität in der deutschen Revolution*, Düsseldorf, 1965.

Epstein, F., 'Zur Interpretation des Versailler Vertrages', *Jahrbücher für Geschichte Osteuropas*, 5:3, 1957, pp. 315–35.

Epstein, K., *Matthias Erzberger and the dilemma of German democracy*, Princeton, NJ, 1959.

Erdmann, K. D., 'Deutschland, Rapallo und der Westen', *Vierteljahrshefte für Zeitgeschichte*, 11, 1963, pp. 105–65.

'Gustav Stresemann. The revision of Versailles and the Weimar parliamentary system', 1980 Annual Lecture at the German Historical Institute, London, 1980.

'Das Problem der Ost-oder Westorientierung in der Locarno-Politik Stresemanns', *Geschichte in Wissenschaft und Unterricht*, 6, 1955, pp. 133–62.

Euler, H., *Die Aussenpolitik der Weimarer Republik 1918–1923*, Aschaffenburg, 1957.

Farr, P., *Soviet Russia and the Baltic republics*, London, 1944.

Fechner, H., 'Das Ende der deutschen Ostpolitik im Baltikum', *Ostbrief. Mitteilungen der Ostdeutschen Akademie* (Lüneburg), April 1956, pp. 233–7.

Felix, D., *Walther Rathenau and the Weimar Republic. The politics of reparations*, Baltimore–London, 1971.

Fink, C., 'Defender of minorities. Germany in the League of Nations, 1926–33', *Central European History*, 5, 1972, pp. 330–57.

The Genoa Conference. European diplomacy 1921–22, Chapel Hill, NC, 1984.

Firks, Baron w. von, 'Lettländische Innenpolitik und Wir', *Baltische Monatsschrift*, 58:3, 1927, pp. 178–85.

'Volkstum und Bodenständigkeit', *Baltische Monatsschrift*, 58:1, 1927, pp. 35–43.

Fischer F., *Griff nach der Weltmacht. Die Kriegszielpolitik des kaiserlichen Deutschland*, Düsselfdorf, 1961.

Fischer, L., *The Soviets in world affairs*, New York, 1960.

Frauenstein, A. M., *Die Zentraleuropäischen Randstaaten mit besonderer Berücksichtigung des baltischen Dreibundproblems, Lettland, Estland und Litauen*, Riga, 1921.

Freund, G., *The unholy alliance. Russian–German relations from the Treaty of Brest–Litovsk to the Treaty of Berlin*, London, 1957.

Freymann, R, von, 'Die lettländische–russische Friedensvertrag und seine Verwircklichung', *Rigasche Zeitschrift für Rechtswissenschaft*, 1:4, 1926–7.

Fromme, E., *Die Republik Estland und das privat Eigentum*, Berlin, 1922.

Frommelt, R., *Paneuropa oder Mitteleuropa. Einigungsbestrebungen im Kalkül deutscher Wirtschaft und Politik 1925–33*, Stuttgart, 1977.

Garleff, M., *Deutschbaltische Politik zwischen den Weltkriegen. Die parlementarische Tätigkeit der deutschbaltischen Parteien in Lettland und Estland*, Bonn, 1976.

Gasiorowski, Z., 'The Russian overture to Germany of December 1924', *Journal of Modern History*, 30:2, 1958, pp. 99–117.

'Stresemann and Poland after Locarno', *Journal of Central European Affairs*, 18:3, 1958, pp. 292–317.

'Stresemann and Poland before Locarno', *Journal of Central European Affairs*, 18:1, 1958, pp. 25–47.

Gathorne-Hardy, G. M., *A short history of international relations*, London, 1934.

Gatske, H. W., *Germany's drive to the west. A study of Germany's western war aims during the First World War*, Baltimore, Md, 1966.

'Russian–German military collaboration during the Weimar Republic', *American Historical Review*, 63, 1957/1958, pp. 565–97.

'Von Rapallo nach Berlin. Stresemann und die deutsche Russland-Politik', *Vierteljahrshefte für Zeitgeschichte*, 4:1, 1956, pp. 1–29.

Gernet, B., 'Lettlands auswärtige Handelsbeziehungen', in J. Bokalders, eds, *Lettlands Oekonomist*, Riga, 1929, pp. 22–45.

Gordon, H. J., *The Reichswehr and the German Republic, 1919–1926*, Princeton, NJ, 1957.

Görlitz, W., *Die Nordostdeutschen. Führungsschichten und ihre Umwandlungen seit dem Ersten Weltkrieg*, Hamburg , 1963.

Gorodetsky, G., *The precarious truce. Anglo–Soviet relations, 1924–7*, London, 1977.

Graham, Malbone Watson, *The diplomatic recognition of the border states*, Publications of the University of California at Los Angeles in social Sciences, vol. 3, nos. 3 (Estonia) and 4 (Latvia), Berkeley, Calif., 1939–41.

Graml, H., 'Die Rapallo-Politik im Urteil der westdeutschen Forschung', *Vierteljahrshefte für Zeitgeschichte*, 18, 1970, pp. 366–91.

Grathwol, R. P., *Stresemann and the DNVP. Reconciliation or revenge in German foreign policy, 1924–1928*, Lawrence, Kan., 1980.

Grimm, C,. *Vor den Toren Europas 1918–1920. Geschichte der baltischen Landeswehr*, Hamburg, 1963.

Grundmann, K.-H., *Deutschtumspolitik zur Zeit der Weimarer Republik. Eine Studie am Beispiel der deutsch–baltischen Minderheit in Estland und Lettland*, Hanover–Döhren, 1977.

Halecki, O., *Borderlands of Western civilization. A history of eastern central Europe*, New York, 1952.

Hallgarten, G. W. F., 'General Hans von Seeckt and Russia 1920–1922', *Journal of Modern History*, 21, 1949, pp. 28–34.

Haltenberger, M., *Die Baltischen Länder. Gehört das Baltikum zu Ost–Nord oder Mitteleuropa*, Dorpat, 1925.

Handwörterbuch des Grenz- und Auslandsdeutschtums, vols. 2 and 3, Breslau, 1936–9.

Hartmann, W., *Die Balten und ihre Geschichte*, Berlin, 1942.

Hasselblatt, W., 'Deutsch–baltische Kulturarbeit in Estland. Zehn Jahre deutsch–baltischer Politik in Estland', *Jahrbuch des baltischen deutschtums in Lettland und Estland*, 7, 1929, pp. 66–70.

'Gedanken über Sicherung des baltischen Raumes', *Baltische Monatsschrift*, 59, 1928, pp. 12–23.

Haupts, L., *Deutsche Friedenspolitik 1918–19. Eine Alternative zur Machtpolitik des Ersten Weltkrieges*, Düsseldorf, 1976.

'Zur deutschen und britischen Friedenspolitik in der Krise der Pariser Friedenskonferenz', *Historische Zeitschrift*, 217, 1973, pp. 54–98.

Hehn, J. von, *Die baltischen Lande. Geschichte und Schicksal der baltischen Deutschen*, Kitzingen am Main, 1951.

Die Entstehung der Staaten Lettland und Estland, der Bolschewismus und die Grossmächten, Berlin, 1956.

'Der Kampf gegen den Bolschewismus und der baltischen Ostfront im Jahre 1918/1919', *Deutsches Archiv für Landes und Volksforschung*, 6, 1942, pp. 696–702.

'Vom baltischen Deutschtum in den letzten 20 Jahren. Bemerkungen zu seiner Geschichte in der Nachweltkriegszeit und zur Umsiedlung', *ibid.*, 5, 1941, pp. 216–41.

Die Umsiedlung der baltischen Deutschen – das letzte Kapitel baltisch–deutscher Geschichte, Marburg–Lahn, 1982.

and Kenez, C. J., eds., *Reval und die baltischen Länder. Festschrift für Hellmuth Weiss zum 80. Geburtstag*, Marburg–Lahn, 1980.

Helbig, H., *Die Träger der Rapallo-Politik*, Göttingen, 1958.

Hesse, A., *Die Wirkungen des Friedens von Versailles auf die Wirtschaft des deutschen Ostens*, Jena, 1930.

Heyking, Baron A., *The main issues confronting the minorities of Latvia and Estonia*, London, 1922.

Hiden, J. W., 'The Baltic Germans and German policy towards Latvia after 1918', *The Historical Journal*, 13:2, 1970, pp. 295–317.

'The "Baltic problem" in Weimar's Ostpolitik', in V. R. Berghahn and M. Kitchen, eds., *Germany in the age of total war*, London, 1981, pp. 147–69.

'The significance of Latvia. A forgotten aspect of Weimar Ostpolitik', *The Slavonic and East European Review*, 53:132, 1975, pp. 389–413.

'The Weimar Republic and the problem of the Auslandsdeutsche', *Journal of Contemporary History*, 12, 1977, pp. 273–89.

Germany and Europe. 1919–1939, London, 1977.

Hildebrand, K., *Das deutsche Reich und die Sowjetunion im internationalen System 1918–32. Legitimät oder revolution*, Frankfurt, 1977.

Hillgruber, A., '"Revisionismus"–Kontinuität und Wandel in der Aussenpolitik der Weimarer Republik', *Historische Zeitschrift*, 237, 1983, pp. 597–621.

Himmer, R. 'Rathenau, Russia and Rapallo', *Central European History*, 9, 1976, pp. 146–83.

'Soviet policy towards Germany during the Russo–Polish war, 1920', *Slavic Review*, 35:4, 1976, pp. 665–82.

Hinkkanen-Lievonen, Merja-Liisa, *British trade and enterprise in the Baltic States, 1919–1925*, Helsinki, 1984.

'Exploited by Britain? The problems of British financial presence in the Baltic States after the First World War', *Journal of Baltic Studies*, 14:4, 1983, pp. 328–39.

Hoetsch, O., 'The Baltic states, Germany and Russia', *Foreign Affairs*, 10:1, 1931, pp. 120–33.

Hoffman, R. J. S., *Great Britain and the German trade rivalry 1875–1914*, New York, 1964.

Holborn, H., 'Diplomats and diplomacy in the early Weimar Republic', in G. A. Craig and F. Gilbert, eds., *The diplomats*, Princeton, NJ, 1953.

Höltje, C., *Die Weimarer Republik und das Ostlocarno Problem 1919–1934*, Würzburg, 1958.

Hovi, K., *Alliance de Revers. Stabilization of France's alliance policies in East Central Europe 1919–1921*, Turku, 1984.

Cordon Sanitaire or Barrière de l'Est? The emergence of the new French Eastern Europe alliance policy 1917–1919, Turku, 1975.

Interessensphären im Baltikum. Finnland im Rahmen der Ostpolitik Polens 1919–1922, Helsinki, 1984.

Hovi, O., *The Baltic area in British policy 1918–1921. From the Compiègne armistice to the implementation of the Versailles treaty*, Helsinki 1980.

Hubatsch, W., *Entstehung und Entwicklung des Reichwirtschaftsministeriums 1880–1933. Ein Beitrag zur Verwaltungsgeschichte der Reichsministerien*, Berlin, 1978.

Hurwicz, E. *Der neue Osten*, Berlin, 1927.

Jacobsen, J., 'Is there a new international history of the 1920s?', *American Historical Review*, 88, 1983, pp. 617–45.

Locarno diplomacy. Germany and the West, 1925–1929, Princeton, NJ, 1972.

Janssen, K.-H., 'Die baltische Okkupationspolitik des deutschen Reiches', in H. von Rimscha and H. Weiss, eds., *Von den baltischen Provinzen*, vol. 1, pp. 217–54.

Jonsson, S. H., 'The coup d'état that failed', *Baltic Review*, 22, 1961, pp. 49–51.

Jordan, W. M., *Great Britain, France and the German problem 1919–1939*, London, 1943.

Kaasik, N., 'L'évolution de l'union baltique', *Révue générale du droit international publique*, 41:5, 1934, pp. 631–47.

Kaiser, D. E., *Economic diplomacy and the origins of the Second World War: Germany, Britain, France and Eastern Europe 1930–39*, Princeton, NJ, 1980.

Kaur, U., *Wirtschaftsstruktur und Wirtschaftspolitik des Freistaates Estland, 1918–1940*, Bonn, 1962.

Keeton, G. W., *Russia and her Western neighbours*, London, 1942.

Kimmich, C. M., *The free city. Danzig and German foreign policy 1919–1934*, New Haven–London, 1968.

Kirby, D., 'A great opportunity lost? Aspects of British commercial policy toward the Baltic states, 1920–24', *Journal of Baltic Studies*, 5:4, 1974 pp. 362–78.

Knorre, W. von, 'Vom Wirtschaftsleben des baltischen Deutschtums', in M. H. Boehm and H. Weiss, eds., *Wir Balten*, Salzburg–Munich, 1951.

Kochan, L., *Russia and the Weimar Republic*, Cambridge, 1954.

Koehl, R. L., 'A prelude to Hitler's greater Germany', *American Historical Review*, 59, 1953/1954, pp. 43–65.

Kollman, E. C., 'Walther Rathenau and German foreign policy. Thoughts and actions', *Journal of Modern History*, 24, 1952, pp. 127–52.

Korbel, J., *Poland between East and West. Soviet and German diplomacy towards Poland, 1919–1933*, Princeton, NJ, 1963.

Krekeler, N., *Revisionsanspruch und geheime Ostpolitik der Weimarer Republik. Die Subventionierung der deutschen Minderheit in Polen*, Stuttgart, 1973.

Kroeger, E., *Die rechtliche Stellung des Ausländers in Lettland*, Berlin–Grunewald, 1930.

Krüger, P., *Die Aussenpolitik der Republik von Weimar*, Darmstadt, 1985.
Deutschland und die Reparationen 1918/1919. Die Genesis des Reparationsproblems in Deutschland zwischen Waffenstillstand und Versailler Friedensschluss, Stuttgart, 1973.

Krummacher, F. A., and Lange, H., *Krieg und Frieden. Geschichte der deutsch–sowjetischen Beziehungen. Von Brest–Litovsk zum Unternehmen Barbarossa*, Munich, 1970.

Küpffer, K. R., 'Über die Herdergesellschaft', *Jahrbuch des baltischen Deutschtums*, 1927, pp. 29–33.

Kürbs, F., *Die osteuropäische Staaten Polen, Litauen, Lettland, Estland als Staats- und Wirtschaftskörper*, Tübingen, 1931.

Laqueur, W., *Germany and Russia. A century of conflict*, London, 1965.

Laubach, E., 'Maltzans Aufzeichnungen über die letzten Vorgänge vor dem Abschluss des Rapallo-Vertrages', *Jahrbücher für Geschichte Osteuropas*, Neue Folge, 22, 1974, pp. 556–79.
Die Politik der Kabinette Wirth 1921/1922, Lübeck–Hamburg, 1968.

Laue, T. H. von, 'Soviet diplomacy: G. V. Chicherin, People's Commissar for Foreign Affairs 1918–1930', in G. A. Craig and F. Gilbert, eds., *The diplomats*.

Lauren, P. G., *Diplomats and bureaucrats. The first institutional responses to twenti-eth century diplomacy in France and Germany* Stanford, Calif., 1976.

Lehnich, O., *Währung und Wirtschaft in Polen, Litauen, Lettland und Estland,* Berlin, 1923.

Lemberg, E., 'Zur Geschichte der deutschen Volksgruppen in Ost–Mitteleu-ropa'; *Zeitschrift für Ostforschung,* 1:3, 1952, pp. 321–45.

Lenz, W. Jr., 'Vom politischen Schicksal des baltischen Deutschtums', *Jahrbuch des baltischen Deutschtums in Lettland und Estland,* 1959, pp. 62–9.

'Zur britischen Politik gegenüber den baltischen Deutschen', in R. von Thadden *et al.,* eds., *Das Vergangene und die Geschichte,* Göttingen, 1973, pp. 272–82.

Linke, H. G., *Deutsch–sowjetische Beziehungen bis Rapallo,* Cologne, 1970.

Lippelt, H., '"Politische Sanierung". Zur deutschen Politik gegenüber Polen 1925/1926', *Vierteljahrshefte für Zeitgeschichte,* 19, 1971, pp. 323–73.

Lizkowski, U., ed., *Russland und Deutschland,,* Stuttgart, 1974.

Loennroth, E., 'The diplomacy of Osten Unden', in G. A. Craig and F. Gilbert, eds., *The diplomats,* pp. 86–99.

Lukacs, J. A., *The great powers and Eastern Europe 1917–1952,* New York, 1953,

Macartney, C., and Palmer, A. W., *Independent Eastern Europe,* London, 1962.

Maddison, E., *Die nationalen Minderheiten Estlands und ihre Rechte,* Tallinn, 1930.

Maier, C. S., *Recasting bourgeois Europe. Stabilization in France, Germany and Italy in the decade after World War I,* Princeton, NJ, 1975.

Mann, B., *Die baltischen Länder in der deutschen Kriegszielpublizistik, 1914–1918,* Tübingen, 1965.

Manning, C., *The forgotten republics,* New York, 1952.

Manteuffel-Katzdangen, *Deutschland und der Osten,* Munich, 1926.

Marks, S., 'The myths of reparations', *Central European History,* 11, 1978, pp. 231–55.

Martel, R., *The eastern frontiers of Germany,* London, 1930.

Matthias, E., *Die deutsche Sozialdemokratie und der Osten 1914–45,* Tübingen, 1954.

Maxelon, M.-O., *Stresemann und Frankreich 1914–1929. Deutsche Politik der Ost–West Balance,* Düsseldorf, 1981.

Maydell, K. Baron von, 'Die Baltendeutschen vor ihrer Umsiedlung. Ein statistischer Rückblick', *Jomsburg,* 4, 1940, pp. 59–90.

Medlicott, W. N., *British foreign policy since Versailles,* London, 1968.

Megerle, K., *Deutsche Aussenpolitik 1925. Ansatz zu aktivem Revisionismus,* Berne–Frankfurt, 1974.

Michalka, W., and Lee, M. M., eds., *Gustav Stresemann,* Darmstadt, 1982.

Ministère des Affaires Étrangères de Lettonie, *La Lettonie en 1921,* Paris, 1922.

Morgan, R. P., 'The political significance of German–Soviet trade negotia-tions 1922–5', *Historical Journal,* 6, 1963, pp. 253–71.

Munter, W. R., 'Die Wirtschaftsverträge der baltischen Staaten', in J. Bokalders, ed., *Lettlands Oekonomist*, Riga, 1929, pp. 5–21.

Nelson, H. I., *Land and power. British and Allied policy on Germany's frontiers 1916–1919*, London–Toronto, 1963.

Neré, J., *The foreign policy of France from 1914–1945*, London, 1975.

Newman, W. J., *The balance of power in the interwar years, 1919–1939*, New York, 1968.

Nicolson, H., *Curzon. The last phase*, London, 1934.

Peacemaking 1919, London, 1963.

Page, S. W., *The formation of the Baltic states. A study of the effects of great power politics on the emergence of Lithuania, Latvia and Estonia*, Cambridge, Mass., 1959.

'Lenin, the national question and the Baltic states 1917–1919', *The American Slavic and East European Review*, 7:1, 1948, pp. 20–6.

Pärming, T., *The collapse of liberal democracy and the rise of authoritarianism in Estonia*, London–Beverly Hills, 1975.

Pärn, H., 'Die Einführung der Selbstbesteurung innerhalb des Volksgemeinschaft der Deutschen in Lettland', *Jahrbuch des baltischen Deutschtums*, Riga, 1927.

Pick, F. W., *The Baltic nations*, London, 1945.

Pieper, H., *Die Minderheitenfrage und das Deutsche Reich 1919–1933/34*, Hamburg–Frankfurt, 1974.

Plieg, E. A., *Das Memelland 1920–1939*, Würzburg, 1962.

Pogge von Strandmann, H., 'Grossindustrie und Rapallopolitik. Deutsch–sowjetische Handelsbeziehungen in der Weimarer Republik', *Historische Zeitschrift*, 222, 1976, pp. 265–341.

'Rapallo-strategy in preventive diplomacy: new sources and new interpretations', in V. R. Berghahn and M. Kitchen, eds., *Germany in the age of total war*, London, 1981, pp. 123–46.

Pohl, K. H., *Weimars Wirtschaft und die Aussenpolitik der Republik 1924–6. Vom Dawes–Plan zum internationalen Eisenpakt*, Düsseldorf, 1979.

Polonsky. A., *The little dictators. The history of East Europe since 1918*, London, 1975.

Polvinen, T., 'Zur Erforschung der jüngeren politischen Geschichte Finnlands', *Jahrbücher für Geschichte Osteuropas*, 13:2, 1965, pp. 231–46.

Post, G., Jr, *The civil–military fabric of Weimar foreign policy*, Princeton, NJ, 1973.

Puchert, B., 'Die Entwicklung der deutsch–sowjetischen Handelsbeziehungen von 1918 bis 1939', *Jahrbücher für Wirtschaftsgeschichte*, 14:4, 1973, pp. 11–36.

Pusta, K. R., 'Die Baltenstaaten im europäischen Staatenbund', in *Baltisches Handbuch*, Danzig, 1930, pp. 102–4.

'For a free Baltic', *Baltic Review*, 1, 1953, pp. 17–21.

The Soviet Union and the Baltic states, New York, 1942.

Radek, K., *Die auswärtige Politik Sowjetrusslands*, Hamburg, 1921.

Rauch, G. von, *The Baltic states. The years of independence, Estonia, Latvia, Lithuania 1917–1940*, London, 1974.

'Die baltischen Staaten und Sowjetrussland 1919–1939', *Europa Archiv*, 9, 1954, pp. 6859–68, 6965–72.

'Der Revaler Kommunistenputsch', *Baltische Hefte*, 1, 1955, pp. 19–23.

Raud, V., *The smaller nations in the world's economic life*, London, 1943.

Reddaway, W. F., *Problems of the Baltic*, Cambridge, 1940.

Rheinbaben, W., 'Deutschlands Ostpolitik in Locarno', *Aussenpolitik*, 1,1953, pp. 33–40.

Ribhegge, W., *August Winnig– eine historische Persönlichkeitsanalyse*, Bonn, 1973.

Riekhoff, H. von, *German–Polish relations 1918–1933*, Baltimore–London, 1971.

Rimscha, H. von, *Aufgabe und Leistung der Baltendeutschen*, Berlin, 1940.

'Die Baltikumpolitik der Grossmächte', *Historische Zeitschrift*, 177, pp. 281–309.

'Paul Schiemann als Minderheitenpolitiker', *Vierteljahrshefte für Zeitgeschichte*, 4, 1966, pp. 43–61.

'Paul Schiemann. Memorial', *Jahrbücher für Geschichte Osteuropas*, 2:4, 1954, pp. 475–8.

'Die Politik Paul Schiemanns während der Begründung der baltischen Staaten im Herbst 1918', *Zeitschrift für Ostforschung*, 5, 1956, pp. 68–82.

'Der sogenannte Geheimbefehl Major Fletchers vom 16 Juni 1919', in R. von Thadden, ed., *Das Vergangene und die Geschichte*, Göttingen, 1973, pp. 288–97.

Die Staatswerdung Lettlands und das baltische Deutschtum, Riga, 1939.

Rimscha, H. von, and Weiss, H., eds., *Von den baltischen Provinzen zu den baltischen Staaten 1917–1918. Beiträge zur Entstehungsgeschichte der Republiken Esland und Lettland*, vols. 1 (*1917–1918*) and 2 (*1918–1920*), Marburg–Lahn, 1971–7.

Ritter, E., *Das Deutsche Ausland-Institut in Stuttgart 1917–1945*, Wiesbaden, 1976.

Rodgers, H., 'Latvia's quest for an Eastern Locarno 1925/7', *Eastern European Quarterly*, 5:1, pp. 103–13.

Search for security. A study in Baltic diplomacy, 1920–1934, Hamden, Conn., 1975.

Romas, I., *Die wirtschaftliche Struktur der baltischen Staaten und die Idee einer Zollunion*, Rytas, 1934.

Ronimois, H. E., *Russia's foreign trade and the Baltic sea*, London, 1946.

Roos, H., *Geschichte der polnischen Nation 1916–1960*, Stuttgart, 1961.

Rosenfeld, G., *Sowjetrussland und Deutschland 1917–1922*, E. Berlin, 1960.

Rothfels, H., 'The Baltic provinces. Some historic aspects and perspectives', *Journal of Central European Affairs*, 4:2, 1944, pp. 117–46.

Rothschild, J., *East Central Europe between the two World Wars*, Washington DC, 1974.

Ruge, W., 'Die Aussenpolitik der Weimarer Republik und das Problem der europäische Sicherheit 1925–1932', *Zeitschrift für Geschichtswissenschaft*, 22, 1974, pp. 273–90.

Stresemann. Ein Lebensbild, E. Berlin, 1965.

Rutenberg, G., *Die baltischen Staaten und das Völkerrecht*, Riga, 1928.

Samts, J., 'The achievements of Meierovics' last European trip', *Journal of Baltic Studies*, 7:3, 1976, pp. 247–54.

Scheibert, P., 'Zur Intervention der Westmächte in Nordrussland', *Jomsburg*, 4, 1940, pp. 91–101.

Schieder, T., 'Die Entstehungsgeschichte des Rapallo-Vertrages', *Historische Zeitschrift*, 204:3, 1967, pp. 544–609.

Schiemann, P.,'Aus deutsch–baltischer Kulturarbeit in Lettland', *Jahrbuch und Kalendar des Deutschtums in Lettland*, 1925, pp. 15–18.

Ein europäisches Problem. Die Minderheitenfrage. Unabhängige Betrachtungen zur Minderheitenfrage, Vienna–Leipzig, 1937.

'Politischer Jahresüberblick', *Jahrbuch des baltischen Deutschtums in Lettland und in Estland*, 1930, pp. 4–9.

Schierenberg, R., *Die Memelfrage als Randstaatenproblem*, Berlin, 1925.

Schröder, H.-J., 'Zur politischen Bedeutung der deutschen Handelspolitik nach dem Ersten Weltkrieg', in G. Feldman *et al.*, eds., *Die deutsche Inflation. Eine Zwischenbilanz*, Berlin–New York, 1982.

Schroeder, H., *Russland und der Ostsee*, Riga, 1927.

Schuker, S. A., *The end of French predominance in Europe. The financial crisis of 1924 and the adoption of the Dawes plan*, Chapel Hill, NC, 1976.

Schulz, G., *Revolutions and peace treaties*, London, 1972.

Schulze, H., *Freikorps und Republik*, Boppard, 1969.

'Der Oststaat-Plan 1919', *Vierteljahrshefte für Zeitgeschichte*, 18, 1970, pp. 123–63.

Senn, A. E., *The emergence of modern Lithuania*, Morningside Heights, NY, 1959.

The great powers, Lithuania and the Vilna question 1920–1928, Leiden, 1966.

Sepols, G., *Za kulisami inostrannoy interventsii v Latvii*, Moscow, 1959.

Seraphim, H. J., and Wollenweber, H., *Ergebnisse einer Studienreise durch Lettland*, Berlin, 1933.

Seton-Watson, H., *Eastern Europe between the wars 1918–1941*, New York, 1945.

Sidzikauskas, V., 'Our tradition of cooperation', *Baltic Review*, 1, 1953, pp. 35–41.

Siew, B., *Lettlands Volks- und Staatswirtschaft*, Riga, 1925.

Slavenas, J. P., 'General Hans von Seeckt and the Baltic question', in V. S.

Vardys and R. J. Misiunas, eds., *The Baltic states in peace and war 1917–1945*, pp. 120–5.

Spekke, A., *A history of Latvia. An outline*, Stockholm, 1957.

Spenz, J., *Die diplomatische Vorgeschichte des Beitritts Deutschlands zum Völkerbund 1924–1926*, Frankfurt–Zürich, 1966.

Stavenhagen, K., 'Das Deutschtum in Lettland', *Taschenbuch des Grenz- und Auslandsdeutschtum*, Heft 20, Berlin, 1927.

Stürmer, M., *Koalition und Opposition in der Weimarer Republik 1924–1928*, Düsseldorf, 1967.

Strazhas, A., 'The Land Oberost and its place in Germany's Ostpolitik 1915–1918', in V. S. Vardys and R. J. Misiunas, eds, *The Baltic states in peace and war 1917–1945*, pp. 43–62.

Sullivan, C. L., 'The 1919 German campaign in the Baltic. The final phase', V. S. Vardys and R. J. Misiunas, eds., *The Baltic States in peace and war 1917–1945*, pp. 31–42.

Sweet, D. W., 'The Baltic in British diplomacy before the First World War', *Historical Journal*, 13:3, 1970, pp. 451–90.

Tarulis, A., *American–Baltic relations 1918–1922. The struggle over recognition*, Washington DC, 1965.

Soviet policy towards the Baltic states 1918–1940, Notre Dame, Ind., 1959.

Taube, Baron A. von, *Baltische Köpfe*, Bovenden, 1953.

'Das Auswärtige Amt und die estnische Frage 1917–1918', *Jahrbücher für Geschichte Osteuropas*, Neue Folge, 17:4, 1969, pp. 542–80.

'Die Entstehung der estnischen Eigenstaatlichkeit 1917–1920', *Jomsburg*, 3:1/2 1939, pp. 24–36.

'Das Reichskommissar Graf Robert Keyserling und die deutsche Politik in Livland und Estland im März/April 1918', *Zeitschrift für Ostforschung*, 19, 1970, pp. 601–31.

Thimme, A., 'Gustav Stresemann. Legende und Wirklichkeit', *Historische Zeitschrift*, 181, 1956, pp. 287–358.

Thompson, J. M., *Russia, Bolshevism and the Versailles peace*, Princeton, NJ, 1966.

Torma, A. and Raud, V., *Estonia, 1918–1952*, London, 1952.

Trachtenberg, M., *Reparations in world politics. France and European economic diplomacy, 1916–1923*, New York, 1980.

Turner, H A., Jr, *Stresemann and the politics of the Weimar Republic*, Princeton, NJ, 1963.

Ullmann, R. H., *Anglo–Soviet relations 1917–1921*, 3 vols., Princeton, NJ, 1961–72.

Unfug, D., 'The Baltic policy of Prince Max of Baden', *Journal of Central European Affairs*, 23, 1963, pp. 152–65.

Uustalu, E., *The history of the Estonian people*, London, 1953.

Vahter, L., 'The ill-fated Soviet coup in Estonia', *Baltic Review*, 23, 1961, pp. 24–31.

Vardys, V. S. and Misiunas, R. J., eds., *The Baltic states in peace and war, 1917–1945*, Philadelphia, Penn, 1978.

Varmer, A., 'Die Aussenpolitik Estlands während der Eigenstaatlichkeit', *Acta Baltica*, 8, 1968/1969, pp. 159–94.

Volkmann, H.-E.,'Das deutsche Reich und die baltischen Staaten 1918 bis 1920', in J. von Hehn *et al.*, eds., *Von den baltischen Provinzen etc*, vol. 2.

'Ökonomie und Machtpolitik. Lettland und Estland im politisch–ökonomischen Kalkül des Dritten Reiches, 1933-1940', *Geschichte und Gesellschaft*, 2, 1976, pp. 471–500.

'Probleme des deutsch–lettischen Verhältnisses zwischen Compiègne und Versailles', *Zeitschrift für Ostforschung*, 14, 1965, pp. 713–26.

Die russische Emigration in Deutschland 1919–1929, Würzburg, 1966.

Vries, Axel de, 'Das Deutschtum in Estland', *Taschenbuch des Grenz- und Auslandsdeutschtums* (Berlin), 21, 1927.

Wachtsmuth, W., *Von deutscher Arbeit in Lettland 1918–1934. Ein Tätigkeitsbericht. Materialien zur Geschichte des baltischen Deutschtums*, 3 vols., Cologne, 1951–53.

Wagner, G., *Deutschland und der polnisch–sowjetische Krieg 1920*, Weisbaden, 1979.

Walsdorff, M., *Westorientierung und Ostpolitik. Stresemanns Russland-politik in der Locarno-Ära*, Bremen, 1971.

Walters, M., *Baltengedanken und Baltenpolitik*, Paris, 1926.

Lettland. Seine Entwicklung zum Staat und die baltischen Fragen, Rome, 1923.

Wandycz, P. S., *France and her Eastern allies 1919–1925. French–Czechoslovak–Polish relations from the Paris Peace Conference to Locarno*, Minneapolis, Minn., 1962.

Soviet–Polish relations 1917–1921, Cambridge, Mass., 1969.

Weiss, H., 'Der deutsch–baltische Beitrag zur Lösung der Minderheitenfrage in der Zeit zwischen den beiden Weltkriegen', in *Leistung und Schicksal. Abhandlungen und Berichte über die Deutschen im Osten*, Cologne, 1967.

'Das Volksgruppenrecht in Estland vor dem zweiten Weltkrieg', *Zeitschrift für Ostforschung*, 1, 1952, pp. 253–5.

Wengst, U., *Brockdorff-Rantzau und die aussenpolitischen Anfänge der Weimarer Republik*, Berne–Frankfurt, 1973.

Wertheimer, F., *Deutschland, die Minderheiten und der Völkerbund*, Berlin, 1926.

Von deutschen Parteien und Parteiführern im Ausland, Berlin, 1927.

White, S., *Britain and the Bolshevik revolution. A study in the politics of diplomacy 1920–1924*, London, 1979.

Wittram, R., *Das Nationale als europäisches Problem. Beiträge zur Geschichte des Nationalitätenprinzips*, Göttingen, 1954.

'Wendepunkte der baltischen Geschichte. Gegebenheiten und Betrachtungen', in M. H. Boehm *et al.*, eds., *Wir Balten*.

Wrangell, Baron W., 'Ausschnitte aus der estnischen Politik 1918–1920', *Baltische Monatsschrift*, 1930, pp. 521–42.

Wurm, K., *Die französische Sicherheitspolitik in der Phase der Ostorientierung 1924–1926*, Frankfurt, 1979.

Zimmermann, L., *Deutsche Aussenpolitik in der Ära der Weimarer Republik*, Göttingen–Zurich–Frankfurt/Main, 1958.

Zinghaus, *Führende Köpfe der baltischen Staaten*, Kaunas–Leipzig–Vienna, 1938.

Index

DATE DUE